THE TRIALS OF ACADEME

Amy Gajda

The Trials of Academe

The New Era of Campus Litigation

HARVARD UNIVERSITY PRESS

Cambridge, Massachusetts, and London, England

2009

Library of Congress Cataloging-in-Publication Data

Gajda, Amy.
    The trials of academe : the new era of campus litigation / Amy Gajda.
       p.   cm.
    Includes bibliographical references and index.
    ISBN 978-0-674-03567-6 (alk. paper)
    1. Universities and colleges—Law and legislation—United States.   I. Title.
    KF4225.G35   2009
    344.73'074—dc22   2009022123

This book is for my father, Leo Gajda, a scholar at heart who could only dream of college.

Contents

Acknowledgments

I owe deep thanks to a large number of people who have helped me throughout the course of researching and writing this book. First thanks must go to Elizabeth Knoll of Harvard University Press, whose vision and creativity helped shape the project from the start. Thanks also to colleagues at the University of Illinois College of Law—especially John Colombo and Jennifer Robbenault—who offered helpful comments and suggestions on early chapters during a faculty retreat. Other Illinois law faculty offered additional helpful suggestions: Matt Finkin, Dick Kaplan, and Dean Bruce Smith. Thanks also to colleagues in the Department of Journalism at Illinois, especially Walt Harrington, who not only shared ideas about the project with me but also saw to it that I had time to write.

Tina Gunsalus, another Illinois colleague, has my undying gratitude for reading through early drafts of chapters, offering very helpful ways of thinking about the topic, and for jump-starting the project. Len Gajda was a careful reader of early drafts.

I have had numerous helpful discussions with other scholars while writing the book (Norm Denzin, Sam Gove, Steve Helle, Sue Kieffer, Barbara Lee, Rich Martin, John Nerone, Bob O'Neil, and Kyu Ho Youm among them), and those discussions helped me tremendously throughout the process.

Thanks also to the amazing Michael Olivas, who gave me an early opportunity to present ideas from this project at a higher education law roundtable at the University of Houston Law Center and who has supported this project in other ways too numerous to catalogue. Thanks to Bill Kaplin, who offered help during the roundtable and also found time to read and comment on a later draft, and Leland Ware, who talked with me about the work during both the more formal proceedings and, later, on a more informal basis. Thanks also to other participants at the round-table who offered helpful ideas and suggestions: Dennis Gregory, Paul Horwitz, John LaNear, and Rhonda Vonshay Sharpe.

I am grateful to the anonymous reviewers who generously read and commented on the proposal, early drafts, and final manuscript.

Thanks to Deanna Shumard and Golda Lawrence for helping me in multiple important and supportive ways during crucial stages of my work on the book, and to John Donohue and Joanne Moryl for careful copy-editing. I am grateful as well to all students in my Law of Higher Education seminar at Brooklyn Law School during Spring 2008; our classroom discussions helped me think about these issues in new ways. And, of course, thanks to the multitude of professors and administrators who have shared their ideas and, sometimes, their worries regarding campus litigation on a more informal basis.

Special thanks, finally, to my husband, David Meyer, for his unflagging support and encouragement; and to my helpful, wise, and tolerant sons, Michael Meyer and Matthew Meyer.

THE TRIALS OF ACADEME

CHAPTER 1

An Introduction

In 1970, with the shockwaves of the Kent State tragedy still reverberating, a group of professors, administrators, and lawyers gathered in Ann Arbor, Michigan, to discuss the role that law might play in restoring order to the nation's campuses. The mayhem at Kent State University, in which Ohio National Guardsmen shot dead four students and injured nine others in response to a turbulent anti-war demonstration, had unleashed revolts across the country. In all, some 760 college and university campuses were ultimately forced to shut down. In response, some universities had turned to the courts, seeking injunctions or other legal sanctions against rabble-rousing students. With the dust settling, here was a chance for university counsel and outside lawyers to compare notes on what worked. John Holloway, counsel at the University of Colorado, related, for example, how a novel, "self-executing" injunction served on student leaders as they marched to reoccupy the university's administrative offices had stopped them in their tracks on the steps of Regent Hall and persuaded them to disperse.[1]

But some contributors to the seminar saw potentially more trouble in the offing. The upheavals of 1970 had brought others into court as well. Students, faculty, and parents complaining of the universities' handling of the crises sought court orders to close campuses, or to reopen them, or to recover compensation for injuries or classes missed due to strikes.[2]

The lawsuits produced mixed results. Kent State's campus was closed for six weeks under a court order.[3] A state judge ordered the University of Miami to reopen a day after it had closed in response to student unrest, but later softened the directive to affirm the university president's authority to excuse class attendance.[4] A New York small-claims court ordered New

1

York University to refund $277.40 in tuition to the father of one student for classes cancelled in the wake of student strikes.[5] But other, larger actions, some seeking millions of dollars in damages, failed.[6]

In this sudden swell of lawsuits demanding judicial review of campus management, Robert O'Neil saw "the ominous prospect of governance by injunction."[7] O'Neil, then a law professor at the University of California at Berkeley who would go on to become president at the universities of Wisconsin and Virginia, cautioned that by enlisting the courts in disciplining unruly students, universities were potentially opening the door to broader and less welcome forms of judicial oversight: "An initially narrow range of questions committed to a court may steadily expand, because of the quest and counter-quest of various campus constituencies for protection against each other, until vital decisions about the way the university functions are being made by judges who have no particular expertise or sensitivity in these matters."[8]

Indeed, the expansion was already afoot, some participants observed. Holloway pointed out, with some amusement, that "in Colorado we were sued by a coed seeking a grade of *B* in English Literature 101."[9] The trial judge had run that case out of court, telling lawyers, "If you think this court is going to sit here and grade papers in English Literature 101, you're crazy."[10] But Richard Goodman, a Detroit trial lawyer with experience in representing students, saw potential merit in a new sort of legal claim: "It would not surprise me to see lawsuits brought by students against universities, perhaps under a contract theory, basing complaints on poor curricula or incompetent faculty. These actions will say to the university, 'You promised us a good education and we're getting a lousy education. You have breached your contract. Now pay up.' Why shouldn't a lawsuit for damages be brought under such circumstances?"[11]

Karl Bemesderfer, an assistant to the president of the University of Chicago, thought Goodman "a prophet." In fact, Bemesderfer pointed out with obvious dismay, a Wisconsin court was already entertaining a lawsuit challenging a denial of tenure.[12] As "bizarre" as this development seemed, Goodman pointed out that litigation once considered similarly novel in other contexts—over collective bargaining by employees, for example— had come in time to be accepted as perfectly routine.[13]

With nearly four decades' hindsight, the conversation in Ann Arbor seems both quaint and prescient. Quaint, of course, because astonishment over a tenure lawsuit is impossible to muster in an age when such litigation has become entirely commonplace. But prescient also in foreseeing the expanding role law might play on campus—and the risks it might pose for academic communities. Within two years of the Ann Arbor conference, Robert O'Neil observed that "the federal courts have become forums for the litigation of a broad range of [academic] issues that one would not have thought justiciable a decade ago."[14]

Today, lawsuits are such an established fact of university life that a guidebook for new faculty devotes an entire chapter to "Legal Issues and the Professorate."[15] Alongside chapters on mastering "the art of grantsmanship" and "getting published," the volume alerts new professors to "the litigious environment of academe" and offers practical tips for steering clear of liability toward students, colleagues, and other potential plaintiffs.[16] A guidebook for college administrators contains a similar chapter, offering as a tip about difficult personnel decisions, "[d]o not do anything without advice at every step from the lawyers."[17] Yet another volume is dedicated entirely to advising faculty on minimizing their legal risks, and warns that "[t]he days are long past when a college teacher had to pay little or no attention to the possibility of being sued in connection with being employed to teach."[18]

Of course, university lawyers are quick to agree that campuses have become "legal minefields."[19] Kathleen Curry Santora, leader of the National Association of College and University Attorneys, wrote in 2004 that "[p]reventive law" was one of the most pressing imperatives for higher education in the immediate future: "Institutions must educate people on their campuses about the legal implications of their actions, identify areas of significant risk, and establish internal mechanisms to forestall legal action."[20]

There is no doubt that the number of legal claims involving colleges and universities has ballooned significantly in recent years.[21] According to one survey, the number tripled within the span of just five years during the mid-1990s.[22] Both the number and role of in-house university counsel have swelled, as have average expenditures by universities on outside legal counsel (nearly tripling between 1983 and 1992 alone).[23] But equally significant is the expanding subject matter of these legal disputes. The substance of some claims is familiar. Lawsuits alleging unlawful discrimination in hiring or promotion—however "bizarre" they seemed in 1970—are now plentiful and multiplying.[24] In one sample, academic race-discrimination suits nearly quadrupled between 1991 and

1997.[25] The growing number of legal tangles over intellectual property rights and other fruits of academic inquiry is also well known.[26]

But, in addition to these, a mounting number of what might be seen as normal academic scraps have landed in court. "Anyone who has served time as an academic administrator," Frederick Schauer of the University of Virginia School of Law has wryly observed, "is familiar with the frequency with which academics shout 'academic freedom' whenever they are confronted with mandatory grade curves, grading deadlines, schedule changes, and numerous, even less plausible, assertions of academic freedom."[27] In past eras, these routine tussles over academic privilege went no farther than the dean's office. Today, "[a] remarkable number" are ending up in court.[28]

A small sample of recent court decisions finds students suing over grades, tuition increases, and the reuse of old exam questions; faculty claims that administrative oversight of course content, student evaluation, and classroom teaching violates the First Amendment; rival scholars suing one another for defamation over bruising scholarly critiques; graduate students and junior faculty seeking redress from their mentors or supervisors for faulty advice; and professorial claims of decanal abuse arising from the allocation of faculty offices. In one case, a faculty plaintiff included a claim against a former colleague "whose offense was to clean out [her] refrigerator and throw away her noodles at some point during the spring of 2003."[29]

There is much more to this story than merely a smattering of oddball or frivolous complaints of the sort one might find in any walk of life. The important development is that, as far as litigation and the courts are concerned, academia is beginning to resemble other walks of life. Significantly, members of academic communities are increasingly inclined to think about their interactions in legal terms.[30] And, of at least equal significance, judges are increasingly receptive to mediating these campus conflicts.

Until relatively recently, colleges and universities operated with something close to legal impunity.[31] "There were few legal requirements relating to the educational administrator's functions," Professors William Kaplin and Barbara Lee have noted, and "[t]he higher education world . . . tended to think of itself as removed from and perhaps above the world of law and lawyers."[32] In part, this was simply because potentially applicable laws were few. Well into the twentieth century, the employment relationship remained largely a matter of private bargain in all contexts, and universities were often shielded from liability under doctrines of governmental or charitable immunity.

Beyond this, even when general legal principles might otherwise seem to apply, lawsuits were bounced out of court on the basis of a particular reluctance to intervene in academic disputes. Writing in 1979, Harry T. Edwards and Virginia Davis Nordin summed up the traditional attitude: "Historically, American courts have adhered fairly consistently to the doctrine of academic abstention in order to avoid excess judicial oversight of academic institutions. The courts have also frequently stepped in to prevent the intrusion by other governmental agencies into the affairs of institutions of higher education, particularly with respect to issues pertaining to intellectual freedom."[33] First by way of common-law doctrine and later as a matter of constitutional principle protecting academic freedom, courts allowed universities to run their own shop.

Even in 1979, however—less than a decade after the Ann Arbor roundtable on campus disorder—Nordin, and Edwards, a Michigan law professor who would be nominated later that year to the federal bench, saw the ground beginning to shift. Although the case law was still sparse, they observed that "in recent years the courts seem to have overcome their reluctance to hear cases concerning academic institutions, so that an increasing number of decisions are beginning to define legal rights and responsibilities of the university and its constituent parts."[34] By 1980, Dean Helen Gouldner of the University of Delaware despaired that "[b]eing in court, preparing for cases, and trying to stay out of court have all become an integral part of the university's regular affairs."[35]

The greater court involvement was spurred partly by federal and state civil rights statutes providing new remedies for discrimination, and partly by developments in constitutional law recognizing broader student rights to free speech and due process. Between 1972 and 1974, Congress enacted a raft of measures directly regulating colleges and universities. In 1972, Congress amended Title VII of the Civil Rights Act of 1964, extending its prohibition of race and sex discrimination expressly to academic employment;[36] Title IX of the Educational Amendments of 1972 barred other forms of sex discrimination by educational institutions receiving federal funds;[37] the Rehabilitation Act of 1973 imposed a similar ban on discrimination against "qualified handicapped individual[s]";[38] and the

Buckley Amendment of 1974 regulated the use of information in student files.[39]

These enactments required courts to open their doors to at least some academic plaintiffs, but judges continued to tread softly, regularly lacing opinions siding with university defendants with lofty tributes to institutional autonomy. In 1987, Congress was forced to amend Title IX and the Rehabilitation Act to overturn court decisions that had "unduly narrowed" the laws' application to favor university defendants.[40] A study of court decisions reviewing tenure denials found in 1993 that "[d]espite the 1972 amendments to Title VII, the courts have continued to defer to the judgments of institutional officers and have claimed that they do not have the expertise to evaluate academic qualifications and standards."[41] The study's author, Terry Leap, noted a handful of then-recent decisions favoring plaintiffs but concluded that it was too early to know whether those cases were merely "short excursions off the well-beaten anti-interventionist path," or instead "mark[ed] a turning point for federal courts."[42]

Fifteen years after Leap's survey, however, there can be little doubt that courts have turned the corner. Plaintiffs challenging tenure denials on grounds of discrimination still face an uphill fight, and courts continue to express caution about second-guessing academic judgments. But, as one former staff counsel to the American Association of University Professors recently observed, "[w]hile courts continue to pay lip service to the 'deference' owed academic decisions within colleges and universities, the application of the law to the facts suggests otherwise."[43] Court decisions for discrimination plaintiffs, encompassing both final judgments of liability and preliminary rulings finding cases to be substantial enough to proceed to trial, once only a trickle, are now a steady stream.[44]

Outside the tenure context, as well, courts have shown increasing willingness to intervene, as "litigation [has] extended into every corner of campus activity."[45] Whether upholding the asserted First Amendment rights of individual faculty members or students against university administrators, weighing defamation claims arising from peer review, or supervising the "reasonableness" of academic conduct under tort law, judges are more and more treating academic actors like any other. Georgetown University law professor J. Peter Byrne, a leading legal scholar of academic freedom, detects "increased judicial distrust of academic decision making."[46] Examining judicial interpretations of constitutional academic freedom in the decade preceding 2004, Byrne found that "[w]hat unifies these decisions, otherwise an uncouth mishmash, is that they enhance the power of judges to set basic policies for colleges and universities."[47]

A 2005 case out of Vanderbilt University illustrates the new attitudes prevailing both on campus and in the courts.[48] In February 2002, chemistry professor B. A. Hess returned graded exams to his organic chemistry students, as was his custom, by stacking them on a table outside his classroom so that students could retrieve them on their way into class. Nicklaus Atria, an aspiring pre-med student, was disappointed with his grade, a B-minus. He later approached Hess and asked him to "re-grade" the exam on the ground that one of Atria's answers was erroneously marked as incorrect. To guard against the possibility that students might alter their answer sheets before seeking a "re-grading"—a sadly recurring phenomenon in Hess's experience—the professor kept photocopies of all original answer sheets before returning them to the students. When Atria insisted that his answer to question six was actually correct, Hess produced the photocopy of Atria's original answer sheet, proving that the answer had been altered.

Hess referred Atria to Vanderbilt's Honor Council for investigation. At a subsequent disciplinary hearing, Atria contended that the answer in question could have been somehow smudged, from "a" to "c," in his book bag.[49] The Council was unmoved, and found "clear and convincing evidence" that Atria himself had altered the answer in an attempt to improve his grade from a B-minus to a B; it ruled that Atria should receive a failing grade for the course. When Atria appealed, the university refused to allow him to introduce the results of a private polygraph test, citing concerns about reliability of the evidence. In addition, the professor who chaired the university's Appellate Review Board concluded that Atria's appeal—which now theorized that he had been framed by an unknown student seeking to move up the grading curve by eliminating rivals—was meritless and did not warrant an appellate hearing before the full review board.[50]

Out of options on campus, Atria then sued in federal court, alleging that Professor Hess was negligent by returning graded exams in a way that made it possible for a rival student to frame him and that Vanderbilt had breached its contractual obligations in rejecting his administrative appeal. The district court summarily rejected Atria's claims, reasoning in classic fashion that "a federal court is an inappropriate forum in which to challenge academic matters."[51]

On appeal, the Sixth Circuit Court of Appeals disagreed with the trial judge and reinstated Atria's lawsuit. With respect to Atria's claim that Hess had been negligent, the appeals court brushed aside the university's argument that it was inappropriate to invite jurors to decide whether Hess's method of returning exams was "reasonable." The court answered, "Given that Tennessee law requires a juror to put himself in the place of a surgeon to determine whether 'the defendant failed to act with ordinary and reasonable care when compared to the custom or practices of physicians from a particular geographic region,' we do not think it unreasonable to ask a juror to place himself in the shoes of a professor, even a professor in an advanced level course, who hands back graded tests."[52]

The appeals court also held that the trial court had improperly rejected Atria's breach-of-contract claim. Atria claimed that Vanderbilt's student handbook, including its listing of procedural rules for Honor Council proceedings, constituted an enforceable contract with students, and that the university had breached the contract by denying him a full appellate hearing and rejecting his polygraph evidence.

The federal appeals court agreed with Atria that " 'the student-university relationship is contractual in nature' " and that "[c]atalogs, manuals, handbooks, bulletins, circulars and regulations of a university may help define this contractual relationship."[53] The court further agreed that Vanderbilt's student handbook, in particular, constituted an implied contract with students, notwithstanding that the handbook itself expressly underscored that its provisions "are not intended to be all-inclusive and do not constitute a contract."[54]

The court then held that a jury could reasonably conclude that Vanderbilt had breached its duties under the handbook by failing to provide a full appeals hearing and by excluding his polygraph test. The handbook expressly authorized the review board chair to summarily reject appeals without a hearing, but the court found an arguable ambiguity in an earlier set of procedures and ruled that a jury should decide on the proper course.[55] The handbook similarly said nothing about the right to introduce polygraph evidence, but because it did not "expressly *prohibit* a petitioner from submitting polygraph evidence," the court thought that jurors should decide.[56] Because the university allowed the introduction of hearsay evidence at discipline hearings, "[a] reasonable juror could conclude that Vanderbilt's decision to accept some forms of unreliable evidence but not others was an arbitrary decision and a breach of its implied contract with Atria."[57] (This, despite the fact that federal courts have long followed precisely the same practice, broadly excluding polygraph evidence while admitting multiple categories of hearsay.[58])

The appellate court's readiness to find merit in Atria's claim that he was framed is remarkable enough. Atria's claim—that another student risked everything to inch up the grade curve by adulterating a B-minus exam in the hopes that the student would thereafter seek a "re-grade" and be dropped from the course for academic fraud—shares some of the same quality of criminal defendants who seek to avoid conviction on the grounds that unknown adversaries must have planted their DNA at the scene.

Even more remarkable, however, are the lengths to which the court was prepared to go to find a legal basis upon which Atria could press his theory. In upholding the soundness of Atria's contract claim, the court had to disregard the student handbook's own disclaimer that its terms constituted a contract and find it plausible that the handbook, through silence, impliedly guaranteed students the right to introduce forms of evidence widely held inadmissible in other legal and quasi-legal proceedings. In allowing his negligence claim, the court reasoned that a professor is no different from a surgeon or any other professional or commercial actor subject to ordinary negligence principles requiring "reasonable" conduct.

More broadly, in rejecting the trial court's suggestion that courts have no business superintending such "academic matters," the appeals court answered that Atria's case "involves a disciplinary action by the university, and does not arise in the context of any academic finding, and may appropriately be brought in this court."[59] The appellate court's exceedingly narrow conception of the "academic" judgment to which courts might owe some deference starkly illustrates just how far courts have traveled from the academic abstention doctrines that once strongly protected the autonomy of colleges and universities. In fact, a year before the *Atria* case was decided, Michael Olivas, a law professor at the University of Houston, put "[c]onsumer and educational malpractice" claims at the top of his list of "the most pressing legal issues that higher education institutions will confront in the next five years."[60]

The growing resort to legal process to resolve academic disputes is not merely a parochial concern for academics. It should be of vital interest to the broader society because it threatens to undermine values of academic freedom that have served American society extremely well.

Notwithstanding the periodic (and sometimes legitimate) criticisms leveled at colleges and universities, there is little dispute that higher education has been an essential engine driving the phenomenal technological, social, medical, and economic accomplishments of the past century. "The quality of life enjoyed by the people of the United States in the opening years of the new millennium," observed Frank Rhodes, president emeritus of Cornell University, "rests in substantial part on the broad foundation provided by the American university during the twentieth century."[61] "[Higher education] has been the path to social attainment for millions from impoverished backgrounds, the generator of the nation's leaders in every area of life, the key to vastly improved professional services from health care to technology. It has been the foundation of growing national economic prosperity and manufacturing success, vast improvements in the products of agriculture and industry, and undreamed-of access to new means of communication."[62]

American universities, Derek Bok agreed, are "the nation's chief source for the three ingredients most essential to continued growth and prosperity: highly trained specialists, expert knowledge, and scientific advances others could transform into valuable new products or life-saving treatments and cures."[63] Moreover, "[b]ecause knowledge has become the dominant economic force, the importance of the university can only grow."[64] American society, therefore, has an obvious and enormous interest in the continued vitality of the academic enterprise.

The strength of colleges and universities, in turn, and their ability to meet the accelerating demands of society for innovation and transmission of knowledge depend upon academic freedom. "Academic freedom," as Richard Hofstadter noted in his classic history of the subject, "is a modern term for an ancient idea."[65] Reaching back to the Middle Ages, universities were granted a large measure of autonomy and "internal matters of institutional government were in the hands of those immediately connected with learning."[66]

Granting universities freedom to define and direct their own academic missions, and granting individual scholars freedom to pursue knowledge, without external constraint, has proved enormously important in creating the conditions for creativity and discovery.[67] "For over nine hundred years," Frank Rhodes has observed, "the effectiveness of the university has been dependent upon a social compact under which society supports the university financially and grants it a remarkable degree of autonomy, while the university uses its resources and its freedom to serve the larger public interest."[68]

Universities have achieved most greatly where they have been most free. Rhodes has attributed the distinctive success of American universities in the twentieth century, during which U.S. institutions have widely overtaken and surpassed their counterparts in Europe and elsewhere, in large part to their greater autonomy:

> Decentralized, feistily independent, uncoordinated, pluralistic, American universities have been opportunistic, adaptive, creative, and responsive to new opportunities . . . [T]heir independence from central government planning and control gives them a vigor that has proved more elusive in the regulated European institutions, where faculty members are often civil servants and where central government control extends not only to management of institutional enrollment and programs, but also to regulation, budgeting, and evaluation of individual academic departments.[69]

The same pattern arguably can be seen when drawing comparisons among American universities. Some have suggested, for example, that the preeminence of the universities of California and Michigan among U.S. public institutions might derive partly from the peculiarly robust support those states have given to academic freedom and institutional autonomy.[70]

Part and parcel of this success have been the unique norms of self-governance that have taken root within this "autonomous society-within-society."[71] "The American university remains an organizational enigma, whose loosely coupled structure and collegially based organization defy the established canons of management. But the very flexibility of the internal organization of the American university has nurtured its entrepreneurial spirit."[72] Intensifying legal scrutiny is already crimping the decentralization and creativity upon which this system depends. When the *Chronicle of Higher Education* asked university counsel in 2004 to identify the most urgent trends reshaping higher education, one listed "[c]reating a risk-conscious environment":[73] "Faced with rising litigation costs and escalating premiums for liability and property insurance, colleges will be forced to weigh carefully the risks of their novel programs. To make decision makers more sensitive to such risks, many institutions have adopted risk-management models that take a holistic approach—one that assesses and works to control risks that transcend the boundaries of various divisions and departments."[74]

Perceptions of new legal risks are doing more than simply raising obstacles to programmatic innovation at the margins; they are encroaching on the very core of the academic enterprise. The backbone of self-governance in academe is peer review, the determination and enforcement of academic standards of merit by colleagues with expertise in the field, guided by "the conventions of the scholarly community."[75] Indeed, as Matthew Finkin and Robert Post point out, the very idea of academic freedom rests upon unfettered peer review. "In essence," they observe, "academic freedom consists of the freedom to pursue the scholarly profession according to the standards of that profession."[76] The genius of this system is that it enlists faculty who, in Derek Bok's words, "are in the best position to appreciate academic values and insist on their observance," not only because of their specialized knowledge but also because "they have the greatest stake in preserving proper academic standards and principles, since these values protect the integrity of their work and help perpetuate its quality."[77]

The growing recourse to the courts by academics, and the increasing willingness of judges to accept the invitation and resolve campus disputes, pose a substantial threat to this heart of academic self-governance. Cases reviewing tenure decisions are only the most obvious examples. By ordering an award of tenure to a faculty member, perhaps based entirely on a judicial evaluation of the candidate's scholarly record in comparison to others previously tenured, a court may well shape an academic unit's scholarly identity and direction for decades to come.

Lawsuits targeting peer reviewers, then, threaten the core mechanism for determining academic merit. In 2004, for example, a California appeals court sent back to the trial court an associate professor's defamation and invasion-of-privacy suit against an external reviewer who had included a three-sentence comment critical of the professor's availability to student advisees in an evaluation of an academic program.[78] In 2006, a federal court in Illinois heard a case involving an unsuccessful tenure candidate who sued her dean for tortious interference with contractual relations, on the theory that he had interfered with her employment relationship with the university by writing a negative review of her performance.[79]

The court ended up rejecting the claim on the least plausible of all grounds—namely, that the dean's negative recommendation had not actually caused her loss of tenure—but opened the door to future claims whenever a negative internal review might be thought "unjustified" or "malicious."[80] A federal court in Philadelphia set the stage for similar claims based on faculty evaluation of student work, allowing a graduate student to challenge his advisors' critical evaluation of his master's thesis as arbitrary discrimination in violation of the Constitution's equal protection clause.[81]

Legal actions such as these will not commonly succeed. The standard for liability remains high, and yet the courts' willingness to subject academic judgments to searching review is itself cause for concern. The vitality of the academic community depends directly on the willingness of its participants to engage in rigorous peer review. "Negative evaluations on professional grounds are as necessary for this system as is respiration for the body," Peter Byrne has observed. "[W]ithout such collective rejections, disciplines would lose coherence and academia's claim to advance knowledge would suffer."[82] Yet, the prospect of being subjected to burdensome lawsuits may well dampen the ardor of busy scholars for the process of peer review.[83]

Court decisions vindicating the First Amendment rights of individual students and faculty members in opposition to university policies pose their own unique risks. Academic freedom assumes "the freedom to pursue the scholarly profession according to the standards of that profession," as Finkin and Post observe; yet that balance of scholarly freedom and professional norms "would be lost if academic freedom were reformulated as an individual right that insulates scholars from professional regulation."[84] Nevertheless, on the rationale that students and faculty do not "shed their constitutional rights to freedom of speech or expression at the schoolhouse gate,"[85] courts have intervened with growing frequency to resolve tussles by students, professors, and administrators over academic criticism and the content of classroom discussion.[86]

Borrowing wholesale from legal doctrine developed in the context of secondary schools, a growing number of courts have held that such conflicts should be resolved by determining whether the challenged policy or practice is " 'reasonably related to legitimate pedagogical concerns.' "[87] Thus, a federal appeals court held that a student was entitled to a trial to assess whether the University of Utah had legitimate pedagogical reasons for insisting that she recite a script containing offensive language as part of an acting clinic.[88] Another similarly weighed the University of California at Santa Barbara's " 'legitimate pedagogical concerns' " for rejecting as nonconforming a graduate student's thesis containing a profane "disacknowledgements" section.[89] A third held that the same standard should control whether the University of Alabama could direct one of its professors to refrain from interjecting his Christian beliefs into his exercise physiology classes.[90]

Although the legal test is meant to leave room for "reasonable" academic policies concerning classroom speech and course content, the reality remains that the courts' willingness to review academic policies "transfer[s] authority over internal disputes about teaching from the schools to the courts."[91] If courts insert themselves without appropriate sensitivity for the values at stake, they risk doing real damage to the academic enterprise.

In one well-known case, for example, a federal court barred the University of New Hampshire from acting against a professor who insisted upon using vivid sexual analogies in teaching technical writing because, in the court's view, the professor's pedagogical reasons for larding his writing instruction with sexual allusions "overwhelmingly" outweighed the university's pedagogical concerns with the approach.[92] The court minimized the university's interest as simply coddling "adult students [who] found his choice of words to be outrageous."[93] And yet the university was responding to substantial evidence that the professor's allegedly habitual resort to sexual innuendo, both inside and outside of class, had left students feeling demeaned and fearful to interact with a professor who was leading a course required for their graduation.[94] Surely, quite aside from any fears of potential liability to students, the university had substantial and legitimate concerns with the learning environment experienced by students in the class, and yet those received little weight in the court's pedagogical accounting. Free speech values on campus are different from those in civil society—paradoxically, at once both broader and more qualified, as Robert O'Neil has cogently pointed out[95]—and yet the trend of court decisions is to treat them identically.

This book describes and evaluates the growing resort to courts and legal process in campus disputes over scholarship, teaching, and academic governance.

In some ways, the deepening interaction between universities and the courts parallels the spreading entanglement between universities and corporations. In *Universities and the Marketplace,* Derek Bok acknowledged that "[c]ommercial practices . . . are hardly a new phenomenon in American higher education."[96] In 2007, the University of Alabama's $4-million-per-year contract with new football coach Nick Saban stirred new anxiety about the commercialization of college athletics, and yet Bok pointed out that "[i]n 1905, Harvard was concerned enough about its profitable football team to hire a 26-year-old coach at a salary equal to that of its president and twice the amount paid to its full professors."[97] Even so, notwithstanding such precedents, Bok is surely correct that the "unprecedented size and scope" of today's commercial influences mark an important and possibly portentous development for academia.[98]

Similarly, although legal actions have been a part of academe for more than 200 years, both the quantity and character of litigation has changed dramatically. "What is new and different today," according to Lawrence White, a veteran counsel for colleges and universities, "is the aggressiveness with which courts and legislatures intrude in academic decisions as fundamental as the selection of students, the awarding of scholarships, and the determination of curriculum."[99] White adds, "[o]urs is the age of judges and legislators who routinely second-guess decisions with which they disagree, even if it means substituting their own views for the considered judgments of educational professionals."[100]

The causes for this turn are complex and are explored in greater depth in the chapters that follow.[101] In part, the changes have come from outside of campus—the extension of civil rights laws and an ever-expanding range of other federal and state regulation to higher education, the development by the Supreme Court of broader due process and First Amendment protections, the deepening tendency of all Americans to think of their wants and expectations in terms of "rights," and what Robert Kagan has called a general and distinctively American culture of "adversarial legalism."[102]

In part, however, the turn to law has been spurred by changes from within the university. The dramatic growth of many modern universities into sprawling, fragmented "multiversities,"[103] coinciding with the dramatic diversification of faculties and students in recent decades, has challenged the sense of community that long facilitated shared governance and accommodation.[104] As universities undertake a broader range of roles—landlord, health care provider, law enforcement, agricultural advisor, venue for major entertainment events—they are encountering new fields of regulation and contractual entanglements.[105] At the same time, as campus communities have grown more diverse and polarized, norms of collegiality and accommodation that once inhibited legal battle have weakened. The growing reliance on non–tenure track faculty has stirred a new field of legal questions relating to their employment status and academic privileges.[106] One lawyer on the front lines of litigation involving academia noted that law has not yet "begun to respond in earnest to the evolving demographics of a professoriate in which record numbers of faculty members are neither tenured nor on tenure track."[107]

Relatedly, of course, the "legalization" of academia is tied to its "commercialization." The more universities reach out to and reshape themselves in the model of commercial and other nonacademic enterprises, the more likely they are to be viewed by outsiders, including courts, as essentially like their nonacademic partners.[108] Thus, in the *Atria* case, involving the altered chemistry exam, the appellate court was quick to apply ordinary tort principles to academics on the rationale that professors are no different from physicians and others who must answer for the "reasonableness" of their conduct.[109] In another case from Florida, overturning a university's decision to dismiss a medical student for academic deficiencies as "arbitrary," a judge deflected the university's appeal for deference to its academic judgment as out of step with "contemporary values": "The deeply rooted . . . judicial deference to university conduct toward students becomes increasingly less defensible as bottom-line, commercial concerns motivate university actions and students seek a more consumer friendly product."[110] Indeed, to the contrary, today " 'higher education is both a product and a relationship that begs for external review.' "[111]

There is another important element at work—the very success of universities in enlisting the courts' aid in protecting academic freedom. For most of history, respect for academic freedom has been predominantly a matter of "custom, usage and scholarly comment," rather than law.[112] When disputes did find their way into court, judges mostly refused to enter the fray under doctrines of academic abstention, but not out of the conviction that the Constitution forbade their intervention.[113] It was only in the 1950s, in response to McCarthy-era attacks on academics, that explicit legal protection for academic freedom began to emerge in a series of Supreme Court opinions.[114]

In 1957, in Sweezy v. New Hampshire, the Supreme Court barred the state's attorney general from probing a visiting lecturer about the content of his remarks at the University of New Hampshire.[115] In intervening, the Court explained that the vitality of democracy depended upon respect for free academic inquiry and the pursuit of knowledge: "Scholarship cannot flourish in an atmosphere of suspicion and distrust. Teachers and students must always remain free to inquire, to study, and to evaluate, to gain new maturity and understanding; otherwise our civilization will stagnate and die."[116] While Chief Justice Warren, for the majority, had attributed this academic freedom directly to "[t]eachers and students," Justice Frankfurter's concurring opinion focused more directly on the autonomy of academic institutions. Academic freedom, he wrote, must encompass " 'the four essential freedoms' of a university—to determine for itself on academic grounds who may teach, what may be taught, how it shall be taught, and who may be admitted to study."[117]

The Court's recognition in *Sweezy* and a handful of subsequent cases of a basis for constitutional protection of academic freedom has served universities well.[118] It staved off some of the predations of the McCarthy era. It undergirded the Court's grudging acceptance of limited affirmative action measures in pursuit of a diverse student body.[119] And, most recently, it has been credited by some with fostering legal and social norms that prevented a recurrence of McCarthy-like repression in the immediate aftermath of the terrorist attacks of September 11, 2001.[120]

Yet, the Court's decisions have left unresolved the basic tension underlying the conceptions of academic freedom outlined in the Warren and Frankfurter opinions in *Sweezy*. The academic freedom valued by the Constitution—the principle excluding "governmental intervention in the intellectual life of a university"[121]—can be seen to comprehend both the right of individual "[t]eachers and students" to inquire, teach, and learn, and the right of the university to define itself as an institution.

What is clear is that the Supreme Court's broad and undifferentiated embrace of "academic freedom" as a constitutional value has thrown open the courtroom doors to an expansive range of internal disputes over speech, process, and governance. The university's right to "determine for itself on academic grounds who may teach, what may be taught, [and] how it shall be taught"[122] is answered in court with the individual professor's right "to inquire, to study, to evaluate"[123] as she sees fit. One faculty member's constitutional right to speak freely in the classroom without penalty contends with another's constitutional right to criticize through peer review.[124]

Courts cannot realistically avoid the dilemma by categorically excluding one set of claims or claimants. Some courts have tried that approach, with deeply troubling results. Faced with a lawsuit brought by a group of public university professors challenging a Virginia statute restricting access to sexually explicit Web sites on state-owned computers, the federal court of appeals briskly dispatched the claim on the ground that the academic freedom protected by the Constitution belongs to academic institutions, not to individual faculty.[125] This provides a tidy, but entirely unsatisfactory, solution. The same principle, "that the state owns and may dictate the professional speech of professors at state universities, just as fully as it does the information given out by a clerk at the department of motor vehicles, could justify the state insisting on the topics and even opinions that a professor may express in class or in scholarship."[126] And yet, as Robert O'Neil observed, nearly two decades before the Virginia decision, "Whatever may be said of the need to safeguard other parts of university life such as research, extramural statements, promotion and tenure decisions, admission and evaluation of students, and the use of campus facilities, it is the core of speech in the classroom that should most clearly claim our solicitude and that of the courts."[127]

Most courts—and virtually all scholars—agree that a conception of academic freedom robust enough to fulfill its function of igniting discovery and nurturing democracy must encompass both individual and institutional rights.[128] Without effective protection against abusive administrators, many—perhaps most—individual professors would shrink from pushing boundaries and challenging convention: "Difficult as the 'chilling effect' often is to document in first amendment litigation," writes Matthew Finkin, a leading scholar on academic freedom and labor relations, "it is richly documented in the annals of AAUP investigations."[129]

Likewise, any view that denied independent legal protection to the autonomy of colleges and universities, apart from the individual liberty of their faculty, would leave them vulnerable to encroachments that chip away at the conditions necessary for a vibrant scholarly community, "even though no individual scholar can be shown to have been threatened for what he teaches or publishes."[130] Finkin, who otherwise thinks it a misnomer to describe educational institutions as possessing rights of "academic freedom," points out that "for an institution that seeks to maintain intellectual freedom, there must, at some points, be freedom *of* the university if there is to be freedom *in* the university."[131] The "Statement on Academic Freedom" produced by the Global Colloquium of University Presidents, convened at Columbia University in 2005, captured the common understanding: "The activities of preserving, pursuing, disseminating, and creating knowledge and understanding require societies to respect the autonomy of universities, of the scholars who research and teach in them, and of the students who come to them to prepare for lives as knowledgeable citizens and capable leaders. The autonomy of universities is the guarantor of academic freedom in the performance of scholars' professional duties."[132]

These dual concepts of academic freedom are not always in conflict; in felicitous cases, all interests within an academic community "make common cause against an external threat."[133] But, when the academic sensibilities of institution and individual scholar collide, there is no avoiding the need to balance the contending interests. This reality, as much as any other, makes clear that it is impossible for courts somehow to disentangle themselves entirely from academic disputes. Unwilling to surrender the hard-fought gains of recent decades in protecting both individual scholars and academic institutions, we can only search for ways to manage the tension and minimize the risks of judicial involvement.

The cases and court decisions recounted in the succeeding chapters—involving claims of discrimination, free speech, defamation, property rights, torts, and contract—illustrate the ways in which resort to the courts can damage the academic enterprise. But they also point the way toward possible responses. Just as academics and judges have each contributed to the "legalization" of the academy in recent years, each can play roles in minimizing the threat that the turn to law poses to academic freedom. Academic institutions must continually work to "'educat[e]' the courts about the issues and the way academic institutions operate."[134] And judges must respond by becoming far more sensitive than they presently are to the risks for academic freedom that attend judicial resolution of disputes over university discipline, faculty appointments, admissions, peer review, and other facets of academic life.

Universities can contribute positively by consciously seeking to restore a stronger sense of community on campus, as suggested by Frank Rhodes and other academic leaders.[135] As in any institution, greater care in anticipating and managing human relations can go some distance toward avoiding some number of lawsuits.[136] So, too, universities can reduce litigation by crafting more effective mechanisms for resolving disputes internally. More than thirty-five years ago, at the Ann Arbor gathering called in the wake of the Kent State crisis, Robert O'Neil warned that "increasing resort to the courts for settlement of campus disputes [may] cause the internal organs of conflict resolution to atrophy."[137] Ensuring that students, faculty, and other members of the academic community have means at hand for grieving perceived wrongs and resolving conflicts, including exploring the viability of emerging new methods of alternative dispute resolution, may eliminate some lawsuits. Increasingly, for example, colleges and universities are providing ombudspersons to investigate and mediate claims of mistreatment, or exploring ways of mandating arbitration of disputes by neutral decision makers who have a firm understanding of the ways in which academic institutions operate.[138]

Beyond these measures, universities may need to think as fundamentally about the direction of higher education as about the direction of the courts. At the University of Illinois, President B. Joseph White, a former business school dean who once took a six-year respite from academia to serve as a corporate executive, staked part of the university's future on the creation of a profit-making, online education division; the operation—originally branded as a virtual "fourth campus" to be staffed primarily with a new stable of non–tenure track instructors and organized as a limited liability corporation—promised to serve as a profit center for the university, generating a $27 million annual return within five years.[139] Illinois ultimately scaled back some of its ambitions for the initiative, partly because of faculty skepticism and partly because of thin market demand.[140] But as more universities turn to such explicit business models, as the public sees universities "grow more complex and the[ir] presidents become more like chief executives than stewards of academic life,"[141] it will understandably become ever harder to persuade judges that universities deserve to be insulated from the legal scrutiny applied to ordinary commercial enterprises. At least, academic leaders, having already recognized that "[t]he increasing commercialization of universities and the expanded role of private industry in university research threaten[s] to compromise the academic mission,"[142] must also recognize the creeping "legalization" of the academy as a collateral cost of that trend.

As all understand, no steps now will drive the courts entirely out of academia, nor would anyone want that result. In 2001, Steven Poskanzer, then a senior administrator at the SUNY system who had spent eight years as counsel at the University of Pennsylvania, surveyed the burgeoning law of higher education and concluded that "[o]n balance, the law has added real value and fairness to American higher education while maintaining the ability of faculty and institutions to fulfill their academic missions."[143]

But just six years later, Poskanzer, having been named president of SUNY–New Paltz, found himself a named defendant in an academic lawsuit and found his name part of the caption of a trial court decision reinstating two students who had been suspended for harassing a campus administrator. The court, in Holmes v. Poskanzer, found that the students were likely to prevail in their lawsuit asserting a due process right to have lawyers present during their campus disciplinary hearing.[144]

Parting ways with its president's earlier benign assessment of the impact of law on campus, the university warned that "[i]nserting lawyers" would transform "matters [that] should be educational in nature" into "intricate, time-consuming, and costly" judicial proceedings.[145] And, indeed, it would take more than a year before the court finally dismissed the student complaint.[146]

CHAPTER 2

A World Apart:
A Short History of the
Rise of Academic Deference

In 1779, American and British forces clashed in bloody battles stretching from Savannah in the south to the coast of Maine. Virginia, for the moment, was spared the brunt of the fighting; the full-scale British invasion of the commonwealth was still two years distant. Yet, in this relative calm before the storm, another battle of sorts was unfolding on the campus of the College of William and Mary.

For years, even before the war, there simmered a "long-lasting feud between the faculty and the Board of Visitors over the internal control of the college."[1] The William and Mary faculty were viewed with growing suspicion and contempt by more ardently patriotic Virginians. Amid the rising revolutionary fervor, faculty members—comprised mostly of English-born Anglican clergy—appeared maddeningly aloof or, worse, openly sympathetic to the royal government. The turmoil extended to the college's academic program. In 1773 and 1774, mounting public dissatisfaction with the college's undistinguished and rigidly traditional curriculum, narrowly focused on the classics, philosophy, and divinity in the Oxford model, generated spirited calls for reform. Critics urged the college to offer modern languages and literature, history, and science; to permit students more freedom in structuring their studies; and to jettison the grammar school—a preparatory program for boys—in order to elevate the seriousness of the academic environment. The faculty would not budge.[2]

Open rebellion, however, accomplished what barbed criticism could not. Virginia's declaration of independence and the royal government's collapse drove virtually the entire faculty from campus, with many fleeing to England. One of the last holdouts, the college's English-born president and head of the Anglican Church in Virginia, John Camm, refused to recognize the authority of the new government and was dismissed by the Board of Visitors in 1777.[3] With the Tory faculty decamped, James Madison, a Virginia-born professor of natural philosophy and the only Patriot among the prewar faculty, assumed the presidency of the struggling college. Madison, a cousin of the future president of the United States of the same name, is thought by one historian to have been the author of an earlier series of anonymous commentaries calling for curricular reform and broader state support of the college. In any event, as president he now energetically pursued the same agenda, along with allies on the Board of Visitors.

A particularly important ally was Thomas Jefferson, who had returned from Philadelphia in 1776 to immerse himself in the affairs of his home state, first in the House of Delegates and then as governor in 1779. Jefferson first sought to remake his alma mater through the legislature, introducing a package of bills that would transform the college into a university at the apex of a comprehensive system of public education. When his ambitious proposals foundered in the legislature, Jefferson, who was also a member of the college's Board of Visitors, joined with Madison in a plan to reinvent the college from within. In December 1779, they persuaded the Visitors to overhaul the college from the ground up, effectively "manipulating and stretching to the utmost the powers already granted to the Board, under the old Colonial charter."[4] The Visitors reorganized the curriculum to include modern languages, law, and medicine; introduced an elective system, giving students new control over their course of study; and secularized the academic program, abolishing a chair in divinity and recasting the duties of an endowed chair in Indian missionary work from converting the tribes to studying their cultures, languages, and origins. The Visitors also closed the college's grammar school, terminating the position of its master, Rev. John Bracken, who had been hired in the revolutionary turmoil two years earlier as a professor of humanity.[5]

Bracken's immediate resistance may have been sidelined by the approach of war. With the British invasion of Virginia, the college was closed in 1781 as General Cornwallis's forces passed through Williamsburg, and then was occupied by French soldiers and partially destroyed during the ensuing siege of nearby Yorktown. For whatever reason, it was not until 1787 that Bracken sought to reclaim his faculty position by legal process, setting up the first major encounter between academia and the American courts.

Bracken's petition for a writ of mandamus, to compel the Visitors to re-store him to his faculty position, was transferred directly to the Virginia Court of Appeals "on account of difficulty" of the case. Bracken's legal claim was premised on the charter by which King William and Queen Mary had created the college in 1693. His lawyer argued that the charter established the faculty, Visitors, and Trustees essentially as "three branches of government" within the college, and that the Visitors had grossly over-stepped their bounds by presuming to redefine the membership of the faculty. Professors, Bracken contended, attained a vested legal interest in their position which could be extinguished only by formal legal process on proof of serious misconduct. In light of the faculty's constitutive roles in the college, "[i]t would be very strange indeed," Bracken's lawyer con-cluded, "if they could be deprived of them by the mere will of the Visitors, and could have no relief in this Court."[6]

And yet that was precisely the conclusion urged by John Marshall, a one-time law student at William and Mary who would go on to become Chief Justice of the U.S. Supreme Court, in presenting the college's hard-nosed defense. Marshall's first argument was that the court had no juris-diction over the matter at all. Marshall insisted that William and Mary, like all colleges, was an eleemosynary enterprise whose directors oper-ated beyond the power of the court's direction. Even if the court had ju-risdiction, Marshall argued in the alternative, the Visitors plainly acted within their lawful authority in reorganizing the college and terminating Bracken's position: "The Visitors or Governors have power to make such laws for the government of the College, from time to time, according to their various occasion and circumstances, as to them should seem most fit and expedient." A broad and flexible understanding of the Visitors' powers was necessitated, he argued, not only by the words of the 1693 charter, but also by the nature of the academic enterprise: "It was proper, that this discretion should be given to the Visitors, because a particular branch of science, which at one period of time would be deemed all im-portant, might at another, be thought not worth acquiring." Since "the Visitors have only legislated on a subject upon which they had a right to legislate," Marshall contended, "it is not for this Court to enquire, whether they have legislated wisely." The Court of Appeals sided with

Marshall in a conclusory forty-word order: "Let it be certified that, on the merits of the case, the General Court ought not to award a writ of mandamus to restore the plaintiff to the office of grammar master and professor of humanity in the said College."[7]

Bracken can hardly be considered an unqualified blow for academic freedom. Most obviously, the court's brief order offered no real statement of legal principle (although another decision would later say that the court had not been persuaded by Marshall's jurisdictional argument).[8] More fundamentally, the decision upheld an administrative restructuring that pointedly stripped faculty of status and authority. Before the Revolution, William and Mary had followed the English model of Oxford and Cambridge, in which collegiate governance rested squarely with the faculty; in Germany, too, the professoriate assumed authority to direct the universities largely free of external meddling.[9] *Bracken*, however, reinforced what then emerged as a distinctively American model of academic organization, in which managerial power was lodged in a strong executive leader and a lay governing board.[10] An essential part of William and Mary's 1779 reform, after all, had been to subject the faculty to closer control by the Board of Visitors, requiring that "all future questions involving curriculum, appointments, or any other college matter would be decided only after due consultation between President and faculty on one side of the table and a standing committee of six Visitors on the other."[11] Indeed, it would take more than a century and a half before courts would really begin to take seriously the academic freedom claims of individual scholars and teachers.[12]

Yet, while Marshall's victory in *Bracken* shifted power within campus, it did importantly preserve and entrench the power of the university to direct its affairs from within. Though Jefferson's first resort had been to the legislature, the reforms vindicated in *Bracken* were ultimately effected through internal channels of governance, however contested they might have been. In persuading the court to stay its hand, moreover, Marshall had won implicit acceptance of the idea that colleges enjoy broad authority to chart their own course.

In the first major litigation involving an academic dispute, the court had deferred to campus authority. In this way, *Bracken* laid the first foundation stone in what would in time emerge as a powerful, albeit loosely defined doctrine of academic abstention in American law. In matters of academic policy and governance, courts would stay their hand. For generations following the Virginia court's decision, aggrieved professors, students, and other campus constituents would learn, like John Bracken, that university officials, for all intents and purposes, *were* the law.

For Bracken himself, who was nothing if not persistent, vindication would ultimately come two decades later through the very internal channels his lawsuit had unwittingly affirmed. Having failed in his quest for a court order reinstating him to the faculty, he returned to court in a new lawsuit to compel payment of his faculty salary and was again rebuffed.[13] Throughout, he remained a prominent fixture in Williamsburg as rector of Bruton Parish Church, located a mere 1,675 feet from the gate of the president's house on campus. In 1812, upon Madison's death, Bracken was chosen to succeed the man who had turned him out of the faculty thirty-three years before. He became William and Mary's ninth president.[14]

A Large Victory for a "Small College"

Bracken turned out to be only the first of John Marshall's contributions to academic autonomy. Nearly three decades later, Marshall was in his nineteenth year as Chief Justice of the Supreme Court when it decided Trustees of Dartmouth College v. Woodward, a landmark case establishing constitutional protection for the independence of private colleges and universities.[15]

As in *Bracken*, the case grew out of an internal struggle over campus governance. Dartmouth's president, John Wheelock, had strongly disagreed with his governing board over the Trustees' support for sectarian programs, including "organized revivals and novel moral reforms like temperance."[16] When Wheelock resisted the Trustees' determination, they dismissed him for insubordination in 1815.[17] The quarrel figured prominently in New Hampshire's legislative and gubernatorial elections the following year, contributing to "a political revolution in the State."[18] A new Republican majority swept into the statehouse, determined to bring the Trustees to heel and to put Dartmouth on a more ecumenical course. In June 1816, the legislature passed measures effectively seizing control of the college. The statute revised the college's charter to expand the size of Dartmouth's Board of Trustees from twelve to twenty-one, with the new members to be appointed by the state's Republican governor, and to subject all major campus decisions to review by a new, twenty-five-member Board of Overseers also appointed by the governor. For good measure, the statute renamed Dartmouth College as "Dartmouth University."[19]

Pursuant to the law, the governor appointed nine new Trustees, who then convened a meeting, along with two of the original Trustees, and asserted control of the new "University." A majority of the old Trustees resisted at every turn. While the legislation was pending, several pleaded with the legislature that the measure would constitute a dangerous and unprecedented invasion of academic independence:

> If the provisions of this bill should take effect, we greatly fear that the concerns of the college will be drawn into the vortex of political controversy . . . The whole history of the United States for the last twenty years teaches us a lesson which ought not to be kept out of view. Our literary institutions hitherto have been preserved from the influence of party. The tendency of this bill, unless we greatly mistake, is to convert the peaceful retreat of our college into a field for party warfare.[20]

After the legislature brushed aside their concerns and rewrote Dartmouth's charter, nine of the original Trustees resolved to press their cause in the state courts, contending that the state was powerless to interpose itself in the administration of the college.

Initially, the Trustees met with utter frustration. The New Hampshire Supreme Court, in an opinion written by a chief justice recently appointed to the court by the new Republican governor, could find no basis for concluding that the governance structure provided in Dartmouth's original charter was somehow beyond the reach of legislative revision. Indeed, in Chief Justice William Richardson's hands, the special character of education became an argument not for deference, but for active state supervision:

> No man prizes more highly than I do, the literary institutions of our country, or would go farther to maintain their just rights and privileges. But I cannot bring myself to believe, that it would be consistent with sound policy, or ultimately with the true interests of literature itself, to place the great public institutions, in which all the young men, destined

for the liberal professions, are to be educated, within the absolute control of a few individuals, and out of the control of the sovereign
power . . . [M]ake the trustees independent, and they will ultimately
forget that their office is a public trust—will at length consider these institutions as their own—will overlook the great purposes for which their
powers were originally given, and will exercise them only to gratify their
own private views and wishes, or to promote the narrow purposes of a
sect or a party.[21]

Indeed, the court affirmed not only the propriety of legislative supervision, but pronounced its own readiness to intervene as necessary to curb
future abuses of campus power: "The officers and students of the college
have, without doubt, private rights in the institution—rights which
courts of justice are bound to notice—rights, which, if unjustly infringed,
even by the trustees themselves, this court, upon a proper application,
would feel itself bound to protect."[22]

When the case reached the U.S. Supreme Court, however, the Trustees
found a more receptive forum. Daniel Webster, who argued Dartmouth's
case, framed the matter as a David-and-Goliath struggle against external
interference: "It is, Sir, . . . a small College. And yet, there are those who
love it." Webster pressed two arguments. The first was that the state's action invaded the vested property interests of the college's president and
faculty on the theory that their "college livings" constituted "sacred" and
legally protected "freeholds."[23] This argument was probably not well calculated to appeal to Marshall, who three decades earlier had inveighed
against precisely this propertied view of faculty positions in *Bracken*.[24]

Webster prevailed, however, in his second argument, that the state's
effective seizure constituted an unconstitutional impairment of the college's contract rights under its original charter. Marshall's opinion for the
Court echoed the arguments he had made on behalf of William and Mary
nearly three decades before. Dartmouth, he reasoned, was not made an
organ of the state by its charter, but was rather a "private eleemosynary institution."[25] As such, its charter was a contract with the state protected
against future state impairment by the Constitution. Dartmouth's founders, he reasoned, "contracted for a system, which should . . . retain forever
the government of the literary institution they had formed, in the hands of
the persons approved by themselves."[26]

For the New Hampshire Supreme Court, the nature of the educational enterprise had been an argument for subjecting universities to democratic control; for Marshall, it was an argument for limiting state power to interfere. The Constitution's framers, he noted, had "withdrawn science, and the useful arts, from the action of State governments" by asserting exclusive federal authority over patents; by the same token, he reasoned, the Constitution should be understood to value and protect "contracts made for the advancement of literature."[27]

Like *Bracken* before it, the *Dartmouth College* decision was less than a four-square victory for academic freedom. As in the Virginia case, Dartmouth's legal claim to autonomy derived somewhat narrowly from the terms of its charter, rather than from the Constitution itself or any general principles of academic deference. In fact, the landmark status of the *Dartmouth College* decision to this day comes from its declaration of constitutional protection for private and commercial contracts generally, not from the happenstance that the case involved an academic claimant.[28] "For Marshall," observes Professor Matthew Finkin, "the question was not what was congenial to education, but what was consistent with the college founders' intentions" as manifested in their underlying contract.[29]

Nevertheless, *Dartmouth College* offered a significant new measure of protection to the operational independence of colleges and universities. As in *Bracken*, the power of a college's governing board to steer the institution through an internal crisis had been affirmed. But, in addition, Marshall's opinion recognized a constitutional right shielding the college's internal governance from external state interference. In doing so, the Court effectively "embrace[d] a fundamental commitment to institutional pluralism."[30] True, the scope of this constitutional right might be confined to private colleges, which could invoke contract rights against the state.[31] But, as Professor John Thelin has argued, even that limitation can be overstated, given the murkily blended public and private character of colleges at the time of the decision. According to Thelin, because "there is reasonable doubt that anyone in the early nineteenth century made a substantive distinction between 'public' and 'private' colleges in the United States," Marshall's "delineation of clear, strong powers for the academic corporation of Dartmouth College was a 'victory' for *all* colleges and universities, whether they are what we would today call 'private' or 'public.'"[32]

Whatever its original scope, the *Dartmouth College* decision indisputably recognized a new legal basis for protecting the autonomy of at least a major share of the nation's academic institutions. And in doing so, Marshall's opinion, not incidentally, rejected a line of reasoning in the state court that would have exposed all colleges, public or private, to free-ranging supervision by legislatures and courts alike. If *Bracken* had strengthened the institutional autonomy of colleges by turning back a legal challenge by a disgruntled individual professor, the *Dartmouth College* decision had done something much more. It gave institutional autonomy indirect constitutional protection capable of repelling a direct assertion of public control.

As it happens, nearly two centuries later, in 2007, a power struggle over the Dartmouth College Board of Trustees landed back in court. This time, the struggle pitted the college's administration and its allies on the board against certain alumni who hoped to gain control of the board through elections and steer the college in a more libertarian direction. To thwart the insurgency, the college announced plans to enlarge the board, from eighteen to twenty-six members, effectively diluting the influence of the alumni-elected Trustees. An alumni group filed a lawsuit to block the plan, alleging that past practice amounted to a contractual guarantee of alumni influence (a legal claim more fully explored subsequently in Chapter 9). The college moved to dismiss, arguing that "[t]he Board's judgment concerning what is best for Dartmouth" was not a matter for the courts.

This time, a plan to restructure the Board of Trustees would succeed against a claim of contract rights, though not because of a court decision: a spirited fight within the alumni group led it to withdraw the suit in June 2008.[33] Again, an appeal for external control of university governance had fallen short and internal channels had prevailed.

Bitter Medicine and the Constitutionally Autonomous State University

Notwithstanding *Dartmouth College*'s strong protection of the independence of private colleges, many fledgling state universities were subject to incessant meddling by shifting legislative factions in early years. The University of Michigan, founded in 1817, just two years before Dartmouth's victory in the Supreme Court, found that the decision offered no shield against the legislature's excessive, proprietary attentions. At one time, the legislature commanded the university to maintain a branch in every judicial district in the state. By 1840, the hobbled university was considered "practically a failure" and the legislature appointed a select committee to diagnose the problem. Its conclusion, in substance, was that the University of Michigan lacked Dartmouth's institutional autonomy. The university's legislative patrons, the committee reported bluntly, had acted

> [a]s if, because a university belongs to the people, that were reason why it should be dosed to death for fear it would be sick, if left to be nursed, like other institutions, by its immediate guardians. Thus has state after state, in this American Union, endowed universities, and then, by repeated contradictory and over legislation, torn them to pieces with the same facility as they do the statute book, and for the same reason, because they have the right.[34]

The committee's prescription, to place management of the university beyond the reach of the legislature, was effected at a state constitutional convention in 1850, when provisions were added to place "the general supervision of the university, and the direction and control of all [its] expenditures," securely in the hands of an elected Board of Regents.[35] The constitutional shift of power did not altogether stop the legislature from seeking to dictate terms, but it proved to be as effective a shield for the University of Michigan as the contract clause had proved for Dartmouth.

The utility of constitutional status to the University of Michigan, as well as the undaunted persistence of the legislature, is illustrated by a four-decade struggle between the Regents and the legislature over the teaching of homeopathy on campus. Homeopathy, a system of alternative medicine conceived by German physician Samuel Hahnemann in the eighteenth century, held that diseases could be combated by administering extremely diluted quantities of substances capable of producing symptoms similar to those of the disease in healthy persons. It was derided by adherents of mainstream medicine as having roughly the same healing efficacy as the Michigan legislature's early ministrations to the state's university. It could not quite be said that homeopathic practitioners "dosed [their patients] to death," as the select committee had said of the legislature's mismanagement of the university, because the central complaint against homeopathy was, in fact, that its prescribed dosages were of no consequence whatsoever.[36] But the medical establishment, and the faculty of the University of Michigan's medical college to a one, plainly wanted nothing to do with a practice they considered akin to quackery.[37]

Yet the Michigan legislature evidently had greater enthusiasm for the promise of homeopathy. In 1855, the legislature amended the university's governing statutes to order the university to maintain "always . . . at least one professor of homeopathy in the department of medicine." When the Regents ignored the edict, a private citizen filed suit to compel compliance. The university tried to evade by pleading that more time was needed to study the feasibility of integrating homeopathy into the medical school, particularly given the antipathy of its faculty. The Michigan Supreme Court dismissed the lawsuit on the ground that the citizen-plaintiff lacked a sufficiently personal interest to bring the suit, but it hinted strongly that the legislature's directive was, in any event, probably an unconstitutional invasion of the Regents' prerogatives to manage the university.[38]

After a dozen years' inaction confirmed the university's intention to flout the 1855 directive indefinitely, the legislature revived the cause, but with a new strategy. This time the legislature would seek to purchase what it could not command. In the years immediately following the Civil War, the university's financial situation had grown dark and the Regents turned to the state for aid. The state, which had never before spent tax dollars to support the university, responded with legislation to provide an annual revenue stream worth roughly $16,000—on one condition: "that the regents of the university shall carry into effect the law which provides that there shall always be at least one professor of homeopathy in the department of medicine."[39] After a year of agonizing, the Regents answered that they would accept the aid and "comply" with the condition by creating a new "Michigan school of homeopathy" to be located in some city *other* than Ann Arbor. The state balked, and the Regents filed suit to compel the release of the promised funds. A divided Michigan Supreme Court (without the participation of eminent Chief Justice Thomas Cooley, who remained one of the three founding professors of the university's law school) held that the university's stratagem of exile did not constitute compliance. The state could not compel the university to teach homeopathy, but the state was free to starve it.

The impasse was broken in 1875 when the legislature offered the university a $6,000 annual appropriation to fund a school of homeopathy apart from the medical school. The university took the deal and the homeopathy school operated modestly out of the campus home of one of its two professors.[40] What appeared to be a palatable solution to the long-running controversy returned to court, however, for a final time in 1896 after the legislature enacted legislation ordering that the school it had long insisted be located in Ann Arbor now be relocated to Detroit. The Michigan Supreme Court, in a third visit to the controversy, issued a final and emphatic declaration of the university's autonomy. The state's constitution gave the Regents an extraordinary independent status, coequal with that of the legislature, and as to matters of campus governance and spending the Regents' authority was "absolute and unqualified." Pursuant to its constitutional status, the Board of Regents had consistently "denied the power of the legislature to interfere with its management or control, and for 46 years ha[d] declined obedience to any and every act of the legislature which they, upon mature reflection and consideration, . . . deemed against the best interests of the institution. This court has sustained them in that position, and has on every occasion when asked denied its writ to interfere with their action."[41] The court finished by adding its own strong support of this approach:

> It is obvious to every intelligent and reflecting mind that such an institution would be safer and more certain of permanent success in the control of such a body than in that of the legislature, composed of 132 members, elected every two years, many of whom would, of necessity, know but little of its needs, and would have little or no time to intelligently investigate and determine the policy essential for the success of a great university.[42]

The court's decision thus recognized an important new foundation for university autonomy against external control in state constitutional law. But it also recognized a principle of potentially far broader significance: as a matter of sound public policy, quite apart from the particular language of any given charter or constitution, colleges and universities are best managed by their own; in the context of higher education, direct accountability to the people is not a virtue, but a threat to the academic mission.

The judgment of history ultimately favored the Michigan medical faculty's assessment of homeopathy over that of the legislature. The "dozens of departments and freestanding schools" of homeopathy that sprang up across the United States during the late nineteenth century, observes medical historian John Haller, dwindled sharply in the first years of the twentieth century under mounting regulatory pressure from medical education associations. Perhaps ironically, when the University of Michigan finally closed the doors to its Homeopathic College in 1922, it was one of the last three institutions in the United States to offer instruction in the field.[43] It seemed that a "branch of science," to borrow from John Marshall's argument to the Virginia court in *Bracken*, deemed at one time by some to be "all important," was ultimately thought "not worth acquiring"; but, as Marshall had urged, the decision was the university's alone.

Dismissals, Discipline, and Deference: The Rise of "Academic Abstention"

The value of constitutional protection for universities is also amply demonstrated by the early travails of the University of Missouri. The *Dartmouth College* case shielded most private colleges from legislative restructuring. And roughly a fifth of the states, like Michigan, granted similar autonomy to their public universities by way of state constitutional status.[44] But the University of Missouri, a public university founded by statute in 1839, fell outside both sorts of protection and so fell prey to regular political predations. Its first president, John Lathrop, resigned and took up the founding presidency of the University of Wisconsin in 1849, after suffering bruising indignities at the hands of the legislature and the fledgling university's Board of Curators. The atmosphere was so bitter that at a farewell dinner, attended by thousands of supporters despite bad weather, Lathrop unleashed a rebuke of the legislature and the Curators so "caustic, we never expect to hear its like again," according to an approving report in the local newspaper. In response, the Curators nearly refused the gift of a portrait of Lathrop by celebrated Missouri artist George Caleb Bingham, ultimately acceding only, in the words of a proposed resolution, to demonstrate "the Christian principle of overcoming evil with good."[45]

One source of trouble appears to have been the legislature's habit of controlling the university by periodically vacating *en masse* the offices of the university's curators, president, and faculty. Lathrop's successor, James Shannon, was turned out in one such purge in 1855; when the new Board of Curators offered him reappointment the following year, he refused.[46] That same 1855 purge cleared the way for the appointment of Bolivar S. Head, previously a mathematics tutor, as professor of mathematics and head of the university library. The term of Head's appointment was for six years, but within three years the legislature passed yet "another act vacating, from the 4th day of July, 1860, the offices of all the professors, tutors, and teachers connected in any manner with the university, and providing also that a new board of curators should be elected in the place of the existing board, and that elections should be had to fill the offices by the act made vacant."[47] In the house-clearing that followed, Head was not reinstated. (Head's replacement, in fact, stayed only briefly himself before deserting campus to enlist in the Confederate cause.)

Like the Rev. Bracken before him, Professor Head apparently waited some years before seeking to overturn his ouster in the courts. As in Bracken's case, the delay may well be explained by the onset of war; the Civil War closed the Columbia campus and left the university in shambles and essentially bankrupt for years. When the university regained its financial footing, Head filed suit and eventually took his case to the U.S. Supreme Court, representing himself without an attorney. He lost emphatically at every turn. The state court ruled that "the university was a public corporation, and therefore subject to the unrestrained control of the legislature"; the U.S. Supreme Court agreed further that boilerplate in Head's six-year contract, stating that his appointment was "subject to law," implicitly meant that his tenure was "subject to whatever law the State legislature might think fit to pass," including one simply cancelling the contract altogether. Having obtained his job in precisely such a legislative coup, the Court observed, the professor could hardly express surprise.[48]

The decision in *Head* illustrates the abject vulnerability of some public universities to legislative meddling, but also the strong inclination of courts to steer clear of campus disputes. In case after case through the nineteenth and early twentieth centuries, courts briskly upheld the essentially absolute power of universities to dismiss faculty members as they saw fit. In part, this reflected the simple absence of legal restrictions on employers generally. In the age of at-will employment, before the enactment of modern labor and civil rights laws, those who were fired typically had no legal ground available to complain. In this sense, academic employees stood on no worse ground than workers in other fields, whose employers also enjoyed a broad "autonomy" in the employment relationship.[49] But the pattern of decisions favoring universities during this era was so strong, in cases involving faculty dismissals, student discipline, and other academic matters, as to suggest that something else was at work.

Even when existing law provided plausible grounds of complaint, courts seemed determined to affirm university authorities. In Darrow v. Briggs, for example, the Missouri Supreme Court showed obvious impatience with a professor's complaint that he had been defamed and wrongfully fired by the president of Drury College, in violation of a contractual promise of indefinite employment, for donating a controversial book on "theosophy" to the local library. The court affirmed dismissal of the lawsuit on the ground that the college's bylaws reserved "a very broad discretion" to remove faculty whenever the board of trustees considered that "the interest of the college shall require it."[50] In Ward v. Board of Regents of Kansas State Agricultural College, a federal appeals court similarly upheld a public college's power to fire a professor midway through a fixed-term contract on the theory that its statutory authority to "remove any professor whenever the interests of the college shall require" became an implicit term in every contract.[51] In Gillan v. Board of Regents of Normal Schools, the Wisconsin Supreme Court went a step further, ruling that even a calculated effort by a public college to tie its own hands concerning dismissal, such as by making a contract unambiguously barring removal except on proof of misconduct, would be legally ineffective where the college's statutory authority to dismiss was unqualified.[52] As Professor Peter Byrne observed, a striking pattern emerged from the case law: "the dilution of contract principles as a binding ground for decision . . . invariably led to deference toward academic officials."[53]

Indeed, even where a governing statute itself placed limits on a college's authority to dismiss, courts might construe the grant to give the university unreviewable authority to act. In Hartigan v. Board of Regents of West Virginia University, a professor of anatomy protested that he had been summarily fired even though the relevant statute gave West Virginia University the power to remove faculty only "for good cause." Though modern law distinguishes "good cause" employment from at-will employment, the West Virginia Supreme Court discerned no limits to the Regents' powers:

> [The statute] makes that power very wide, because it does not specify any cause constituting ground of removal such as incompetency, immorality or other specific cause, but leaves it to the regents to [be the] judge of the cause of removal, to say what is good cause . . . No intimation is breathed by the statute of their accountability to any court . . .
>
> Some one will ask, is the Board of Regents to do as it pleases, without control, erroneous as its action may be? Yes, so far as the courts are concerned.[54]

Courts followed the same approach in student-discipline cases. When E. Harley Pratt was ejected from Wheaton College for belonging to a temperance organization known as the Good Templars, in violation of a college rule barring membership in secret societies, his resort to the Illinois courts was categorically rebuffed. The Illinois Supreme Court held:

> [W]hether the rule be judicious or not, it violates neither good morals nor the law of the land, and is therefore clearly within the power of the college authorities to make and enforce. A discretionary power has been given them to regulate the discipline of their college in such manner as they deem proper, and so long as their rules violate neither divine nor human law, we have no more authority to interfere than we have to control the domestic discipline of a father in his family.[55]

Nominally, the court's opinion left open the possibility of judicial correction of campus disciplinary measures that violated "the law of the land," but practice made clear that this possibility was largely theoretical. The U.S. Supreme Court echoed the same theme of deference nearly fifty years later in disposing of a would-be law student's challenge to a similar ban on Greek organizations at the University of Mississippi.[56] "The notion," explained Robert Bickel and Peter Lake, "was that the university—not the law—was sovereign in this domain."[57] The university, in effect, occupied a world apart, beyond the meddling and supervision of the courts.[58]

The *Pratt* court's comparison of collegiate and parental authority was not incidental. It helped lay the foundation for judicial recognition of the *in loco parentis* doctrine, under which colleges held broad authority to impose order and protect the moral welfare of their students, in the same manner as parents.[59] The analogy was telling. Even today, courts regard parental discipline and internal family governance as significantly insulated from judicial review.[60] Evolving attitudes concerning domestic violence have eroded judicial inhibitions in recent years, but especially at the time of the court decisions establishing the parent-like authority of college authorities, notions of "family privacy" left very little room for judicial review of paternal power.[61]

Thus, when Stetson University suspended a sophomore for "ringing cow bells and parading in the halls of the dormitory at forbidden hours, cutting the lights," and other such "subversive" activities, the Florida Supreme Court readily deferred to campus administrators.[62] The Michigan Supreme Court was equally unmoved by the plight of eighteen-year-old Alice Tanton, who was barred from returning to Michigan State Normal College (now Eastern Michigan University) on the ground that "she smoked cigarettes on the public streets of Ypsilanti" and was observed riding "in an automobile on the lap of a young man." The court curtly disposed of her legal challenge, praising "the motherly interest" demonstrated by the college dean and emphasizing the broad regulatory latitude vested in college officials: "That, in the absence of an abuse of discretion, the school authorities and not the court shall prescribe proper disciplinary measures is, we think, settled by the text-writers and the adjudicated cases."[63] Four years later, a New York court similarly upheld Syracuse University's dismissal of junior Beatrice Anthony on the ground that she was not, in the university's sober estimation, "a typical Syracuse girl." The court agreed that this was not much of a reason to dismiss a student, but held that ultimately "no need for dismissing need be given"; instead, it was the student's burden to show the *absence* of grounds relating to the "ideals of scholarship" or "the University's moral atmosphere." The court added: "[T]he University authorities have wide discretion in determining what situation does and what does not fall within the classes mentioned, and the courts would be slow indeed in disturbing any decision of the University authorities in this respect."[64]

In both the faculty-dismissal and student-discipline cases, significantly, courts offered rationales for judicial deference that went well beyond the particular wording of university statutes or bylaws. Just as the Michigan

Supreme Court had warned in the homeopathy dispute that legislative supervision imperiled academic excellence, courts worried generally that judges were similarly ill-equipped to second-guess academic judgments and that opening the doors to campus litigation would risk serious harm to the uniquely valuable missions of universities. In *Hartigan*, for example, the West Virginia Supreme Court warned that if courts undertook to review academic judgment in dismissing a professor, "every case of removal may, probably would, be made the subject of protracted litigation. In the meanwhile the incompetent professor would go on, and the harm to the university would be, or might be, very great."[65] Similarly, in the *Stetson University* case, the Florida Supreme Court cautioned that broad judicial deference in reviewing student complaints was necessary to ward against "vexatious litigation" that "would very materially impair the discipline and usefulness of an institution of learning."[66]

These policy considerations led courts to adopt a deferential attitude across the full spectrum of lawsuits challenging academic decision making, without regard for the nature of the underlying cause of action or the identity of the academic defendant as public or private. Professor Byrne, writing in 1989, aptly summed up the lay of the land:

> It would be inappropriate to describe academic abstention as a doctrine, because courts have never developed a consistent or thorough body of rationales or followed a uniform group of leading cases. Yet the consistency of result and invocation of the need for judicial restraint whenever internal university decisions are challenged by an unhappy student or professor has been sufficiently impressive that a competent practitioner today would advise such a student or professor that her chances of success are low or nil.[67]

Other scholars, surveying the same landscape, have felt less inhibition about describing the cases as reflecting a clear and cognizable "doctrine of academic abstention."[68]

Whether described as a doctrine or merely an attitude, the judicial disinclination to engage in serious review of academic actions was plainly strong and widely acknowledged. But, being at most a common-law doctrine, it was subject to override by a determined legislature. Developments in the 1950s and 1960s, however, would provide a constitutional foundation for academic deference—a development that at once both strengthened and weakened universities' claim to be free from judicial oversight.

Of Subversives and Straitjackets: Constitutional Protection for Academic Freedom

Paul M. Sweezy was a man of no small complexity. The son of a wealthy Wall Street banker, Sweezy was educated at Philips Exeter and Harvard, where he was president of the *Harvard Crimson* and, later, a star graduate student in economics. Sweezy, the economist Paul Samuelson wrote admiringly many years later, "was the best that Exeter and Harvard can produce," and "early established himself as among the most promising economists of his generation." Yet, his left-wing politics were problematic. A sojourn at the London School of Economics during the darkest days of the Great Depression had inspired a conversion to Marxism and socialism. When he later became convinced that his Marxist beliefs had cost him a shot at a tenured professorship at Harvard, Sweezy left full-time academia and retired to his native New Hampshire. There, he founded a socialist journal called *Monthly Review* and, living off an inheritance drawn from the J.P. Morgan banking empire, devoted himself to a life of writing on the failures of capitalism.[69]

Soon thereafter, in the gathering chill of the Cold War, New Hampshire attorney general Louis Wyman was tasked by the state legislature, as "a one-man legislative committee," to investigate " 'whether subversive persons . . . are presently located within this state.' "[70] Sweezy seemed like a good prospect. In 1954, Wyman summoned Sweezy and demanded to know, among other things, about the content of a lecture Sweezy had delivered to a humanities class at the University of New Hampshire. In particular, the attorney general wanted to know whether Sweezy had opined in his lecture about the inevitability of socialism or "the theory of dialectical materialism." Sweezy would allow that he was "a classical Marxist," but refused, as a matter of constitutional principle, to disclose his political beliefs or the substance of his university lecture. After the state supreme court affirmed Sweezy's conviction for contempt, the U.S. Supreme Court took up his case. The New Hampshire legislature, whose attempted takeover of Dartmouth College in 1816 had provided universities with their first constitutional protection, had set the stage for another, even more direct contribution to academic freedom.

The Supreme Court ruled for Sweezy 6–2, with one justice (appointed to the Court after oral argument in the case) not participating. Chief Justice Warren rested the plurality's decision on a relatively narrow due process ground—that the record left doubt whether the legislature had really meant to authorize the disputed line of questions—but it also endorsed a significantly broader ground: that the First Amendment shielded Sweezy's university lecture as an exercise of "academic freedom." The plurality wrote that "there unquestionably was an invasion of petitioner's liberties in the areas of academic freedom and political expression—areas in which government should be extremely reticent to tread." Warren then explained at some length "the essentiality of freedom in the community of American universities":

> No one should underestimate the vital role in a democracy that is played by those who guide and train our youth. To impose any strait jacket upon the intellectual leaders in our colleges and universities would imperil the future of our Nation . . . Scholarship cannot flourish in an atmosphere of suspicion and distrust. Teachers and students must always remain free to inquire, to study and to evaluate, to gain new maturity and understanding; otherwise our civilization will stagnate and die.[71]

Justice Frankfurter, joined by Justice Harlan, agreed that Sweezy's conviction was unsustainable, but he attributed that result directly to a substantive constitutional prohibition against "governmental intervention in the intellectual life of a university." Frankfurter rationalized this rigorous constitutional protection directly on "the dependence of a free society on free universities": "For society's good—if understanding be an essential need of society—inquiries into [the "mysteries of nature" and basic social] problems, speculations about them, stimulation in others of reflection upon them, must be left as unfettered as possible. Political power must abstain from intrusion into this activity of freedom, pursued in the interest of wise government and the people's well-being, except for reasons that are exigent and obviously compelling."[72] Five years earlier, Justices Frankfurter and Douglas, another former law professor, had each written separate opinions in cases suggesting constitutional protection for academic freedom, but *Sweezy* was the first occasion on which a majority of justices agreed that the Constitution protected "academic freedom" by name.[73]

The emergence of constitutional protection for academic freedom was obviously no small matter. Before *Sweezy*, protection for academic freedom had been tenuous at best. The American Association of University Professors (AAUP) had made important strides in securing respect for academic freedom on American campuses through influential declarations on the subject in 1915 and again in 1940. Indeed, the AAUP's 1940 Statement of Principles on Academic Freedom and Tenure, asserting that "[t]eachers are entitled to full freedom in research and in the publication of the results," as well as to "freedom in the classroom in discussing their subject," in time won "nearly universal institutional acceptance."[74] The AAUP's labors in articulating these principles and in monitoring campus compliance with them through formal investigation and censure had vastly improved the conditions and security of academic employment.[75] But its protections depended ultimately on the willingness of university authorities to go along; the AAUP's 1940 Statement was therefore, in William Van Alstyne's apt description, "very soft law."[76] By recognizing First Amendment protection for academic freedom, the Court provided means to enforce the guarantees of academic freedom in court, even against the predations of legislators and prosecutors. The 1940 Statement itself, Walter Metzger observed, was intended "not to reinforce legal claims, but to provide a feasible substitute for them."[77] Yet, by embracing key elements of the AAUP's conception of academic freedom as First Amendment values, the Supreme Court ensured that legal and campus protections for academic freedom would be mutually reinforcing. And "[i]n comparison with the soft law of the 1940 Statement," Van Alstyne notes, "the first amendment is very hard law indeed."[78]

Ten years later, *Sweezy*'s implicit consensus became explicit in the Court's opinion in Keyishian v. Board of Regents of the University of the State of New York. In *Keyishian,* the Court overturned a New York law that required all state university personnel to disclaim allegiance to the Communist Party. Justice Brennan's majority opinion located protection for academic freedom squarely in the First Amendment:

Our Nation is deeply committed to safeguarding academic freedom, which is of transcendent value to all of us and not merely to the teachers concerned. That freedom is therefore a special concern of the First Amendment, which does not tolerate laws that cast a pall of orthodoxy over the classroom . . . The classroom is peculiarly the "marketplace of ideas." The Nation's future depends upon leaders trained through wide exposure to that robust exchange of ideas which discovers truth "out of a multitude of tongues, [rather] than through any kind of authoritative selection."[79]

New York's required disclaimer was all the more dangerous, the Court warned, because the activities and allegiances it proscribed were so ambiguous, chilling even permitted inquiry and expression by scholars wary of misjudging the line.

Sweezy and *Keyishian* protected academic freedom in the classic sense contemplated by the AAUP's 1940 Statement of Principles, as the right of individual scholars to teach and study free from penalty or constraint. Yet, in Regents of the University of California v. Bakke, a case that would come a decade after *Keyishian*, Justice Powell relied on both decisions to recognize First Amendment protection for the "academic freedom" of a university as an institution. The issue in *Bakke* was the constitutionality of an affirmative action program used at the University of California at Davis. With the rest of the Court split evenly into two camps, Justice Powell's opinion effectively decided the case. In considering the university's argument that it had a compelling interest in admitting a racially diverse student body, Powell emphasized that the Court owed deference to the professional judgment of university administrators. "The freedom of a university to make its own judgments as to education," Powell wrote, "includes the selection of its student body."[80]

Powell's conception of academic freedom encompassing academic institutions as well as individual academics was not torn from the blue. As Powell noted, Justice Frankfurter's influential concurrence in *Sweezy* had described academic freedom both in terms of individuals and institutions. Quoting from the famous Statement of Remonstrance by the Open Universities in South Africa, Frankfurter had insisted that "the spirit of free inquiry" required " 'the four essential freedoms' of a university—to determine for itself on academic grounds who may teach, what may be taught, how it shall be taught, and who may be admitted to study."[81] Now Powell relied on the same observation to conclude that "in arguing that its universities must be accorded the right to select those students who will contribute the most to the 'robust exchange of ideas,' petitioner invokes a countervailing constitutional interest, that of the First Amendment."[82]

A quarter-century later, in 2003, Powell's view was formally adopted as that of a Court majority in Grutter v. Bollinger, upholding the use of affirmative action by the University of Michigan Law School. In *Grutter*, Justice O'Connor's majority opinion agreed with Powell that the First Amendment specially safeguards the "educational autonomy" of universities:

> We have long recognized that, given the important purpose of public education and the expansive freedoms of speech and thought associated with the university environment, universities occupy a special niche in our constitutional tradition. In announcing the principle of student body diversity as a compelling state interest, Justice Powell invoked our cases recognizing a constitutional dimension, grounded in the First Amendment, of educational autonomy . . . Our conclusion that the Law School has a compelling interest in a diverse student body is informed by our view that attaining a diverse student body is at the heart of the Law School's proper institutional mission, and that "good faith" on the part of a university is "presumed" absent "a showing to the contrary."[83]

Grutter thus suggested that constitutional respect for university autonomy blunted the application of other constitutional principles, at least when a university defendant could plausibly argue that its conduct was intertwined with its good-faith academic judgment.

Indeed, even well before *Grutter*, the Court had effectively followed the same course in turning aside constitutional challenges by students to their academic dismissals. In Board of Curators of the University of Missouri v. Horowitz, the Court showed no enthusiasm for taking up a medical student's claim that her dismissal following poor clinical evaluations violated her due process rights. Even assuming that students have some protectable "liberty" interest in avoiding dismissal, the Court ruled, the university had given her ample "process" in ousting her. Then-Justice Rehnquist's majority opinion saw no real good—and no small danger— in importing more judicial process into campus disputes:

> [W]e decline to ignore the historic judgment of educators and thereby formalize the academic dismissal process by requiring a hearing. The educational process is not by nature adversary; instead it centers around a

continuing relationship between faculty and students, "one in which the teacher must occupy many roles—educator, adviser, friend, and, at times, parent-substitute" . . . We decline to further enlarge the judicial presence in the academic community and thereby risk deterioration of many beneficial aspects of the faculty-student relationship.

The same considerations led the Court to conclude that any *substantive* limits on universities' power to set their own academic policies, under the guise of constitutional substantive due process, must also be kept to a minimum. "Courts are particularly ill-equipped," Rehnquist warned, "to evaluate academic performance."[84] Justice Powell concurred, emphasizing that "[u]niversity faculties must have the widest range of discretion in making judgments as to the academic performance of students and their entitlement to promotion or graduation."[85]

In Regents of the University of Michigan v. Ewing, too, the Court emphasized the same considerations in rebuffing a medical student's substantive due process challenge to his dismissal for poor academic performance. The student's score on a crucial examination was indisputably abysmal, but he argued that his dismissal was nevertheless "arbitrary and capricious," in violation of fundamental due process guarantees of fairness, because the university had let other failing students (whose scores were admittedly not quite so low as the claimant's) retake the exam while denying the same opportunity to him. The Court, in an opinion by Justice Stevens, followed *Horowitz* in holding that the university satisfied any requirement of b asic fairness, even assuming that students have a protectable "property" interest in continuing their studies. "Considerations of profound importance," Stevens wrote, "counsel restrained judicial review of the substance of academic decisions": "When judges are asked to review the substance of a genuinely academic decision, . . . they should show great respect for the faculty's professional judgment. Plainly, they may not override it unless it is such a substantial departure from accepted academic norms as to demonstrate that the person or committee responsible did not actually exercise professional judgment."[86] By this approach, constitutional review of academic decisions comes to an end once the court is satisfied that the judgment was, in fact, "academic" in nature; and, as *Grutter* affirmed, judges are directed to presume "good faith" in such decision making. In rationalizing this limitation on judicial review,

Justice Stevens emphasized that courts are simply not "suited to evaluate the substance of the multitude of academic decisions that are made daily by faculty members of public educational institutions—decisions that require 'an expert evaluation of cumulative information and [are] not readily adapted to the procedural tools of judicial or administrative decisionmaking.'"[87]

This rationale is, of course, familiar. By "recognizing a constitutional dimension, grounded in the First Amendment, of educational autonomy"—one which requires that courts "defer" to the good-faith academic judgment of university decision makers—the Supreme Court's decisions have effectively constitutionalized the traditional common-law doctrine of academic abstention. At least it is fair to say, as Professor Byrne has, that "[t]he constitutional right of institutional academic freedom appears to be a collateral descendant of the common law notion of academic abstention."[88]

Dissension in the Devils' Den: New Openings for Judicial Involvement

The Supreme Court's recognition, in the 1950s and beyond, of First Amendment protection for academic freedom, including the "educational autonomy" of academic institutions, substantially strengthened traditional legal protections for campus prerogatives. Constitutional rights, unlike common-law rights, are not subject to override by determined legislative or judicial actors. But the universities' winning resort to the courts for constitutional protection also carried potential complications, as administrators at Central Connecticut State College were to learn in 1970.

In September 1969, a group of students at the New Britain college (now Central Connecticut State University) sought to organize a campus chapter of Students for a Democratic Society (SDS) and petitioned the college for official recognition. Their request was routed through normal channels to the campus Student Affairs Committee, made up of both students and faculty, which quizzed the applicants about their ties to the national SDS and about their intentions concerning campus disruptions. The students answered somewhat evasively, insisting that they did not take orders from the national SDS but demurring on whether they might ever disrupt classes or incite other unrest, explaining that it would depend on the circumstances. It probably didn't help matters that the committee's deliberations coincided precisely with the Days of Rage in Chicago, during which the ultra-radical SDS offshoot the Weathermen took to the streets, smashing cars and storefronts and battling police. A majority of the campus committee favored recognizing the group, but college president F. Don James declined. Citing the SDS's support for disruption and violence, the president concluded that "approval should not be granted to any group that 'openly repudiates' the college's dedication to academic freedom." President James did little to cool tensions when, after the frustrated students retired to the "Devils' Den" coffee shop in the campus student center to discuss what to do, he dispatched two deans to eject them on the ground that they were not "a duly recognized college organization."[89]

In response, the student radicals took not to the streets, but to the courts, filing a lawsuit claiming that the president's action violated their First Amendment rights. The lower courts ruled against the students, concluding that "the President of the College . . . acted within his broad discretion and comprehensive authority" in denying recognition.[90] But the U.S. Supreme Court, in one of Justice Powell's first opinions on the Court, unanimously reversed. The Court invoked *Sweezy* and *Keyishian*'s constitutional protection of academic freedom, to affirm not the broad discretion of campus administrators, but the students' right to a remedy. "At the outset," Powell's analysis began, "we note that state colleges and universities are not enclaves immune from the sweep of the First Amendment." Indeed, "[q]uite to the contrary," the First Amendment applied with special force to "safeguard[] academic freedom" on campus. While the president might rightfully refuse recognition to students who unambiguously vowed defiance of reasonable campus rules, Powell wrote, he could not act simply on the basis of his "disagreement . . . with the group's philosophy."[91]

Chief Justice Burger concurred in Powell's opinion on the understanding that "[t]he courts, state or federal, should be a last resort" to resolve campus conflicts, but he also acknowledged that times had changed. "The relatively placid life of the college campus of the past," the Chief Justice observed, "has not prepared either administrators or students for their respective responsibilities in maintaining an atmosphere in which divergent views can be asserted vigorously, but civilly, to the end that those who seek to be heard accord the same right to all others."[92]

Justice Douglas, whose dissenting opinion in *Adler* two decades earlier had been the first to invoke constitutional protection for "academic freedom" by name, went even further. The days of obeisance to "[t]he status quo of the college or university"—the "governing body (trustees or overseers), administrative officers, . . . and the faculty"—were over, he wrote. "Education is commonly thought of as the process of filling the receptacles"—that is, the minds of the students—"with what the faculty in its wisdom deems fit and proper." Yet, "[s]tudents—who, by reason of the Twenty-sixth Amendment, become eligible to vote when 18 years of age—are adults who are members of the college or university community. Their interests and concerns are often quite different from those of the faculty. They often have values, views, and ideologies that are at war with the ones which the college has traditionally espoused or indoctrinated." In such matters, Douglas saw no particular reason to privilege the views of the faculty and other figures of the academic establishment:

> Many, inside and out of faculty circles, realize that one of the main problems of faculty members is their own re-education or re-orientation. Some have narrow specialties that are hardly relevant to modern times. History has passed others by, leaving them interesting relics of a bygone day. More often than not they represent those who withered under the pressures of McCarthyism or other forces of conformity and represent but a timid replica of those who once brought distinction to the ideal of academic freedom.

In the inevitable clash of campus constituencies, Douglas insisted that it is "they, the students, [who] speak in the tradition of Jefferson and Madison and the First Amendment."[93]

Healy did not, of course, spell the end of constitutional deference to university officials. *Bakke, Horowitz, Ewing,* and *Grutter,* all yet to come, each significantly affirmed constitutional protection for "educational autonomy" in lawsuits brought by former or would-be students. And, indeed, thirty-five years later, the Court is accurately understood still to regard universities as specially situated "First Amendment institutions," whose "norms and practices" are entitled to unusual deference.[94] But *Healy* did powerfully illustrate that the recognition of explicit constitutional protection for academic freedom would not operate merely as a shield for university communities against external meddling, but would potentially draw courts deeper into campus affairs in mediating intramural disputes over policy and governance.[95] Where the activities of some within a campus community are said to endanger the ability of others to learn or teach, acknowledges First Amendment scholar and former university president Robert O'Neil, it is "not always clear *whose* academic freedom is at stake."[96] And, in such cases, there may be no alternative but for a court to decide.

By the time *Healy* was handed down in June 1972, the national SDS had already come apart at the seams. But the significance of the decision, and the views it implied of the courts' role on campus, was only beginning to emerge. Indeed, in a real sense, its full significance is still being worked out today. Justice Powell's principle of academic deference may have carried the day in Justice O'Connor's razor-thin majority opinion in *Grutter*, but *Healy*'s legacy can surely be seen in the sharp dissents of Chief Justice Rehnquist and Justice Thomas. O'Connor wrote for five members of the Court in embracing a "holding . . . in keeping with our tradition of giving a degree of deference to a university's academic decisions, within constitutionally prescribed limits."[97] Her opinion bowed to the University of Michigan Law School's "educational judgment that [racial] diversity is essential to its educational mission," even while expressing the expectation "that 25 years from now, the use of racial preferences will no longer be necessary to further the interest approved today."[98]

Chief Justice Rehnquist's dissent, on behalf of four members of the Court, flatly "rejected calls to apply more lenient [constitutional] review based on the particular setting in which race is being used," including specifically in the "context of higher education."[99] Justice Thomas's opinion went even further, dripping with populist contempt for the notion that the Constitution embodied any special respect for the self-serving academic judgment of elitist university officials. For Thomas, the "tradition of . . . deference" affirmed by the *Grutter* majority was nothing more than a house of cards built from concurring opinions in *Sweezy* and *Bakke* and empty say-so in the Court's opinion in *Keyishian*.[100] Thomas fumed that "[t]he majority upholds the Law School's racial discrimination not by interpreting the people's Constitution, but by responding to a faddish slogan of the cognoscenti."[101] He insisted that "the Law School's assessment of the benefits of racial discrimination and devotion to the admissions status quo are not entitled to any sort of deference, grounded in the

First Amendment or anywhere else," and derided "the idea that the First Amendment authorizes a public university to do what would otherwise violate the Equal Protection Clause."[102]

The clash between the majority and dissents in *Grutter* highlights just how precarious a foothold institutional academic freedom enjoys in present-day constitutional doctrine. The debate between Justices O'Connor and Thomas, in a real sense, pits respect for universities as uniquely public-minded against a demand for unbridled public accountability through law. For now, the view that the First Amendment requires courts to limit their incursions on university autonomy, balancing the rights of individuals against the interests of the university to define and pursue its own academic mission, remains on top, but only by the narrowest margin. Justice O'Connor may have held the line on the tradition of judicial deference to academic judgment, but Justice Thomas may well speak for the future in expressing profound skepticism that colleges and universities are entitled to special treatment under the law.

In closing his opinion, Thomas mustered half-hearted agreement with one aspect of O'Connor's majority opinion, endorsing "the imposition of a 25-year time limit . . . as a holding that the deference the Court pays to the Law School's educational judgments . . . will itself expire."[103] Judging from the trend line of recent court decisions surveyed in the chapters that follow, subjecting colleges and universities to unstinting legal scrutiny in a dizzying range of academic controversies, the expiration date on academic deference may well be coming even sooner than Justice Thomas had hoped.

CHAPTER 3

Battles over Bias: Anti-discrimination Law on Campus

When George W. McLaurin was admitted to the University of Oklahoma in 1948, his admission was subject to certain conditions crafted by the university president, George Lynn Cross. Mr. McLaurin, a sixty-one-year-old retired college instructor seeking his doctorate in education, was "required to sit apart at a designated desk in an anteroom adjoining the classroom; to sit at a designated desk on the mezzanine floor of the library, but not to use the desks in the regular reading room; and to sit at a designated table and to eat at a different time from the other students in the school cafeteria."[1] The problem that inspired the restrictions was, of course, that Mr. McLaurin was black.

At first, the university had denied McLaurin admission altogether, but by the late 1940s the state's segregationists were running short of options. Earlier lawsuits brought by the National Association for the Advancement of Colored People (NAACP) had established that states were constitutionally obligated to provide substantially equivalent educational opportunities for students of all races.[2] In January 1948, Thurgood Marshall, then the NAACP's legal director, had squared off in the U.S. Supreme Court against officials of the University of Oklahoma's law school over whether the law school was required to admit a qualified African American applicant, Ada Lois Sipuel. Within four days, the Court unanimously ruled that Oklahoma was required to provide Sipuel with a public legal education forthwith.[3] A week later, the state responded, not by admitting Sipuel to the University of Oklahoma but by founding a separate "law school" for Sipuel in three basement rooms of the state capitol. Yet, later faced with the prospect of funding similar separate graduate programs for McLaurin and five other African American applicants in fields ranging from pharmacy to zoology, the state ultimately yielded, allowing black students to attend the University of Oklahoma, but on "a segregated basis."[4]

After McLaurin began his studies, university officials loosened the restrictions a bit, partly in response to resistance from McLaurin's white classmates. His chair, for example, was moved from the anteroom to the rear of the main classroom and a rail surrounding it, marked "Reserved for Colored," was taken down. Yet he was still required to eat and study separately from his white classmates, at specially designated tables. His case therefore provided the NAACP with an extraordinary opportunity to attack the very premise of the odious doctrine of "separate but equal."[5] Could white and black students, sharing the very same classroom, library, and other facilities, obtain an "equal" educational experience if they were nonetheless divided by the color line? The Supreme Court unanimously answered that they could not, at least in the context of graduate education. Chief Justice Vinson's opinion rejected the Regents' contention that the "separations" were "merely nominal," emphasizing instead that "the intellectual commingling of students" was an essential part of advanced university study. By "set[ting] McLaurin apart from the other students," Vinson wrote, "[t]he result is that appellant is handicapped in his pursuit of effective graduate instruction. Such restrictions impair and inhibit his ability to study, to engage in discussions and exchange views with other students, and, in general, to learn his profession."[6]

McLaurin, by recognizing the educational detriment caused by racial barriers in graduate study, helped lay the foundation for the NAACP's frontal assault on segregation four years later in Brown v. Board of Education.[7] In fact, *McLaurin* was part of a deliberate strategy by the NAACP to soften the ground for *Brown* by first using the "separate but equal" doctrine of Plessy v. Ferguson to gain a foothold for equal opportunity in higher education.[8] Between 1938 and 1950, the NAACP had won a series of cases involving graduate and professional schools, culminating in court orders requiring state universities to admit black students on equal terms with whites. On the same day the Supreme Court decided *McLaurin*, it held in a companion case that a separate Texas law school for blacks was not the equal of the University of Texas School of Law, and ordered the University of Texas to admit Heman Sweatt, an African American mail carrier from Houston.[9]

There is a certain irony, perhaps, in the NAACP's choice of higher education as the wedge to open the broader attack on segregation and racial exclusion. It centered the fight for civil rights in a field where courts had long been specially reluctant to intrude, requiring plaintiffs like George McLaurin, Ada Lois Sipuel, and Heman Sweatt to surmount not only prejudice but inclinations toward academic deference as well. The Court's decisions in *McLaurin* and *Sweatt*, after all, preceded by just seven years Justice Frankfurter's declaration in Sweezy v. New Hampshire of the " 'the four essential freedoms' of a university—to determine for itself on academic grounds who may teach, what may be taught, how it shall be taught, and who may be admitted to study."[10]

Yet, other considerations favored the NAACP's strategic focus on higher education. Most obviously, of course, it was anything but clear that race-based decisions in these cases had been based "on academic grounds." In fact, all understood that the true moving forces behind the challenged segregationist policies were to be found off campus, typically in state legislatures. As Ada Lois Sipuel acknowledged, "[m]ost of the university officials whom my suit targeted as defendants were [themselves] victims of these laws."[11]

In addition, compelling considerations of racial justice appeared likely to overshadow abstract notions of academic deference in any event. Indeed, race had previously proved to be a subject on which academic autonomy was notably vulnerable. In 1908, the U.S. Supreme Court had upheld enforcement of a Kentucky statute banning integrated instruction at " 'any college, school, or institution,' " notwithstanding that it violently trampled the defining institutional commitment of Berea College, founded by abolitionists before the Civil War, to educating black and white students together.[12] In its readiness to affirm Kentucky's power to prescribe public policy on race, Professor Matthew Finkin has observed, "the Court chose to blind itself to the college's founding documents and the almost forty years of the institution's history in deciding the college's fundamental purpose."[13] Similarly, though more justly, the Court in *McLaurin* readily subordinated the university's own educational policies to emerging public policy on race. Instead of deferring to university officials, the Court acted directly on its own independent assessment of classroom dynamics and the elements of "effective graduate instruction."

History appears to confirm the wisdom of the NAACP's approach. Internal conference records now establish that the Court that unanimously ruled for McLaurin in 1950 was not, in fact, ready to strike a broader blow for desegregation.[14] The Court, in other words, was willing to enforce constitutional principles of nondiscrimination against colleges and universities that it was not yet willing to apply generally. Indeed, the decisions culminating in *McLaurin* and *Sweatt*, Harvard law professor Michael Klarman observed, "functionally overruled *Plessy* with regard to higher education."[15] At least when it came to constitutional equality, universities were not outside the law; in fact, they were first in line.

The impact of the Supreme Court's decisions on educational opportunity in higher education was dramatic. Shortly after *Sipuel* was handed down in 1948, the University of Arkansas became the first southern university to abandon segregation voluntarily; others soon followed, by choice or by court action. Yet, for the individual plaintiffs who pioneered these victories, the results were decidedly mixed. Lloyd Gaines, whose suit to gain admission to the University of Missouri School of Law provided the first landmark in 1938, never attended law school. In fact, shortly after the Court ruled in his favor, he mysteriously disappeared and was never heard from again. George McLaurin and Heman Sweatt each struggled academically and were forced to abandon their hard-won studies.[16] When Ada Lois Sipuel attended her first class at the University of Oklahoma College of Law—confined, like McLaurin, behind a rail in the rear of the lecture hall in a solitary chair reserved for "colored"—she was shocked to discover that Maurice Merrill, the one-time dean who had unsuccessfully argued against her admission in the Supreme Court, would teach her constitutional law. Yet he turned out to be one of her favorite professors.[17] An excellent student, Sipuel earned her degree and went on to a successful career. In 1992, she became a Regent of the University of Oklahoma, assuming a spot on the board that had once engineered her exclusion.

As a result of the pioneering courage of students like Ada Sipuel and George McLaurin, the constitutional guarantee of racial equality came sooner to college campuses than to grade schools and other public settings. But the Supreme Court's intervention in *Gaines, Sweatt, Sipuel,* and *McLaurin* did not, of course, mean the end of either academic deference or discrimination on campus. Discrimination on many grounds other than race, including sex, age, disability, and sexual orientation, continued to evade serious constitutional review. And when Congress mobilized to fill some of the gaps in constitutional protection by statute, higher education was carved out based on the evident belief that academic judgment properly stood on different legal ground. If *Sipuel* and *McLaurin* had not seemed to implicate academic freedom, the expansion of anti-discrimination law in subsequent years brought the potential conflicts into sharper relief.

Of Statutes and Status: Civil Rights Laws Come to Campus

In 1943, the College of Osteopathic Physicians and Surgeons in Los Angeles, a school that would ultimately become part of the University of California at Irvine, launched a search for a research director for its Institute of Tropical Diseases. It posted the job opening with a Chicago-based academic employment agency, looking for "a man [both] experienced in bacteriology and qualified to do research in tropical diseases." The president of the college, Dr. William Ballentine Henley, would personally negotiate the terms of a contract with the researcher chosen for the job.

A research scientist named William Canavan, then employed as an instructor of zoology in Pennsylvania, expressed his interest directly to President Henley. "I am vitally interested," he wrote, and "would be delighted to sign on the dotted line provided the salary is commensurate." But there was one potential problem, Canavan explained; he had a disability. Canavan had a fine record in bacteriological research and writing, the employment agency would shortly thereafter explain in its own letter to President Henley, but he also had a physical impediment: "Before he had a hunting accident he was a vigorous, athletic man," someone at the agency wrote to the college. "Of course, since the accident he is a very much handicapped man, but I think this should in no way affect his teaching ability."

President Henley responded to Canavan's missive with great interest. Henley wrote that the college had purchased both a house and laboratory space for the new faculty member. Canavan's background seemed a very good fit. Would he accept an annual salary of $3,600? If so, how soon could he arrive in California?

Canavan responded promptly, writing that he found the salary acceptable, and explaining that he could wrap up his work in Pennsylvania in two weeks from the moment he had "received definite assurance that he was employed" by the college. Canavan included his photograph in this second letter and stressed what the employment agency had already explained about his disability. "[P]lease let me know if you have any objections to employing one who is physically handicapped," he wrote, "if such does not impose any restrictions on his ability to carry out the responsibilities of the position."

President Henley responded a few days later indicating that he was "very pleased" to receive Canavan's letter. "You mention a physical handicap," the president wrote in response to Canavan's concerns. "As long as it does not interfere with your research abilities, we would not have any objections whatsoever." President Henley in fact explained that he could imagine that a physical handicap might actually improve one's research ability and assured Canavan that the program was his as soon as he reported to work at the college. Even so, Canavan sent Henley yet another letter before his move to California. He was having problems finding transportation, he explained, because of his disabilities. "I am wondering if you too will turn me down because I am on crutches," he wrote, urging the president to respond with frankness. "I would not want to come out there and find that I have to come right back." Again, Henley reassured him, "If you can do the work, a handicap is no obstacle."

Yet, just two days after Canavan arrived in California and reported for work, President Henley bluntly told Canavan that he had made a mistake in hiring him. He suggested that Canavan would not be suitable for the position because he had too much difficulty getting around and that the college was not ready for someone with such a disability just then. Canavan had lost a job he had barely started.

In the 1940s, with no applicable civil rights statutes and no available claim under the Constitution, William Canavan's only legal resort was to the common law of contracts. He sued the college, but only for simple breach based on the president's promise of employment. California trial and appeals courts readily found in Professor Canavan's favor; they rejected out of hand President Henley's arguments that the two men had not agreed to the precise terms of an employment contract and that Canavan had misrepresented his condition.[18] But Canavan's only remedy, given the common law's traditional hostility to requiring specific performance of employment contracts, was one year's salary as damages. Civil rights statutes, in contrast, would eventually provide relief both more generous and far more flexible, including reinstatement, promotion, back pay, and other equitable, "make whole" remedies.[19] But first, academics had to bring themselves within the scope of federal civil rights laws.

In contrast to the comparatively early foothold that constitutional equality gained in higher education, statutory protections for civil rights were much slower to reach college campuses. When Congress enacted its first major civil rights legislation since Reconstruction, the Civil Rights Act of 1964, it specifically exempted colleges and universities from the provisions covering employment discrimination. Title VII of the 1964 Act broadly prohibited employers from discriminating on the basis of "race, color, religion, sex, or national origin," but pointedly exempted "educational institution[s] with respect to the employment of individuals to perform work connected with the educational activities of such institution."[20] When Congress later acted to prohibit age discrimination, through the Age Discrimination in Employment Act (ADEA) of 1967, it again made special provision for academic employment. In prohibiting mandatory retirement before age seventy, and in later amending the Act further to eliminate any general retirement age, Congress twice specifically allowed colleges and universities wider latitude in forcing out senior tenured faculty.[21]

Legislative history explaining the exemptions is sparse, but Congress was evidently persuaded that full-throttle application of anti-discrimination laws to academic employment carried undesirable risks. Certainly, insulating academic judgment in faculty hiring, promotion, and retention fit naturally with the established "anti-interventionist policy [of the courts] regarding the personnel decisions of colleges and universities."[22] Longstanding concerns about judicial entanglement, reflected in both common-law and constitutional doctrines, emphasized the limited competence of judges to superintend expert judgment in narrow academic specialties and the broad compass properly allowed to universities in shaping their institutional futures.[23] Similarly, academics cautioned that eliminating mandatory retirement would constrain "the influx of new ideas vital to the success of higher education," undermining values of academic freedom and the sustainability of tenure itself.[24]

But, by the early 1970s, Congress was rethinking the privileged status of higher education. In 1972, Congress amended Title VII to eliminate the exemption for academic employment. A congressional committee recommending the revision could find "nothing in the legislative background of

Title VII, nor [in] . . . any national policy . . . to support the exemption." Indeed, if anything, the committee reasoned, "discrimination in educational institutions is especially critical" and deserving of statutory prohibition.[25]

Congress pushed the reach of anti-discrimination law still further in subsequent measures. Title IX of the Educational Amendments of 1972 prohibited educational institutions receiving federal funds from discriminating based on sex, and the Rehabilitation Act of 1973 did the same with respect to discrimination based on disability.[26] When Congress expanded the legal remedies against disability discrimination, in the Americans with Disabilities Act (ADA) in 1990, colleges and universities were covered without reservation.[27] And, finally, in 1993, colleges and universities fell fully within the scope of the Age Discrimination in Employment Act, when the previous amendments excepting tenured faculty from the Act's provisions on mandatory retirement were allowed to expire. Concerns for academic autonomy, the Supreme Court later observed, now took a back seat in Congress to a new resolve to confront "the widespread and compelling problem of invidious discrimination in educational institutions."[28]

Yet, many courts did not immediately share Congress's change of heart. Even after Congress had expressly repealed Title VII's exemption for academic employment in 1972, "[t]he courts initially refused to reexamine the judgments of qualifications made in academia by those charged with tenure decisions."[29] To some degree, the courts' hostility to discrimination claims by academics was one instance of a broader judicial reluctance to apply Title VII fully to all white-collar employment, or what Harvard law professor Elizabeth Bartholet called "jobs in high places."[30] But judges also cited special reasons, unique to the academic context, for treading lightly, including the complex, decentralized, and highly subjective nature of academic evaluation.

Turning aside a sex discrimination claim brought by a medical school instructor just two years after the 1972 amendments, the Court of Appeals for the Second Circuit wrote with obvious impatience in Faro v. New York University: "Of all fields where federal courts should hesitate to invade and take over, education and appointments at the University level are probably the least suited for federal court supervision."[31] "It was almost," wrote George LaNoue and Barbara Lee, in a study of the early cases, "as though the honorable men in the judicial robes could not bring themselves to believe that the distinguished men in the academic gowns could discriminate."[32]

This "judicial posture," Terry Leap observed, "made it exceedingly difficult for women and minority faculty members to use Title VII or other laws in employment discrimination suits."[33] Indeed, writing in 1979, Harry T. Edwards and Virginia Nordin pointed out: "The doctrine of academic abstention has probably had one of its clearest statements, and its most dramatic impact, in the area of academic sex discrimination, where none of the first thirty-odd cases reported have been decided in favor of the plaintiff."[34] LaNoue and Lee's comprehensive review of faculty discrimination litigation between 1971 and 1984 confirmed the assessment on a broader scale, finding that "plaintiffs have won only 34 of the 160 decisions that reached the merits" and that, perversely, "the only environment in which plaintiffs have generally been successful is when whites sued black institutions."[35]

In time, however, courts settled into their new role and their initial refusal to scrutinize faculty hiring and promotion decisions began to fade. As early as 1978, the Second Circuit felt impelled to disclaim any "policy of self-abnegation where colleges are concerned," conceding that "the common-sense position we took in *Faro*, namely that courts must be ever-mindful of relative institutional competences, has been pressed beyond all reasonable limits, and may be employed to undercut the explicit legislative intent of the Civil Rights Act of 1964."[36] By 1989, on the heels of a small but growing number of decisions upholding academic discrimination claims, the Court of Appeals for the First Circuit took the then-unprecedented step of affirming, as a remedy for a court finding of discrimination, that an assistant professor be granted tenure.[37]

Five weeks after the First Circuit's ruling affirming the courts' power to award tenure, the U.S. Supreme Court weighed in, strongly confirming that a new day had dawned for academic discrimination claims. In a lawsuit challenging a denial of tenure at the Wharton School of Business, the Court unanimously rejected the University of Pennsylvania's claim that it was entitled to shield confidential peer-review materials from forced disclosure. Rejecting the university's contention that values of academic freedom required respecting the confidentiality of peer review, the Court emphasized instead Congress's evident intention, in abandoning Title VII's original exemption for academic employment, "to expose tenure determinations to the same enforcement procedures applicable to other employment decisions." And, yet, while the Court seemed thoroughly unpersuaded by the arguments for an academic privilege against disclosure, it also hastened to insist that courts, in scrutinizing the disclosed materials, be careful not to impose their own academic judgments:

> In keeping with Title VII's preservation of employers' remaining freedom of choice, courts have stressed the importance of avoiding second-guessing of legitimate academic judgments. This Court itself has cautioned that "judges . . . asked to review the substance of a genuinely academic decision . . . should show great respect for the faculty's professional judgment." Nothing we say today should be understood as a retreat from this principle of respect for *legitimate* academic decisionmaking.[38]

The *University of Pennsylvania* decision marked a turning point in judicial attitudes toward academic discrimination claims. In its wake, courts have appeared increasingly ready to set aside their qualms and wade into the murky waters of academic evaluation. And yet the Supreme Court's directive—to subject academic employment decisions to "the same procedures applicable to other employment decisions," while simultaneously respecting universities' autonomy in making "*legitimate* academic decision[s]"—was notably two-sided. Going forward, the experience of lower courts would show just how difficult it could be to be faithful to both.

Slurs and Smoking Guns: The University as "Hostile Working Environment"

In 1987, a study of higher education litigation in Iowa found only one reported case asserting a claim of discrimination under federal law (an unsuccessful comparable-worth claim brought by clerical staff at the University of Northern Iowa).[39] Yet, even at the time that study was published, a case was pending in an Iowa trial court that would break new ground in the application of federal anti-discrimination law—becoming one of the first and only cases "in which a faculty member has successfully argued that her academic department constituted a hostile working environment."[40]

Jean Jew, a first-generation Chinese-American who was raised in Mississippi, arrived at the University of Iowa from New Orleans in 1973. A newly minted medical doctor and aspiring research scientist, she had followed her mentor, Dr. Terence Williams, when he was recruited from Tulane to become head of Iowa's anatomy department. Arriving as a postgraduate associate, Dr. Jew earned a spot on the tenure track one year later as an assistant professor.[41]

Yet, from her very arrival in Iowa City, she found the anatomy department an unhappy place. Even before she arrived, the department "was split into factions and morale was poor." And the internal conflicts only intensified after Williams arrived as the new head, with Jew and two other Tulane colleagues. Existing, older faculty in the department chafed at the new guard, and Williams only aggravated matters by projecting "an image to many that he expected their 'loyalty'—that they would get ahead only if they voted his way on departmental matters." It was, the medical college dean later conceded, " 'a department that was just paralyzed' " by tensions and anxieties; " '[i]t was a terrible place to be in a university.' "[42]

This would not be a propitious environment for any untenured faculty member, but it was still worse for Jean Jew. From her first year in the department, Williams's adversaries on the faculty began spreading rumors, sometimes in "locker room language," that he and Jew were having a sexual affair. In the ensuing years, two other professors directed sexual and ethnic slurs at her; sexual graffiti concerning her appeared in the men's room; sexually explicit cartoons, at least one purporting to represent Williams and Jew engaged in sex, were posted outside the laboratory of one of her senior colleagues. "The campaign of sexual slander was extensive," recalls Martha Chamallas, then an Iowa law professor, "reaching students throughout the college, as well as faculty and staff in other parts of the University."[43] Indeed, two male faculty members pursuing their own tenure grievances in the college even offered to prove the alleged affair between Williams and Jew in order to advance their own claims of unfavorable treatment. Dr. Jew was granted tenure in 1979, but she was understandably "hurt, humiliated and ashamed by the incidents, and suffered some health problems because of them."[44]

When Jew became eligible for promotion to full professor in 1983, the balance of power within the department had shifted against her. Williams, her mentor and scholarly collaborator, had been forced out as head of the department just a few months before her candidacy went before the faculty, and his supporters were now in the minority.[45] The department faculty voted five-to-three against Jew's promotion. Williams and two colleagues he brought with him from Tulane voted in Jew's favor; the old guard voted against her, on the ground that Jew, a frequent coauthor with Williams, "had not established her 'independence' in the area of research and publications."[46] After Jew complained about her treatment internally to the provost and other officials, the university appointed a panel of faculty from other campus units to investigate her claims. The panel concluded that Jew had, in fact, been harassed; that two of the senior colleagues who had voted against her were incapable of judging her objectively, and that the university should take strong steps to clear Jew's name and protect her from further abuse. When negotiations between Jew and the university over remedial steps broke down, Jew went to court, filing an action alleging sex discrimination under Title VII.

After a twelve-day trial, a federal trial court ruled in Jew's favor. It found that the slurs, insults, and rumors spread by some of her colleagues had created a "hostile work environment" that substantially interfered with her ability to do her job, and that this harassment was based on sex. District Judge Harold Vietor also concluded that Jew had been denied promotion to full professor based on her sex. He found both circumstantial and direct evidence of gender bias on the part of at least three, and possibly four, of the five senior faculty who voted against Jew's promotion. Two of these professors had been involved in the vicious rumors and slurs; the other two were implicated based on comments made at the faculty meeting discussing Jew's promotion, one suggesting that "women and blacks have it made" and the other that "Dr. Jew had received many more advantages than he had received."[47]

The core of the university's defense—that Dr. Jew had been denied promotion because a majority of her colleagues honestly judged her research accomplishments to be deficient—was held to be pretextual. The court conceded that "[t]here is room for honest difference of opinion as to the adequacy of Dr. Jew's research and publications record." But, given the direct evidence of bias by some of the decision makers, the court ruled, it was the university's burden to show that Jew would still have been judged deficient even in the absence of any sex bias. This it could not do. Drawing strength from the Supreme Court's ruling in the *University of Pennsylvania* case earlier that year, the district court dismissed any suggestion that deference was owed to the university's academic judgment; "academic freedom," the court wrote, "does not include the freedom to discriminate against tenure candidates on the basis of sex." Having found the university guilty of discriminating against Jew, the court ordered that she be promoted to full professor, effective retroactively to the date of the discrimination six years before.[48] Dr. Jew remains on the Iowa faculty to this day, in part, she says, to continue to press for improvements in gender equity; the University's Council on the Status of Women now annually awards the Jean Jew Justice Award in her honor.[49]

Jean Jew's case, like those of George McLaurin and other civil rights pioneers before her, might seem to highlight the compelling need for judicial scrutiny to root out misconduct and bias in higher education. Her case, like McLaurin's, exposed vile conduct and spurred constructive change on campus.[50] In this sense, anti-discrimination law might appear to provide the strongest context for setting aside notions of "academic abstention." In the *University of Pennsylvania* case, for example, the Supreme Court gave a reassuring assessment about the complementary nature of institutional academic autonomy and anti-discrimination law. Judicial scrutiny of campus hiring and promotion posed no "*direct* infringement" of the university's "asserted right to 'determine for itself on academic grounds who may teach,'" because neither the courts nor the EEOC presume to dictate to universities the "criteria [they] . . . *must* use in selecting teachers"; rather, the courts' role is only to ensure that purportedly academic decisions do not rely upon discriminatory considerations— "including race, sex, and national origin—that are proscribed under Title VII."[51]

Yet, courts and universities traditionally have been unusually wary of active judicial review of academic employment decisions. In light of the durability of the tenure relationship, and the central role that faculty appointments play in defining an institution's academic identity and mission, litigation in this context carries profound implications for plaintiff and defendant alike. This is all the more true after the ADEA's abolition of mandatory faculty retirement, when a grant of tenure may now cement a relationship, and preclude alternative appointments, for a period lasting forty or fifty years. The high stakes make it enormously important, then, that courts confine their intervention to cases in which university decision makers have truly acted for illegitimate, nonacademic reasons.

In the modern age, elite decision makers are not likely to helpfully memorialize their racist or sexist designs in the form of *McLaurin*'s reserved seating and wooden railings. Consequently, smoking out illicit considerations is more likely to require drawing inferences from facts that might support several plausible interpretations. Even on the ugly facts in *Jew*, the district court recognized that "some of the harassment of Dr. Jew may have been motivated in part by animosity towards Dr. Williams," and her supporters acknowledged that "Jew suffered from her association with Williams."[52] If courts are not to intervene in every internecine faculty power struggle—many of which involve not merely petty personal frictions but also more substantial disagreements about the character or future direction of an academic unit—they must be sure to differentiate between the different possible motivations.[53] In *Jew*, the court concluded that even disentangling the various hostilities toward Jew, her harassment "remained sex-based." Yet, absent smoking-gun evidence of the sort in that case, teasing out illicit bias may draw courts far deeper into the core of academic evaluation. A case on which the district court in *Jew* relied, Bennun v. Rutgers, graphically illustrates the perils.

Pretext and Peer Review: Judging Academic Merit

When biochemist Alfred Bennun was denied tenure by Rutgers University in 1971, he brought a lawsuit against the university. Because Title VII did not then apply to academic employment, Bennun did not base his case on federal law. Instead, he creatively sued Rutgers and several professors for "maliciously interfering with his right to contract."[54] Rutgers relented and tenured him in 1972, the same year that Title VII was extended to faculty hiring decisions.

When Bennun sought promotion to full professor eight years later, his candidacy percolated through seven layers of internal university review, with mixed results:

The full professors in Dr. Bennun's department recommended in favor of promotion by a 5–0 vote with one abstention, based upon their assessment of his qualifications in the five areas of activity specified in the University's promotion criteria. Applying the same criteria and reviewing the same qualifications, a college-wide committee of faculty members recommended against promotion by a 4–0 vote. The college dean recommended in favor of promotion. The University-wide biochemistry faculty, whose role was limited to evaluating achievements in research accomplishments and scholarly/creative activity, recommended against promotion by a 4–2 vote. The committee advisory to the President of the University, comprised of four distinguished faculty members and the three campus provosts, recommended that Dr. Bennun not be promoted. The President recommended to the University's Board of Governors that Dr. Bennun not be promoted, and the Board of Governors declined to award promotion.[55]

Again Bennun went to court, this time asserting that the university had denied him promotion because he is Hispanic, in violation of Title VII. In contrast to the *Jew* case, Bennun "concede[d] that there [was] no direct, smoking gun evidence" of bias by any decision maker at Rutgers.[56] Instead, he introduced the promotion packets of twenty-seven other faculty members who had won promotion over a six-year period, to show that he was, in fact, qualified to be a full professor and that the university's reservations were pretextual.

The district court agreed with Bennun, resting its conclusion predominantly on a comparison between Bennun's credentials and those of one other faculty member, Dr. Ethel Somberg, who was promoted to full professor in Bennun's department two years before. Examining her curriculum vitae, outside review letters, and evaluative comments made by peers and administrators, the court concluded that Rutgers had judged her more charitably than it had Bennun. Bennun, the court emphasized, had a larger number of publications, lectures, and conference presentations. Moreover, Bennun's outside tenure review letters, the court concluded, were "objectively stronger" and came from "more significant scholars"; the supportive letters in Somberg's file were discounted on the ground that they came from "friend[s]" and "former student[s]."

The university's contrary assessment of their files—Somberg had received strong support at all seven levels of Rutgers' internal review, whereas Bennun had prevailed at only two—was, the court concluded, "simply not believable." Testimony by Rutgers' provost that Bennun did not measure up to the university's expectation that full professors "would have become an influential investigator on the national and international scene" was dismissed as "simply incredible" given the district court's own assessment that "[t]here was no indication that [Somberg] had an impact on the discipline or was an 'influential investigator on the national or international scene.'" For good measure, the district court noted that Bennun's outside letters also compared favorably with those of a Rutgers zoologist and physicist who had won promotion to full professor in other years.[57]

Not surprisingly, Rutgers protested that it was unfair to compare comments drawn from the files of different professors, evaluated by different reviewers, at different times. Rutgers further argued that it was misleading to compare Somberg's and Bennun's research records head-to-head because Somberg's primary strengths were in "teaching, curriculum development, and program-building," whereas "the focus of Dr. Bennun's activities had been research and he had been evaluated, at best, as an average teacher who had done negligible curriculum development work or program-building."[58] Yet, for the district court, that the department had judged Somberg's research to be commendable "'considering her teaching responsibilities,'" while not cutting Bennun the same slack, became just more evidence of the "shifting standard[s] . . . applied to the plaintiff." The court also cast doubt on the university's superior assessment of Somberg's teaching, concluding that its own "objective" comparisons of their peer classroom evaluations found "no real differences."

On this basis, the district court concluded that Rutgers had favored Somberg and disfavored Bennun because of their races, and it ordered that Bennun "be retroactively promoted to full professor with full back pay from the 1980–1981 review."[59] On appeal, the federal Court of Appeals for the Third Circuit unanimously affirmed the district court's analysis, readily agreeing that the trial judge's comparative analysis of the promotion packets "amply shows that Somberg was treated more favorably th[a]n Bennun" and that the university's criticisms of Bennun's candidacy were pretextual.[60]

With *Bennun*, as Judge Delores Slovitor noted in her dissent from the full appeals court's refusal to rehear the case, the courts had finally "abandoned the doctrine of restraint" marked by earlier cases and waded directly into the murky waters of academic evaluation. "[I]t appears," she wrote, "that the district court reassessed every decision made by Rutgers regarding Professor Bennun's qualifications and concluded that the court's assessment of the factors under review was superior to the university's."[61] When Rutgers asked the Supreme Court to review the case, it was supported by a brief filed jointly by the American Council on Education, New York University, Princeton University, and the universities of California, Michigan, and Pennsylvania. Together, they argued that the sort of comparative analysis of subjective merit evaluations undertaken in *Bennun* intruded dangerously on the institutional autonomy of universities and constituted exactly the sort of "second guessing" of academic judgment that the Supreme Court warned against in the *University of Pennsylvania* case.[62]

The Supreme Court ultimately let the decision stand. If it declined to hear the case out of the conviction that it was aberrant or of no broader significance, it was surely mistaken. *Bennun* proved a model for other courts in teasing out evidence of discrimination. And, as statutes have extended anti-discrimination law beyond the contexts of race, national origin, and sex discrimination, the potential for court scrutiny of academic judgment has only broadened.

Discrimination, Disability, and Detriments: New Theories of Liability

In the years since *Bennun*, additional courts have followed its basic approach in seeking to prove discriminatory pretext through direct comparative assessments of faculty qualifications in tenure files. A 2008 court decision in New York City, upholding the sufficiency of a professor's complaint and sending the case on for jury trial, illustrates well the new face of anti-discrimination law on campus. The complaint in Hinton v. City College of New York packaged together no less than four different legal theories of unlawful discrimination, spanning three different statutes. In reviewing the legal soundness of these claims—asserting sex discrimination, disability discrimination, and unlawful retaliation—the court's opinion gives something of a roadmap of the likely course of future litigation.[63]

Laura Hinton, a poet and specialist in contemporary and experimental women's literature, was a tenured associate professor of English at City

College of New York when she first sought promotion to full professor in 2003. Among other works, she is the author of *The Perverse Gaze of Sympathy: Sadomasochistic Sentiments from* Clarissa *to* Rescue 911, in which she advances the thesis that popular sentimental novels, films, and television programs often carry a darker, "sadoerotic" undercurrent.[64] Her first application for promotion to full professor was returned to her immediately on the ground that she filed it late; her second application the following year was turned down on the merits at each of four stages of internal review. In presenting her file to a "divisional" promotions committee comprised of all department chairs in the candidate's division at City College, Joshua Wilner, the English department chair, summed up her case this way: "[Hinton] is intelligent, imaginative, and energetic in areas that engage her interest, but her effectiveness is qualified by a tendency . . . to miss or be late to meetings that don't conform to her schedule and by a tendency to become involved in imbroglios." Wilner added, though, that he might be inclined to support her promotion in the near future "[i]f the current year passes calmly and Prof. Hinton continues to be productive."[65] When she sought promotion a third time, in 2005, her candidacy cleared the departmental promotions committee and Wilner did indeed support her cause before the divisional committee. Nevertheless, that committee and a subsequent college-wide review committee both voted against promotion. In the end, the CUNY president sided with the department and Hinton was promoted—but not before Hinton had already gone to court alleging that she was the victim of wide-ranging discrimination at City College.

In her complaint, Hinton challenged the initial denials of promotion on several grounds. She advanced two different theories of sex discrimination under Title VII: first, that she, like Jean Jew, had suffered sexual harassment amounting to a "hostile work environment"; and, second, that she had been judged more harshly than male colleagues (and, for that matter, than other female colleagues too) when being considered for promotion. Next, Hinton complained that she had been discriminated against because she suffers from disabilities—chronic fatigue syndrome and irritable bowl syndrome—in violation of the ADA and New York state human rights law. Finally, she claimed that she had been mistreated by her colleagues and administrators in retaliation for having complained about discrimination in her department.

She was, the district court recounted, "unhappy with her teaching schedule in the Spring 2003 semester," and resentful that she had been assigned the following semester to teach a seminar in "an 'overstuffed undergraduate room' with 'very uncomfortable chairs without ventilation.'" She was upset that she was not assigned to serve on a hiring committee and that the dean cut funds for a poetry series she ran. She complained that she suffered "'humiliating remarks about her work' and that her 'scholarship [had been] denigrated.'" A former dean, she said, had once called her a "poor baby," and a former department chair in 1994 called her "a sentimental heroine begging for money"—a remark that might have chafed peculiarly in light of the thesis of her later book.[66]

City College asked the federal district court in Manhattan to grant summary judgment in its favor, arguing that the undisputed facts made clear that her claims were meritless. The court ruled partly in the college's favor, holding that the isolated incidents of rude or boorish behavior alleged in her complaint were insufficiently pervasive to constitute a "hostile work environment" under Title VII, and excluding her disability discrimination claims for lack of proof that college officials acted against her on that basis. But District Judge Gerard Lynch also ruled that Hinton was entitled to make her case to a jury on at least two of her major claims—that she had been denied a promotion in 2004 because of her sex and that she had suffered retaliation in the department for having asserted her legal rights. An examination of the court's reasoning sheds light on the shape of litigation to come, not only in Hinton's case but in others that will inevitably look to decisions like this one for guidance in crafting their claims.

First, Judge Lynch held that Hinton had alleged facts sufficient to establish City College's liability for sex discrimination in deferring her promotion to full professor. Hinton had pointed to sexist comments by some former departmental leaders not directly involved in her promotion, but the centerpiece of her sex-discrimination claim, as in *Bennun*, rested on a comparison of her own qualifications with those of a previously promoted male colleague—namely, the man who had shepherded her case for promotion within the humanities division, then-department chair Joshua Wilner. Citing the deposition testimony of one of Hinton's allies on the faculty to the effect that Wilner "doesn't publish a thing"—in fact, his web biography mentions that a book he published the year of his promotion won the Jean-Pierre Barricelli annual book award of the International Conference on Romanticism—the district court held that "[a] reasonable factfinder could . . . conclude that Hinton's application for promotion to full professor was stronger than that of at least one male applicant who had been promoted, Joshua Willner [*sic*]." As in *Bennun*, the legal process—this time a jury—would compare faculty promotion packets to decide whether Hinton deserved promotion in light of past promotions. To City College's objection that Wilner and Hinton "are not similarly situated because of their 'differences in scholarship, academic discipline, and because their applications were decided years apart,'" Judge Lynch held that these matters, too, were for the jury to decide. "A reasonable juror could equally well find Willner [*sic*] better qualified than Hinton, or otherwise find them not similarly situated," the court concluded, "but Hinton has presented sufficient evidence to make this a genuine issue for trial."[67]

Hinton's second major theory of liability—that City College discriminated against her because she has a disability—reflects another important new frontier of anti-discrimination law in higher education. The old case of William Canavan, lured to California and then heartlessly turned away for reporting to work on crutches, was easy; modern claims of disability discrimination, like those raised by Hinton, are often far less certain. In Hinton's case, the district court first expressed uncertainty over whether the professor's stated impairments—chronic fatigue syndrome and irritable bowel syndrome—really qualified as protected "disabilities" under federal law. The court noted that "[o]nly those impairments that 'limit a major life activity' in a 'substantial' manner are statutory disabilities" within the scope of the ADA. The court ultimately found it unnecessary to decide whether Hinton's conditions met this description because it found no evidence in any event that City College had disfavored Hinton on this basis. But the court's indecision over the scope of disability discrimination law highlights issues that are increasingly landing colleges in court.[68]

Hinton's third and final claim against City College—that colleagues and administrators had retaliated against her for complaining about unlawful discrimination—represents another major new front in anti-discrimination law. Title VII, like Title IX, the ADA, the ADEA, and other civil rights statutes, prohibits not only discrimination but also retaliation against any person for having asserted claims of discrimination.[69] The facts of Hinton's case give some sense of the potential significance of that mandate for colleges and universities. Hinton's claim of retaliation rested centrally on the fact that she had a history of "numerous instances in which she complained, formally and informally, of discrimination against her by co-workers and various parts of the [City College] administration." She had, for instance, filed EEOC (Equal Employment Opportunity Commission) charges at the time of her initial tenure review in 1998 and again in 2004 when she was being considered for promotion to full professor; she also complained internally about other acts of perceived mistreatment of herself and colleagues and again later about the handling of those complaints. When a colleague asked the humanities dean, "[W]hy are you harassing Laura Hinton and what did she ever do to you?" he allegedly gestured across the room and shot back, "[T]hat's what she did to us, these two file cabinets."[70]

On this basis, the district court ruled, "a reasonable factfinder could conclude, with ease, that there was a causal connection between Hinton's protected activity [in complaining about discrimination] and the denial of her second promotion." More significantly, perhaps, the court also ruled that Hinton could challenge, under a retaliation theory, the legality of several less dramatic departmental measures affecting her, including her committee assignments and funding of a small poetry series. Some of the alleged reprisals of which Hinton complained—such as her vaguely stated "dissatisfaction with her course assignments"—were "too nebulous or too trivial to permit a finding of retaliation," the court allowed. Yet, Hinton's claim that she had been excluded from a hiring committee that carried particular prestige within her unit, and the dean's decision not to provide several hundreds of dollars in funds to support a poetry series dear to her heart, could be found substantial enough to show unlawful retaliation: "A reasonable jury," the court reasoned, "could conclude, as did Hinton, that in the English Department, the funding process and the hiring process are the 'two ways in which you are acknowledged as a valued and important colleague.'"[71]

The court's decision to green-light Hinton's retaliation claim might reasonably give pause to campus administrators who must routinely assign committee work, classrooms, laboratory space, travel funds, or other perquisites among cantankerous colleagues. As the court observed in

Hinton, Title VII's bar on retaliation encompasses any decision affecting job responsibilities or conditions that a reasonable employee would consider " 'materially adverse' "; "what might not qualify as an adverse employment action under Title VII's anti-discrimination provisions," it noted, "may still violate Title VII's anti-retaliation provisions." Indeed, "even a single act of retaliation, if it satisfies the ["materially adverse"] . . . standard can create liability." Consequently, if a faculty member has previously alleged mistreatment on the basis of race, sex, or national origin, an administrator must tread carefully in doling out classrooms, committee work, and discretionary program funds—calculating at each step the risk that a future jury might infer that these assignments were meant to reflect negatively on the professor's standing as " 'a valued and important colleague.' "

Other cases give a glimpse of the range of potential grievances. One month before *Hinton,* a federal appellate court in Denver turned aside a retaliation claim based on an allegation that faculty colleagues in an appointments meeting had rolled their eyes and snickered at the plaintiffs' opinions about hiring standards, but noted that "[c]onduct such as this, if pervasive enough, may in fact rise to the level" sufficient to trigger liability.[72] That same month, a federal trial court confronted a retaliation claim based in part on a business school's failure to highlight a professor's "intellectual contributions" in its annual report.[73] A federal appellate court expended several pages in the *Federal Reporter* explaining why the assignment of a Monday-Wednesday-Friday teaching schedule (as opposed to the plaintiff's preferred Tuesday-Thursday schedule); the fixing of an uncomfortably cool office temperature; and suffering "the silent treatment" from faculty colleagues, among other slights, fell short of the gravity necessary to state a legal claim.[74]

Not two months after *Hinton,* another federal court in Manhattan grappled with a discrimination claim filed by another CUNY professor. Arthur Whaley sued after he was denied reappointment as an untenured full professor at CUNY's Sophie Davis College. But his claims of race and age discrimination were not confined solely to his reappointment. In addition, his complaint rattled off a long list of slights and insults, including his department chair's "insistence on receiving [a] complete grant package before signing"; "the school's refusal to give him a new computer, rather than a lightly used computer"; "the initial denial of his request for a paid research assistant"; his chair's "failure to invite [him] to become a member of the Health Policy Search Committee"; "the school's initial denial of his request to obtain administrative assistance with grant preparation"; "being 'forced' to assist 'less experienced' faculty with their research"; "being subjected to a barrage of emails"; "being assigned inadequate sites for course meetings"; and "being excluded from a curriculum reform subcommittee."[75]

The court ended up finding that most of these claims were barred by the Title VII's limitations period; and the few fresh incidents—including the failure to appoint Whaley to a hiring committee and assigning him a slightly used computer on his arrival to the college—were not individually substantial enough to trigger Title VII's anti-discrimination provisions. But the court *did* send on for jury trial Dr. Whaley's claim of unlawful retaliation under Title VII. Although the evidence was "thin," the court reasoned, and the college had presented a very substantial case that Whaley was let go for legitimate, job-related reasons, it was ultimately the job of the jury to decide whether the college had, in fact, "used the wrong, 'stricter' standard when deciding whether to reappoint him."[76]

In yet another illustration of the way in which discrimination and retaliation claims can pack a one-two punch, in 2006 a federal court cited *Bennun* in ruling that Camille Smith, then an associate professor of music at the University of Florida, was entitled to a jury trial of her claim that her department refused to promote her to full professor because of her sex. The university had argued that she was denied promotion "in part because she had not published a book." Yet, Smith argued that this was mere pretext, as shown in part by the fact that the university had promoted a male colleague, the director of bands, without insisting on a book. When the dean of the music school answered that "band directors are not expected to publish," the court held that a jury should sort it out. The band director was an "appropriate comparator," the court found, because both he and the plaintiff were music professors, and jurors could be trusted to scrutinize Smith's teaching evaluations and her "numerous articles and papers" and decide for themselves whether the university's assessment of her achievements should be credited.[77]

As it happens, the jury in Professor Smith's case turned out to have some academic expertise. "At one point in the deliberations," the *Gainesville Sun* reported, "a juror who identified himself in court as a UF faculty member and doctor, asked to be dismissed because he felt he could no longer be fair in deliberations." With the professor excused, the jury ultimately found that Smith's department had not discriminated in its refusal to promote her. It did, however, conclude that the department had denied the summer teaching assignments she desired in retaliation for her discrimination claim, and awarded her $150,000.[78]

The point of this survey is surely not to suggest that colleges and universities should be beyond reproach under anti-discrimination law. More than three decades after Congress acted to bring academic actors fully within the scope of Title VII and other anti-discrimination laws, there is broad agreement even among university officials that court scrutiny is entirely proper. But, even in the compelling context of anti-discrimination law, judicial review is not costless. The litigation costs of responding to frivolous or baseless claims may be no greater in the academic context than for other employers. But the costs of legal error in adjudicating nonfrivolous discrimination claims may well be significantly higher in the context of academic employment.

Beyond the unique durability of a court order of tenure, *Bennun, Hinton,* and other recent cases illustrate the peculiar perils of asking judges or—surely no better—jurors to evaluate comparative scholarly accomplishment and to fix the bar of academic merit. It is difficult enough for members of a campus promotion and tenure committee, themselves scholars and steeped in the culture, needs, and norms of a particular institution, to make such judgments in fields as far-flung as psychology, physics, poetry, and photojournalism. In the hands of outsiders who may be both ignorant of the relevant discipline and insensitive or even hostile toward the academic mission of the institution, the risks are infinitely higher. Consider, for example, Justice Thomas's dismissive assessment of the University of Michigan's academic mission in Grutter v. Bollinger. In concluding that the university could not justify the use of racial preferences to ensure the admission of a diverse student body, Thomas disparagingly recharacterized the university's pursuit of academic excellence as little more than an "interest in remaining elite and exclusive" for its own sake.[79] Indeed, Thomas suggested that the University of Michigan might better serve the people of Michigan by altogether abandoning any aspiration to selectivity in its student body.[80] In Thomas's case, his contemptuous disregard for the academic judgment of Michigan's faculty and administrators was at least paired consistently with a sneering skepticism toward the broader principle, suggested in Justice Frankfurter's concurrence in Sweezy v. New Hampshire, that "a 'free society' depends on 'free universities' and [that] 'this means the exclusion of governmental intervention in the intellectual life of a university.' "[81] But for any who continue to recognize real value in academic freedom, entrusting broad oversight authority in such hands carries obvious and substantial risks.

"One of the Last Frontiers of Civil Rights"

Nearly six decades after the Supreme Court effectively ordered the desegregation of higher education in *McLaurin* and *Sweatt*, the role of the courts in combating discrimination seems not to have diminished. Indeed, the inflow of new legal claims appears to be growing. In 2008, the EEOC reported that it had received 82,792 private-sector charges in fiscal year 2007, "the highest volume of incoming charges since 2002 and the largest annual increase (9%) since the early 1990s."[82] While the EEOC does not separate out which of those claims are related to higher education, all indications are that campus-related discrimination claims are growing at least as fast. Studies suggest that about half of all campus legal claims relate to discrimination, and that these claims skyrocketed during the 1990s.[83]

Some have linked the rise in litigation to the increasing number of non-tenured faculty on campus. Others have pointed to a significant rise in tenure standards, arguing that more lawsuits are brought by those who find themselves without a job when peers just a few years before have won tenure on lesser records.[84] But the increase can also be attributed, of course, to what Leland Ware calls the elusive quest for equality on college campuses for minority faculty. As he notes, race discrimination persists: "[M]any of the minority professors who survive the selection process are subjected to racial and gender bias at their institutions," including student confrontations, biased evaluations, and indifferent administrators.[85] Recent studies confirm the same unfortunate reality when it comes to sex discrimination. A 2007 Canadian study reported that, despite gains, women faculty continue to lag significantly in the upper reaches of the professoriate; "[s]ystemic discrimination is alive and well in the academy," laments one of its authors.[86]

And the surging EEOC filings do not even account for the full scale of new litigation touching college campuses. Federal anti-discrimination law prohibits adverse treatment on the basis of race, sex, national origin, disability, and age, but some forms of discrimination continue to fall outside the scope of statutory protections. In such cases, aggrieved parties may seek to expand the safeguards against discrimination through political action, as, for example, in the case of an online petition urging the University of Colorado to ban discrimination against students who miss class because of military service.[87]

In others, as in the case of law professor Peter Hammer, they resort to creative pleading in the courts.

When Peter Hammer left private law practice for an academic career in 1995, he was anxious that law schools might discriminate against him because he is gay. As a result, Hammer says he deliberately remained "closeted" until after he had several job offers in hand. When negotiating to accept an offer from the University of Michigan Law School, however, Hammer felt impelled to raise the issue because it was important to him to determine whether his domestic partner would be covered under the university's health insurance benefits. Officials at Michigan were quick to assure him, he said, both that the university provided benefits to domestic partners and that university policy strictly prohibited discrimination on the basis of sexual orientation. He took the job.

When Hammer came up for a tenure vote in 2002, however, he fell short. After leaving Ann Arbor to join the faculty of Wayne State University Law School in Detroit, Hammer filed suit against the University of Michigan for denying him tenure. Hammer was convinced that some of his Michigan colleagues had voted against him because he is gay. Yet, because neither federal nor state civil rights laws prohibited discrimination on the basis of sexual orientation, Hammer was forced to look elsewhere to make out a legal claim. He found his answer in the same place as had other "pre-statutory" civil rights plaintiffs (including William Canavan and Alfred Bennun)—in his employment contract. Hammer's complaint, filed in state court, alleged that the university had promised not to discriminate against him when it hired him, and that it later breached that promise when it refused him tenure. Hammer says he is the first openly gay candidate to be considered for tenure at the University of Michigan Law School, and the only man to be denied tenure by the institution in at least forty years.

Hammer's lawsuit, which was still working its way slowly through the Michigan courts in 2009, illustrates the shape of litigation at what one of his court briefs describes as "one of the last frontiers in civil rights."[88] (Hammer's lawsuit would also prove remarkable for the extent to which it challenged traditional assumptions of confidentiality in peer review—a feature considered separately in Chapter 6.) Without a statutory cause of action, plaintiffs are often forced to invent their own theories based on contract, tort, or equitable doctrines such as promissory estoppel. One of the notable features of Hammer's lawsuit is that it seeks to establish the university's liability for discrimination based upon the university's voluntary efforts to do more than what was required of it by law: the legal hook for Hammer's claim was that the university itself promised that it did not discriminate based on sexual orientation. In this way, a university's generosity in undertaking to combat or avoid discrimination may ironically provide a basis ultimately for holding it liable. The same effect can be seen in disability discrimination law. In Betts v. Rector and Visitors of the University of Virginia, for example, a pre-med student was found to be protected by the ADA even though he was not, in fact, disabled. Yet, because Virginia's own student services office had offered him services to help with his mild learning impairment, the court found that the university apparently *regarded* the student as disabled, bringing him within the protections of federal disability-discrimination law.[89]

In Hammer's case, proving the truth of his discrimination claim would take him into uncharted territory. Not only did he seek to pioneer a new frontier of anti-discrimination law by establishing a legal remedy for anti-gay bias, he was seeking to prove his case by an unprecedented method: by seeking to expose the culturally conservative leanings of former colleagues and asking a court to disqualify their tenure votes. This was, reported *Inside Higher Ed*, an entirely "new method for fighting bias" and one that left "some experts on tenure and higher education . . . worried that these arguments—whatever the veracity of Hammer's claims—pose dangers to the tenure process."[90]

Hammer's theory was that some number of faculty who voted against his promotion were affected by anti-gay bigotry and that their votes should be struck from the tally on his tenure case.[91] Because there were no "smoking guns" in the faculty's deliberations suggesting consideration of Hammer's sexual orientation, he would have to dig deeper. To identify the culprits, Hammer's lawyer deposed each colleague who had voted against Hammer, probing for possible evidence of anti-gay sentiment. Some were quizzed about their personal views on "hot-button social issues" such as same-sex marriage and abortion rights.[92] In court filings, Hammer pointed to evidence about the churches or synagogues his adversaries attended and to references to homosexuality or same-sex relationships found in their scholarly writing. In one case, an undercover investigator posed as a prospective parishioner and secretly recorded conversations with leaders of a faculty member's church to ascertain its views on homosexuality and abortion.[93] These were, Hammer conceded, unconventional lines of proof, but necessary under the circumstances. "The theory of the case is that you are dealing with this very strong combination of religion and family values," Hammer explained to a reporter for *Inside Higher Ed.* "You've got to get inside somebody's mind and present it in a way that can be objectively verified."[94]

The University of Michigan asked the court to dispose of the case on summary judgment, insisting that Hammer had been denied tenure solely because his scholarship did not meet the law school's standards and arguing strenuously that "the court should not second-guess the University's tenure decision." The university cited a raft of cases stretching back decades emphasizing the "broad discretion" rightfully allowed to universities in matters of academic judgment.[95] In reply, Hammer answered that he was not asking the court to review the merits of his promotion, but only to enforce the promises made to him by the university.[96] The Michigan Court of Claims agreed to dispose of one of Hammer's claims (that his eight-year service to the university had given him "*de facto* tenure"), but ruled that his contract-based discrimination should proceed to trial.

As it happens, at the same time Hammer's tenure-discrimination case was wending its way through the Michigan courts, Hammer was also a plaintiff in another action. But in this action, National Pride at Work v. Cox, Hammer was allied with the University of Michigan and the state's other leading public universities in seeking to overturn an interpretation of the state constitution that would compel the universities to cut off health benefits for their employees' same-sex partners. Michigan voters had amended the state's constitution in 2004 to prohibit public recognition of same-sex "marriage or similar union for any purpose." The question was whether the policy of state universities and other public entities to provide benefits to the domestic partners of gay employees was, in effect, treating same-sex partners as standing in a marriage-like "union."

To defend their right to provide domestic partnership benefits, the universities argued that the marriage amendment should be construed narrowly to avoid impinging on the universities' constitutional right of academic autonomy. The Michigan constitution expressly grants to the state's universities an autonomous power to manage their own affairs (as seen in that battle over homeopathy at the University of Michigan). Moreover, the AAUP argued in a friend-of-the-court brief, the institutional autonomy of universities is protected by the First Amendment, and this "[a]cademic freedom . . . extends to university governance on matters of educational policy, structure, and governance."[97]

In *National Pride at Work*, the tables had turned on the relationship between institutional autonomy and anti-discrimination law. For decades, universities had been in the position of invoking academic freedom and doctrines of academic deference in an effort to curb the reach of anti-discrimination law on campus. Plaintiffs, like Alfred Bennun and Peter Hammer, had been put in the position of arguing that academic autonomy should not be construed so broadly as to immunize universities from the reach of anti-discrimination law. Progressive commentators concerned with advancing the cause of equality argued that universities had no basis for resisting the majoritarian will of Congress, which had resolved to bring college campuses within the compass of Title VII and other civil rights laws. Yet, now the constitutional autonomy of universities was the last and best hope of repelling a majoritarian commandment on civil rights that was anything but progressive. Employees who hoped to retain basic benefits for their families quite reasonably scrambled to invoke the power of their university employers to pursue their own conception of civil rights without interference from the political process. Institutional academic freedom, it turned out, might affirmatively advance the cause of anti-discrimination.

The courts, however, soundly rejected the universities' arguments. The university, wrote the Michigan Court of Appeals, "is not an island": "Within the confines of the operation and allocation of funds of the University, it is supreme. Without these confines, however, there is no reason to allow the regents to use their independence to thwart the clearly established public policy of the people of Michigan."[98]

In 2008, the Michigan Supreme Court affirmed the decision, insisting that "[t]he people of this state have . . . spoken on this issue."[99] As a result, the domestic-partnership health benefits that Peter Hammer had taken such care to secure in launching his academic career in Michigan were declared illegal.

The *National Pride at Work* litigation provides a fitting conclusion to this chapter's review of the inroads made by anti-discrimination law on college and university campuses. It was through anti-discrimination law, particularly constitutional scrutiny of racial segregation and exclusion, that courts made an early and significant breach in the legal norms that had long kept them out of academic life. And, to many, there could be no stronger warrant for court intervention. The image of the dignified George McLaurin looking in stoically on his graduate education classes from his designated desk in an alcove refutes any notion that colleges and universities should somehow occupy "an island" beyond the view of the courts.

Yet, recent cases demonstrate that subjecting colleges and universities to free-wheeling court supervision untempered by any respect for academic autonomy can also be seriously problematic. Few contexts provide an opportunity for so profoundly seizing control of an institution's future identity and mission as the appointment of personnel with academic tenure. In insensitive or overconfident hands, comparisons of scholarly merit may easily lead courts to remake academic departments based ultimately not on improper discrimination but on disagreements over scholarly agendas, methodologies, or institutional ambition. Moreover, as *National Pride at Work* shows, sometimes it is not academic autonomy, but a conception of "equality" dictated by popular government that is the true engine of discrimination. Autonomy may be wielded to make universities "islands" of inclusion as well as of exclusion.

Accordingly, the challenge is to shun the alternative extremes of wholesale immunity and unbridled oversight and to define terms for court intervention that balance interests in nondiscrimination against legitimate interests in academic freedom and autonomy. Awards of tenure or promotion based on unfiltered comparisons of academic merit, as in

Bennun, arguably sacrifice too much academic freedom in pursuit of nondiscrimination. But Congress's pre-1972 decision to place academic employment decisions entirely beyond the purview of the courts just as surely veered too far in the other direction.

As the next chapter, exploring the rise of First Amendment litigation on campus, shows, the difficult task of striking a balance between competing constitutional values is by no means confined to the discrimination cases.

CHAPTER **4**

Free Speech Free-for-All:
The First Amendment on Campus

On April 4, 1991—the twenty-third anniversary of the assassination of Martin Luther King Jr.—a group of students at Virginia's George Mason University joined together in the cafeteria of the student union building. The gathering, however, had nothing to do with King's passing, or at least not deliberately. Instead, the occasion was the "Dress a Sig" contest sponsored by the campus chapter of Sigma Chi, an annual highlight of the fraternity's Derby Days festivities. Six sororities competed to dress Sigma Chi members as "ugly women." In their bid to take top honors, members of the Gamma Phi Beta sorority offered up one of the white Sigma Chi brothers in blackface: "He was painted black and wore stringy, black hair decorated with curlers, and his outfit was stuffed with pillows to exaggerate a woman's breasts and buttocks. He spoke in slang to parody African-Americans."[1] If the team meant this get-up to attract attention and distinguish their entry from a crowded field, they succeeded in droves. Within days, 247 outraged students petitioned the university administration to denounce the performance.

The university's dean for student services, Kenneth Bumgarner, met with students involved and imposed what might have been considered a slate of relatively modest sanctions. No student was individually disciplined and neither of the Greek organizations involved was driven from campus. Instead, the Sigma Chi chapter was placed on social probation for two years, meaning that it could not sponsor social or athletic events without campus approval. The fraternity was also directed to plan an educational program "addressing cultural differences, diversity, and the concerns of women." The Gamma Phi Beta sorority, for its part, was placed on social probation for one year.[2]

Apparently, the women of Gamma Phi Beta accepted the sanction and moved on. Not so the brothers of Sigma Chi. By the end of the semester, they went to federal court in Alexandria, Virginia, contending that the crimping of their social calendar violated the First Amendment of the U.S. Constitution. The plaintiffs readily conceded that the "ugly woman" skit was "hurtful, offensive, and inappropriate"; they allowed that the dressing of a contestant in blackface was "particularly offensive to African-Americans."[3] Yet, they insisted that administrators at a public university—one named for the "Father of the Bill of Rights," no less—were powerless to penalize their free expression.

District Judge Claude Hilton emphatically agreed, granting summary judgment for the students. "Because th[e] fundamental right [of "free, uncensored expression"] extends to students at a state university," he reasoned, "a state university may not hinder the exercise of First Amendment rights simply because it feels that exposure to a given group's ideas may be somehow harmful to certain students." The university offered to prove at trial that the disciplinary response was warranted because of the skit's disruptive impact on the learning environment, but the court saw no need for extended inquiry. Instead, the court considered it obvious that "[t]he student activity at issue in this action is consistent with GMU's educational mission in conveying ideas and promoting the free flow and expression of those ideas."[4]

On appeal, the federal Court of Appeals for the Fourth Circuit in Richmond was equally sure of the students' rights. The university argued that the "ugly woman" contest was "purely mindless and insensitive fraternity fun, . . . devoid of any reasonable claim to political or artistic expression,"[5] but the court saw in the fraternity's antics a deeper message clearly protected by the First Amendment: "What is evident is that the Fraternity's purposefully nonsensical treatment of sexual and racial themes was intended to impart a message that the University's concerns, in the Fraternity's view, should be treated humorously." Citing Supreme Court precedent dealing with nude dancing and theatrical productions, the court saw the case as straightforwardly controlled by "First Amendment principles governing live entertainment"; "short of obscenity," the court held, "it is generally protected." Having recognized the fraternity's performance as constitutionally protected speech, the court viewed the rest of the case as falling easily into place. The university's objection to racially insensitive speech ran afoul of First Amendment precedent barring "viewpoint discrimination" by the government. "The mischief," the court explained, "was the University's punishment of those who scoffed at its goals of racial integration and gender neutrality, while permitting, even encouraging, conduct that would further the viewpoint expressed in the University's goals." Whatever interests the university might have in advancing its "educational endeavors," the court concluded, could certainly not justify "selectively silencing speech on the basis of its viewpoint."[6] Thus, the university was constitutionally prohibited from "imposing any discipline on the plaintiffs as a result of the activity on April 4, 1991."[7]

The courts' ready intervention in the George Mason controversy, finding a constitutional right of undergraduates to continue the "ugly woman" tradition free from administrative meddling, represented a remarkable judicial journey from the courts' traditional reluctance to involve themselves in campus affairs. After all, it was not so many decades ago that courts effectively saw no legal issue—much less high constitutional principle—implicated by campus control of student life. In 1924, for example, the Michigan Supreme Court had breezily upheld the authority of a state college to toss an undergraduate from campus altogether for smoking cigarettes in public, riding openly in an automobile with a young man, and then having the temerity to "air[] her grievances and her defiance of disciplinary measures in the public press." The public college's actions raised no constitutional eyebrows whatsoever. " 'Courts have other and more important functions to perform,' " the court scoffed, " 'than that of hearing the complaints of disaffected pupils . . . against rules and regulations promulgated by [state college officials] . . . for the government of the schools.' " Indeed, the state supreme court capped its opinion by singling out the student's decision "to air her defiance of discipline in the public press" as a particularly meritorious reason to send her packing.[8] Less than a decade earlier, the U.S. Supreme Court had dismissed the notion that the Constitution had anything to say about the University of Mississippi's decision to exclude all fraternity members from campus: "[W]hether such membership makes against discipline," the Court admonished, "was for the state of Mississippi"—not the courts—"to determine."[9]

Of course, First Amendment doctrine had undergone a revolution since those early cases, including its extension to state governments by way of "incorporation" through the Due Process Clause of the Fourteenth Amendment.[10] What was notable about the *Sigma Chi* case, then, was not the courts' holding that First Amendment principles generally prohibit states from penalizing offensive speech. Nor was it that public universities are "state actors" subject to the First Amendment. Decisions of the U.S. Supreme Court going back at least to 1972's Students for a Democratic Society case, Healy v. James, made it clear that students enjoyed constitutional rights on campus, even against their own public universities.[11] Instead, what was notable about the *Sigma Chi* case was the courts' readiness to hold public universities to precisely the *same* First Amendment constraints applied to other state governmental actors.

The point was not lost on Judge Francis Murnaghan, who concurred in the *Sigma Chi* case on appeal but wrote separately to caution that the majority's "reasoning goes unnecessarily too far." Murnaghan agreed that Sigma Chi had been improperly punished, though on the much narrower ground that university officials had limited their own powers by preapproving the event. Absent such a waiver, however, Murnaghan emphasized that college officials should have broader powers over student speech than government possesses off-campus. "The University," he wrote, "does have greater authority to regulate expressive conduct within its confines as a result of the unique nature of the educational forum." Given that "the most fundamental concern of a university is to provide the optimum conditions for learning," Murnaghan reasoned, "the University must have some leeway to regulate conduct which counters that interest, and thereby infringes upon the right of other students to learn."[12]

For the majority, the constraints of the First Amendment were nearly categorical. A state university could no more suspend the partying privileges of an obnoxious fraternity than the state police could throw someone in jail for voting Democratic. Yet, for Judge Murnaghan, the question of campus speech was murkier, pitting the constitutional rights of some—in this case, the fun-loving Sigs—against the constitutional rights of the university to safeguard the learning environment for other students and for its broader academic mission. For Murnaghan, unlike the majority, this would typically require careful, case-by-case balancing of the competing interests. "I wholeheartedly believe that the free exchange of ideas and debate are fundamental to a place of learning," he wrote. "Yet, they comprise only part of a university's mission and must be balanced against a university's other interests, especially those interests which rise to the level of constitutional significance."[13]

Packed into the *Sigma Chi* case, then, can be seen the major dilemmas of the modern First Amendment's reach onto college campuses. The involvement of courts in policing the boundaries of free speech, press, assembly, and religion on campus was the natural and inevitable outgrowth of Supreme Court decisions in the 1950s and 1960s recognizing special First Amendment protection for academic freedom. Those early cases were welcomed by universities because they harnessed the formidable power of the Constitution to repel external incursions on academic freedom. It mattered little, for instance, that the claimant in 1957's *Sweezy v. New Hampshire* was an individual scholar rather than the university as an institution because the interests of both were aligned in resisting interference from outside. Yet, as First Amendment expert Robert O'Neil observes, "[t]he years since 1957 have brought a nearly linear progression in the evolution of judicially recognized academic freedom safeguards."[14] The resulting recognition of constitutional protection for the academic freedom both of individual scholars, in *Sweezy* and similar cases, and of universities to define and pursue their own institutional missions, as in Regents of the University of California v. Bakke, put the values on an inevitable collision course in cases like *Healy* and *Sigma Chi*.[15]

The Supreme Court's own first pass at navigating this intersection did nothing to simplify matters; in fact, it gave mixed signals. In *Healy*, the Court held that a state college's refusal to recognize a campus chapter of the Students for a Democratic Society violated the First Amendment rights of its aspiring student members. On one hand, Justice Powell's opinion for the Court insisted that "state colleges and universities are not enclaves immune from the sweep of the First Amendment," and expressly denied that "First Amendment protections should apply with less force on college campuses than in the community at large." Yet, on the other hand, *Healy* simultaneously allowed that "First Amendment rights must always be applied 'in light of the special characteristics of the . . . environment' in the particular case," and that "[i]n the context of the 'special characteristics of the school environment,' the power of the government" permits it to prohibit "actions which 'materially and substantially disrupt the work and discipline of the school.' " When it comes to universities, Powell observed, "[a]ssociational activities need not be tolerated where they infringe reasonable campus rules, interrupt classes, or substantially interfere with the opportunity of other students to obtain an education."[16]

Healy's seeming ambivalence allowed subsequent judges to pick and choose the guidance they wished to emphasize. In earlier years, courts rooted in generations-old doctrines favoring broad deference to universities tended to emphasize, as Judge Murnaghan did, the allowance for reasonable campus regulations. Yet, increasingly, in keeping with the *Sigma Chi* majority, courts have shifted their emphasis toward *Healy's* insistence that First Amendment rights apply no less forcefully on campus.

The Fourth Circuit's robust enforcement of the fraternity's First Amendment freedoms in the George Mason case was, in fact, just part of a larger burst of judicial decisions in the 1990s aggressively scrutinizing campus speech codes and regulation. A number of these cases—including the *Sigma Chi* case—were shepherded by the Center for Individual Rights (CIR), a conservative public-interest litigation group, as part of a campaign to use the First Amendment to attack "political correctness" on college campuses. In looking to throw the weight of constitutional litigation against liberal orthodoxy, writes political scientist Steven Teles, "[u]niversities provided a happy hunting ground for such cases, and also allowed CIR to adopt the posture of defending individuals against large, oppressive organizations, and to do so by using constitutional claims that liberals had pioneered."[17] As a matter of strategy, CIR initially resolved to focus its efforts, channeled through a newly formed Academic Freedom Defense Fund, specifically on "cases and controversies that have a bearing upon academic freedom and First Amendment rights." A First Amendment campaign, CIR calculated, might tap into strong popular and judicial currents against "the 'PC' movement" and serve as a wedge for later, more ambitious litigation directed against affirmative action in student admissions and faculty hiring. "In this way," the strategy went, "an Academic Freedom Defense Fund might contribute to a productive political 'realignment' on college campuses."[18]

Yet, even if CIR and other organizations had an orchestrating hand in pushing First Amendment litigation on campus, none of the cases was manufactured. Each percolated up from genuine controversies and each reflected the growing inclination of campus combatants to take their grievances to court. In the modern campus environment, Stanley Fish lamented in 2003, "[n]ot only is the First Amendment pressed into service at the drop of a hat (especially whenever anyone is disciplined for anything), it is invoked ritually when there are no First Amendment issues in sight."[19] Yet, as CIR shrewdly calculated, the uncertain boundaries of First Amendment doctrine have provided an excellent basis for inviting willing judges to enter the campus fray.

Politics, Provocation, and Prurience: Free Speech in the Classroom

It did not take CIR long to find its next opportunity to expand the First Amendment's foothold on campus. Within months of Sigma Chi's appellate victory, CIR was back in court, this time championing a professor's rights in the classroom. The University of New Hampshire, whose campus had given rise to the Supreme Court's landmark recognition of academic freedom in Sweezy v. New Hampshire, was again the setting for a First Amendment battle. This time, however, the subject for which First Amendment protection was claimed was not a lecture on Marxist economic theory at the height of the Cold War, but a discussion of technical report writing for animal science students. And the claimed threat to academic freedom came not from the ideological probes of a McCarthy-era prosecutor, but from university officials seeking to enforce a campus policy against sexual harassment.

J. Donald Silva was a long-tenured professor of communications in the university's School of Applied Science. In his first meeting with a new class of freshman science students in the spring semester of 1992, Silva, as he was wont to do, likened effective technical report writing to sex. "I compared focusing the thesis statement of a technical report with the sexual relationships between persons," he would later explain, "and how familiarity and experience are part of the communication, if focus is to occur." Because "[f]ocusing on the central idea of a long technical report is a complex task for freshmen in their second semester," he urged the teenagers instead to approach the challenge as if it were sexual intercourse: "Focusing requires the same long probation, adjustment, centering, a back and forth, give and take relationship until the writer and the subject are connected and fused as one." What others mundanely call a thesis paragraph was, for Silva, a beautiful "act of fusion."[20]

When the class met on February 24, 1992, Silva amplified on the theme: "I will put focus in terms of sex, so you can better understand it. Focus is like sex. You zero in on your subject. You move from side to side. You close in on the subject. You bracket the subject and center on it. Focus connects experience and language. You and the subject become one." Two days later, he tried to sharpen his students' appreciation for the power of "definition" by describing belly-dancing as being "like jello on a plate with a vibrator under the plate." At this point, a number of Silva's students had heard enough. After class, six female students went to express their revulsion and concern to a female faculty member; they "all expressed a fear of going to speak with him directly because they would never wish to be alone with him." Over the next four days, the university received a total of eight written complaints. Students said they felt "degraded," "shocked," "appalled," and "demeaned" by his oddly sexualized description of the writing process in class; in addition, a subsequent hearing found that "students described a number of other encounters with Professor Silva that had sexual overtones and that resulted in students feeling offended, embarrassed and intimidated."[21]

A university panel ultimately concluded that Silva's "repeated and sustained comments and behavior of a sexual and otherwise intrusive nature had the effect of creating a hostile and intimidating academic environment," in violation of the university's policy against sexual harassment. Since Silva had been previously warned by his department chair to stop using "sexual examples" in class, the university suspended him for one year without pay and directed him to seek counseling. Silva sued, with CIR's assistance, claiming a First Amendment right of academic freedom to teach the class as he saw fit.

The case was assigned to a semiretired federal judge, Shane Devine, who granted a preliminary injunction in Silva's favor and ordered his immediate reinstatement to the classroom. Senior Judge Devine, who had himself attended the University of New Hampshire after service in the Army during World War II, first set aside any concern over the "jello" comment by suggesting that students had jumped to wild conclusions by assuming "that the word 'vibrator' necessarily connotes a sexual device." He then dispatched the sanctions for Silva's remaining classroom allusions on the ground that they "were made in a professionally appropriate manner as part of a college class lecture," and could not be punished simply because "six adult students found his choice of words to be outrageous." Applying the university's sexual harassment policy to "Silva's classroom speech is not reasonably related to the legitimate pedagogical purpose of providing a congenial academic environment," Shane wrote, "because it employs an impermissibly subjective standard that fails to take into account the nation's interest in academic freedom."[22]

Professor Silva returned to the classroom and the university trustees agreed to pay him $60,000 in back pay and damages, and $170,000 in legal fees. Silva crowed to the press about his vindication: "The university seemed to feel this was more of a case of students' rights being more powerful than the First Amendment to the Constitution. Well, they were wrong."[23] CIR boasts on its Web site that "*Silva* is considered the first case to address the conflict between free speech and sexual harassment at a university."[24]

Yet, if *Silva* was among the first to explore the legal frontier between a professor's constitutional right to speak and a university's interest in sparing its students a toxic learning environment, it would plainly not be the last.[25] In 2000, a federal appeals court in Denver upheld a $557,100 jury award in favor of a veterinary technology professor who argued that the First Amendment entitled him to discuss tampons, denigrate blonde-haired women, and allude "to human anal and oral sex and male orgasms during a lecture about the transmission of parasites."[26] A federal appeals court in California ruled that a professor who repeatedly used vulgarities and "place[d] substantial emphasis on topics of a sexual nature"—including "consensual" sex with children, pornography, and his own writings for *Hustler* magazine—in teaching remedial English was constitutionally protected because he could not have known that his behavior ran afoul of college policy against "creating an intimidating, hostile, or offensive learning environment."[27]

The First Amendment, then, which little more than a decade ago was assumed to have no serious application to harassment, has emerged as a substantial counterweight to anti-discrimination law—and nowhere more powerfully than on college campuses.[28]

Still, not all courts have been so generous in protecting classroom speech, leaving the law in more than a little disarray.[29] A federal appeals court in Cincinnati, for example, held that an untenured communications instructor could not be dismissed for using the words "nigger" and "bitch" in a frank classroom discussion of "words that have historically served the interests of the dominant culture."[30] Yet, when a white journalism professor cautioned a class of African American students at a historically black university that "[a]nyone who doesn't . . . make opportunities for themselves may be guilty of having what some would call a 'nigger mentality'—the sort of thinking that can keep us all on the back of the bus together," another federal appeals court ruled that he could be cut loose.[31] The U.S. Court of Appeals for the Sixth Circuit, the same court that recognized the First Amendment right of the communications professor to use the word "nigger" in a classroom discussion of derogatory speech, upheld the dismissal of a university basketball coach who deployed the same word in a locker room pep talk, rejecting the claim of academic freedom.[32] The same court, in 2001, also upheld a Michigan community college's power to discipline an English professor who regularly bombarded his students with vulgar sexual remarks in class.[33] "Suffice it to say," observes Professor O'Neil, "that there is little certainty on the degree to which academic freedom protects the use of vulgar and taboo language in the college classroom."[34]

A university's dilemma in the modern legal environment is palpable. Acting to discipline or perhaps even remove a professor who insists on sexualizing classroom discussion may be found, as in *Silva*, to violate the professor's First Amendment rights and expose the university to hundreds of thousands of dollars in liability. Yet, standing by and allowing such behavior to continue may well be found to violate the legal rights of students to a nondiscriminatory learning environment. Under Title IX, students may hold a university liable if it has notice that a professor's sex-based classroom conduct is impairing students' ability to learn and fails to act. In Hayut v. State University of New York College at New Paltz, for example, an undergraduate student sued the university and her former political science professor because the professor had repeatedly referred to her in class by the nickname "Monica" at a time when the sex scandal involving Monica Lewinsky and then-president Bill Clinton was unfolding in the news. The U.S. Court of Appeals for the Second Circuit, in an opinion written by former Yale Law School dean Guido Calabresi, held that the professor's use of a nickname with sexual connotations could be found to have impaired the student's educational experience by "discourag[ing] [her] from more active involvement in his classroom discussions"; "compell[ing] her to avoid taking additional classes taught by [the professor]"; or "simply creat[ing] a disparately hostile educational environment relative to her peers." On this basis, the court found that the university could have been found responsible for sex discrimination; the only thing that spared it from potential liability is that administrators demonstrated their readiness to take adequate protective action, including negotiating the professor's swift retirement.[35]

The difficulty for universities is that they are caught between expanding legal protections for both free speech and nondiscrimination on campus, with relatively little reliable guidance from the courts about how the sometimes conflicting mandates are to be reconciled. The extent of the new legal uncertainty is reflected in *Hayut*. After holding that the university could not be held liable for the professor's classroom remarks because it acted promptly to address them, the court held that the student could go forward with her suit against the professor individually. Judge Calabresi then hastened to acknowledge—but leave entirely unresolved—the question of the professor's possible rights in the matter. The professor had admitted using the nickname in a "joking" manner and occasionally to "discipline" the student for talking or eating in class, but "has never expressly asserted that the comments complemented his classroom curriculum or had any other legitimate pedagogical purpose that might merit the kind of First Amendment protection that has long been recognized in the academic arena." On this question, Judge Calabresi—the former Yale dean and one of the brightest minds on the federal bench—could only punt: "We . . . express no view," he wrote, "on (a) whether such a defense could have been made, or could still be, made, or (b) if made, whether this claim would entail issues of fact or law." The scope of the professor's murky classroom speech rights would be left to be sorted out by others at trial—and, inevitably, on innumerable college campuses across the country.

Head of His Class: Student Speech in the Classroom

The next and still largely unexplored frontier in classroom speech rights concerns the rights of students to express themselves in class. In 2007, a

California appellate court confronted the claim of Stephen Head, an education student at San Jose State University, who argued that his teacher's unfavorable assessment of his classroom performance amounted to viewpoint discrimination in violation of his First Amendment rights. Head, who described himself as "a person who holds generally libertarian or conservative beliefs and viewpoints," felt himself swimming against the ideological tide in a course on "Social, Philosophical and Multicultural Foundations of Secondary Education." He complained about handouts and teaching materials dealing with cultural insensitivity, racism, and the "inability of a color blind approach to address these problems"; he objected that the professor did not permit him to challenge her classroom instruction by citing contrary authorities who "contested" multiculturalism; and he felt chilled by professorial criticism of his class comments suggesting that he might be "unfit to teach." The professor's rejection of his viewpoints in classroom discussion and written work, he argued, violated his constitutional right to speak freely; requiring him to parrot back his professor's or the university's dogma concerning multiculturalism to get a good grade was, he contended, government-compelled speech.[36]

Head's claims could draw qualified support from a decision three years earlier by a federal appeals court in Denver. In that case, a first-year acting student at the University of Utah named Christina Axson-Flynn had objected to performing roles that required her to recite certain coarse language or take God's name in vain. When the acting faculty refused to excuse her from the roles, she sued them for breaching her rights to free speech and religious liberty under the First Amendment. The district court rejected her claims summarily, but the appeals court reversed, holding that she had stated a sufficiently plausible claim to warrant a trial. Insisting that she perform assigned roles was indeed "compelled speech," the court ruled, triggering the protections of the First Amendment. While universities may compel speech based on "legitimate pedagogical concerns," the court held that Axson-Flynn could nevertheless prevail if she could show that the faculty's insistence was motivated by hostility to her religion. Similarly, if the acting program had occasionally allowed other excuses—such as excusing a Jewish student from class on Yom Kippur— the Free Exercise Clause might well entitle Axson-Flynn to the accommodation she sought.[37]

Michael Paulsen, a constitutional law professor who represented Axson-Flynn on appeal, exulted that it was a "breakthrough case in recognizing [that] the discretion of educators at the state university and secondary schools level is not limitless. They cannot, as a requirement to curriculum, require students to utter words or engage in acts that violate their most deeply held religious principles."[38] After the case was sent back for trial, the university settled and agreed to adopt a "religious accommodation" policy for all course requirements—despite fierce objections by "faculty members, mostly from the hard sciences, . . . that altering course content for reasons that have nothing to do with a 'legitimate pedagogical goal' was, by definition, an abdication of the [university's] commitment to academic integrity."[39]

In Head's case, meanwhile, the California appellate court ruled against him, deferring to the university's control over curriculum and classroom discussion. "A university is entitled to set its own curriculum and its selection of course materials will express academic ideas and values it wishes to inculcate," the court wrote. And "[p]ublic university professors are not required by the First Amendment to provide class time for students to voice views that contradict the material being taught or interfere with instruction or the educational mission."

But, at the same time, the court hinted that there might well be broad outer boundaries fixed by the First Amendment on a professor's control of student discussion. The court was careful to note that no evidence suggested that Head's professor had acted with "an impermissible discriminatory or retaliatory purpose," and suggested that "the First Amendment may require an instructor to allow students to express opposing views and values to some extent where the instructor invites expression of students' personal opinions and ideas."[40]

The professor's academic freedom to control the content and direction of classroom discussion—an interest lying at the heart of academic freedom—had now met a new constitutional counterweight. Not only must the professor's free-speech interest be set off against the student's equal-protection right to be free from discrimination, and the university's own First Amendment interests in institutional autonomy, now it must also contend with the student's First Amendment right, under appropriately limited circumstances, to share class time.

Artistic Expression and the Creative Campus Litigant

Head and *Axson-Flynn,* like *Silva* before them, involved clashes over speech in the classroom. But it is not only this core interest of the professoriate that has inspired faculty to take to the courts in defense of academic freedom and the First Amendment. In some cases, faculty have litigated to defend their rights to express themselves more artistically, in campus galleries, quadrangles, or even, in the case of the University of Minnesota at Duluth, on the history department's hallway bulletin board.

In the mid-1990s, the University of Minnesota–Duluth History Club wanted to bring a little levity to the staid halls of the history department and, at the same time, boast a bit about the department professors' broad interests and research areas. So club members asked each faculty member to pose for a photograph with at least one prop that best showed his or her area of historical interest. The photos would be posted beside the professors' academic backgrounds, their heroes from history, and favorite related quotations.

Professor Albert Burnham, whose interests ran toward U.S. military history, chose to pose wearing a coonskin cap and holding a .45 caliber military pistol. His heroes, he said, were John Adams and Davy Crockett.

Professor Ronald Marchese posed wearing a cardboard laurel wreath, and holding a Roman short sword. Homer and Alexander the Great were his historical heroes, and he listed Ancient Greece and Rome and Homeric Literature as his special areas of interest.

Students, faculty, and members of the public would all enjoy the display highlighting eleven faculty members, or so the members of the history club hoped. Some did. A federal judge would later write admiringly that "[m]embers of the department received many compliments on the presentation, as did the students who assembled it."[41]

But one of Burnham and Marchese's colleagues, Professor Judith Trolander, who herself had elected to pose with "three large books," was said to be "shocked by what she saw."[42] Just a few weeks earlier, Trolander had been the object of death threats on anonymous flyers sprinkled throughout campus captioned: "The Imperial Council of Deer Hunters Proclaim Open Season on Judy Trolander[,] Lesbian Feminist Bitch." The flyers followed on earlier death threats by "the deer hunters" against a newly appointed university vice chancellor, Sandra Featherman, who with Trolander had taken a leading role in spearheading campus efforts to promote diversity. The threats against Featherman had warned her to stay away from Duluth or face kidnapping: "There are footsteps crunching on the forest floor—it's the deer hunters coming . . . The deer hunters stalking—getting closer and closer, never giving up the hunt, never putting down their rifles. Overwhelmed by their desire to kill."[43]

The new threats against Trolander suggested that the author had indeed been stalking her. The flyers listed her home address and provided detailed "target information," including the best sniper position for getting a clean shot through her home's "large windows" and the assurance that "[s]he is the only occupant of the house, so it is OK to shoot silhouettes on drawn shades." After warning that any faculty member who cooperated with the university's diversity project would be "sentenced to death along with their pets, children, and spouses," the threat urged sympathetic readers to action: "Get cracking you kill[-]crazy buckaroos."[44]

It was in this context that Professor Trolander felt some alarm when a photograph of her colleague wearing a coonskin cap and brandishing a pistol appeared in the hallway of her department. Both Trolander and another professor who was the chair of the university's Commission on Women (which had been declared "dissolved" by the "deer hunters") complained to university officials; Trolander was reportedly "fearful that the display would inspire whoever was making the death threats."[45]

University chancellor Lawrence Ianni had scrambled earlier in the month, in the immediate wake of the latest threats, to reassure the academic community about the university's commitment to both campus safety and diversity. Now, he appeared before the history department faculty and sought to put out the latest fire. Though he recognized the harmless intentions behind the display, he "tried suggesting to the history department faculty that 'it would be an act of collegiality to remove the photos,'" in light of "'the effect of the agitation on campus.'"[46] But the history department chair and other faculty, apparently jealous of their own prerogatives, refused. "Somehow, this ugly trend of History governance by external administrators and bureaucrats must be called into account," read an internal department memorandum. "[I]f the photo display is our line in the sand, so be it."[47] Ianni then directed campus police to remove the photos of Burnham and Marchese, based on the university's "legitimate interest in addressing the fears of the targeted faculty members, in restoring harmony to the campus and the history department, and avoiding further disruption of university activities."[48]

Ianni's decision to remove the faculty photos swiftly became a cause célèbre, lampooned as the latest episode of the "PC follies." Speaking in the immediate wake of the controversy at a conservative think-tank forum in Minneapolis, University of Minnesota business school professor Ian Maitland suggested the flap was hardly "the stuff of landmark First Amendment cases," but deserved its place in " 'the tragicomic history of political correctness' " on American campuses.[49] Yet, even as he spoke, Burnham and Marchese and the two history students who had organized the exhibit were pressing a lawsuit in federal court, arguing that the chancellor's action had violated their First Amendment rights. In fact, Maitland himself would go on to fight a ten-year legal battle, ultimately with CIR's help, for male pay equity at the University of Minnesota.[50]

The federal district court strongly sided with Burnham and Marchese. The chancellor's decision to selectively remove only photos showing weapons, the court reasoned, was "an impermissible content based restriction." The university could not rely on concerns about the effect on threatened colleagues and the anxious "milieu" of campus death threats, moreover, because the First Amendment does not permit speech to be suppressed merely because " 'its content . . . is offensive to some members of the audience.' " Indeed, the district court held that the professors' First Amendment rights were so "clearly established" that the chancellor could be held personally liable for his actions, setting aside the usual protections of "qualified immunity" for government officers. "It is inconceivable to this court," District Judge Michael Davis wrote, "that the Chancellor of a major University could have failed to know that [the] First Amendment forbade, except in the narrowest of circumstances, the type of conduct at issue here."[51]

But judges could not agree. On appeal, a three-judge panel of the federal court of appeals in St. Paul reversed the district court's judgment. Two judges agreed that in light of the "tense" atmosphere on campus—in which, according to Ianni, "numerous employees" were in tears over "fears that someone would randomly open fire on campus"—"the balance of interests" plainly supported Ianni's decision.[52] Judge C. Arlen

Beam dissented, denouncing the majority's opinion as "an example of the triumph of the political correctness agenda of three or four campus personalities over well-established free speech rights of students and faculty."[53]

Beam would yet prevail. The full ten-member appeals court agreed to reconsider the panel's decision en banc, and all seven additional judges to hear the case sided with the plaintiffs. Now it was Judge Beam's turn to write the majority opinion, and Ianni lost badly. The selective exclusion of Burham and Marchese's photos, the court ruled, was impermissibly motivated by hostility to the viewpoint expressed in the photos—namely, "that the study of history necessarily involves a study of military history, including the use of military weapons." The university's claimed concerns about the impact of the display on the campus's learning environment and academic mission were "totally unproven." And, finally, it should have been obvious to the chancellor that his actions violated the faculty members' "clearly established" First Amendment rights, thus properly exposing him to personal liability.[54]

What began, then, as an impasse between faculty colleagues over a goofy photo display morphed quickly into a clash of principles both sides thought worth defending through years of litigation. The court battle served, moreover, as a test case not only for the free-speech rights of professors, but also for the right of the UMD history department to resist unwanted meddling by the central administration. The tortuous history of the litigation also says something, of course, about the practical costs of the resort to court and about the significant indeterminacy of the relevant legal principles. Ironically, the very question on which three courts flip-flopped in rapid succession was whether the First Amendment rights of the plaintiff-professors were "clearly established."

The case also underscores how unenviable life can be for campus administrators in the modern litigation age. Judge McMillian, dissenting from the final appellate judgment against the chancellor, observed that "it [was] fair to say that Ianni, as the unlucky decisionmaker in this employment-related controversy, was between a rock and a hard place. Regardless of whether he decided to have the photographs removed or left alone, it was reasonable for him to assume that some faculty members would be quite upset."[55] Navigating the shoals between faculty invoking their academic freedom to pose in coonskin caps and colleagues reeling from death threats meant to derail campus efforts to promote diversity, Ianni then confronted the history department's "line in the sand" rejecting bureaucratic meddling. It is surely little wonder that in 2006, eleven years after retiring from the university administration, Ianni published *A Plague on Both Their Houses*, billed as the first of an intended "trilogy of novels . . . deal[ing] with the conflicts and absurdities of the academic life."[56]

Other campus controversies over art displays confirm the dilemma, the disagreements, and the urge to head to court. If administrators exclude or even relocate provocative exhibits out of concern for the sensibilities of passersby, they may well be sued by the artist or exhibitor. An early case involving the now-celebrated artist Chuck Close, then a lowly art instructor at the University of Massachusetts, showed considerable deference to the university's decision to remove a display of Close's work—including vivid nudity and captions such as "I'm only 12 and already my mother's lover wants me"—in a student union corridor regularly used by children. Though the trial court had ruled strongly in Close's favor, holding broadly that university officials "had no right to censor simply on the basis of offensiveness which fell short of lawful obscenity," the federal court of appeals concluded sternly that it was "a case that never should have been brought."[57]

In more recent and less deferential times, however, courts have found university control over art to present a more nuanced question under the First Amendment. In 1985, the federal appeals court in Chicago rejected a challenge to a junior college's decision to relocate three frankly sexual artworks from a faculty art show—including a stained-glass representation of a naked, brown-skinned woman "crouching in a posture of veneration before a robed white male whose most prominent feature is a grotesquely outsized phallus . . . that the woman is embracing"; the college directed that the works be moved from a prominent display off the campus's main student "mall" to a more out-of-the-way upstairs gallery, after a number of students complained.

For the court in Piarowski v. Illinois Community College District 515, in contrast to the approaches of both the district and appellate courts in the Chuck Close case, the matter could not be reduced to bright-line rules favoring either artist or administrator. Instead, Judge Richard Posner, a prominent, longtime academic at the University of Chicago, wrote that the case involved the intersecting academic freedoms of both professor and institution. Balancing the two constitutional values required some reasonable accommodation:

> The college authorities were worried that Piarowski's stained-glass windows, created by the chairman of the college's art department and exhibited in an alcove off the college's main thoroughfare, would convey an image of the college that would make it harder to recruit students, especially black and female students. If we hold that the college was forbidden to take the action that it took to protect its image, we limit the freedom of the academy to manage its affairs as it chooses. We may assume without having to decide that the college's interest was not great enough to have justified forbidding Piarowski to display the windows anywhere on campus, but it may have been great enough to justify ordering them moved to another gallery in the same building.[58]

Piarowski thus gave college administrators leeway to take account of public sensibilities and the college's own interests in responding to complaints about the art, but still left them at peril if they misjudged what a future court would think reasonable.

In fact, in the present environment, there is peril in being sued even if administrators elect *not* to censor controversial art. In 2003, Washburn University's Campus Beautification Committee selected five statues to be temporarily displayed on campus as part of an annual exhibit. One of the statues, entitled *Holier Than Thou*, depicted "a Roman Catholic bishop with a contorted facial expression and a miter that some have interpreted as a stylized representation of a phallus." After receiving many complaints, university president Jerry Farley issued a statement acknowledging that "[t]here is no solution that will be satisfactory to everyone at this point," but deciding to leave the statue in place where it was, along "a high-traffic sidewalk" connecting the student union and the main administration building. Instead of censorship, he urged the community to engage in further dialogue to explore and credit the concerns raised. His pleas for dialogue did not get far. This time, the resulting lawsuit came from a professor and a student who argued that the university's prominent display of the statue effectively endorsed an anti-Catholic message in violation of the First Amendment's guarantee against the establishment of religion. The university ultimately prevailed, but not before spending more than two years in litigation that reached all the way to the U.S. Supreme Court, which declined to hear the case.[59]

As the cases make clear, colleges and universities now face very real litigation risks—even if not always liability—when they make decisions concerning artistic and other nonverbal expression on campus. The relationship between academic freedom and artistic expression has long been cloudy and even the entitlement of nonverbal art to full First Amendment protection is not beyond dispute. Indeed, as Robert O'Neil has observed, the court ruling endorsing Washburn University's defense of artistic expression as a part of the broader academic enterprise is actually "unusually sympathetic to artistic freedom as a component of academic freedom."[60]

Of course, *Burnham* had gone further still in protecting the posting of faculty photographs, yet this may be because the courts in that case regarded the images not so much as artistic expression as "non-verbal conduct" expressing a "particularized message" about military history in the college curriculum.[61] Even the definition of what counts as art, not surprisingly, is in the eye of the legal beholder.

The benefits of the recent infusion of campus litigation are also surely open to debate. Of the leading protagonists in the *Burnham* case, only one—Judith Trolander, the object of the death threats by the anonymous "deer hunters"—remains listed on the history department faculty Web site at the University of Minnesota at Duluth. The faculty Web site includes, however, the photograph of a new departmental colleague standing in front of a bookcase, dressed strikingly in what appears to be a red-and-black plaid woolen jacket and matching cap of the sort commonly seen on hunters.[62]

Hitting the Mark: Grade Litigation

The First Amendment is also called upon in what seems at first blush even less connected to its promise of freedom of expression. Grade litigation is another First Amendment trend.

Brian Marquis, a fifty-year-old undergraduate at the University of Massachusetts at Amherst, for example, was shocked when he checked his grades online in early January 2007. He felt sure that he was entitled to an A-minus in his Philosophy 161 course, "Problems in Social

Thought," but there staring back from his computer screen was a C. He e-mailed the graduate teaching assistant who had served as the instructor, and was informed that his final numerical score in the course was an 84 (not a 92.5, as Marquis had calculated). Moreover, the teaching assistant explained that he had then assigned final grades based on a curve, which dropped Marquis's letter grade to a C. A subsequent appeal to the university ombudsperson provided no satisfaction. After conferring with Marquis's instructor, she confirmed that Marquis had not "been singled out in an arbitrary and capricious manner." She urged Marquis "to accept this grade and continue on with [his] course work." But Marquis, a double major in legal studies and sociology, was not of a mind to be philosophical about his philosophy grade. Three weeks later, he filed a fifteen-count complaint in federal court demanding that the grade be raised to an A-minus.

"It's a tragic incident," Marquis explained to a reporter when the press inevitably picked up on the story. "Perhaps this is one of the ways that they'll listen to me, they'll take my claim seriously."[63] He was particularly concerned, he said, that the C might hurt his chances of getting into law school. By the early fall, the district court had bounced Marquis's suit out of court, dismissing all fifteen counts, including his claim that the disappointing grade violated his First Amendment rights.[64]

For all the media attention his suit attracted, Marquis was not the first to sue his professor for a better grade, arguing that the First Amendment somehow applied. For more than a century, there had been rare instances of lawsuits over grades, but these were almost always based on a claim that the grade had been based on some nonacademic, discriminatory consideration.[65] Yet, now lawsuits were challenging the very standards of academic evaluation. In 2005, part of Stephen Head's case against San Jose State included a demand for "a judicial order requiring the university to change his grade [in his education course from an F] to an 'A' or a 'B.'" Head had argued that he should not be marked down for rejecting the university's approving views of multiculturalism in education, though the court rejected the claim.[66]

Head and Marquis, who had specifically sought damages for the "emotional distress" caused by his C, might be surprised to learn that professors sometimes feel the same emotional investment in grades. Increasingly, student grade lawsuits are sharing courthouse dockets with those brought by faculty. A dental school professor at the University of Michigan, for example, invested more than six years and untold personal funds litigating through two separate court systems his challenge to a dean's decision to allow two students to retake a test on which he had assigned failing grades.[67] Professor Keith Yohn had pleaded, among other things, that relieving the students of his failing grade had caused him severe emotional distress and violated his First Amendment rights. "A scholastic grade is one of the most sought after jewels in education," he explained to the courts. "Teachers expend a lot of time, energy, and emotional distress in determining a student's grade."[68] The U.S. Supreme Court twice declined to hear his appeals.[69]

Just a month after the federal court in Springfield, Massachusetts, dismissed Marquis's bid to raise his grade, Carey Stronach, a long-tenured physics professor at Virginia State University, went to federal court in Richmond in a bid to lower one of his student's grades, from an A to a D—and money damages to salve the "anxiety, emotional distress, and humiliation suffered as a result of the grade dispute." Stronach's saga began when he gave one of his students a D in Physics 112 after the student had failed three of five quizzes. When the student complained to Stronach's department chair and offered evidence that he had, in fact, aced the quizzes (evidence that Stronach disputed), the chair raised the student's grade to an A; Stronach's dean and provost confirmed the grade change over the professor's staunch protest.[70]

In early 2008, the district court dismissed the claim that the grade change violated Stronach's First Amendment right to academic freedom. The court pointed to decisions in three federal courts of appeals rejecting professors' constitutional grading claims. The only case that offered Stronach any support, the court reasoned, was distinctly qualified. The U.S. Court of Appeals for the Sixth Circuit had held in Parate v. Isibor that, under the First Amendment's protection for academic freedom, an "individual professor may not be compelled, by university officials, to change a grade that the professor previously assigned to her student."[71] Yet *Parate* had gone on to make clear that a university was free to change the grade itself, so long as it did not force the objecting professor to do the deed herself, so it, too, offered no help to Stronach.[72]

But the precedent the *Stronach* court found most compelling was one from the Richmond court's own appellate circuit that rejected distinctive constitutional protection for professorial academic freedom across the board, not only in matters of grading. In 2000, in Urofsky v. Gilmore, the U.S. Court of Appeals for the Fourth Circuit rejected a First Amendment challenge brought by professors to a state law generally prohibiting state employees from accessing pornographic Web sites from state computers. The professors offered plausible claims why their research might require access to forbidden sites and argued that the law violated their First Amendment rights of academic freedom. But the appellate court ruled against the professors in a way that deprived them of far more than Internet sites. The *Urofsky* court held that the First Amendment's "special concern" for academic freedom protects only universities' institutional interests in autonomy; "[s]ignificantly, the [Supreme] Court has never recognized that professors possess a First Amendment right of academic freedom to determine for themselves the content of their courses and scholarship, despite opportunities to do so."[73] Given this precedent in the court's own circuit, *Stronach* concluded that "[h]owever definite the university's right to academic freedom is . . . it is clear that it is the *university's* right and not the *professor's* right."[74]

As veteran university counsel Lawrence White observed, *Stronach* marks "a significant departure" in the law governing grading disputes. The earlier grading cases on which *Stronach* relied had been distinguishable. "The plaintiffs in earlier cases," he pointed out, "were faculty members who had refused to comply with reasonable institutional grading policies—for example, a policy against grade inflation or requiring the assignment of an 'incomplete' rather than a failing grade to a student with a specified number of class absences." *Stronach*'s sweeping rejection of any protectable professorial interest in evaluating student performance was consistent with the Fourth Circuit's decision in *Urofsky*—a decision many academic freedom scholars find alarming—but took it out of step with courts in other parts of the country.

White's seasoned advice: college administrators considering a grade change should consult first with campus counsel.[75]

Taking Stock of the Modern First Amendment on Campus

College administrators may also wish to check with counsel before assigning teaching packages. Course assignments, too, have First Amendment implications, or so a dean at the University of Montana discovered recently.

When a spot opened up to teach constitutional law at the University of Montana School of Law in 2004, longtime faculty member Robert Natelson volunteered. Natelson had joined the Montana law faculty in 1987, primarily to teach property law courses, but had developed a substantial scholarly interest in constitutional law and had written a number of law review articles in the field. By his own account, Natelson had also led "a colorful life outside the law school," hosting a talk radio show, leading an anti–tax ballot initiative, and twice seeking the Republican nomination for governor.

The dean, after consulting with the faculty appointments committee, resolved to plug the hole with an adjunct or emeritus professor while conducting a national search for a constitutional law scholar. Natelson, who had been rebuffed for years in his efforts to teach the constitutional law course, was convinced that his outspoken conservative views were the reason for his frustration. "The law school apparently views this course as politically sensitive," he explained, "and has kept it in liberal hands for over 20 years."[76]

Natelson appealed directly to the state Board of Regents to overturn the dean and allow him to teach constitutional law. He also called on the Regents to order the law school "to reassess its policies and practices to assure that faculty members of all viewpoints receive equal opportunity and treatment in hiring, promotion, work practices, merit pay and faculty awards, and that there is greater viewpoint diversity among faculty." Viewpoint discrimination by a public university, he told the Regents, is unconstitutional under both the federal and Montana constitutions.[77]

Natelson never needed to press his legal claim in court. University president George Dennison appointed an outside lawyer, Donald Robinson, to investigate the professor's claims. After a hearing, at which both Natelson and his dean were represented by counsel, Robinson found a different basis for ruling in Natelson's favor: that the professor's reliance on a loosely followed past "custom and practice" of accommodating faculty preferences in course assignments gave rise to an enforceable expectation on Natelson's part that he would teach constitutional law.[78] The university president accepted the lawyer's findings and directed the law school dean to assign the constitutional law course to Natelson.[79] The president's directive caused some grousing at the law school, and the dean expressed concern over precedent narrowing decanal discretion in course assignments. But, according to a news report, one of Natelson's faculty colleagues insisted there would be no hard feelings over Natelson's resort to a "legal remedy" for faculty politics: "We can't hold a grudge against someone for exercising his rights," said Professor John Horwich, "especially not here—in the Law School."[80]

Natelson's case offers a useful vehicle for assessing the impact of First Amendment claims on academic life and governance. On one hand, there should be an obvious and fundamental compatibility between academic values and the First Amendment's guarantees of free speech and inquiry. "The classroom is peculiarly the 'marketplace of ideas,'" the Supreme Court has often observed.[81] Guaranteeing the freedom to study, challenge, speak, and collaborate—the very First Amendment values universities have successfully invoked to repel external interference—should, in theory, advance rather than obstruct the academic mission. After all, "[t]he very mission of a college or university," Robert O'Neil notes, "depends upon broad latitude for viewpoints in the pursuit of truth and understanding."[82] Yet academic life regularly involves conflicts requiring accommodation of the competing rights of individuals and the broader institution. The danger, in practice, is that enlarging the role of judges and juries in crafting those accommodations may do more harm than good.

In Natelson's case, for example, the claim of viewpoint discrimination was complicated by the facts. Even aside from Natelson's politics, the hearing officer found "a high degree of 'personal animus' toward Professor Natelson by the Law School faculty generally." There were, in addition, legitimate concerns advanced about Natelson's student evaluations in required courses, his record of service and civility with students and colleagues, and the "domino effect" of course reassignments that would follow from shifting him from property to constitutional law.[83] Moreover, even if the motives of the various actors involved could be accurately identified and untangled, the proposition that public universities are barred from considering ideological viewpoints in making faculty appointments "turns out to be a complex and, in my view, unsolved First Amendment issue," remarks UCLA law professor and First Amendment expert Eugene Volokh—and one that might require balancing Natelson's constitutional rights against those of the university itself.[84]

In Natelson's case, the matter was ultimately resolved on campus without resort to the courts. Whatever role legal principles may have had in shaping the outcome (and it appears they contributed significantly), it was ultimately the university president, an academic officer, who decided how to weigh the conflicting claims relating to teaching, service, collegiality, and the implications for other faculty course assignments.

The willingness of courts to protect speech and academic freedom more generally on college campuses has been undeniably valuable in fending off outside attacks on free inquiry and has significantly bolstered the status and independence of faculty.[85] Yet, there are at least three reasons for possible concern about the broadening judicial role in enforcing First Amendment rights on campus. The first is that judges appear increasingly inclined to treat public colleges and universities just like any other governmental entity for purposes of the First Amendment. As many thoughtful First Amendment scholars have recognized, there are substantial reasons to think differently about speech rights on campus. "[T]he university," argues academic-freedom scholar Peter Byrne, "has a fundamentally different relationship to the speech of its members than does the state to the speech of its citizens."[86] In some regards, of course, the toleration for speech and inquiry should be broader on campus than elsewhere. The idea that a faculty member at a public college should enjoy no more liberty to discuss research in the classroom than does a civil-service employee to grouse about a work assignment ought to be, Professor O'Neil rightly observes, "deeply troubling."[87] At the same time, the academic context sometimes justifies more control of speech than would be tolerated elsewhere. Concern for the learning environment, and the need to manage intense competing demands for limited resources, calls for alteration of the usual principles defining "public forums," for instance.[88] As Professor Kenneth L. Marcus, former head of the U.S. Commission on Civil Rights, points out, "[c]ollege campuses are both public places *and* student homes—and, at various times and in various places, they bear precisely the attributes that have led courts both to apply the First Amendment strictly and to abstain from doing so."[89]

Even more fundamentally, the educational function necessarily involves institutional judgments about the content of speech.[90] In the town square, the First Amendment requires government officials to maintain neutrality about contending claims; but academia routinely employs "collective criteria" to judge the value of inquiry and debate. Legislatures may not penalize belief in "intelligent design," for example, but universities may surely conclude that it does not belong in the science curriculum.[91] "The academic speech of the teachers and the students is subject to disciplinary norms deemed to facilitate criticism and discourse," Byrne notes. "[T]hose who do not meet the standards of speech set by the university are subject to penalties—students through grades and faculty through the denial of promotion or tenure."[92] None of this requires the conclusion that the First Amendment has no application to campus, but it does require sensitive recognition that free-speech principles must be tailored to the unique environment of the academic mission. Yet, as *Sigma Chi, Burnham,* and many more cases reflect, courts today often wholly disregard or discount the significance of the academic context in enforcing the First Amendment.

A second concern is that even when courts do recognize the special significance of the academic context, they sometimes only crudely perceive the relevant values at stake. Sometimes, as in *Silva,* courts emphasize professorial freedom and barely recognize the contending academic interests of the university, faculty colleagues, and students. Other times, courts veer in the opposite direction, as when *Urofsky* emphasized universities' autonomy rights to the wholesale exclusion of professorial academic freedom. Such categorical fixes do not accord with most academics' understandings of the complexity of the problems. Professor O'Neil, for example, points out that "[m]ention of academic freedom reminds us not only that campus speech and its treatment may differ from speech in the larger community but also that special factors within the academy may shape the scope of those differences."[93] Judith Areen, former dean of Georgetown's law school, has persuasively argued that the scope of First Amendment protection, and ultimately of judicial deference to university defendants, should vary according to the nature of the decision at stake. Constitutional protection for the speech of individual faculty members should depend in the first instance on whether it is genuinely related to an academic matter; the constitutional authority of the university as an institution to override and discipline that speech should then depend, at least in part, on the extent to which its action reflects the collective judgment of the broader faculty.[94] Yet if protecting free speech on campus requires a nuanced, case-by-case balancing of conflicting academic values—as courts sometimes recognize, as in the *Axson-Flynn* case involving the Utah acting student—it is at least fair to prefer that this balancing be done by judges and juries only as a last resort. However controversial the outcome, there is greater reason to trust the judgment respecting Professor Natelson's course assignment because it resided with the university president rather than with a local judge.

Finally, there is a third concern with the turn to the courts to resolve free-speech debates on campus: the trajectory of court decisions pushing the boundaries of the First Amendment encourages and channels ever more campus controversies into court. When a university fires a tenured professor after he gives an inflammatory speech provoking public outrage—as the University of Colorado did in the well-publicized case of Professor Ward Churchill in 2007—a First Amendment claim is hardly unexpected.[95] Yet, increasingly, far more mundane disagreements that once were resolved internally, through the normal give-and-take of academic governance, are likewise cast as contests of great constitutional principle and turned over to lawyers and judges to be sorted out in court. "Nowadays," observes Professor Marcus, former head of the U.S. Commission on Civil Rights, "it is not surprising to hear the First Amendment invoked in virtually any campus controversy."[96]

Examples abound. While University of Montana president George Dennison was deliberating over Robert Natelson's claim of a constitutional right to teach constitutional law, he was also a named defendant in Flint v. Dennison. In that case, the student senate president—sanctioned by his colleagues for spending $214 on pizza and campaign posters, in violation of a student-government bylaw limiting campaign spending to $100—litigated all the way to the U.S. Supreme Court his claim that the bylaw violated the First Amendment.[97] A graduate student at the University of California at Santa Barbara went the same distance (with equal futility) in asserting a First Amendment right to university acceptance of a master's thesis on calcium carbonate containing a "disacknowledgments" section listing "special *Fuck You*'s" to the dean, Regents, governor, and "Science" itself.[98] In 2007, when the University of Illinois abandoned its controversial mascot, "Chief Illiniwek," two students who portrayed the Chief at football games sought an emergency injunction on the ground that ending their performances would violate their "constitutional right[s] of freedom of speech, freedom of expression and academic freedom"; the previous year, a state appellate court had rejected a lawsuit by a different group of students contending that the half-time performances violated *their* civil rights by reinforcing ethnic stereotypes.[99] In another case from the same campus, a physics graduate student asserted a constitutional right to present data her university supervisors believed to be deeply flawed at a scientific conference, free from academic sanction.[100]

And, of course, faculty members have been no less emboldened. Courts have had to contend with professors' claims of First Amendment rights not to hand out student course evaluations,[101] to abstain from providing specific feedback to their students,[102] and to defy campus policies requiring faculty to submit grading materials.[103] A University of Arizona professor suspended after a campus disciplinary hearing for allegedly feeding his unwitting Spanish students marijuana-laced cookies at their final exam went to court to defend his "First Amendment right to teach his classes as he saw fit."[104] Wolfgang Hirczy de Mino, as part of a long-running dispute with the University of Houston over its treatment of adjunct professors, alleged in court that the university's practice of suspending the e-mail accounts of adjunct faculty during nonteaching semesters, as well as its use of an apparently vexing spam filter, violated his right of free speech under the First Amendment.[105] When de Mino was terminated for engaging in an affair with a student in one of his classes, he again invoked the First Amendment, filing suit asserting that penalizing the affair violated his constitutional right of free association.[106]

The year after a Texas court rejected de Mino's claim, Paul Abramson, a longtime psychology professor and sex researcher at UCLA, published a book-length argument in support of the view that "university romance policies are constitutionally unjust."[107] Abramson argues extensively that the First and Ninth Amendments of the Constitution confer on university professors and students a fundamental right to engage in intimate liaisons, and invalidate campus policies of the sort that got de Mino into trouble. Abramson's volume on *Romance in the Ivory Tower* is not likely to be regarded as an impressive contribution to the literature on constitutional theory; yet, that a veteran scholar of psychology and human sexuality saw fit to undertake a project focused on constitutional theory as applied to campus policy is an impressive marker of just how far rights-thinking has insinuated itself into academia.

Back to the Future: The Brothers of Sigma Chi

As it turns out, the "ugly woman" contest was not the last contribution that George Mason University's Sigma Chi chapter would make to the jurisprudence of the First Amendment on campus. In 2005, the brothers held two separate parties at which, university authorities alleged, under-age guests were given alcohol and then sexually assaulted by two different Sigma Chi members. A few months later, a university administrator saw a number of Sigma Chi members and pledges gathered near the campus library, singing and marching, in what she took to be a hazing ritual; later, members were seen wearing their Sigma Chi letters at an orientation carnival, at a time when the chapter was suspended and members were barred from associating with the fraternity.

This time, the university threw the book at the fraternity, banning it from campus for ten years. Again, the brothers returned to federal court, claiming that the penalty violated their rights of free speech, association, equal protection, and due process. District Judge Leonie Brinkema, who two years earlier had presided over the trial and sentencing of al Qaeda conspirator Zacarias Moussaoui, seemed to have less patience with the fraternity, however. She found ample evidence and fair process to support the fraternity's ejection from campus.

But Judge Brinkema threw out the First Amendment claims on somewhat more equivocal grounds. Though the "singing and dancing" outside the library was expressive activity protected by the First Amendment, the fraternity lacked standing to complain since the other misconduct abundantly supported the sanctions in any event. Similarly, the challenge to the discipline of members for wearing their Sigma Chi letters failed because the brothers had named the wrong defendant. The court's ruling left Sigma Chi banned from campus, but also left open the possibility that other fraternities, with properly pled complaints, could fight hazing charges on First Amendment grounds in the future.[108]

When the George Mason campus newspaper, the *Broadside*, reported on Sigma Chi's latest resort to the courts, some students were evidently offended by its recitation of the misconduct charges against the fraternity.

"You guys at the [B]roadside have dragged fraternities['] names through the dirt for as long as I've been at this university," wrote one reader. "You should prepare yourselves for a lawsuit because not only is this information innaccurate [*sic*] and one-sided, it's defamatory."

But that is another chapter.[109]

CHAPTER 5

Prerogative and Profit:
Battles over Intellectual Property

In 1901, William Townsend Porter, an associate professor of physiology at Harvard Medical School, founded a company that he called Harvard Apparatus. It produced and sold medical research equipment, such as kymographs, inductoriums, and, in time, an innovative syringe device known as the "Harvard Pump." The name of the company, and its celebrated pump, was fitting because Harvard Apparatus operated directly out of Harvard Medical School, which was especially convenient given that all of the company's products were manufactured in the medical school's machine shop.

The undertaking was spurred by Porter's efforts to remake physiological instruction at Harvard in the German model, substituting laboratory experimentation for book-learning and lectures. The new model required the provision of enormous supplies of specialized equipment to fill Harvard's laboratories, yet "the cost of such . . . equipment made on the old lines would be beyond the means of any large school," Porter lamented. Porter's solution was to design and mass produce his own on site, supported by capital helpfully provided by Harvard's president, Charles W. Eliot. The plan was as inventive as it was essential to the school's mission. Writing triumphantly in 1903, Porter insisted that "[t]he supply of apparatus of this type bears the same relation to the advance of physiology that the commissariat bears to the advance of the army."[1]

Over a six-year run at the medical school, business in the machine shop boomed. The operation hummed along so efficiently, in fact, that Harvard Apparatus was able to market its surplus products to other universities and laboratories. Yet, in President Eliot's view, business was actually getting *too* good. In 1907, just two years before he closed out four decades as Harvard's president, Eliot ordered Porter to pack up "Harvard Apparatus" and move it off campus. The problem, as Eliot saw it, was that the enterprise's "quasi-mercantile status" was at odds with the academic mission and might well violate the university's charter.[2] As it happened, Porter's medical supply operation was not the only quasi-mercantile influence Eliot was then seeking to drive from campus. During the same year that he resolved to oust Harvard Apparatus, Eliot was also pushing bravely to abolish football at Harvard on the ground that the game was not "fit for college."[3]

Professor Porter dutifully relocated Harvard Apparatus to a barn on his farm in nearby Dover, about eighteen miles southwest of Cambridge. From this bucolic setting, it continued to supply Harvard's medical laboratories, though now "as a complete outsider" as the university required.[4] In time, even Porter himself was ready to close up shop. When he retired from the Harvard medical faculty in 1928, he offered to give away Harvard Apparatus to the American Physiological Society, but the learned society "declined to accept the gift."[5]

Harvard Apparatus eventually changed hands. One hundred years after the company set up shop in Porter's barn, the annual report of its new parent company, "Harvard Bioscience," describes itself as "a global developer, manufacturer and marketer of a broad range of specialized products, primarily apparatus and scientific instruments, used to advance life science research at pharmaceutical and biotechnology companies, universities, and government laboratories worldwide." Annual revenue in 2008 was $88 million.[6] In 1996, new owners decided to update the company's corporate logo and created a company Web site on which the Harvard name appeared in a Harvard crimson-like color and in a distinctly Harvard-like font. The word "Apparatus" was relegated to the shadows in a diminutive, gray font. The new appearance, a court later acknowledged, was "virtually identical" to the familiar mark of Harvard University.

In 2001, Harvard took notice of its distant relative and decided the jig was up. Harvard the University sued Harvard the Company for multiple invasions of its intellectual property: trademark infringement, trademark dilution, unfair competition, and cybersquatting, a legal claim surely beyond the imagination of William Townsend Porter, based on the company's use of "Harvard"-named Web sites.

The legal defense raised by Harvard Bioscience and Harvard Apparatus was straightforward: Harvard had simply waited too long to complain. Company officials suggested that if Harvard wanted to stop the use of its name, it should have acted promptly as soon as "Harvard Apparatus" products started emerging from Porter's barn. Under the legal doctrine of "laches," even a valid legal claim can expire if a claimant delays unreasonably in asserting it. The federal trial judge who heard the case in Boston sided readily with the company. "Harvard University's one hundred year delay in interposing an objection to the use of the name Harvard Apparatus by a company that it virtually fathered," he wrote, "is beyond the rim of anything a court considering a laches defense has found to be even remotely reasonable." The judge suggested that the use of the Harvard trademark color and font (being a more recent incursion on the university's identity) was actionable, but "[t]he use of the unadorned name 'Harvard Apparatus,'" the judge wrote, "is a gift of time."[7]

In 2009, Harvard Apparatus boasts two separate medical products Web sites, www.harvardapparatus.com and www.harvardbioscience.com. "Harvard" still looms in a font size nearly twice the size used for "Apparatus" or "Bioscience," but the words appear in an unassuming white, separated by a thin line more red than crimson.

The *Harvard Bioscience* case is a useful starting point for considering the expanding interrelation of courts and higher education through the law of intellectual property. It provides an example of the ways in which universities seek legal protection not only for marketable inventions, but also for their marketable identity, with increasing attention paid to "branding" and cyber rights. More notably, however, the case provides a striking reminder of just how far academic attitudes have traveled concerning business opportunities and marketing.

Charles Eliot—today often revered as "a dreamer who [would] take risks and challenge the Harvard community to push itself to its limits" and a visionary "giant in the evolution of higher education" more generally[8]— was evidently unable to foresee the coming age of "technology transfer" and "academic capitalism."[9] A century later, the dramatically changed environment on campus would be compactly captured in the dual professional identity listed for one of Eliot's modern-day successors, economist Lawrence Summers, holder of a chair named in Eliot's honor. After stepping down as president (but before his return to government service in the

Obama administration), Summers was identified in 2007 as "Charles W. Eliot University Professor at Harvard and part-time managing director with D. E. Shaw Group, an investment and technology development firm."[10]

Even at the time President Eliot was seeking to drive Harvard Apparatus (and football) from campus, the seeds of change on the nation's campuses were beginning to take root. The very same 1906 issue of the *American Educational Review* that reported on Eliot's campaign against college football also contained an item titled "College Men in Industry," taking note of industry's burgeoning interest in the brain power of America's campuses—and of its transformative potential for higher education. "The laboratory and the shop of the technical school are as different from the library and the cloister of the college as the equator is from the poles," the *Review* crowed. "Our educational system is undergoing the most practical readjustment that it has experienced in all its history."[11]

In that readjustment, any aspiration of banishing commerce from campus would prove as hopeless as Eliot's campaign to prohibit the pigskin. Today, as David Kirp writes, "American higher education is being transformed by both the power and the ethic of the marketplace."[12] The classic metaphor of the classroom as the "marketplace of ideas" increasingly provides a literal description of the modern university. Colleges and universities have always worried about revenue, of course, but "[w]hat is new about today's commercial practices is . . . their unprecedented size and scope," notes Derek Bok. "Today, opportunities to make money from intellectual work are pursued throughout the university by professors of computer science, biochemistry, corporate finance, and numerous other departments."[13] The opportunities are most abundant in science—described by former Cornell president Frank Rhodes as "[t]he center of gravity of the New American University"[14]—but extend far beyond. From "Big Science" to online "virtual education," Kirp notes, "[e]ntrepreneurial ambition, which used to be regarded in academe as a necessary evil, has become a virtue."[15]

This new entrepreneurial spirit has brought academics into more frequent contact not only with corporations, but also inevitably with the courts. Indeed, the law of intellectual property—through which universities harness the market power of their discoveries and creative products through patents, copyrights, and assorted legal doctrines—has opened up a major new interface between campus and courts. "Higher education is a major supplier of intellectual property through its research, scholarship, and dissemination of knowledge," observes Professor Michael Olivas, an expert on higher education law, "and is perhaps the greatest consumer of intellectual resources, through hiring and use of intellectual property."[16] The number of patents granted to academic institutions grew by 1,325 percent between 1979 and 2000, far outstripping the growth of patents generally.[17] And the pace shows no signs of letting up. In 2006, universities introduced 697 new products into the market, and started 553 companies; that same year, they filed 11,622 separate patent applications, up from 6,397 just five years before.[18]

This "commercialization" of higher education has been as lucrative as it has been controversial. In 2006, universities earned more than $1.2 billion from patent licensing, forked over by companies that have bargained for the opportunity to commercialize university inventions. That figure is up tenfold from the comparatively paltry $123 million that universities reaped from such licenses in 1991.[19] Some individual colleges and universities earn millions of dollars from licensed apparel and memorabilia sales alone.[20] The increased revenue has enabled universities to pursue their academic missions—financing new programs, faculty lines, and laboratories—but has also stirred anxieties that the profit motive may be corrupting and redefining those missions. David Kirp warns that money has never before exerted such "raw power" over "so many aspects of higher education."[21] Jennifer Washburn calls the new business orientation "the single greatest threat to the future of American higher education."[22] Others have been more sanguine, but most agree with William Kaplin and Barbara Lee's observation that "[t]he potentials and problems arising from universities' and faculty members' research relationships with industry have garnered more attention than almost any other higher education development of the past thirty years."[23]

Unsurprisingly, given the enormous money and other stakes involved, legal claims over ownership and other commercial rights relating to academic activities are increasingly finding their way into court. "Disputes over academic intellectual property have, until recently, been treated as mere footnotes to the respective histories of the university, patents, and copyrights," notes Corynne McSherry, "but they are taking on new prominence as IP becomes a crucial source and guarantor of title on the elusive 'knowledge frontier.' "[24]

The amount of money at issue can be extraordinary.

A New Day on Campus

In 2008, Cornell University won a jury verdict against Hewlett-Packard Corporation (HP) on the claim that HP had borrowed technology invented and patented by a Cornell engineering professor, Hwa Torng, without first bargaining for a license. In 1989, Torng had developed a process that enabled computers effectively to "multi-task," carrying out multiple commands at once, thereby greatly improving their speed. Cornell alleged that HP had incorporated Torng's breakthrough in supercomputers built for the federal government and for Boeing Corporation. A jury in Syracuse, New York, agreed and awarded Cornell $184 million. If it survived appeal,[25] it would be the tenth-largest damages award in the history of the United States, and the fourth-largest for a patent-infringement action. Professor Torng, now retired, stands to get a $46 million slice from the award, under Cornell's standard profit-sharing agreement with its faculty; he said he intended to give at least 80 percent of it to charities in the Ithaca area.[26]

Even though the amount was a good deal smaller than the $900 million in damages Cornell had initially sought, the university was rightfully gleeful. "This has the potential for being a fundamental case for all universities," a Cornell spokesperson told a reporter. "It's very important to protect intellectual property, and you have to make sure people know that this happened."[27]

Cornell's spokesperson need not have worried. The word is already out about the importance of protecting intellectual property—and the dazzling financial rewards that can come from doing so. Cornell's verdict presented the happy occasion (though not for HP) when university and researcher stand side-by-side against alleged infringement by a corporate deep-pocket. But with such dizzying financial incentives, universities now find themselves sometimes fighting their own over the IP booty.

Consider the case of chemistry professor John Fenn. By his own account, when Fenn first set foot in New Haven as a graduate student in 1937, he was "a wide eyed small town youth from Kentucky," utterly "awed by[] the splendor of Yale's campus."[28] When he decamped New Haven for good fifty-seven years later as an emeritus professor, it was with a good deal less reverence, and the two would forever share opposite sides of a case caption in the federal courts.

Through his years on Yale's faculty, Fenn had a history of disagreements with Yale over the share of profits the university allowed faculty to keep from their academic discoveries. Fenn's affections for Yale were said to be further diminished when he was forcibly retired upon turning seventy in 1987 (before federal law was amended to prohibit such mandatory retirements).[29] Yet, Fenn persevered in his research as an emeritus professor at Yale and one year later developed a process to analyze biological macromolecules through electrospray ionization. When Yale administrators inquired about his discovery, Fenn is said to have downplayed its commercial potential; meanwhile, Fenn himself quietly patented the process and sought to bring it to market through a company he co-owned with a former graduate student.[30]

Fenn's invention, as it turned out, was of great value. *Investor's Business Daily* reported that the breakthrough had "enormous applications in drug research" and put the market in mass spectrometry instruments at $2 billion.[31] When Yale found out about Fenn's patent in 1993 and demanded that he assign it to the university, Fenn refused. After relocating to Virginia Commonwealth University in 1994, Fenn was the first to strike in the courts. He sued Yale on a battery of legal theories ranging from theft to unfair trade practices, accusing the university of effectively trying to steal his invention; Yale responded with an equally impressive array of counterclaims, accusing Fenn of stealing *its* property rights in the invention.

After nearly a decade of litigation, Fenn lost badly. Just as the case was finally nearing trial in Hartford, Fenn was awarded the 2002 Nobel Prize in chemistry for his disputed discovery. It probably did not help Fenn's cause—given Yale's claim that he had denied the invention had much commercial value—that the Nobel Foundation hailed Fenn's discovery as "revolution[izing] the development of new pharmaceuticals" and offering "promising applications . . . in other areas, for example foodstuff control and early diagnosis of breast cancer and prostate cancer."[32]

Federal trial judge Christopher Droney ruled that Yale's patent policy—requiring professors to report all discoveries and inventions for patenting by the university—was "a valid and enforceable part of the contract of employment" with faculty. As a professor, the court held, "Dr. Fenn owed Yale the duties of a fiduciary, including the duties to make full disclosures and maintain an undivided loyalty." His failure to alert Yale about the significance of his discovery and to turn it over for exploitation by the university not only breached his contract and his fiduciary duties, the court ruled; it also amounted to outright larceny. Fenn, the judge found, had in effect embezzled the university's property—albeit intangible, intellectual property—just as a bank teller would be liable for stealing money from the change drawer. The finding of theft meant that Fenn had to pay the university both treble damages—three times the royalties Yale would have received under the patent—as well as punitive damages for showing "reckless indifference" to the university's property rights, altogether more than $1 million.[33] A federal appeals court upheld the judgment in 2006.[34]

At the same time Fenn was litigating against Yale, he was also ensnarled in litigation against his former graduate student and the company they had jointly founded to market his inventions. In 2007, one month after Virginia Commonwealth University celebrated Fenn's ninetieth birthday with a symposium in his honor, Fenn lost again.[35]

As Fenn's case illustrates, the enormous economic value of some research or a history of grievances can strain the legal assumption that researchers and their academic employers occupy a cozy relation of "undivided loyalty." In the modern environment, where universities may spend "upwards of $20 million to attract a star biochemist, complete with retinue and laboratory,"[36] researchers might be forgiven if they think of themselves more naturally as free agents than as Mr. Chips. Even universities seem to acknowledge that faculty member and university often stand at arm's length. Saint Louis University, for example, recently asked a judge in an intellectual property dispute to keep certain evidence, including university marketing plans and licensing agreements, out of the hands of the tenured professor-defendant because such plans and agreements were information "to which a tenured professor in one department of the University [was] not ordinarily given access."[37]

The respective rights of universities and researchers are now routinely spelled out in research contracts or legally binding university patent policies. But that has not stopped a steady stream of litigation over their interpretation, and matters are easily complicated when policies evolve over time or research projects are carried from one institution to another in the ongoing competition for scholars.[38] Typically, university policies claim the lion's share of patent revenue for themselves while allowing faculty members responsible for the invention a smaller slice.

Meanwhile, when it comes to academic works protected by copyright, another intellectual property conception, university policies are often more generous.

The University of Illinois, like many others, moved to make its copyright provisions more explicit after Congress changed copyright law in 1978 to give all employers, including universities, ownership over any "work for hire," including faculty scholarship. At the university, the creators of "traditional academic copyrightable works" generally retain all rights to their creations. Those works include just about anything a professor might write: "class notes, books, theses and dissertations, educational software . . . articles, non-fiction, fiction, poems, musical works, dramatic works including any accompanying music, pantomimes and choreographic works, pictorial, graphic and sculptural works, or other works of artistic imagination that are not created as an institutional initiative."[39] Professors retain copyrights in their projects generally unless terms explicitly say otherwise, works are directly commissioned by the university, or the work is "a specific requirement of employment or as an assigned University duty," though that third provision has been interpreted narrowly and very much in favor of the author-professor, given that professors typically must publish to receive tenure.[40] The American Association of University Professors (AAUP) has argued that policy, practice, and academic freedom all require that professors retain the copyright in nearly all of their work.[41]

Patents and copyrights, though both under the intellectual property umbrella, are treated differently within the university for both academic and economic reasons.[42] First, there is worry that it would restrict academic freedom if creative work automatically became the property of the university.[43] In addition, written work traditionally has not been a huge money-maker—certainly not on the order of computer codes and mass spectrometry—and requires much smaller start-up costs, diminishing the university's incentive to demand a return on investment. In fact, the different treatment of patents and copyrights might be seen as confirming the foresight of the *American Educational Review,* which in 1906 had predicted a coming transformation of higher education that would cleave "the laboratory and the shop" of technoscience from "the library and the cloister" of the traditional academy.[44]

If the law defining the respective rights of universities and their creative employees is sometimes unclear, at least there is typically a written contract or other document to go by. When it comes to the legal rights *among* university researchers or authors, the potential for confusion—and thus for litigation—is often many times greater.

The Case of the Star-Crossed Astronomers

A few days before Christmas 1876, Hamilton College astronomy professor Christian Peters sent an excited letter to *The Utica Morning Herald* about what he described as a "new star" with an intense brightness. The sudden "flare up"—a nova, or "a world on fire"—had first been seen at an observatory in Athens, Greece, about one month before, he explained, but had just been detected and confirmed the previous night at the Litchfield Observatory on the Hamilton campus. The new star's position, he reported to readers, "shows, by comparison with the catalogues, that no star brighter at least than ninth or tenth magnitude had been in that place before."[45]

A little more than ten years after the *Herald* published that letter, the catalogues that Professor Peters had referenced would be the subject of a nasty legal battle in the New York courts.

Peters was an astronomer of world renown. By the time he joined the Hamilton College faculty, he had discovered multiple new asteroids.[46] The catalogues were a project he had been working on at the upstate New York campus for several years. Eventually, Peters hoped, they would be compiled into one definitive star catalogue, a publication that would feature thousands of star placements and positions, creating an entire map of the sky.

Peters hired Charles A. Borst, a former student, to aid in the effort, though the precise employment agreement between the two was not clear and would become a key part of the lawsuit. Borst took some of Peters' original charts and added his own calculations and star positions to them. The entire work would become a manuscript more than 3,500 pages long.[47]

Borst completed the star catalogue sometime in 1888. When Peters asked to see the work, Borst produced a title page that indicated it had been authored by Borst "under the direction of Christian H. F. Peters." Professor Peters, it is said, read the page Borst had handed him, "tore up the paper, opened the stove door, put the fragments into the fire, and then turned on [Borst] with the simple order, 'Bring me the catalogue!' "[48]

Borst refused. So Peters filed a lawsuit, asking the court to rule that the star catalogue belonged to him as its original creator. Borst argued in response that he had added the vast majority of star placements. The local sheriff would be called to take custody of the star catalogue for the duration of the legal dispute.[49]

Though lawsuits among academics were far from usual back then, Peters had turned to law before in his academic dealings. He told a colleague who had asked about funding for the observatory at Hamilton that he had retained a lawyer in a dispute regarding his previous year's salary. "The trustees here too," he warned, "will find that there are 'fighting astronomers.' "[50]

Peters, the fighting astronomer, would win the first round. In November 1889, a New York trial judge ruled that Peters was the rightful owner and author of the star catalogue. The judge—seemingly a bit overwhelmed by the literal and figurative star power in the courtroom and later criticized by others as not up to the task of understanding academic work[51]—first decided that the work itself did not belong to Hamilton College, because Peters's work on the manuscript stretched back to 1858, predating his arrival on campus. Then he found little to corroborate Borst's claims that he and his sisters had put nearly the entire project together at home, noting that young persons often believe they know and do more than they do. "Real, true ability, ordinarily, is modest and unassuming," the judge wrote, and "has respect for age and eminence won by long years of study and labor."[52]

At the time of the trial, Professor Peters was seventy-six years old. But whatever respect for his age and eminence the judge had shown would be of little value. Peters died of an apparent heart attack on the way to the Litchfield Observatory at Hamilton College just eight months after the verdict on July 18, 1890.[53] Some said that the stresses of the star catalogue ordeal killed him.

Four years later, New York's highest court would overturn the decision in favor of Peters. The justices decided that Charles Borst, by then affiliated with Johns Hopkins University,[54] deserved a new trial because of a bad evidentiary ruling. Just as the trial court had sided with Peters, the appellate court seemed taken with Borst's evidence and testimony. "That Borst, as a mere assistant of Peters, should not only help him during observatory hours . . . but should devote to his service all time of his own, working late into the night and absorbing every spare moment," the court wrote, "only to magnify the reputation of Peters, and on a salary of only six hundred dollars a year," was "too painful to contemplate."[55] Based on "the subject matter involved and the peculiar relations between the parties," the court decided, Borst deserved a new trial.

A new trial would never happen. In the five years it would take the litigation to make its way from trial to the highest court in New York, those involved in the project lost the ability and interest to pursue the star catalogue. The warring academics and the plodding course of justice brought any notion of publication to a halt. The star catalogue would never be published, a victim of those who cared so much about it that they had invited the courts to decide its fate.

A Modern Battle of the Stars: Campus Meets Copyright

The trial judge in the Peters-Borst star catalogue dispute assured readers that the case involving two academics was an unusual one. "Fortunately," the judge wrote in his opinion, "it is not often we have to deal with such controversies as this, in which the real question in issue relates, not to money considerations, but to the credit to be given parties for scientific or literary productions."[56] Yet, ten years after the final decision in the case, astronomer Simon Newcomb had a broader perspective. The case was "of scientific interest," he wrote in a book chronicling his own career in astronomy, because, "although the question was a novel one to come before a court, it belongs to a class which every leader in scientific investigation must constantly encounter in meting out due credit to his assistants."[57] Perhaps the most important lesson, Newcomb suggested, was that the case "affords an instructive example of the possibility of cases in which strict justice cannot be done through the established forms of legal procedure."[58]

If so, the lesson might be said to have been lost on Dr. Heidi Weissmann. Almost precisely 100 years after the trial court's decision favoring academic mentor over mentee, Dr. Weissmann was in federal court in Manhattan testing the same waters. Weissmann was an extraordinarily promising medical researcher and "a rising star" on the faculty at Yeshiva University's Albert Einstein College of Medicine in the Bronx.[59] Since arriving at Einstein's Montefiore Medical Center as a fourth-year resident, Weissmann had worked closely with Dr. Leonard M. Freeman, chief of nuclear medicine at Montefiore and vice chair of Einstein's department of nuclear medicine. Freeman was himself a star in the field, a former president of the Society of Nuclear Medicine and "a prolific author [who was] . . . a much sought-after speaker at national and international meetings."[60] For a decade, they collaborated closely on a number of articles and research projects. The relationship between the "enterprising junior associate" and her prominent mentor was, the *New York Times* later observed, "productive, seemingly harmonious and fairly typical in science."[61] The trial court later summed up their division of labor: "To a large extent it was [Weissmann's] part of the joint enterprise to write down the results of their activity, with [Freeman] always on top of what was in progress, by actually supervising the investigations, writing portions of papers, reviewing drafts, commenting on the scripts and lending credibility thereto and to the project by his standing, reputation, knowledge, perception, and experience."[62]

The partnership unraveled in 1987. Freeman, preparing to give a lecture at a seminar on nuclear medicine at Mt. Sinai School of Medicine, submitted under his own name a paper summarizing the state of the art in the field to be distributed to those attending the seminar. The paper had previously been prepared by Weissmann for use at similar review courses and was pieced together in substantial part from earlier papers jointly authored by Weissmann and Freeman. When Weissmann learned that Freeman planned to distribute the paper under his own name, she complained to the seminar's organizers and Freeman readily agreed to give the lecture without handing out the paper. The next day, Weissmann sued Freeman in federal court for infringing her copyright in the paper. Weissmann was tired of sharing credit for her work. Freeman was "dumbfounded." "I feel she had no right to take credit for the entire paper based on our joint work," he told the *New York Times*.[63]

The Weissmann-Freeman dispute was a modern restaging of the Borst-Peters saga from a century before. Once again, courts were confronting what they called "an uncommon controversy" involving "the problems that arise when a long relationship between accomplished professor and brilliant assistant come to an end."[64] And, in some ways, this modern battle of the stars played out in much the same way, with the trial court siding admiringly with the mentor and the appeals court showing greater sympathy with the claims of the assistant. Yet, whereas the *Borst* saga ended inconclusively, the outcome in *Weissmann* seemed to point the way toward a new legal regime for academic collaborations.

The trial court dismissed Weissmann's claim on the ground that it simply had no business in the courts. The work in which Weissmann claimed a copyright was a product of her collaboration with Freeman, an "evolutionary stock piece" patched together from their earlier, jointly authored work. Within the context of the parties' collaborative relationships, it was fair game for the mentor to lift from work of his erstwhile coauthor that itself had cribbed from their joint efforts. In Judge Milton Pollack's view, it was a case of Weissmann biting the hand that fed her; after all, he noted, "it was the defendant who opened the doors for Dr. Weissmann, making all of her research and writing possible and professionally recognized." Her "resort to the courts," Pollack concluded, was a sorry act of "misguided ego," and her mentor was "amply vindicated as a professional matter by exposure of the facts."[65]

The federal appeals court in Manhattan, however, had a very different view. It chided Judge Pollack for straying from the law and for focusing instead "on the parties' long-standing and close professional relationship."[66] Pollack's assumption that the professors' close collaborative relationship controlled the case "stands copyright law on its head." Under copyright law doctrine protecting "derivative works," the only questions were whether Weissmann, in revising the prior collaborative work, had intended to claim the revision as her own and whether her tinkering had added something that could be considered "more than trivial." Weissmann's paper passed that bar, the court concluded, and she was therefore entitled to assert ownership rights. In addition, her mentor's use of her property could not be classified as "fair use" under the law. Although Freeman did not "stand to profit" in a conventional sense from exploiting Weissmann's work (Freeman earned his modest $250 honorarium for the lecture even without distributing the paper), Freeman "stood to gain recognition among his peers in the profession." "Particularly in an academic setting, profit is ill-measured in dollars," the court reasoned; Freeman had stolen the coin of the academic realm: scholarly reputation as an author.[67]

The contrast between the approaches of the trial and appellate courts in *Weissmann* illustrates a striking shift of judicial attitudes toward scholarly disputes. Judge Pollack had effectively resolved the matter on the basis of governing academic norms. The loose, back-and-forth borrowing of written work was, for Pollack, permitted by the nature of the parties' collaborative relationship. Yet, on appeal, as Corynne McSherry notes, "the court treated academic authorship like any other authorship dispute"; the scope of permissible use was, for the appellate court, determined not by academic norms, but by the strict terms of the Copyright Act.[68] For Judge Pollack, the scholarly dispute plainly belonged "in another forum";[69] for the appellate court, it rightfully belonged in court.

The readiness of the appellate court in *Weissmann* to sort out a dispute over scholarly credit between coauthors stands in sharp contrast to a decision just two years earlier by a federal appeals court in Chicago. In that case, Weinstein v. University of Illinois, a former assistant professor of pharmacy sued his one-time colleagues over revisions they made to a jointly published article before publication—including one change that lowered the plaintiff's name in the list of coauthors. In an opinion by former academic Frank Easterbrook—and joined by another former tenured professor, Richard Posner—the court regretted that the matter had ever come to court. "If war is the extension of diplomacy by other means, this suit—like other litigation a form of warfare—is the extension of academic politics by other means," Easterbrook wrote. "Weinstein and Belsheim [one of his coauthors] were unable to compromise, and Weinstein has dragged his fellow scholars and the University into the contest." In that case, the disgruntled scholar had rather outlandishly framed the loss of authorial credit as a violation of his constitutional rights to due process. In rejecting the claim, the court briefly noted that the defendant's revision of the work was consistent with copyright law, but the bottom line of the opinion was clear enough that disputes like this really had no business in court.

Yet, *Weissmann*, by effectively insisting that academic norms are not above the law and that ordinary intellectual-property principles would be strictly applied to allocate rights to academic "property," seemed to throw open the courthouse doors to a potentially broad range of academic quarrels. Moreover, a significant feature of the court's analysis—its recognition, in McSherry's words, of "academic persona—professional identity . . . as property"[70]—invited an entirely new sort of intellectual-property claim wholly apart from the world of patents and copyrights. If universities traded on the academic reputation of their faculty for financial gain, they might then be liable to their faculty under the common-law doctrine of "misappropriation," the use of another's name or likeness without permission. It is not a suggestion without support. In a recent case, for example, Rama Nemani, a research assistant professor of pharmacology at Saint Louis University, sued the university for having listed his name on a successful NIH grant application without first obtaining his consent. The grant was approved, but not in an amount sufficient to cover the professor's salary, and his position was terminated. When Nemani later found out his name had been used on the grant application, he sued the university for the misappropriation of his valuable scholarly identity—the same theory by which celebrities can recover if advertisers use their names to endorse products without permission. A St. Louis jury agreed and awarded Professor Nemani $300,000. The award could have been a lot higher; jurors were said to have asked if they might add punitive damages, but the judge refused.[71] The verdict was set aside on appeal on the ground that Nemani had impliedly consented to the use of his name on grant applications through his grant-funded employment, but leaves other academics without such a history another possible, albeit unusual, intellectual property-related cause of action.[72]

Nemani was left disillusioned by the loss. "It's not science," he lamented to a reporter, "these people are out for money."[73]

Loose Lips Sink Ships—and Patents

Weissmann illustrates the use of intellectual property litigation to challenge customary norms of academic collaboration—"the 'medieval' guild structure of academia."[74] It was possible to see in *Weissmann* and similar cases, observes McSherry, that "[t]he agents of change were resentful graduate students and junior researchers, who were turning to the legal system to resist the appropriation of their research by their mentors— takings prompted, in turn, by increasing anxiety about publications rates and productivity." More broadly, as McSherry and others have pointed out, the growing "propertization of academic work" poses a basic challenge to traditional academic norms concerning the exchange and ownership of knowledge.[75] When Professor Christian Peters detected for himself the exciting "new star" in 1876, he rushed to report his finding the next day in a letter to the *Utica Morning Herald*. Today, an academic who discovers something of potential commercial value is advised to keep his cards close to his vest.

Consider the unhappy experience of Carol Klopfenstein, a professor emeritus of grain science at Kansas State University. Klopfenstein and a colleague applied for a patent for new methods of producing cereal products containing soy cotyledon fiber (SCF). A description of the new product might not suggest, at least to the uninformed reader, an obvious market appeal in the breakfast-cereal aisle—SCF is said to be "comprised mainly of cell wall material and . . . a by-product derived from processing dehulled or defatted soybean flakes into soy protein isolates or concentrates."[76] Nonetheless, research suggested that the product yielded health benefits by lowering serum cholesterol levels while raising levels of HDL, the so-called good cholesterol.

But Klopfenstein's patent application was rejected by the Patent and Trademark Office on the ground that she and her colleagues had previously shared information about their discovery with others. The prior disclosure that rendered their discovery unpatentable was a "poster presentation" consisting of printouts of fourteen PowerPoint slides pasted onto poster board. The poster board had been displayed, more than a year before the patent application, at a three-day meeting of the American Association of Cereal Chemists and again, more briefly, at an Agriculture Experiment Station at Kansas State. Upholding the rejection of the patent application, the U.S. Court of Appeals for the Federal Circuit held that the academic inventors had effectively given their invention to the public by summarizing their findings without extracting promises of confidentiality from conference-goers.[77]

The *Klopfenstein* court was not an outlier; other courts also have struggled to define the sort of academic disclosure that will preclude an inventor from later patenting a discovery. A student's disclosure of an invention in the course of defending a thesis to a faculty committee, for example, will not necessarily defeat patentability, but indexing the thesis in the university library likely will.[78] In Massachusetts Institute of Technology v. Harman International Industries, a court considered whether a graduate student's earlier field trials of an invention through the streets near the university should invalidate a patent. For his doctoral thesis at MIT in 1989, Jim Davis had invented the technology for the now-ubiquitous computer-aided navigational systems for drivers—a project he called "the

Back Seat Driver." In developing and refining his device, Davis had a number of MIT undergraduates and others test drive a specially equipped car—
leading ultimately to the truly impressive claim on the patent application
that the device had "successfully guided drivers unfamiliar with Cambridge, Mass., to their destinations." MIT got its patent but when it later
filed an infringement action against the maker of Harman/Kardon "Traf-
ficPro" for stealing its technology, Harman defended partly on the ground
that Davis's prior flaunting of his invention on the streets of Cambridge defeated its patentability. The court deferred Harman's claim for trial.[79]

Courts have acknowledged the concern that penalizing prior disclosure naturally undercuts "the incentive for inventors to participate in academic presentations or discussions."[80] To mitigate the problem, *Klopfenstein* insisted that courts are less likely to characterize a prior disclosure as
fatal "[w]here professional and behavioral norms entitle a party to a reasonable expectation that the information displayed will not be copied."[81]
Yet, as intellectual property principles are used to wear away preexisting
academic norms of collaboration and sharing, as in *Weissmann,* even this
leeway for guarded academic disclosure may shrink. At bottom, as University of Virginia law professor Margo Bagley notes, *Klopfenstein* "seems
sure to result in a further stifling of scholarly discourse prior to the filing
of patent applications."[82]

Studies suggest that patent law's incentives for prefiling secrecy have already affected the behavior of many academic scientists, leading to delay
in disclosing discoveries at conferences and through publication.[83] There is
even a suggestion that patent law may be partly responsible for a down-
turn in the collective contributions by U.S. academics to global scholarly
discourse, as measured by publications in top journals.[84] "While not
amenable to precise quantifications," Bagley writes, "the stifling of discourse and the erosion in the norms of sharing and colloquy historically
associated with the scholarly enterprise are costs that must be balanced
against the technology transfer gains."[85]

Bagley and other scholars have identified "the growth of patent-related
litigation involving universities" as an additional, related concern.[86] Jennifer Washburn, for example, relates the example of a patent obtained by
the University of Utah on a human gene related to hereditary breast cancer. When the chair of the genetics department at the University of Pennsylvania attempted to use the gene in cancer research, he was threatened
with litigation by the company to which Utah had licensed its patent.[87]

Moreover, the impact on scholarly discourse is likely to grow in the years ahead. Patent law scholar Arti Rai notes that "the legal system has also done its part to encourage the patenting of basic research," and that a series of rulings by the federal appeals court responsible for patent law has steadily expanded the boundaries of patentability.[88] As a result, observes NYU law professor Rochelle Cooper Dreyfuss, intellectual property law has "expanded to cover an array of creative efforts that were previously largely ignored or considered ineligible for protection."[89]

As in the contexts of anti-discrimination law and First Amendment rights, the turn to law in matters of campus innovation is both inevitable and, in many respects, constructive. Without doubt, legal protection of invention and authorship has enriched scholars and universities alike and supported investment in additional research and discovery. Moreover, whatever the equities of the particular *Borst* and *Weissmann* sagas, there have surely been exploitative and abusive academic collaborations. Providing a legal remedy for such abuses and securing the parties' reasonable expectations may well remove disincentives to collaborate, facilitating productive relationships and additional innovation. The challenge, however—as with anti-discrimination law and First Amendment rights—is to import legal doctrines in a way that is sensitive to the academic context and cognizant of its potential costs. Woodenly applying expectations of pre-patent secrecy developed in commercial contexts, for example, or propertizing scholarly reputation on the model used for Hollywood celebrities risks displacing long-standing and socially beneficial academic norms of sharing and collaboration.

IP for a Cause

The ever-expanding reach of intellectual property law on campus is not solely a product of greed or generous court rulings. In addition, campus combatants are discovering that intellectual property law provides a handy new legal tool for pressing grievances that may be only distantly related to property interests. In this way, intellectual property law may share common ground with the First Amendment as an emerging vehicle for litigating all variety of campus beefs.[90]

At the same time Heidi Weissmann was pressing her copyright infringement action against her former mentor, she was also suing her university for sex discrimination over her salary and a deferred promotion.

In trying to make sense of Weissmann's motivation for pressing her copyright claim in court, District Judge Pollack speculated that the suit may well have sprung from her anger over having been deferred for promotion; in any event, the court surmised, her motivations "go beyond and are outside of a claim of copyright infringement."[91] Looking at Weissmann's double-barreled litigation, Corynne McSherry suggests that ultimately "both suits represent[ed] an effort to claim a space of equality in a hierarchical institution."[92] Anti-discrimination law provided a basis for challenging traditional hierarchies based on sex, race, or religion, while intellectual property law provided a way of attacking a hierarchy of academic status by enforcing a formal conception of property rights in ideas and written work. "The [copyright] lawsuit," McSherry observed, "threatened the hierarchy embedded in mentorship: a decision in Weissmann's favor would have suggested that mentor and mentee were equal and autonomous."[93]

Collateral campus hostilities also seem to have been behind lawsuits brought by professors in an unsuccessful effort to bar universities with which they were once affiliated from selling their textbooks in the campus bookstore and from using their textbooks in classes on campus—a surprising anti-education stance for college instructors.[94] The plaintiff "appears to believe that a copyright entitles the author to determine how a work is used and thus to prevent the book's adoption as a teaching text," one court reported. "Not at all."[95] More understandably, professors at the University of Connecticut in 2005 successfully invoked intellectual property principles to fend off a demand by a student under the state's Freedom of Information Act for electronic copies of all PowerPoint slides used in class. A state appellate court agreed that "any educational materials developed by the teachers are the intellectual property of those teachers, and it is the decision of each instructor whether to provide the PowerPoint presentation files to a student."[96]

More recently, intellectual property law provided a last resort for supporters of Chief Illiniwek, abandoned in 2007 as the mascot of the University of Illinois under strong pressure from the NCAA. As all other tactics were proving futile—including appeals to the legislature and even a constitutional lawsuit based on claims of academic freedom brought by the students who portrayed the so-called Chief in half-time performances—an alumnus who had designed the university's distinctive "Chief" logo back in

1980 stepped forward to claim ownership of the iconic symbol much revered by some fervent Illinois students and alumni. He argued that the trademarked symbol—of a "stern-faced Chief in blue and white, surrounded by a blue and orange headdress"—having been abandoned by the university, should revert to him.[97] If he gained control of the symbol, he could presumably thwart the university's plans to retire the controversial figure by keeping campus shops forever abundantly stocked with Chief Illiniwek t-shirts, banners, and baseball caps. A federal court tossed the suit in 2008, but the artist's lawyer promised more litigation, possibly even in another jurisdiction. "We are certainly not going to give up, whether it's with another court or direct appeal," the lawyer vowed to Champaign-Urbana's *News-Gazette*. "The Chief is not easily defeated."[98]

Final Notes

Intellectual property plaintiffs often seem to have the same level of fortitude as the so-called "Chief" and his counsel, even in matters that might have been thought long settled. Who owns what after note taking during a typical classroom lecture is a current, yet very old, puzzlement.

In 1825, a surgeon named Abernethy delivered lectures on surgery to medical students at Saint Bartholomew's Hospital in London, England. He was surprised to come across parts of his lectures in the medical journal *The Lancet*, all of which had been published without his permission. Dr. Abernethy asked a court for an injunction to stop future publication and the court agreed, using, by analogy, the traditional control that a professor had over his lecture notes. "We used to take notes at [professors'] lectures," a judge wrote, apparently drawing from his own educational experience, "but it was never understood that those lectures could be published;—and so with respect to any other lectures in the university, it was the duty of certain persons to give those lectures but it never was understood, that the lectures were capable of being published by any of the persons who heard them."[99]

Fast forward nearly 200 years and that seemingly basic principle appears very much up for grabs. In 2008, a University of Florida professor named Michael Moulton was also surprised to see his classroom lectures appear for sale by a company that called itself Einstein's Notes. Einstein's Notes, like similar operations on other campuses across the nation, hires students to take detailed notes in class, which are then sold to other students who wish to avoid wrist strain or early morning classes. Moulton has asked a federal trial court in Florida for an injunction to stop publication of those lecture notes, asserting both copyright and misappropriation claims.

The copyright argument should be of special interest to students across the United States. According to Moulton's lawyers, *all* student notes taken in class are "a copy or close derivative work of that professor's intellectual property," and so technically infringe on the professor's copyright; students who keep their notes to themselves fall within copyright's exemption for "fair use," while those who sell them to others must answer in court.[100]

Meanwhile, Moulton told the *Chronicle of Higher Education* that his lawsuit has nothing to do with money and everything to do with what students learn in his lectures. "What bothers me the most," he said, "is sometimes the notes will get things wrong."[101] But a lawsuit that Moulton had heard about years ago also bothered him. There, he remembered, a court granted the note-sellers permission to publish professors' lectures over university copyright claims. And, indeed, in 1996, a federal appeals court upheld a jury verdict rejecting a claim by the University of Florida, which had tried to use copyright law to stop commercial distribution of one of its professor's class notes. The appellate opinion does not describe in depth the precise issues and legal arguments before the jury, concluding only that the record contained "competent support" for the judgment against the university.[102] The *Chronicle*, however, reported at the time of the decision a finding sure to unsettle hardworking faculty: that the jury believed that a professor's lectures were made up "of facts or ideas that do not belong to anyone."[103]

Moulton's own lawsuit—which "aims to clarify one simple fact: professors own their own lectures"[104]—stumbles into an old yet increasingly contested territory that is, as Corynne McSherry points out, anything but simple. Indeed, the very much open question of who, if anyone, owns the intellectual content of classroom lectures touches on "a 'second academic revolution'": "Ascribing property rights in lectures inevitably 'propertizes' academic work in general," she notes, "helping to reposition scholarship and pedagogy at the center of a web of commercial relations—a market economy."[105] A headlong rush to the courts to assign ownership and specify permissible uses of ideas expressed in class entails regulating and restricting the transmission of knowledge at the very heart of the academic enterprise. As much as discrimination or First Amendment claims, such property claims threaten to remake the classroom experience and open a new avenue for external supervision and control of "the intellectual life of a university."[106]

Faulkner Press, Moulton's publisher, is the named plaintiff in the case. On a Web site devoted to the dispute, Faulkner says it is "proud to protect the rights of Professor Moulton and the rights of all professors."[107] That Web site—devoted solely to the note-publishing case, outlining the principles the Press hopes to establish through intellectual property litigation—links lawsuits and academe in a telling way.

The Web address is, fittingly, www.thefutureofhighered.org.

CHAPTER 6

Privacy in Peril:
Peer Review Meets Judicial Review

It was nearing midnight on February 20, 2002, and the University of Michigan Law School's tenured faculty had just voted on a difficult tenure case. Assistant Professor Peter Hammer—whose discrimination lawsuit was considered in Chapter 3—was universally regarded as an outstanding teacher and had spearheaded an innovative and highly valued legal services program in Cambodia, but his scholarship had received mixed reviews. In fact, when Hammer had first come up for tenure in 2000, the faculty deferred his case for two years so that he could make an all-out effort to improve his scholarship. Now, after nearly nine hours of agonizing debate spread over two nights, the faculty voted 18–12 in favor of tenure—four votes short of the two-thirds approval required under law school rules. It was only the second time in forty years that the faculty had voted to deny tenure.

Jeffrey Lehman, then dean of Michigan's Law School, addressed the tenured professors in the room. He would inform Peter Hammer of the result, and he reminded the professors that everything said during their long deliberations was strictly confidential.[1] In a follow-up e-mail, Lehman reiterated to the tenured faculty the importance of maintaining confidentiality:

> At the end of the day, although I understand that reasonable people might have a different view, I continue to believe that the right norm for the Law School is that as individuals we should not discuss with Peter the process that led to the faculty's decision. That includes not talking about the actions of the committee, of the tenured faculty as a whole, or of individual colleagues. It also includes not talking about our own actions in

that process, including statements we made to our colleagues during the process, or votes we cast. And it includes declining to answer questions that ask us to reveal or affirm any actions we took in the process.[2]

Dean Lehman called Hammer at home after midnight following the faculty vote to break the news. Hammer's shock soon turned to frustration over his inability to get a detailed accounting of what went wrong. As he later recalled:

> All he would say was that I had failed to receive the two-thirds vote necessary to send an affirmative recommendation for tenure to the central administration. He would not tell me the actual vote count. He would not tell me whether the Tenure Committee Report was favorable or unfavorable. He would not tell me whether the opposition was internal or external. He did tell me, however, that no faculty member would be able to tell me any of these things either. He stated that faculty members were expressly prohibited from revealing anything that happened at the meeting, even to the point that they could not express their own views on the merits of the case or how they voted as individuals.[3]

In the days that followed, Hammer pressed for more information. He wanted to see the external reviews of his scholarship and the official report of the law school's tenure committee; he wanted to know what the vote had been before the committee and the full tenured faculty. Aside from providing a general description of the concerns over Hammer's scholarship, Dean Lehman remained steadfast.

Lehman obviously believed, in company with many academics, that confidentiality is essential to the integrity and rigor of the peer-review process. And he evidently fully expected to be able to limit Hammer's access to information about what had been said about him. It is likely that the scholars who had provided internal and external reviews of Hammer's scholarship similarly expected that their identities and comments would remain a secret. Some letters soliciting peer reviews of tenure candidates, after all, promise that any appraisal will be held in confidence.[4]

Yet, Hammer would not be deterred from uncovering the judgments that had derailed his promising career at Michigan. When his efforts to persuade Lehman to release more information failed, he turned to the law. In May 2002, he filed a request under the Michigan Employee Right to Know Act demanding access to his full personnel file. In response, the law school produced redacted versions of some reviews and communications, but withheld other peer-review material including the tenure committee's confidential report. Hammer then filed a formal grievance claiming, among other things, that the law school's refusal to provide a "reasonable level[] of openness regarding the decision making process" was both "illegal and fundamentally unfair."[5] The law school rejected the grievance.

In 2005, two years after Hammer had resettled at Wayne State University Law School in Detroit and Lehman had left for the presidency of Cornell University, Hammer sued the University of Michigan. Among other claims, he alleged that his former colleagues had discriminated against him because he is gay, in violation of a contractual promise of nondiscrimination. What followed shows vividly the power of judicial review to remake the basic assumptions of peer review.

During eleven months of pretrial "discovery," Hammer was able quickly to ascertain the votes and views of all persons involved in reviewing his file. His lawyer deposed twenty-one Michigan professors and administrators involved in his tenure denial, including the dean, the provost, and colleagues who had voted against his promotion, probing their conduct, judgments, and, in some cases, political views and religious affiliations. He obtained full, unredacted copies of all documents connected with his tenure file, including the reports of the tenure committee and all internal and external review letters. In addition, he obtained copies of a large volume of e-mails and other correspondence between various colleagues and administrators making reference to his tenure case and its aftermath.

The clash between what Dean Lehman called "the right norm for the Law School" on confidentiality and the court-enforced norm of "generous and wide-ranging discovery provided by the Federal Rules of Civil Procedure" could hardly be more glaring.[6] When one of Hammer's former colleagues was informed by the associate dean that his negative assessment of Hammer's work would be turned over to Hammer in the litigation, his e-mail reply consisted of a single, four-letter expletive. That e-mail, too, was produced.

Much of this material is now posted on the Internet, on two different Web sites dedicated to Hammer's grievance and lawsuit.[7] As a result, curious Web surfers may now peruse the full twenty-one-page majority report of the tenure committee, as well as a seven-page dissenting opinion and a five-page concurring opinion.[8] There, they may find a detailed account and assessment of the evaluative comments offered by each of seven named external reviewers and five internal reviewers, or they may choose to read PDF versions of some of the reviews in full for themselves. The reviews dissect Hammer's scholarship (and that of his coauthor, a long-tenured Columbia law professor) and offer direct evaluative comparisons between Hammer and several named contemporaries at other law schools. Readers may examine the minutes of the two faculty meetings held to discuss the tenure case, complete with shorthand summaries of comments attributed to specific colleagues ("He's a bad writer," pronounced one; "Poor choice for a research project . . . Don't see paper leading to antitrust debates down the road," opined another). Dean Lehman's "confidential" letter to Michigan's provost summarizing the substance of the faculty's deliberations is also available.[9]

All together, observed one academic blog, "the documents, including e-mails, letters and depositions of two dozen or so profs, represent one of the most comprehensive portraits of a tenure decision and the institutional personality of a law faculty that is ever likely to be publicly available."[10] Yet what is remarkable about Hammer's case is mostly that these documents are posted online. For those enterprising enough to journey to a courthouse, similarly revealing collections of once-confidential peer-review documents can be found in the public case files of numerous other tenure lawsuits.[11]

The growing frequency and breadth of court-ordered disclosure are not just catching attention in the blogosphere. They are reshaping basic assumptions about peer review and the ways in which universities govern themselves. At one time, courts hesitated to pierce the veil of secrecy surrounding academic peer review; historically, not only review letters but even the membership of tenure committees was considered sacrosanct. Today, as Hammer's case shows, all information relating to personnel decisions is readily discoverable once a lawsuit is filed.

The implications of the trend toward free-wheeling disclosure go far beyond the context of tenure and promotion. Peer review is the backbone of academic evaluation throughout the university. In hiring and promotion, "[p]eer review is the canonical procedure for determining 'who will teach.' "[12] Yet, it is also the foundation for decisions about what shall be published by leading academic journals and university presses, and about what shall be studied, through the process of research approvals and grant funding. Subjecting the competition for research dollars to the rigor of the peer-review system, notes former Cornell University president Frank Rhodes, is "one of the great strengths of the research enterprise in this country," and largely explains the preeminence of American universities in basic research.[13]

Indeed, it may not be too much to say, as academic-freedom scholar Peter Byrne has claimed, that "[a]cademic freedom has no meaning without peer review."[14] The peer-review process of academic self-evaluation, after all, underlies the claim to professorial and institutional autonomy. That universities entrust core academic judgments—judgments that are as institution-defining as those concerning tenure and the research mission—to specialists in the field is a basic reason for deference by courts and other state actors. Peers possess scholarly expertise and judgment that courts do not and cannot, and have a peculiarly powerful self-interest in ensuring the future integrity and standards of their guild.

Yet, in recent years, courts have been called upon with increasing frequency to examine the role of confidentiality in effective peer review in matters affecting hiring and promotion, publication, and research support. A central issue in these debates is whether the scholars who participate in the peer-review system, the ballyhooed backbone of the academic enterprise, themselves have the personal backbone required to dish out criticism in the bright sunlight of public scrutiny. Judges, as in the Supreme Court decision described below, seem increasingly sure that peer review can operate in the open. Many academics continue to insist that sensitive academic judgments cannot be made in a fishbowl; but plaintiffs like Hammer insist that is the only way to see the sharks.

"Stand Up and Be Counted": Peer Review in the Glare of Judicial Scrutiny

In 1985, the University of Pennsylvania's Wharton School denied tenure to Rosalie Tung, an associate professor specializing in international management, with a special interest in Asia-Pacific business. When Tung heard that Wharton based its decision "on the ground that the Wharton

School is not interested in China-related research," she was convinced that this was "simply their way of saying they do not want a Chinese-American, Oriental, woman in their school." She complained of discrimination to the Equal Employment Opportunity Commission (EEOC), alleging that her "qualifications were 'equal or better than' those of five named [faculty] members who had received more favorable treatment." The EEOC investigated and asked Wharton for copies of all six tenure files, but the University of Pennsylvania refused. It argued that "confidential peer review information" should be off limits to external scrutiny absent a more specialized showing of need.[15]

The EEOC then armed itself with a court order directing the university to turn over the files. The university fought to the U.S. Supreme Court, which agreed to hear the case in order to settle a split in the lower courts over whether colleges and universities enjoy a "qualified privilege" to withhold confidential peer-review information. Several federal appellate courts had recognized a qualified privilege to keep things confidential, similar to the privilege protecting lawyer–client communications, while others had ruled that peer-review materials should be freely available so long as they were relevant.[16] Parties on both sides quickly saw the case as a major test of the relationship between academe and the courts. The National Organization for Women Legal Defense and Education Fund filed a brief supporting the EEOC; the AAUP, the American Council on Education, Harvard, and Stanford each filed briefs supporting Penn. Peter Byrne, writing while the case was pending, warned that "[a] cavalier disregard for the interests of the university in the process of peer review would be disastrous" for academic freedom.[17]

Despite Byrne's warning, the Supreme Court ruled unanimously and emphatically against the universities. Even if it were true that "confidentiality is important to the proper functioning of the peer review process," the Court reasoned, "[t]he costs that ensue from disclosure . . . constitute only one side of the balance." On the other side is the "great, if not compelling, governmental interest" in "ferreting out . . . invidious discrimination."[18] Uncovering illicit motivations requires ready access to any information that might be relevant to the university's decision making: "[I]f there is a 'smoking gun' to be found that demonstrates discrimination in tenure decisions," the Court wrote, "it is likely to be tucked away in peer review files." Indeed, even if there were no smoking gun, " 'confidential material pertaining to other candidates for tenure in a similar time frame may demonstrate that persons with lesser qualifications were granted tenure or that some pattern of discrimination appears.' "[19]

The Court dismissed as "speculative" and "extremely attenuated" the university's argument that the risk of public disclosure would have "a 'chilling effect' on candid evaluations and discussions of candidates."[20] The justices suggested—in what the *New York Times* described as "a forceful tone that bordered on sarcasm"[21]—that they would not "assume the worst about those in the academic community": "Although it is possible that some evaluators may become less candid as the possibility of disclosure increases, others may simply ground their evaluations in specific examples and illustrations in order to deflect potential claims of bias or unfairness," the Court concluded. "Not all academics will hesitate to stand up and be counted when they evaluate their peers."[22]

The decision was perhaps not as disastrous for the universities as possible, though it was close. Justice Blackmun's opinion for the Court reaffirmed that values of academic freedom protected by the First Amendment require judicial "respect for *legitimate* academic decisionmaking." The Court insisted that it need not address "the precise contours of any academic-freedom right" against judicial control of tenure decisions, because it was enough to reject what it termed "an *expanded* right of academic freedom to protect confidential peer review materials from disclosure."[23]

Blackmun's opinion, moreover, left open whether colleges and universities might be allowed to redact the materials they produced in order to shield the identities of peer reviewers. Some courts since the *University of Pennsylvania* decision have allowed redaction, although most seem to agree that "[t]he strong language of [the Court's opinion] . . . indicates that the Supreme Court did not intend to give universities special treatment."[24] An opinion of the Ohio Supreme Court captures the consensus: "It seems the antithesis of academic freedom to maintain secret files upon which promotion and tenure decisions are made," the court wrote, adding that scholars ordinarily are expected to go in for the rough-and-tumble of academic debate.[25]

Academics may or may not appreciate the courts' high confidence in their fortitude. No matter what assurances colleges and universities may offer in their letters requesting tenure reviews, scholars who answer the call must be prepared to have anything they write published in a court opinion or even, as in Hammer's case, posted in PDF form on the Internet. In calculating the risks of that disclosure, moreover, reviewers must consider not only the odds that the candidate about whom they are writing will sue, but also the chance that any other candidate in that person's department or college will end up suing in the years ahead. In Alfred Bennun's race-discrimination lawsuit against Rutgers University, for example, Bennun had introduced the promotion packets of twenty-seven other faculty members who had won promotion over a six-year period to show that he was, in fact, qualified to be a full professor and that the university's reservations were pretextual.[26] In a later discrimination action against Columbia University, another plaintiff asked for—and received—all "personnel files and tenure dossiers of Barnard and Columbia faculty in the departments of biology, mathematics and physics who were considered for tenure from 1985 [to 1996]."[27] Eventually, at least ninety-four separate tenure and personnel files became a part of the evidence in that case.

The information contained in these collateral files, moreover, can then find its way into published court opinions, in sometimes excruciatingly candid detail. In Bennun's case, the court focused on the file of Dr. Ethel Somberg, one of Bennun's coworkers who had been promoted several years before Bennun filed his lawsuit. The court described in detail not only each of the internal and external evaluations in Bennun's promotion dossier but also in those of Somberg and several other colleagues, cataloguing the "deficiencies" in each. The court disparaged by name each of the external reviewers in Somberg's file as cronies who could not be considered "renowned scientists." Turning to another file, the court noted that a departmental colleague had been promoted despite the judgment of an external reviewer from MIT that the candidate "was not a leading light in his field."[28] In Hammer's case, the comments of one reviewer comparing Hammer head-to-head with other up-and-coming scholars in the same field found their way into a court exhibit and from there onto the Internet.

While it is true that most scholars are accustomed to openly debating one another's ideas, it is quite uncommon for them to publicly rank-order colleagues in their field or frankly opine on whether junior scholars at other institutions would be judged tenure-worthy at their own. Indeed, broadcasting such views would likely be viewed as uncollegial, destructive, or even incendiary. Yet these are precisely the sorts of evaluative judgments that are often most valued by promotion and tenure committees struggling to decide whether to make a decades-long investment in an emerging scholar. It is hardly fanciful to imagine that, for many reviewers, the risk of future publication will temper their willingness to provide candid comparative assessments.

The modern trend toward generous access is illustrated by a 2008 decision by distinguished federal trial judge Louis Pollak of Philadelphia. Pollak is himself a former academic, having served as the dean of both Yale Law School and the University of Pennsylvania Law School before his appointment to the bench in 1978. While presiding over a faculty lawsuit against Villanova University, Pollak initially limited discovery to other promotion files in the same academic year in which the plaintiff was denied promotion. His view had been that "the sensitivity of personnel information tipped the balance against producing dossiers and committee reports from years other than the one in which [the plaintiff] was allegedly retaliated against." Yet, a year later, Pollak reconsidered and reversed himself. He had come to see that the limited access to comparative information had hamstrung the plaintiff in resisting the university's motion for summary judgment, and he decided to fall in line with "the accepted approach of limiting the time period to a few years before and a few years after the alleged retaliatory decision."[29]

"Mindful that ours is a liberal discovery regime in which parties are generally entitled to relevant evidence," Pollak concluded, "the court is convinced that its previous ruling was in error, and that there are no compelling reasons for preventing plaintiff from accessing a few years' worth of promotion applications so that she can more fairly assess whether she was treated differently from her colleagues." Accordingly, the court ordered Villanova to turn over "the dossier materials and all materials reflecting the views and decisions the various decision makers for candidates from the college of arts and sciences, for promotion from assistant to associate professor," between the 1998 and 2004 academic years.[30]

At the same time, the dean-turned-judge suggested a possible middle-ground solution for the future: that the parties and the court limit the damage by "scrupulously using acronyms or aliases in their public filings." In a later proceeding, Pollak himself would compare the plaintiff's tenure dossier with dossiers from professors he identified by alphabetical letters only, moving in order from Dr. A through Dr. N.[31]

Pollak's suggestion could certainly mitigate the damage to peer review from court-ordered disclosure. Yet, despite its promise, it appears for the time being that most courts are more inclined to follow the anything-goes approach to disclosure found in the *Hammer* and *Bennun* cases.

The rationale given by the U.S. Supreme Court for ordering disclosure in the *University of Pennsylvania* case was the "great, if not compelling, governmental interest" in ferreting out employment discrimination. Increasingly, however, some litigants are riding its momentum to compel disclosure of confidential research information entirely outside the context of employment and discrimination, opening entirely new legal fronts challenging academic freedom.

Cats, Courts, and Confidentiality in Academic Research

Michael Podell is a veterinarian with a specialty in pet neurology whose office is in Northbrook, Illinois. If you send a question to a syndicated pet column and ask about seizures in a dog, the author might turn to Dr. Podell for the definitive answer.[32] Dr. Podell's Web site suggests that he offers both compassionate care and the most advanced medical treatment available for family pets.[33]

Dr. Podell used to be a tenured professor at Ohio State University. It was there that he received a grant from the National Institutes of Health, and where the trouble that would propel Professor Podell to his new career away from academe in a suburban Chicago veterinary clinic started.

Podell's research, funded by a $1.68 million grant from the National Institutes of Health, focused on a suspected connection between the progression of AIDS and use of the drug methamphetamine. The research involved infecting cats with the feline immunodeficiency virus and then giving the animals methamphetamine to determine how the drug might affect the virus's progression in the brain.[34] In May 2002, Dr. Podell published preliminary results of his research in the *Journal of Neurovirology*, finding that methamphetamine dramatically accelerated the spread of the feline immunodeficiency virus, a result with important implications for AIDS progression in human beings.[35]

By the time Podell announced those initial results, a related lawsuit filed by an animal rights group called the Physicians Committee for Responsible Medicine (PCRM) had been working its way through federal court for six months. As part of the lawsuit, PCRM demanded access to Podell's NIH grant application under the federal Freedom of Information Act. The court action, according to the plaintiffs, was designed to reveal "that [Podell's] experiments should have never been approved" or funded by NIH[36] and "to expose the scientific inadequacies of Dr. Podell's study" in general.[37] Those backing Podell called the lawsuit nothing less than an attack on biomedical research.[38]

While PCRM had already received portions of Dr. Podell's grant application by the time it filed its lawsuit—enough to criticize Podell's spelling and math abilities in strident letters to both the NIH and the president of Ohio State[39]—the group wanted Podell's complete grant application without redaction. A full application would show that Podell had not sufficiently explained why animal use was necessary in his experiments, PCRM suggested, and would reveal the study's "serious scientific shortcomings."[40]

NIH argued in response that parts of the grant application detailing Podell's research design and preliminary data should be exempt from public disclosure under a FOIA exception for trade secrets and private commercial or financial information. According to the NIH, "the development of the feline model of neuroAIDS and drug abuse is proprietary research, because this model system has the potential for pharmaceutical drug development." Podell, NIH contended, would suffer "potential commercial harm or competitive disadvantage if the information [were] released in its entirety, as several laboratories are currently working on similar projects in the area of drug abuse and HIV infection." As a result, Podell's "research design properly can be viewed as a commercially valuable plan used in the processing of a trade commodity," bringing it within FOIA's trade-secrets exemption. In addition, NIH noted, premature disclosure of the research design and preliminary results could affect Podell's "ability to publish his research in journals whose policies dictate that they will not publish research that previously has been disclosed."[41]

Of course, from the point of view of an organization like PCRM, whose goals were to deter the research from ever being undertaken, these consequences of disclosure were all to the good.

In 2004, federal District Judge Reggie Walton in Washington, D.C., reviewed Podell's full sixty-six-page grant application in chambers and concluded there was no reason to keep it under wraps. Notwithstanding the booming modern business in patented university research, Judge Walton apparently thought it far-fetched to think of an academic scientist having a "commercial" interest in research. "The fact that Dr. Podell was engaged in research for the university renders the possibility of a trade interest in his research design remote," Walton wrote. Indeed, relying heavily on a 1974 case to the same effect—a decision that predated by six years the 1980 Bayh-Dole Act which facilitated the patenting of government-funded research and propelled the recent commercialization of academic research—the court suggested that it simply " 'defied common sense to pretend that . . . [an academic] scientist is engaged in trade or commerce.' "[42] The concerns about forced disclosure interfering with later academic publication, moreover, struck Judge Walton as similarly makeweight.

Yet, by the time the court ordered NIH to turn over Podell's full grant application to the animal rights group, his interests in future academic publication were largely moot. An embattled and embittered Podell had left academia two years before, just a few months after the PCRM had filed its lawsuit. When Podell quit, PCRM declared victory in a news release.[43] "We don't have anything personally against Dr. Podell," a spokesperson explained to a local reporter, "[b]ut we don't like the research that he is doing."[44]

The Foundation for Biomedical Research, an organization that supports scientific research using animals, warned that society should be alarmed that "unbearable harassment" had caused an abandonment of valuable peer-reviewed research.[45] Podell's dean called the forty-four-year-old researcher "arguably the finest clinical neurologist in the country, maybe the world"; his departure was a "huge loss for all of veterinary academia."[46] *Time* magazine counted the damage even larger, describing Podell's exit as "an ominous turning point for the research community."[47]

Obviously, it was not the court's decision to open Podell's grant application to the public that caused Podell to leave academia; he had complained about a barrage of phone calls, e-mails, activist confrontations with his children, and even death threats from animal rights activists.[48] Podell was also upset that Ohio State, likely concerned about drawing more heat from animal rights activists nationwide, had done too little to support him publicly.[49] But the prospect of court-ordered disclosure of confidential research data in the midst of a project, with its attendant risks for both future publication and patentability, could only have added to the disincentives to tough it out.

In one sense, Judge Walton's refusal to attribute commercial interests to an academic research scientist might be seen as refreshing. After all, many have decried the "propertization" of science and the infusion of market-based thinking in campus research. As discussed previously, there are significant worries that the incentives for secrecy and controlled access to information created by intellectual property law threaten the defining values of academic research. Yet there is a difference. The conventional critique of the propertization of academic research is that vesting control of knowledge in the hands of an inventor will choke off further research and discovery that might build on the inventor's insights. In Podell's case, in contrast, the point of gaining access was not to advance research but to prevent it. PCRM, the group that sought and won access to Podell's research data, made no bones about the fact that its lawsuit was intended to help put an end to Podell's research activity.

Dr. Podell himself hinted at the link between the law and his leaving in an article in the *Chronicle of Higher Education*. He told a reporter that he hoped that universities would not disclose too much information about their professors' research activities to avoid making them targets. "I'd like," he said, "to see universities provide researchers the security and safety to pursue academic freedom."[50]

With Dr. Podell quietly resettled in suburban veterinary practice, the 17th International AIDS Conference in Mexico City in August 2008 saw the release of two new studies. One, attracting worldwide headlines, concluded that the actual number of Americans infected with HIV is 40 percent higher than previously estimated; the other found an alarming incidence of methamphetamine use (30 percent) among HIV-infected men and urged a new focus in prevention efforts.[51]

Meanwhile, that same summer, the PCRM filed another official complaint against university research. This time, it was with the U.S. Department of Agriculture, targeting what it said was unlawful use of live pigs by the University of Medicine and Dentistry of New Jersey.[52]

Restoring a Sense of Balance to Disclosure Debates

In both the *University of Pennsylvania* and Podell cases, dealing with tenure files and research grant applications, courts sided strongly with disclosure of confidential academic information. In both cases, the courts displayed skepticism, even impatience toward claims that public exposure would threaten basic components of the academic enterprise such as peer review or research. Such losses—particularly the University of Pennsylvania's drubbing in the U.S. Supreme Court—create a danger of legal momentum leading to compelled disclosure in still more realms of academic life. Since the Podell decision, for example, at least two courts have faced private subpoena requests for university institutional review board (IRB) applications, in which professors lay out their research plans for university approval. One court granted the subpoena request after refusing to find a privilege rooted in academic freedom, and the other denied the request without analysis.[53]

Beyond IRB submissions, there are other areas in which courts once firmly rebuffed demands for disclosure, but which might be closer calls today. Consider, for example, the case of K. C. Wu, who sued the National Endowment for the Humanities in an effort to unmask the peer reviewers who had shot down his application for grant funding. In 1972, a federal appeals court turned back his request for disclosure in an opinion that emphasized the danger disclosure would pose to effective peer review.[54]

Similarly, in 1987, a California appellate court refused to order a professor to disclose what he had said at a faculty appointments meeting concerning a candidate's qualifications for an endowed chair. The unsuccessful candidate, an authority on Polish history named Ivor Davies, sued Stanford University history professor Harold Kahn and "thirty Does" for defaming him at the appointments meeting by suggesting "that plaintiff's scholarship was defective." When Kahn refused to testify in a deposition about the appointments discussion, Davies asked the court to compel disclosure. But the California Court of Appeals sided with Kahn, recognizing a qualified privilege rooted in constitutional protection for academic freedom to keep appointments discussions private. "[I]n California," the court wrote, "the fostering of academic excellence finds support in the constitutional right to privacy."[55]

The *Wu* and *Kahn* cases both predate the Supreme Court's decision in *University of Pennsylvania*, and might be considered out of step with the times. Courts considering similar controversies today might well be inclined to take their lead from Justice Blackmun's sturdy skepticism toward claims about the indispensability of confidentiality in peer review. Whereas the California Court of Appeals had readily accepted that "the peer review process is central to the maintenance of academic standards and that confidentiality is indispensable to that process,"[56] Blackmun had considered the claimed "injury to academic freedom [to be] . . . speculative" and pointed out that "confidentiality is not the norm in all peer review systems."[57] In fact, *Kahn* had relied in part on federal appellate precedent finding a qualified academic privilege—cases that the Supreme Court later rejected in *University of Pennsylvania*. The California court's solicitousness for a professor asked to describe his comments at an appointments meeting seems hard to square with more recent cases like that of Peter Hammer, who successfully deposed twenty-one colleagues.

Yet, it would be a mistake to regard the reasoning or outcomes in *Wu* and *Kahn* to be obsolete. To the contrary, they rightly emphasize that questions of disclosure require a sensitive balancing of conflicting public values—pitting a plaintiff's and the public's need for effective scrutiny against societal interests in academic freedom—and that this balance may well be struck differently in different contexts. The Supreme Court itself in *University of Pennsylvania* had framed its analysis as a "balance" in which the interests of effective peer review were outweighed by the "great, if not compelling, governmental interest" in eradicating "invidious discrimination."[58] In *Kahn*, the California appellate court noted that the propriety of disclosure may depend on the nature of the plaintiff's claim. *Kahn* acknowledged that arguments for an academic privilege had sometimes failed in discrimination cases where the privilege was "pitted against legislation of the 'highest priority,'" but concluded that the balance tipped differently where the claimant's interest was only in obtaining money damages for allegedly "false and derogatory statements" concerning the quality of his scholarship.[59]

Close attention to the balance of competing interests would limit disclosure of academic information to contexts where it is truly justified and under conditions, such as redaction or the use of nonidentifying initials or pseudonyms in public court filings, that avoid unnecessary damage to legitimate interests in peer review.

Such balancing could also help courts see their way through yet another related area in which they have struggled: cases in which private parties seek to compel disclosure of professors' working research notes. As in peer-review contexts, professors have argued that an academic privilege similar to a reporter's privilege shields them from divulging their background research data. Historically, claims for a scholar's privilege have often met with a chilly reception in the courts. Yet, as the following conflict between Microsoft and two business professors shows, more substantial attention to the academic interests at stake can lead courts to draw the line against the trend toward disclosure.

David and Goliath: The Scholar's Privilege Fights Back

David B. Yoffie is the Max and Doris Starr Professor of International Business Administration at Harvard Business School. Michael A. Cusumano is the Sloan Management Review Distinguished Professor of Management at MIT's Sloan School of Management, and Yoffie's coauthor. In Web biographies, both men similarly describe the close attention given their book in the landmark antitrust case brought by the U.S. Department of Justice against the software giant Microsoft. *Competing on Internet Time: Lessons from Netscape and Its Battle with Microsoft* . . . played a central role in the Microsoft anti-trust trial," Cusumano's Web site asserts.[60] Yoffie's Web site adds that the book "became a highly publicized part of the Microsoft-Department of Justice anti-trust trial."[61]

But it was not just what was written in the book that deeply intrigued Microsoft Corporation and other players in the antitrust action: it was also material left out of the book. Cusumano and Yoffie's *Competing on Internet Time* used interviews with Netscape officials to chronicle the company's losing battle with Microsoft for Web browser domination. *Business Week* called the Netscape executives whom the authors interviewed "the lab mice of Silicon Valley" because they were so very willing to explain what went wrong with company strategy and why they believed the company's market share plummeted in a very short amount of time.[62] It was key information about a failed business plan.

It was also why Microsoft wanted the professors' notes from the book project. Those notes and other unpublished material, Microsoft attorneys believed, could help prove that it was Netscape's own inept business strategy that had killed its market share, not any illegal squeeze by Microsoft.

But the professor-authors had promised their Netscape contacts confidentiality and did not wish to turn over 200 hours of tape-recorded interviews, 2,000 pages of interview transcripts, or their working notes to Microsoft. Professor Cusumano's dean, himself an expert witness for Microsoft during the trial, maintained that the two authors should "fiercely resist the Microsoft subpoena" on grounds of academic freedom.[63] So Cusumano and Yoffie asked the court to quash Microsoft's request, arguing that "few prominent business executives would give interviews to scholars if they feared that the unedited interview notes could end up in court someday."[64]

A scholar's research privilege had been tried before under similar circumstances, but without much success. The deck plainly seemed to be stacked against it: in 1972, in Branzburg v. Hayes, the Supreme Court had rejected a similar privilege claim on behalf of reporters to withhold disclosure of their sources.[65] Then, in 1990, in the *University of Pennsylvania* case the Supreme Court had relied on *Branzburg* to reject what it considered an analogous privilege claim by universities to withhold confidential peer-review materials.[66] The claim of a so-called scholar's privilege to shield preliminary research data and working notes would not be an easy sell.

And yet both the federal trial and appellate courts upheld Cusumano and Yoffie's right to keep their tapes, interviews, and notes confidential. The U.S. Court of Appeals for the First Circuit in Boston reasoned that a scholar is an information gatherer and disseminator, not unlike a journalist, and that "an academician, stripped of sources, would be able to provide fewer, less cogent analyses." The court used a balancing test, one that recognized little heft in Microsoft's need for the information versus "brim-full" concern about effects on academic investigation should it grant the subpoena. If business people saw that their background comments to an academic researcher could be disgorged for the benefit of competitors at the drop of a legal complaint, their willingness to be take part would likely evaporate, endangering qualitative research. "First Amendment values are at stake," the court decided.[67]

A lawyer for MIT lauded the decision as "a signal step in recognizing the validity of confidentiality in this kind of academic research." A delighted Cusumano told the *New York Times* that "the work of scholars at business schools across the country" had been at stake.[68]

Yet, despite the outcome in *Cusumano* more than a decade ago, legal recognition of the scholar's privilege remains tenuous. The First Circuit continues to recognize a scholar's research privilege, only recently upholding the right of a professor not to testify about his work in a textbook dispute,[69] but most other courts have forced scholars to turn over all or portions of their research-related materials, including unfunded grant proposals, in circumstances essentially similar to *Cusumano*.[70] Courts have held over the years that scholars must testify about their research regarding rollover accidents,[71] must release certain raw field notes on the sociological trends in restaurants,[72] and must turn over raw data from research on smoking.[73] In 1996, the federal appeals court in Washington, D.C., forced scholars to release working data, writing that it could not find "an established or well-settled practice of protecting research data in the realm of civil discovery on the grounds that disclosure would harm a researcher's publication prospects."[74] In most cases, the researchers in these cases were not parties to the underlying action; they just happened to have information of value in resolving an issue presented in the case.

Some would say it is beyond time for courts to take more seriously the potentially disruptive impact of public disclosure on academic research and to balance that cost sensitively against the benefits that would flow from exposure. Dr. Paul Fischer, one proponent, titled his chapter in the book *Rescuing Science from Politics* in the form of a question: "Science and Subpoenas: When Do the Courts Become Instruments of Manipulation?" The chapter focuses on his experience as the lead scientist in the well-known "Joe Camel" study documenting children's ready recognition of the iconic tobacco logo. R. J. Reynolds Tobacco Company subpoenaed from Fischer an overwhelming amount of research data:

> the names and telephone numbers of all the children who participated in the study; all drafts of the study design; all notes, memos, and videotapes pertaining to the study: the names, addresses, telephone numbers, background information, and occupations of all interviewers; hard copy tabulations and data tapes; originals of all test materials; all correspondence

related to the research; the names, addresses, and background information of all consultants; the names and addresses of all funding sources;
and the names and telephone numbers of all respondents who were excluded from the study.

Eventually, because of what Fischer describes as a series of frustrating decisions made by others, those records were all turned over to R. J.
Reynolds.

Dr. Fischer closed his essay by predicting that "the uneasy relationship
between law and science" will continue, especially in the subpoena area,
mostly because law and science are "worlds apart" in the values they uphold and the rules they follow. Judges, he urged, must have "a better understanding of the impact of their decisions on the progress of science."[75]

There are some very tentative signs that this might be happening. In
March 2008, a federal court in Illinois rejected a subpoena request by the
pharmaceutical company Pfizer directed at the *Journal of the American Medical Association* (JAMA) for all information, analyses, evaluations, and peer
reviews of articles, whether accepted or rejected, concerning Pfizer's drugs
Bextra and Celebrex. The peer-review process and its promise of confidentiality would be harmed, the court explained, if it forced JAMA to release
all that information.[76] A federal trial court in Boston reached the same
conclusion two weeks later in turning back a similar Pfizer request directed
to the *New England Journal of Medicine.* Following *Cusumano,* the court balanced Pfizer's "limited" need for the data against what it found to be the
Journal's "persuasive" concerns for the integrity of the peer-review process
in article selection:

> [The *Journal*] maintains that the confidentiality of the peer reviewers
> permits the reviewers to "be as frank as possible in their assessments of
> submitted science" and that if reviewers thought their names or reviews
> would be subject to disclosure in unrelated litigation, there would be
> "chilling effect" on the peer review process and as a result, upon the
> medical community. It believes that its ability to attract peer reviewers
> would be impaired by disclosure of their identities or comments. It fur-
> ther states that disclosure of the comments themselves, even without
> identifying the peer reviewer by name, may well disclose the reviewer's
> identity because in the small scientific community, an opinion may con-
> stitute a recognizable "intellectual signature." Finally, it suggests that re-

viewers lacking confidentiality might face retaliation from those authors whom they have criticized.[77]

These courts' willingness to credit the subtle ways in which disclosure might endanger effective peer review, and to support confidentiality in contexts not involving discrimination, could point the way toward a more balanced judgment in academic disclosure disputes.

Nonetheless, law professor William G. Childs told the *Chronicle of Higher Education* that journal editors and peer reviewers should draw only limited comfort from these rulings. Based on a wealth of legal precedents, the balance could well tip toward disclosure in a future case in which a journal submission was itself the subject of litigation. Indeed, in the same article, former Stanford University president and *Science* editor Donald Kennedy suggested that it might well be time to update the journal's solicitations to peer reviewers. In the new legal environment, reviewers should probably be forewarned that the journal "might not be able to protect them against a subpoena."[78]

Kennedy's uncertainty underscores just how much law is unsettling traditional expectations and interactions in academic criticism and exchange. At the very time that the law respecting intellectual property is eroding traditional academic norms of openness and information sharing in deference to legal notions of ownership, courts are simultaneously challenging traditional academic norms of secrecy in peer review spanning from research funding to tenure to publishing. As with the legal inroads relating to intellectual property, discrimination, and free expression, the law's incursion on privacy interests in academia is certainly not all bad. Impenetrable confidentiality in academia, as elsewhere, has sometimes cloaked discrimination, incompetence, and other misfeasance. The challenge here, as when importing legal norms concerning intellectual property, discrimination, and free expression, is to avoid inflicting undue damage to academic norms that have served colleges and universities—and the broader society—very well. Just as courts must be alert not to superimpose their own judgments of academic merit in scrutinizing tenure decisions, and to avoid woodenly privileging student or faculty speech to the detriment of the broader academic enterprise, courts must also be careful in demanding openness in peer review not to needlessly cripple a mechanism that for generations has been central to the success of American higher education.

Some judges and scholars have suggested ways to limit the potential damage from disclosure with only modest sacrifices to legitimate legal interests; what remains to be seen is whether courts increasingly inclined to view academic actors as no different from commercial ones will be willing to take heed.

CHAPTER **7**

War of the Words:
The Rise of Academic Defamation

Frank Sulloway is a scholar's scholar. He has written scores of journal articles and two celebrated books on evolutionary theory and the history of science. He has taught at MIT, Harvard, Dartmouth, University College London, and, most recently, at the University of California at Berkeley. He has garnered a raft of prestigious fellowships and awards, including a MacArthur Foundation "genius grant."[1]

And he does not take criticism lying down. When Sulloway learned that a man with a less heady curriculum vitae was preparing to criticize his work in print in a small interdisciplinary journal, he lashed back. In a letter to the journal's editor, Sulloway charged that the article's abstract contained statements that were "factually incorrect," "preposterous," and "tendentious," and that "[t]he text itself [was] littered with malicious and untenable claims."[2] In a later writing, Sulloway contended that his critic had departed from the conventions of scientific argument and language and demonstrated "obvious discomfort with probabilistic and statistical relationships."[3]

Yet, Sulloway's response itself strayed from the conventions of scientific argument, lobbing decidedly nonscientific terms including attorney, defamation, and libel. The intended criticism of Sulloway's work, he warned the journal's editor, was so deeply flawed that it was, in effect, illegal. "Science," he would explain, "is not above the law."[4]

Sulloway, Frederic Townsend, and Gary Johnson are the leading protagonists in a drama that one Berkeley newspaper rightly styled "one of the nastier academic debates in recent memory."[5] Sulloway, high-flying scholar, is perhaps best known for *Born to Rebel,* his work on birth order and political drive. The book created something of a sensation when it hit

157

bookstores in 1996, attracting "lavish praise from distinguished scholars and scientists."[6] Sulloway's curriculum vitae, published on his personal Web site, boasts of the book's many excellent reviews and of his national media appearances discussing it. Ten years after publication, the book was still mentioned in the popular press as having reshaped common understanding of family influences on political and social personality.[7]

Frederic Townsend is, in some ways, Sulloway's antithesis. Townsend has toiled far from the leafy preserves of Berkeley and Cambridge, as a lawyer in Washington, D.C., and as a trader on the Chicago Board of Trade.[8] Townsend's publication credits include a review of *When Genius Failed*, a book about a bond-trading firm's rise and fall,[9] and a letter to Roger Ebert's "Movie Answer Man" column musing about certain dialogue in *Casablanca*.[10] His 1996 opinion piece about Orange County, California's financial woes earned *Financial World* magazine a dart in *Columbia Journalism Review's* (*CJR*) "Darts and Laurels" section when *Financial World*, *CJR* wrote, took Townsend's piece and made it its own lead editorial.[11]

Gary Johnson, the third main player, is the former editor of *Politics and the Life Sciences*, the semiannual journal of the Association for Politics and the Life Sciences. Johnson is a political science professor at Lake Superior State University in Sault Ste. Marie, Michigan. Lake State, as it is known locally, touts itself as the smallest public university in Michigan, in the state's oldest city, a former fur trading post, and able to offer personalized attention to its 3,000 students. The university is perhaps best known outside the iron-ore country of northern Michigan for its "Banished Words List," a tongue-in-cheek check on overused, faddish language.[12]

What caused an internationally known scholar to enter with such vengeance the world of an armchair scholar and a professor from a small school in Michigan's Upper Peninsula is not entirely clear. As Sulloway himself has noted, he probably should have bowed out in the beginning.[13]

Johnson's account of the episode, "Science, Sulloway, and Birth Order: An Ordeal and an Assessment," serves as the closing article in the September 2000 roundtable edition of *Politics and the Life Sciences*, published in early 2004, after years of wrangling. Johnson writes that he had accepted Frederic Townsend's paper criticizing Sulloway's *Born to Rebel* and suggested a roundtable that would give Sulloway and other scholars a chance to respond in print.[14]

At first, Sulloway agreed but then changed his mind, according to Johnson's account.[15] And it is the way in which he relayed his change of heart that likely took Johnson's breath away. Sulloway's letter, excerpted years later in Johnson's article, contained at least nine separate mentions of the potential for legal action. "I am . . . writing to inform you that I consider [the Townsend] manuscript to be defamatory in its current form," Johnson quotes Sulloway as writing. Sulloway explained that he was "an independent scholar" who depended on his reputation for his livelihood and was therefore "prepared to take any legal steps that are necessary to protect this reputation from potential libel."[16] Sulloway asked if Johnson was "prepared to defend the truth of [a statement in Townsend's abstract] in a court of law."[17] Toward the end of the missive, Sulloway promised to turn the matter over to his New York attorney if there was no satisfactory resolution by a certain date.[18]

Later letters from Sulloway, Johnson wrote, confirmed that Sulloway's attorney had indeed found Townsend's work to be defamatory,[19] and included a new warning that any suggestion that Sulloway was " 'attempting to avoid scholarly criticism' may be a defamation in its own right."[20] Sulloway, according to Johnson, also wrote both to the president of Lake Superior State University and to the university's legal counsel to complain about Johnson's editorial actions and to accuse him of professional misconduct.[21]

Sulloway, in his own account of the saga posted on his Web site, disclaimed any desire to suppress scholarly criticism, but insisted that scholars do not forfeit their rights as ordinary citizens simply by entering the academy.[22] "Academic or scientific criticism is one thing," he wrote. "Outright lies and personal attacks are another."[23] Legal duties extended not only to potential critics but to scholarly publishers as well. "As every journal editor knows," Sulloway wrote, "freedom of expression does have certain legal limits, and it is the job of the editor to enforce those limits."[24] Editors, he continued, "have a professional responsibility not to recklessly publish unsubstantiated accusations, especially those that are being made by individuals who lack the training and expertise to judge the underlying work."[25]

Sulloway suggested that, far from impinging on academic freedom, resort to the courts could constructively aid in the scholarly quest for knowledge. After all, "the mere publication of . . . defamatory accusations can damage an innocent person's reputation," he wrote.[26] "Scientists are particularly vulnerable to such smear tactics, as their profession is that of 'searching for the truth.' "[27] Shielding scientists from undue attack could, therefore, ensure the continuation of fruitful debate.

It did not take long for this academic squabble to spill into the pages of the popular press. A *Chicago Sun-Times* article, appearing just after the roundtable issue of *Politics and the Life Sciences* reached subscribers, reported that Sulloway had rebuffed Townsend's initial request for information supporting claims made in *Born to Rebel*. Sulloway responded dismissively, according to the *Sun-Times*, that he would never share his raw data with "unqualified individuals including people lacking graduate degrees in the behavioral sciences and a serious record of scholarly publications"[28]—and certainly not with Townsend, whom he considered a "small-minded and ill-informed crank."[29]

All of this left Gary Johnson, the editor from usually placid Lake State, in the middle of a tempest. Besides the unpleasantness of suffering through "a brand of contentiousness seldom seen in science and scholarship,"[30] Johnson saw in the ruckus something more portentous. "Sulloway's legal threats," he wrote, had created a "virtual terror."[31] He warned that "contemporary science must adapt to a changed socio-legal environment" and that there was real danger that journals could be cowed by "the threat of catastrophic legal costs."[32] Indeed, Johnson himself had seriously considered dropping the Townsend roundtable because of the prospect of staggering legal bills.[33]

Even though Johnson ultimately decided to proceed, and Sulloway never actually filed suit, the years of defensive maneuvering occasioned by his threats had, Johnson warned, inflicted its own damage. "Prior to the commencement of this ordeal," Johnson wrote to fellow members of the Association for Politics and the Life Sciences, "both the journal and the association had been growing at an impressive pace, and the establishment of our own independent annual meeting promised a bright future for both the organization and the field of study. With the publication delays [occasioned by the threats of litigation], however, the health of the journal and the association are threatened."[34]

Johnson implored his fellow scholars to bolster the flagging organization through journal subscriptions, membership dues, and voluntary contributions "to help offset the many costs associated with this long sequence of events."[35] He then closed the disputed issue of *Politics and the Life Sciences* with an editorial call for the creation of a "multidisciplinary legal defense fund" to help embattled scholars defend the "open dialogue and critical exchange that is the lifeblood of science and scholarship."[36] A standing fund is needed, he argued, to "reduce the likelihood that legal threats can succeed in stifling research and publication in the natural and social sciences."[37]

If Johnson's call seems a bit dramatic, the fact is that such a fund would not go untapped. Johnson's ordeal was not the first instance where academics and publishers were forced to circle the wagons against defamation claims brought by objects of scholarly criticism, and it would not be the last.

From Newton to *Neary*

Stinging rebukes among scholars over research findings or methodologies are, of course, nothing new. Acrid debate has been a part of academic life at least since Isaac Newton clashed with Robert Hooke in the Royal Society over theories of optics and the inverse square law of gravitation.[38] Indeed, Newton was so wounded by Hooke's repeated barbs and challenges that he periodically withdrew from the rough-and-tumble of scholarly presentation. "Philosophy is such an impertinently litigious Lady," he complained to Edmond Halley in 1686, "that a man has as good be engaged in lawsuits, as have to do with her."[39] Newton intended his remark to be ironic. Today, the observation seems more prosaic. As indignant as Newton was over charges that he borrowed Hooke's ideas without proper credit, he never hired a barrister. Today, defamation claims represent a significant new inroad in the ongoing encroachment of law on academic life.

The point of a defamation action is straightforward: it provides a legal remedy for a person whose reputation has been sullied by false statements of fact. In order to recover, plaintiffs ordinarily must prove that (1) the defendant communicated (or "published") to another, (2) false statements of fact, and (3) those falsehoods were "defamatory"—that is, they harmed the plaintiff's reputation so "as to lower him in the estimation of the community or to deter third persons from associating or dealing with him."[40]

The defamation action itself is relatively old, but claims arising from scholarship and academic debate are a relatively recent phenomenon. In the century or so following the first reported U.S. case alleging defamation by a professor, only about a dozen reported cases involved an academic suing for defamation and not a single one was directed against a fellow academic or an academic journal.[41] So, when a California jury in 1988 socked the University of California with a $7 million verdict for libeling a rancher in a scientific study, the judgment understandably "jolted research universities."[42] A state lawmaker had asked veterinarians from the veterinary school at Davis to investigate the rancher's suspicions that pesticides had killed his cattle herd; the resulting university report blamed conditions at the ranch instead, and the rancher sued the university and the three veterinarians who conducted the study for defamation.[43] The decision in Neary v. Regents of the University of California, noted an eminent California litigator, sent a "chill wind" over "researchers accustomed to freely searching out the most promising avenues to new knowledge."[44] The litigator, who would go on to become president of the American Law Institute, cautioned that "researchers, editors and university officials should become conversant with the essentials of defamation law."[45]

Within two years, the National Association of College and University Attorneys (NACUA) published a guidebook to "Defamation Issues in Higher Education," warning that "[c]ollege and university campuses provide fertile ground for defamation claims."[46] The biggest potential for claims, the NACUA guidebook suggested, arose from the evaluation of faculty, staff, or students and from university-sponsored publications. The booklet offered practical "guidelines for minimizing and avoiding the risk of defamation liability," but concluded that "[t]he simplest advice—to 'speak no evil'— cannot be heeded in an educational community which aspires to rigorous professional and academic standards, and which recognizes free expression as the currency of the marketplace."[47]

Academics would simply have to find some way to carry on, balancing their scholarly pursuits against the emerging new risks from defamation law. Although the NACUA guidebook was generally reassuring in describing the dangers, there was little doubt that the newfound readiness of some scholars to resort to litigation to defend their reputations, when Newton himself would not think of it, portended changes in the tenor and habits of academic debate, even for those who never receive a demand letter or a summons from the sheriff.

Of Cranks, Incompetents, and Low-Down Souls:
The Boundaries of Defamatory Meaning

One day, around 1900, Alfred Nolan Martin, a former Oxford University professor, opened a newspaper in New York to find this account of his troubles:

SAVANT CANNOT MAKE A LIVING.

OLD OXFORD PROFESSOR AND FAMILY IN SAD STRAITS.

That the battle for existence is not won by brains alone is illustrated in the sad plight of Prof. Alfred Nolan Martin, at Richmond Park, Staten Island. A man of extraordinary attainments in classical learning and once a professor in Oxford University, he is now in sad straits because his education hampers him in earning a living. He is living with his young wife and two small children in a house which has not a single door or window inclosed. He is too poor to ask aid. His neighbors say he is starving.

Martin, outraged at the suggestion that his "overeducation" had led him to destitution, sued and persuaded a New York court that the newspaper's ridicule was libelous per se.[48] And thus arguably began academia's sideways entry into the law of defamation, establishing court recognition of an academic's legitimate prickliness about his smarts and his scholarly reputation. Today, in company with *Martin*, courts routinely recognize that "a scholar's reputation among his peers is crucial to his or her career."[49]

Martin's acknowledgment of the scholar's professional stake in his reputation laid an essential foundation for modern defamation law's "ride into the groves of academe."[50] The heart of a defamation claim is that a false utterance has inflicted real injury to the plaintiff. Given the important value assigned to intellectual reputation, then, and the ease with which it can be bruised by the daily barbs and knocks of academic criticism, it might be anticipated that a defamation claim lurks around every campus corner. Fortunately, the courts have not been so expansive in their understanding of defamation. Instead, courts have sought to limit liability to speech with true "defamatory meaning"—that is, content that inflicts true reputational harm.

Consider, for example, the case of William Dilworth, "an obscure engineer" and occasional author of articles in mathematics journals, who

regrettably caught the eye of Underwood Dudley, a mathematics professor writing a book entitled *Mathematical Cranks.*[51] To Dilworth's understandable consternation, Dudley chose to feature Dilworth as a "crank"
based on an article Dilworth had published challenging something described as "Cantor's diagonal process" in set theory. Dudley's book went
on to mock Dilworth as a closed-minded amateur who had overlooked a
basic refutation of his thesis—a point which even "bright undergraduates" could pick up with "a few seconds' thought."[52] The account was,
fair to say, savaging.

But the unfortunate Dilworth found no relief in the federal courts. The
trial court dismissed his complaint out of hand and the court of appeals affirmed, in an opinion written by Judge Richard Posner. Posner, a longtime
professor at the University of Chicago Law School before his appointment
to the bench, who continues to author academic books at a dizzying pace,
displayed little sympathy for Dilworth. The black eye from Dudley, Posner
explained, goes with the territory of being a scholar: "By publishing your
views you invite public criticism and rebuttal; you enter voluntarily into
one of the submarkets of ideas and opinions and consent to the rough
competition of the marketplace. If Dilworth publishes an article saying that
Cantor was wrong, he invites Dudley to publish a book in which he says
that Dilworth was wrong for saying that Cantor was wrong."[53] Under almost any circumstances, Posner wrote, calling someone a "crank" cannot
amount to defamation; the word falls, instead, into a doctrinal category of
"rhetorical hyperbole" for which the law provides no recovery.

Posner added that the case for nonliability "is especially clear where, as
in this case, the word is used in a piece of scholarship."[54] "[J]udges," Posner emphasized, "are not well equipped to resolve academic controversies, of which a controversy over Cantor's diagonal process is a daunting
illustration, and scholars have their own remedies for unfair criticisms of
their work—the publication of a rebuttal."[55] But he was also careful "not
[to] suggest that scholars can never maintain a suit for defamation." To
the contrary, "If a professor is falsely accused of plagiarism or sexual harassment or selling high grades or other serious misconduct, rather than
of having unsound ideas, he has the same right to damages as any other
victim of defamation."[56]

Other courts have similarly attempted to draw the line between actionable defamation and nonactionable insult. In Katz v. Goldstone, an
author of a historical reference on General George Armstrong Custer

claimed that he had been defamed in an unfavorable book review which, he thought, implied that he "was not qualified as a historian of the works of General Custer."[57] The case came before District Judge José Cabranes, who rose to the federal bench after service as a law professor and general counsel of Yale University. Judge Cabranes granted summary judgment in favor of the book reviewer, "find[ing] nothing in the review that is capable of defamatory meaning."[58]

In *Katz*, Cabranes distinguished previous cases in which commentaries on published works had been found to be potentially "defamatory," and suggested that those criticisms had crossed the line because they had attacked the character of the plaintiff-author personally, rather than the quality of the plaintiff's work. For example, where a reviewer "referred to the author as a 'low-down soul,' as well as to the book as 'teeming with ugly words, of which even a mule driver would be ashamed,'" a defamation claim was valid.[59] In contrast, reviews that are "critical but impersonal; addressed to the character of the work rather than the character of the author—are not defamatory as a matter of law."[60]

Cabranes's distinction between personal attack and scholarly criticism—closely paralleling Judge Posner's suggested distinction between being accused of "serious misconduct" versus having "unsound ideas"—appeared calculated to cordon off legitimate academic criticism from scrutiny under the defamation laws. But, elsewhere in his *Katz* opinion, Judge Cabranes seemed to leave the academy open to future claims. In response to the plaintiff's claim that the review had implied his lack of qualification as an "historian of the life of General Custer," Cabranes did not say that such statements would be immune from tort liability. Instead, he held only that the book review in question did not actually convey that message: "Assuming, *arguendo*, that a direct statement of this sort would be defamatory, as injurious to plaintiff's professional reputation and as tending to discourage people from dealing with him in that capacity, we must determine whether the words defendant actually wrote are susceptible of interpretation to mean that plaintiff 'is not a qualified historian of the life of General Custer.'"[61] The judge then concluded that the review had suggested only that the plaintiff had failed to write a quality book, not that he was incapable of doing so.

Cabranes's distinction between capability and performance was sufficient to dispose of the claim in *Katz*, but provides precarious immunity to more far-reaching scholarly criticism that suggests another's inability to measure up to academic standards. The recent imbroglio between John Lott and Steven Levitt illustrates the danger.

More Lawsuits, Less Guff?

John R. Lott does not mind stirring the pot. Like Frank Sulloway, Lott has spent most of his career transiting through elite institutions as a visiting professor, fellow, or research scholar.[62] On his Web sites, in academic papers, and op-ed articles, the economist has taken swipes at affirmative action in police hiring, liberal bias in the media, and the sentencing of Martha Stewart.[63] He has injected himself into political firestorms over the 2000 presidential election in Florida and the Iraq insurgency—offering empirical support to bolster Republican victory claims and, in 2003, backing then–Defense Secretary Donald Rumsfeld's suggestion that Baghdad had a lower murder rate than Washington, D.C.[64]

But Lott is best known for his thesis, spelled out in his 1998 book, *More Guns, Less Crime,* that increasing the supply of legal handguns drives down crime.[65] Lott claims to prove, through complex data analysis spanning eighteen years and covering more than 3,000 U.S. counties, that laws allowing citizens to carry concealed weapons level the playing field with armed criminals and effectively deter crime. A follow-on book five years later argued that the media systematically underreport the crime-deterrent benefits of guns.[66] Lott's Web site lists a host of admiring comments about his books from satisfied readers including Fox Television's Sean Hannity and Ted Nugent, the self-described "gun-toting rock n' roll star" and author of *Kill It & Grill It,* who hails Lott as his "academic hero."[67]

Lott's empirical claims have won him acclaim from gun-rights advocates, but also many detractors. For years, Lott has been dogged by critics who claim that he plays fast and loose with his data and that his conclusions have been driven by ideological objectives.[68] Frustrated, Lott complained in a 2000 interview that many of the criticisms were simply cheap shots, baseless smears made with knowledge that few listeners would ever study Lott's work to decide for themselves.[69] "I've never been involved in a debate like this," he lamented, "because in your normal academic debate, where there are 10 people involved and they've all read the paper, if somebody says 'Professor X didn't account for other gun laws,' everybody else in the room would laugh, because they would know it was an absurd claim."[70] Indeed, Lott's frustration was so palpable that he resorted to engaging his critics in Internet debates under a female pseudonym, Mary Rosh.[71] When skeptics attacked Lott's motives or methodologies, they would sometimes get a rebuke from Mary Rosh, who described herself as an admiring former student of Lott's.[72]

Lott's gun thesis ultimately set him on a collision course with Steven Levitt, a University of Chicago economist with an equally provocative theory about the drop in crime rates in the 1990s. Levitt, the Alvin H. Baum Professor in Economics at Chicago, had won the John Bates Clark Medal in 2003, awarded to the American economist under age forty who has made the biggest mark in the field, and in 2006 was named one of *Time* magazine's "100 People Who Shape Our World."[73] His book, *Freakonomics: A Rogue Economist Explores the Hidden Side of Everything,* coauthored with Stephen Dubner, was a publishing sensation and remained atop the best-seller list for well more than a year after its 2005 publication.[74]

In *Freakonomics,* Levitt advanced the startling idea that much of the crime drop in the 1990s was traceable to the legalization of abortion in the early 1970s. The widespread availability of legal abortion, he suggested, had resulted in fewer unwanted children, especially those who otherwise would have been raised with disadvantages correlated with later criminality. The drop in crime rates in the 1990s came just as these never-born children would have been reaching their mischief-making teenaged years.

As one reviewer observed, "this conclusion managed to offend nearly everyone. Conservatives were outraged that abortion was seemingly being promoted as a solution to crime. Liberals detected a whiff of racist eugenics."[75] But surely none was offended more than John Lott. In advancing his thesis, Levitt had paused briefly to knock down Lott's alternative explanation for the spike in lawfulness. Lott's eventual defamation complaint, filed in federal court in Chicago in 2006, quoted the four sentences from *Freakonomics* that became the basis for Count I in Lott v. Levitt: "Then there was the troubling allegation that Lott actually invented some of the survey data that supports his more-guns/less-crime theory. Regardless of whether the data were faked, Lott's admittedly intriguing hypothesis doesn't seem to be true. When other scholars have tried to replicate his results, they found that right-to-carry laws simply don't bring down crime."[76]

Count II alleged that Levitt had defamed Lott again in a subsequent e-mail message. After *Freakonomics* was released, John McCall, a one-time mentor of Lott's at UCLA, e-mailed Levitt to challenge his dismissal of Lott's research. Had not the *Journal of Law and Economics* published papers replicating Lott's work, McCall asked. Levitt replied: "It was not a peer refereed edition of the Journal. For $15,000 he was able to buy an issue and put in only work that supported him. My best friend was the editor and was outraged the press let Lott do this." In his lawsuit, Lott contended that "the statements about him in *Freakonomics* and the email . . . qualif[y] as defamation *per se* because they imply that his results were falsified or that his theories lack merit, and thus impute a lack of ability and integrity in his profession as an economist, academic, and researcher."[77]

In 2007, the federal district court gave Lott a partial victory. It ruled against Lott on the claim based on *Freakonomics*, but allowed the claim based on the e-mail to proceed to trial.[78] It was, the *Chronicle of Higher Education* observed, "a ruling that might make scholars a bit more wary of pressing the 'send' button" after jotting an e-mail.[79] But the decision illustrated more than simply the peculiar perils of instant communication; it demonstrated just how indefinite the line is that separates permissible criticism from sanctionable slander.

The court agreed with Lott that false statements implying that a person is "unable to perform" or "lacks ability" in his profession are defamatory *per se* under Illinois law (the law it found governed Lott's lawsuit). But it ruled for Levitt on the ground that the passage in *Freakonomics* is "reasonably capable of an innocent construction."[80] Lott had argued that "the only reasonable meaning of the last sentence [in the disputed passage of *Freakonomics*] is that he falsified his results because 'the term "replicate" has an objective and factual meaning in the world of academic research and scholarship.' "[81] The court answered, however, that the meaning of the challenged phrase was to be determined by the lights of the "reasonable reader in . . . the general population," not the specialized " 'world of academic research and scholarship.' "[82] And "[i]n everyday language, replicating 'results' does not necessarily mean analyzing identical data in identical ways"; instead, it could be understood to mean only that other scholars, using their own data or methodologies, disagreed with Lott's conclusions.[83]

Merely expressing disagreement with a scholar's research findings, as contrasted with impugning his integrity or competence, is not defamatory, the court explained. It supported its conclusion by pointing to an

Illinois decision that had exempted from liability statements that appeared to toe the line even more aggressively. In Haberstroh v. Crain Publications, Inc., an associate professor of advertising at Virginia Commonwealth University sued after Chicago-based *Advertising Age* published letters from readers objecting to an essay the professor had penned blasting the advertising industry.[84] One reader accused the professor of not "traveling with a full set of luggage"; another asked, "Why would anyone study a subject from a guy who obviously doesn't understand it?"[85] The professor contended that the statements were libelous because they "question his capability as a teacher, and tend to prejudice plaintiff in his profession."[86] But the Illinois court turned aside the professor's claim on the ground that reasonable readers would recognize the letter writer's language as using "rhetorical hyperbole" or "mere name-calling" in expressing "an assessment of the merits of plaintiff's views," not a literal assertion of his professional incompetence.[87]

Turning to Lott's second defamation claim, however, the federal district court applied the same principles and sustained Lott's claim. Levitt defended his e-mail by pointing to Lott's acknowledgment that he had "raised the funds to pay the . . . printing and mailing costs" for a special issue of the *Journal of Law and Economics* devoted to papers from a conference on Lott's gun thesis.[88] But the court held that "the email statements qualify as defamatory *per se* because they impute a lack of ability in Lott's profession"[89]: "[T]he accusation that Lott 'bought' the Journal and put in only work that supported him is not reasonably capable of a construction other than one attacking Lott's skill and integrity in the profession, especially in light of Levitt's suggestion that the Journal's editor was 'outraged' by this practice."[90]

The *Lott* court's distinction between the statements in *Freakonomics* and the e-mail in defining "defamatory" meaning offers only fragile protection for scholarly criticism. For one thing, in tying liability to the common understandings of a nonacademic audience, the court's approach suggests that scholars must anticipate possible meanings of their speech that scholars themselves would not attach to the words. More fundamentally, the boundary line suggested in each of these cases, from *Dilworth* to *Katz* to *Lott*—separating disparagement of a scholar's research (permissible) from comments implying "a lack of ability" (defamatory), or the imputation of having "unsound ideas" (permissible) from being engaged in "serious misconduct" (defamatory)—will not always be clear. Nor will it provide any sanctuary at all to criticism that unavoidably suggests scholarly incompetence or misconduct.

In August 2007, Lott and Levitt settled their dispute regarding the e-mail-based defamation claim. Levitt agreed to send a clarification letter to John McCall explaining that he did not mean to imply that Lott had improperly influenced editorial process and that, in fact, the journal issue in question had been peer-reviewed. The *Chronicle of Higher Education* would suggest that Lott had "won little from his 15 months of litigaton," but it also warned that the lawsuit "may yet roar back to life."[91]

The *Chronicle*'s prediction would hold true. In the spring of 2008, the parties filed opposing briefs in the Seventh Circuit federal appellate court over the original Count I *Freakonomics* defamation claim. Lott argued that the trial court had wrongly dismissed the claim, and Levitt argued in response that it was rightly dismissed.[92] In early 2009, approximately four years after *Freakonomics'* publication, the appellate court affirmed the trial court's decision, writing that Lott was "barking up the wrong tree" when he complained about "an attack on his ideas, and not his character." The court wrote, "The remedy for this kind of academic dispute is the publication of a rebuttal, not an award of damages."[93]

Matters of Opinion

In his brief to the Seventh Circuit, Steven Levitt argued, among other things, that the *Freakonomics* claim brought by Lott was not a viable one because the offending statement was a "non-actionable expression of opinion." Opinions, precedent readily recognizes, cannot be the basis for a defamation claim. But that legal principle is not as easy as it seems.

When Daniel Curzon-Brown, a longtime English professor at San Francisco's City College, learned of a new Web site allowing students to post anonymous reviews of their professors, he was dismayed at what he found. Several of the posts about Curzon-Brown—calling him "pompous," for example, or "the worst teacher I have ever had the opportunity of knowing"—stung; others commenting on the openly gay professor's sexual orientation were crude or downright vicious.[94] He felt demoralized and depressed; he could "barely stand going to class."[95]

Curzon-Brown might have responded by trying his best to shake off the barbs. Or, he might have returned fire, posting comments critical of his students. Or, he might have followed the example of John Lott and posted pseudonymous comments gushing over himself. (Lott admitted that he had once, under the identity of his alter ego, former student Mary Rosh, posted the following comment: "I have to say that he was the best professor that I ever had . . . There were a group of us students who would try to take any class that he taught. Lott finally had to tell us that it was best for us to try and take classes from other professors more to be exposed to other ways of teaching graduate material."[96])

Instead, Curzon-Brown sued, styling his lawsuit a class action on behalf of all 1,750 teachers at City College and demanding money damages and an order stopping any further defamatory reviews.[97] But Curzon-Brown's lawsuit failed miserably. A year after filing, he agreed to drop the suit and to cover $10,000 of the defendant's legal bills (for fear of being ordered by a court to pay *all* of the defendant's expenses, which had already topped $100,000).[98] Undoubtedly, one reason Curzon-Brown came to doubt the prospects for his lawsuit is the treatment of opinions in defamation law. Under principles of both common law and constitutional doctrine, statements of opinion are shielded from tort liability.[99]

Accordingly, courts sometimes decline to impose liability for evaluative comments made about students, professors, or administrators. For example, where a department head made comments both internally and to the campus newspaper to the effect that "neither the quantity nor the quality of [a junior professor's] scholarly published work justified a grant of tenure," an Illinois court held that the statements merely reflected the head's "opinion of the plaintiff's qualifications for tenure."[100] By the same token,

> If, for instance, a student at the university, in formulating his schedule for the next semester, asked a present student of [the plaintiff-professor] whether or not he should take a course from [the professor], it cannot be said that an expression of opinion by [the professor's] present student that the course was not taught well is defamatory. Nor could plaintiff complain of a review of his published works in a scholarly journal even if the reviewer criticized the plaintiff's work.[101]

Similarly, where a newspaper editorial criticized a professor in charge of an academic support program for student-athletes for being "part of the corruption of college athletics" and "interested chiefly in maintaining the athletic eligibility of his charges, not in their academic progress or career prospects," the West Virginia Supreme Court classified the commentary as nonactionable opinion.[102]

Yet, the breathing space created by the exemption for opinion is less sweeping than might be imagined. "[S]eparating opinion from fact is inherently difficult," notes constitutional law scholar Erwin Chemerinsky. "Is calling a public official 'stupid' a statement of fact, because IQ can be measured, or of opinion?"[103] Determining on which side of the line a given statements falls is often debatable, and sometimes turns on whether listeners would interpret the statement literally or as mere "rhetorical hyperbole."[104] The claim by one Egyptologist in an Internet tit-for-tat that her academic rival had obtained her degree from a "box of Cracker Jacks" was one that obviously belonged in the second category.[105] Similarly, an appeals court did not agonize in holding that references on an anonymous Web site criticizing university management calling the plaintiff, the university's vice president of external affairs, "the 'hatchet man,' the 'Vice-President of Excremental Affairs,' or a member of the 'sewer staff' could not reasonably be interpreted as stating actual fact."[106]

But others are harder to classify. A Louisiana court did not pause, for example, in upholding a defamation award against the law professor who had called a female student a "slut" during class,[107] while a Minnesota court held that a professor's calling a student "homophobic" in class and in a faculty meeting was plainly opinion,[108] though it is not clear that one term is any more "verifiable" than the other.

The unpredictable dividing line between "opinion" and "fact" necessarily leaves academics guessing about how far they can go in criticism and debate. In John Lott's suit against Steven Levitt, for example, the district judge ruled that Levitt's e-mail statements—that the special symposium issue of the *Journal of Law and Economics* organized and funded by Lott was not "peer refereed," and that Lott was able to "buy" the issue and "put in only work that supported him"—qualified as statements of fact.[109] Judge Ruben Castillo held that both statements reasonably appeared to be "precise, readily understood, and susceptible of being verified as true or false," and therefore fell on the "fact" side of the line.[110]

But how is a jury to go about "verifying" such assertions? Levitt contended, for example, that the guns issue was not genuinely peer-reviewed in the usual sense because screening standards are greatly relaxed for special conference issues. According to the *Chronicle of Higher Education:* "The journal sent the guns-and-crime conference papers out for peer review, but—according to several accounts—with the understanding that all or nearly all would be approved for publication. By contrast, the journal accepts fewer than 10 percent of the papers that are submitted for publication in its normal issues."[111] Had jurors been asked to resolve the question, they would have done so according to their own understanding of peer review, since the court found that the legal test looks to the judgment of the "reasonable reader," not the academic insider.[112] In other contexts courts have recognized a strong interest in leaving "breathing space," or play in the joints, in regulating the accuracy of speech, to avoid unduly inhibiting participation by the risk-averse.[113]

In 2004, in Fischbach v. Trustees of California State University, a state appeals court reinstated a defamation lawsuit against a department chair and two external reviewers brought by an associate professor who was taken to task in the external review.[114] The report identified a "glaring area of lack of responsible advising" in the university's Health Education program and, in the allegedly defamatory sentence, charged that the responsible "faculty member does not appear to be meeting the standard for a tenured university professor and it is resulting in a weak program."[115] In sending the case back for trial, the appellate court implicitly found this to be a factual statement suitable for jury verification or refutation.

If this view were to hold elsewhere, defamation claims might serve as a major new pathway for judicial scrutiny of tenure standards. Already, university counsel have noted that defamation claims have become an increasingly common add-on to lawsuits challenging tenure or promotion decisions under the civil rights laws or the First Amendment.[116] The *Fischbach* decision hints, however, at the possibility that defamation claims could provide a new, stand-alone means of subjecting university assessments of tenure standards to external supervisory review: anytime a college or university "falsely" determined that a tenure candidate did not measure up to the institution's expectations (and confirmed that judgment in a communication to others), the candidate might sue for defamation, alleging that the communication has wrongfully injured his or her professional reputation. At least if the plaintiff can plausibly allege some malice on the part of the decision maker (a burden that seems rather easily met, judging from the case law), he or she would stand a decent chance of reaching a jury.

Back to the Future?

At this point, two points should be apparent. First, defamation claims, once a freakish oddity on college campuses, are now common. As recently as 2001, the Baltimore *Daily Record* reported on a professor's defamation lawsuit against a colleague with a sense of wonderment.[117] Jonathan Knight, associate secretary of the AAUP's Committee on Academic Freedom and Tenure, observed then that cases in which "one faculty member says to another faculty member 'you've defamed me, that's hurt my reputation' are highly unusual."[118] Since then, however, a cluster of high-profile scholarly dust-ups—Frank Sulloway and John Lott among them[119]—hint at a changing landscape. Students and even university administrators are joining in increasing numbers, including a freshman at Miami University in Ohio who, passed over during sorority rush, sued her suspected blackballers for defaming her.[120] Accordingly, a veteran higher-education lawyer was surely right in recently observing that "[c]olleges and universities provide fertile soil for defamation claims" and "[t]he scenarios seem endless."[121]

Second, the ordinary tools of defamation law—at least as they are now being applied in the courts—are not well suited to safeguard important values of academic freedom. The heightened proof required of public figures, rules limiting defamatory meaning, and exemptions for opinions offer imperfect protection for legitimate academic debate. Many potential academic plaintiffs are untouched and therefore unconstrained by constitutional limitations on defamation claims; judges and juries seem increasingly emboldened to trust their own judgments in setting the boundaries of academic criticism or classroom discussion; it is sometimes difficult to predict whether a future judge will regard a given statement as nonactionable opinion or sanctionable fact. Because defamation law directly regulates the content of communication—the lifeblood of academic freedom—these openings for further legal intrusions in this field are troublesome indeed.

At the same time, few would doubt the legitimate and valuable role that law—including defamation law—can and should play in building an academic community. The files of courthouses contain frivolous claims, to be sure, such as the $850,000 defamation claim by a Virginia Tech administrator for having been crudely labeled "Director of Butt Licking" in a student newspaper. (The lawsuit rationalized liability on the theory that the title imputed to the administrator "the commission of a crime involving moral turpitude and therefore constitutes defamation."[122])

Court records also, however, detail vile and reprehensible conduct that almost all would agree has no legitimate place in an academic community. The sustained mistreatment of Dr. Jean Jew by a group of senior colleagues on the University of Iowa medical faculty is one example.[123] The constant, backstabbing whispers about Jew's supposed sexual conduct in the office with her colleague were found to be slander.[124] Similarly, in Smith v. Atkins, the law professor's repeated use of the coarse sexual epithet directed at a particular female student in class seems quite properly sanctionable.[125]

Yet, although the results in *Jew* and *Smith* seem correct, it is troubling that neither court gave substantial attention to the considerations of academic freedom implicated by judicial regulation of speech in a classroom or faculty meeting. The courts' incursions may well seem justified in both cases, but it would be reassuring to see an articulation of a principle capable of limiting future interventions to the right cases. For its part, *Smith* does not seem to consider the academic setting of the conduct relevant to its finding of liability (one concurring judge did consider it explicitly in measuring damages, increasing the penalties on the ground that the classroom setting made the defamation "especially egregious"[126]). Rather, the court appeared to analyze the defamation claim in essentially the same way it would if the conduct had occurred in a grocery store, a manufacturing shop floor, or movie theater.

Jew did pause toward the end of its opinion to deflect the defendant's contention that the First Amendment limited the court's power to penalize academic speech. But the court did not need to tarry long, because it had a categorical answer: "Free speech and academic freedom considerations might preclude Title VII liability if the sexual relationship rumors were true, but I have found that the rumors were not true. Rights of free speech and academic freedom do not immunize professors from liability for slander or their universities from Title VII liability for a hostile work environment generated by gender-based slander."[127] This answer implies that the constitutional protection for academic speech under defamation law is strictly limited to truth. There is, in other words, no constitutional solicitude for error in academic speech—or, rather, at least none peculiar to the academic context. Essentially, this denies the propriety of any special respect for academic freedom in enforcing civil rights statutes and tort law.

A case can be made that *Jew*, though perhaps right in its result, was wrong in this reasoning. *Jew, Smith,* and most other contemporary academic defamation cases assume that legitimate academic interests in speech are adequately protected by the ordinary background rules of defamation law and that those rules will leave much academic speech vulnerable to burdensome challenge in the courts.

The prospect of being sued is worrisome in any context, of course. But there are special reasons to be wary in the university setting. First, in contrast to most walks of life, speech and intellectual exchange are at the core of academic life; proposing and challenging ideas, and disseminating the results of research and learning, are what colleges and universities are all about. Accordingly, legal restraints on speech are of particular concern to scholars and students.

That speech and public engagement is, for all practical purposes, a required aspect of the scholar's work may well justify special legal protection. At common law, special privileges or immunities from suit were provided to speakers in selected occupations or settings—such as judicial or legislative proceedings—where hard-hitting speech was essential to an enterprise of high public value. The added protection was rationalized based on recognition that, otherwise, speakers might be inhibited by "fear that their actions in that position might have an adverse effect upon their personal interests. To accomplish this, it is necessary for them to be protected not only from civil liability but also from the danger of even an unsuccessful civil action."[128]

The chilling power of defamation law may be all the greater in the academic setting because of the financial vulnerability of most individual scholars and academic journals. Universities and publishers sometimes pay the legal expenses of employees or authors who are sued for their academic communications, but not always, which can make academic speakers easy targets for legal bullying. In a series of recent cases, small, poorly funded academic journals have simply withdrawn published articles when faced with threats of a defamation lawsuit. In 2005, for instance, Merle Weiner, a family law professor at the University of Oregon, was threatened with a defamation suit by a man whose court case was mentioned in a law review article Weiner wrote about child custody cases and domestic violence. Her university disclaimed any obligation to represent her in legal action arising from her publications.[129] The man also threatened the journal that published Weiner's article, the *University of San Francisco Law Review,* which then promptly eliminated the disputed references from the article on the journal's electronic archives, on the advice of university counsel—advice driven solely by a practical assessment of the costs of litigation.[130]

Similar episodes have transpired at other academic journals. Pity, in particular, the editors of the *Denver Journal of International Law and Policy* at the University of Denver. After the Boise Cascade Corporation complained strongly that it had been defamed by a *Journal* article discussing the company's environmental practices in Mexico, the editors withdrew the article from electronic databases and published an "errata" statement explaining that the article "was not consistent with [its] editorial standards" and contained statements about Boise Cascade that were "clearly inappropriate."[131] The *Journal* was then sued by the authors of the article, who claimed to have been defamed by the retraction; the editors ultimately settled with the authors for an undisclosed sum and an apology.[132]

The relative financial vulnerability of academics, some judges and lawyers have acknowledged, might reasonably support granting them special protection from threats of defamation lawsuits. Judge Frank Easterbrook, himself a professor at the University of Chicago before his appointment to Chicago's federal appeals court in 1985, wrote in Underwager v. Salter:

> [T]he private need for [a defamation] privilege may well be greater in the case of scholars . . . than in the case of newspapers and broadcasters. Newspapers, magazines, and broadcast stations reap considerable profits from their endeavors, and the obligation to pay damages to those they injure is unlikely to put them out of business or even substantially temper their reports . . . Psychologists compiling monographs with the aid of research grants . . . do not receive comparable rewards. Exposing such persons to large awards of damages is more apt to lead to silence than are comparable awards against media defendants.[133]

Easterbrook made this observation simply to justify giving academic defamation defendants the *same* legal protection enjoyed by media defendants in suits by public figures. (Supreme Court precedents had left unresolved whether the constitutional protections of the "actual malice" standard are enjoyed only by media defendants.[134]) Nevertheless, Easterbrook's acknowledgment that academics may be vulnerable to *greater* chilling influences than journalists would provide a rationale for recognizing a new and broader privilege for academic speakers.

The threat to academic freedom is obvious. "The dangers to the first amendment are more threatening in the academic research context," agrees Michael Traynor, the longtime California litigator who served as president of the influential American Law Institute from 2000 to 2008. "A preoccupation with avoiding litigation, and its exorbitant damages, could discourage not only forthright factual reporting, but also the publication of innovative ideas."[135]

When Traynor wrote in 1990—just on the heels of the first major defamation verdict against an academic institution in *Neary*—it was still possible to phrase his statement in the predictive future tense. Today, the threat posed to academic freedom by unrestrained defamation litigation is no longer hypothetical. At Oregon, for instance, Professor Weiner acknowledges that she is more "cautious" now in selecting projects and that she has already "turned down at least one writing project because she feared it would require her to write about cases involving people who might sue."[136] Quite reasonably, she worries that "other professors will be sued by plaintiffs who know that faculty members lack the resources to defend themselves," and that the threat of litigation will become a new "tool" used by groups opposed to certain lines of research or scholarly argument.[137]

It should be a matter of serious concern that even just the threat of defamation litigation has been used effectively to withdraw controversial scholarship from the public realm and to reshape the research agendas of scholars who work in such fields. Given the Supreme Court's recognition that academic freedom is a "special concern" of the First Amendment,[138] there is certainly a plausible argument in favor of recognizing stronger and more particular protection for academia in defamation law. In defamation actions, as with other legal interventions considered elsewhere, colleges and universities and individual academics must be given sufficient leeway to set their own course without punishing oversight. The challenge, of course, is locating a workable and defensible balance

point between the social interests in academic autonomy and those favoring social justice, antidiscrimination, and other objectives of legal intervention. What is needed, in other words, is a way in the modern age
of regulation to restore an appropriate measure of deference to the academic judgments of university actors, without sacrificing too much by
way of essential countervailing values.

Interestingly, the court's opinion in *Jew* might point the way toward
such an alternative, broader view of the deference due to academic actors.
After seemingly rejecting any constitutional breathing space for academic
defamation, the court included a footnote at the first reference to "slander." That footnote allowed that "[a] professor of a state college or university in Iowa might, however, find immunity under state statutes if he can
prove that he spoke his slanderous words while acting within the scope of
his employment."[139] (In *Jew*, the jury found that the defendant's workplace commentary was uttered outside "the scope of his employment."[140])

The statutory immunity cited by the court is not specially tailored to academic settings; indeed, it is a generalized governmental immunity and
would not extend to private colleges and universities at all. Yet, although
it is not geared toward academia, the immunity provision nevertheless
suggests one possible approach to articulating a balance point between
appropriate judicial intervention and academic autonomy. In immunizing
conduct "within the scope of employment," the provision starts with a
presumption of immunity, and requires proof that the employee has engaged in crass self-dealing or some other "substantial deviation from the
employer's business or interests."[141]

A roughly parallel immunity from court intervention might be imagined for academic actors. The principle would start with a presumption
that academic judgments of college and university decision makers—
including the assessment of which judgments truly qualify as academic—
normally deserve deference. Judicial imposition despite that deference
would then require a confident finding that the academic decision maker
had betrayed its basic, public-interested values as by engaging in self-
dealing or discriminating, in disregard of both civil rights laws and academic principles. However expressed, the basic idea would be for courts
to commit themselves to return to a more sensitive engagement with academic communities—reserving the power to step in where social interests clearly and substantially require it.

Making Your Own Reality: Academic Deference
for the Real World

One of the longest-running feuds in academia provides potential insight into how a revived notion of academic deference might operate. The feud features two academic experts on Mexico's Huichol Indian culture. Huichol Indians create art pieces from fine, woven strands of yarn. Tiny lines of brightly colored threads form lines that become birds and ears of corn and sun symbols, all glued with beeswax in a vivid woven painting that evokes both a child's crayon drawing and a sketch artist's precise lines. The pieces are said to symbolize the Huichol belief that we all create our own realities.[142]

The harmony represented in the Huichol artwork could not provide a starker contrast with the enmity that defines the relationship of two of their foremost scholars. Peter Furst, Ph.D., was one of the very first researchers to focus on Huichol Indian culture.[143] He was the first scholar to witness Huichol Indian religious practices and he has written extensively about the Huichols and their art since the 1960s. He is considered an "elder statesman" in anthropology for his ground-breaking work with the Huichol people.

Jay Courtney Fikes, Ph.D., is Furst's junior by thirty years. He, too, has devoted much of his life's work to studying the Huichols. And, as a budding scholar, he came to question some of Furst's work—sometimes caustically. His book, *Carlos Castaneda: Academic Opportunism and the Psychedelic Sixties,* stridently disputes some of Furst's research about the Huichols' use of peyote and other rituals, calling Furst's research "the most complicated and fascinating anthropological hoax of the 20th century."[144]

So started what an appellate court labeled Fikes's "crusade" to discredit Furst's work and Furst's retaliatory "quest" to discredit Fikes, a saga the *New York Times* called a "take-no-prisoners legal battle."[145] Furst admits that he sent letters to publishers of Fikes's work, urging them not to support it. He also sent a letter to the University of New Mexico, suggesting that Fikes would not be a good candidate for a position there.

What makes the Fikes–Furst dispute so compelling for academia is not only that it spilled outside the ivied walls and into the courts, but that the courts themselves could not agree whether Furst's aggressive criticism of Fikes and his scholarship was defamatory or not. The intermediate appellate court found troubling two lines of commentary made by Furst against Fikes.[146] The first involved statements to other scholars that Fikes was not "qualified" to study the Huichol. The second involved Furst's alleged assertions that Fikes had been "disowned" by his doctoral program and that faculty there regretted ever granting his degree. Both kinds of statements, the court found, could be interpreted as fact and not opinion. It reinstated those portions of Fikes's original defamation claim but rejected liability for "opinion" statements that Fikes attributed to Furst, including claims that Fikes was a "lousy anthropologist," "paranoid," "crazy," "anti-Semitic," "racist," "ethnocentric," and a "religious fanatic" who was "incapable of doing a competent job" as an editor.

The New Mexico Supreme Court rejected Fikes's defamation lawsuit in total.[147] Unlike the intermediate appeals court, it found the statements to be nonactionable because Furst had shown that those who heard the statements did not believe them to be fact and, therefore, they were incapable of defamatory meaning. The witnesses had testified that the disparaging remarks were "typical" of what was said within the anthropological scholarly community, "not outside the range of what goes on in academic talk,"[148] and not to be taken literally. The slashing remarks were not "defamatory," the court reasoned, because they are par for the course in academia.

In some ways, the supreme court's disposition seems quite unsatisfactory. For one thing, it reflects a rather cynical view of the nature of ordinary academic debate. As Robert O'Neil, former president of the universities of Virginia and Wisconsin, has pointed out, in functional academic communities, "the very nature of academic discourse actually imposes higher standards than does the general community."[149] In addition, it seems artificial and perhaps even disingenuous to suggest that such brickbats as Furst and Fikes hurled at one another do not wound.

But the court's opinion captures a sense of rough justice in resolving the feud, one perhaps appropriate for a court sitting in the Old West. The core intuition of the court's ruling is that there ought to be immunity for the rough-and-tumble of academic debate within the broad boundaries of decorum fixed by, in effect, its historical high- and low-water marks. Whether this is achieved by redefining what is considered "defamatory" in academia, as the court did, or by recognizing an independent privilege for academic debate is of secondary concern. Most important is that, in some manner, courts find a way to act on *Fikes*'s recognition that "[c]riticism of the work of scholars is generally commonplace and acceptable in academic circles."[150] Because, if courts fail to curb the reach of defamation law on campus, that robust academic criticism, and the scholarly innovation it feeds, may become a good deal less commonplace.

CHAPTER **8**

Of Injuries and Insults:
Tort Law on Campus

Kenneth Abraham is the David and Mary Harrison Distinguished Professor of Law at the University of Virginia Law School and one of the nation's leading scholars in field of torts, the system of law that provides a civil remedy for victims of accidents and other personal injuries. Many first-year law students across the country learn the subject using his basic text, *The Forms and Functions of Tort Law.*[1]

Gary Munneke teaches about 375 miles to the northeast of Charlottesville in White Plains, New York, at Pace Law School. He, too, teaches torts and has written a book familiar to some first-year law students. His volume *How to Succeed in Law School* includes a chapter titled "Studying the Law," with a section subtitled "The Classroom Experience." In the book, Munneke acknowledges the jitters felt by many first-year students as they approach their first law school classes: "You will find yourself in a lecture hall with roughly one hundred more or less equally frightened souls," Munneke writes. "Your sense of anonymity and privacy will be invaded by the seemingly all-knowing professor, armed with a seating chart and an uncanny ability to identify the least prepared student in the class to discuss the case at hand."[2]

The advice seemed tailor-made for one of Professor Munneke's own students, thirty-year-old Denise DiFede. In August 2000, during the first week of fall semester classes, Professor Munneke was preparing to teach his new first-year students a landmark case involving the tort of battery. In tort law, battery is defined as an intentional harmful or offensive touching of another person. The classic case that was the subject of Munneke's class involved a five-year-old boy who, in an apparent prank, pulled a chair out from beneath an older woman as she was sitting down, causing her to fall to the ground and break her hip.[3] The lesson of the case is that a child can be held liable so long as he acted with malicious purpose or with knowledge to a "substantial certainty" that his act would cause the woman to hit the ground. DiFede says that she e-mailed Munneke before class to tell him that she had not been able to read the case and to ask him not to call on her.[4] In class, however, Munneke called on DiFede, summoned her to the front of the classroom, and invited her to sit in a chair. As she complied, she claims, Munneke allegedly whisked the chair away, causing DiFede to fall to the ground, neatly replicating the facts of the case under discussion. DiFede, in turn, sought to replicate the legal principle established in the case by suing her torts professor for $5 million.[5]

One year later, in August 2001, Professor Abraham was teaching another famous battery case to a group of entering Virginia law students. He tapped a student on the shoulder during a class in which he was explaining the so-called "eggshell plaintiff" rule, a torts concept that gives even plaintiffs with very thin skins—literally and figuratively—the right to recover for wrongful injuries that would not harm an ordinary person. Unbeknownst to Professor Abraham, the student was precisely the subject of his lecture; she had been molested and raped when she was eleven years old and even the slight touch in the classroom rekindled traumatic memories.[6] She sued Abraham for battery and demanded $35,000 in damages. "You take your victim as you find them," the student's lawyer later explained. "[N]ormally a touching [like this] might not seen by anybody as offensive . . . He just picked the wrong victim."[7]

Both cases were "resolved" on undisclosed terms before trial. Not surprisingly, they generated a flutter of mostly amused commentary in the press; predictably, the New York *Daily News* jumped on Munneke's story with a student-teaches-professor glee.[8] But some academics reacted with palpable horror, especially to the suit against Abraham. "Given the stuff I teach, this scares me out of my wits," said Anne Coughlin, one of Abraham's colleagues on the Virginia law faculty. "The thought that you'd have to so carefully police yourself in the classroom that a misspoken word might generate not just a student coming up to you after class but a lawsuit . . . is really troubling."[9] Former Virginia dean Richard Merrill wrote a letter to the law school's student newspaper warning about "the impact this suit could have on the classroom experience . . . The anxiety and embarrassment that the possible need for a defense in court will surely create, indeed has already created, will discourage any teacher."[10] In another letter, four colleagues added that

> [r]ecent . . . demonstrations in our law school classrooms have included drug-sniffing dogs in a criminal investigation class; a mock intruder with a water-gun who squirted both students and the professor to illustrate the limits of eyewitness testimony; [and] grabbing students' books in class to illustrate the meaning of "conversion" . . . [I]f professors cannot use reasonable methods for making issues come to life, and push students to think hard about difficult and controversial matters, both legal education and our community will be much the worse.[11]

In *The Paper Chase,* the novel and movie about a student's harrowing first year at Harvard Law School, when the protagonist declines to answer a question in class, he is summoned to the front of the classroom by his contracts professor, the fearsome Professor Kingsfield, and handed a coin. "Mister Hart, here is a dime," Kingsfield tells the student. "Take it, call your mother, and tell her there is serious doubt about you ever becoming a lawyer."[12] In the book and film, circa 1970, the student has some sharp words for the professor and eventually retakes his seat. Nearly four decades later, a similarly wounded student might well hasten to court in hopes of ensuring that the dime is only the first of many the professor would be handing over. In fact, in 2001, two law students at the University of Louisville sued the dean and a professor, R. Thomas Blackburn, for an assortment of torts and civil rights violations—including the claim that Blackburn had been " 'abnormally distant, arrogant, and rude' and would not give them a direct answer to their questions." A federal trial court in Louisville kindly but firmly ruled against the students. The plaintiffs' claims, the court explained, "aptly describe law school in America. And the Court can sympathize with law school assignments that are too long, and with law school professors who will not squarely answer a question. But, without doubt, there is absolutely no relief the Court can grant for these claims."[13]

Yet, judging from the barrage of recent tort suits involving colleges and universities, the court might have been too categorical in ruling out the possibility of a legal remedy. "Insurance statistics," observe higher-education law experts Robert Bickel and Peter Lake, "show steady, and in some cases alarming, rates of growth in college student injury claims."[14]

And as the number of claims has soared, courts have presided over an ongoing revolution in legal doctrine that has opened the courthouse doors ever wider to claims of wrongful injury by students, faculty, staff, and outsiders.

Until the 1960s, colleges and universities were heavily insulated against potential tort liability by immunity doctrines. Public universities were shielded by broad governmental tort immunity, and private universities typically enjoyed similar protection under charitable immunity doctrines. The *in loco parentis* doctrine, which regarded college officials as standing in for parents, amounted for all practical purposes to a "university immunity" for potential injury claims by students.[15] Even when immunities were formally peeled away in the 1960s, courts continued to shield colleges and universities by construing tort law narrowly to recognize few legal duties to protect students from harm.[16]

Over time, however, the reluctance of judges to apply ordinary tort principles to campus actors has worn away, drawing courts ever deeper into academic life. As Peter Lake summed up the tenor of campus tort litigation in 1999, "[h]ere, there, and everywhere, with few exceptions, universities are held to the standards that typical businesses are held to."[17] The first steps were largely unremarkable. If a university truck driver negligently ran over a pedestrian on a city street or a college allowed a dormitory to fall into dangerous disrepair, it seemed only a small step to hold them to the same standards of care required of other drivers and landlords.[18] Yet, even as courts broadened the accountability of universities for injuries that had little directly to do with the academic enterprise, they continued to insist that judges not second-guess genuinely academic judgments under the guise of tort law.

Thus, a student could sue her college for negligence if unsafe conditions in the classroom caused physical injury—as a Penn State student did in 2007 when she was struck in the head during a biology exam by a mounted moose head that fell from a classroom wall[19]—but not for "educational malpractice" or some other tort theory based on substandard academic quality.[20] "The prohibition against allowing educational malpractice claims 'recognizes that universities are empowered to set their own academic standards and procedures,'" explained one federal trial court. "Decisions made by a University regarding a student's academic performance are best left to the educators themselves and should not be subject to review in the courts."[21] Besides concerns over "the lack of a satisfactory standard of care by which to evaluate an educator," courts have cautioned that judicial standard-setting and "oversight might be particularly troubling in a university setting where it necessarily implicates considerations of academic freedom and autonomy."[22]

Yet, as the cases described in the following section suggest, the supposed wall separating (permissible) "non-academic" tort claims from (impermissible) "academic" tort claims is already crumbling.

"Educational Malpractice" and the Reasonable Professor

Adrian Zachariasewycz—or Adrian Zack, as he prefers to be called—graduated in 2004 from the University of Michigan Law School, one of the nation's most elite law schools. Yet he believes that the value of his degree has been lowered by the low grades he received in law school. And, in fact, Zack says he spent several years after graduation fruitlessly searching for permanent legal employment.[23]

In 2006, Zack sued his alma mater and several of the law school's professors and administrators. He claimed that the defendants had tortiously interfered with his future prospects as a lawyer by administering exams that disadvantaged slow typists such as himself. "Certain exams taken by Mr. Zack that required students to be skilled touch-typists in order to produce a competitive response," he explained in his complaint, "resulted in borderline failing grades by virtue of the low volume of prose Mr. Zack could type in the time allotted as compared with other students."[24] He complained that the law school "made no generally adequate accommodation to students with deficient typing skills" (though it did allow them to handwrite their exams if they preferred), and that the dean and several professors effectively covered up the importance of typing speed to effective exam performance. One of the professors named as a defendant was Peter Hammer, who had his own discrimination lawsuit against Michigan Law School.[25]

Zack also added claims against several law school administrators. Two career services officers named as defendants were said to have given Zack job-hunting advice that was "highly disadvantageous to his particular circumstances." Another staff member was sued for having, "without credible justification[,] denied Mr. Zack accommodation during a 24-hour exam when he was forced to take an approximately two-hour break during the exam to handle a personal matter that unexpectedly and unavoidabl[y] arose."[26]

Zack's prospects for prevailing in his lawsuit appear no brighter than the employment prospects of which he complained. But he has good company. In 2007, a law student at the University of Dayton sued the school for negligence for using exam software that, he said, contained a loophole that allowed some classmates to cheat by copying and pasting text into their essay answers. He has claimed that others' cheating caused him to get a low grade in his criminal procedure course; he has asked a federal court in Ohio to award him $200,000 in compensatory damages, $1 million in punitive damages, and a spot on the law review.[27]

Notwithstanding that Zack styled his complaint as one for intentional interference with prospective business relations, it is clear that the substance of both lawsuits is essentially one for educational malpractice. Courts have regularly dismissed such claims on the ground that judges have no business reviewing the substance of academic evaluations. In 2005, for example, a Tennessee court refused a dental student's invitation to regrade his Gross Anatomy exam, turning aside the student's negligence claim on the ground that courts must defer to the professional judgment of educators.[28] The Tennessee court took its cue in part from decisions of the U.S. Supreme Court emphasizing the importance of deferring to academic authorities in the context of constitutional challenges to student dismissals.[29] Courts elsewhere have similarly rejected tort claims challenging the "pedagogical evaluation of . . . test grades" or other academic determinations as beyond the competence of the courts.[30] "[D]etermining a law student's proper grade in a given class has been a mystery for the ages," wrote one weary federal judge in 2002, "and this court is far less well-suited to attempt to do so than a law-school professor."[31]

But that judicial hesitation hasn't stopped students from trying. Thus, in 2002, a student at the Fashion Institute of Technology sued when the school refused to allow him to present menswear as a final graduation project instead of the women's wear and children's wear required by an assignment.[32] In 2003, a student at the University of Bridgeport sued, arguing that classes and instructors were not of sufficient quality.[33] And that same year a student at Columbia sued partly because he was unhappy that graduate students were teaching some courses.[34]

Perhaps closest to the facts of Zack's complaint, a federal court in Kentucky in 2001 dismissed a law student's claim that she had been disadvantaged—in violation of her constitutional rights to equal protection and due process—by her law school's policy of requiring typists to turn in their exams in the separate classroom used by students who handwrote their exams. She argued that the policy had caused her to lose precious time in transit that could have been used to improve her exam score, yet the court found "no fundamental Constitutional right to equal time on a law school exam."[35]

Notwithstanding this bleak track record, however, Zack might take heart from evidence that some courts seem to be overcoming their historical reluctance to review pedagogical judgments. In recent cases, several courts have allowed negligence claims based on shoddy teaching to go forward by shrinking their conception of what counts as an impermissible claim of "educational malpractice." In Doe v. Yale University, for example, the Connecticut Supreme Court held that a medical resident could hold Yale liable for inadequately training her in performing a medical procedure during which she accidentally infected herself with HIV through a needle stick. The court reaffirmed that students cannot sue for "educational malpractice" on a general claim of receiving a substandard education, but distinguished lawsuits in which a student claims that negligent instruction results in physical injury.

Of course, as the *Doe* court readily acknowledged, allowing negligent-instruction claims involving physical injury results in "the kind of judicial oversight of the educational process that, for policy reasons, [the court had] eschewed" in other educational malpractice cases:

> What tips the balance here, however, . . . is the result of the claimed educational inadequacy. When the claimed result is an inadequate education, there is no viable claim because we are unwilling to recognize such a legal duty as a matter of public policy. When, however, the result is physical harm, as in the present case, we are willing to recognize the claim because it falls within the traditionally recognized duty not to cause physical harm by negligent conduct. The fact that the harm is caused in an educational setting is not sufficient to remove the claim from that traditionally cognizable claim.[36]

On the facts of *Doe,* the balance not only tipped against the university, but tipped hard. A jury found Yale negligent and awarded the former resident

$12.2 million, though the state supreme court sent the case back to consider a workers-compensation defense.[37] The exception made in *Doe* is broader than it might seem. It could permit negligent-instruction claims not only for student injuries in university-sponsored laboratory experiments, athletic competitions, field work, and vocational training, but conceivably for any workplace injury plausibly traceable to a lack of better instruction in college.

Five years after *Doe*, the federal appeals court in Cincinnati recognized a different and potentially broader exception to the bar against educational malpractice claims. In Atria v. Vanderbilt University, the court ruled that a jury should be allowed to decide whether a professor was "negligent in the manner in which he redistributed the graded answer sheets from his Organic Chemistry exam."

Atria, it may be recalled, was the pre-med student who had been found guilty by Vanderbilt's Honor Council of doctoring one of his returned exams in an attempt to plead for a higher grade. When his professor produced a photocopy of the original exam, showing that it had been altered, Atria theorized that another student must have doctored the exam before he picked it up in the hope that Atria would discover the error, seek a "regrade," and be found guilty of an honors code violation, thereby marginally improving the standing of all other students on the grading curve. When Vanderbilt found the theory unpersuasive, Atria sued, alleging that he had been victimized by his professor's negligent method of handing back exams. A federal trial court tossed the claim on summary judgment, but the court of appeals found merit in Atria's theory and reinstated his negligence claim. "Atria's is not a claim for educational malpractice because it does not challenge the adequacy of the education that Vanderbilt provided," the appeals court reasoned. "Rather, Atria's challenge is to Professor Hess's method of handing back the graded answer sheets, which Atria claims was negligent and proximately caused Atria's injury." The court could see no reason why jurors, who are routinely asked to pass judgment on the conduct of surgeons and other professionals, are not also perfectly capable of determining how professors should hand back exams.[38]

Atria himself went on successfully to medical school, but the legacy of his lawsuit for higher education may be less cheery. The court appears to have concluded there was nothing particularly "academic" about Professor Hess's judgment concerning how to hand back exams. Yet entrusting courts with the task of deciding which matters of classroom instruction are essentially "academic," and which are not, provides arguably tenuous protection from judicial overreaching. Certainly, Professor Hess saw his method of distributing exams as very much a matter of "academic freedom."[39] Moreover, *Atria*'s likening of professors to surgeons and other professionals suggests a potentially far broader allowance for educational malpractice claims.

Other courts have similarly opened the door to educational malpractice claims, so long as students are clever enough to tie their complaints to specific promises.[40] In a number of states, for example, courts permit students to sue if "the educational institution failed to fulfill a specific contractual promise distinct from any overall obligation to offer a reasonable program."[41] Applying this rule, a Connecticut court found insufficiently specific promises in Yale University's policies to support a student's lawsuit complaining that she had been assigned "a 'revolving door' of advisors," hindering her academic progress.[42] Yet, following the same rule, a Minnesota appeals court reversed summary judgment for a college and reinstated students' complaints that "instructors were frequently tardy or absent and wasted class time by complaining about personal problems."[43] As Peter Lake observed of the Minnesota case, "the kinds of allegations that the Minnesota Court of Appeals permitted to survive as being specific enough to defeat an issue of educational malpractice are the types of allegations that could be routinely made in any other type of suit."[44] Indeed, in 2000, an appellate court had rejected an educational malpractice case against Oklahoma City University in which the student-plaintiff had alleged that his professor had arrived late and frequently cancelled classes.[45]

The potential breadth of the exceptions recognized in recent decisions can be seen by testing their reasoning against the facts of a straightforward educational malpractice case out of Louisiana. In Fall 2000, Leonce J. Miller III was a part-time student studying law in the evenings at Loyola University of New Orleans. He registered for a legal ethics course called "The Legal Profession" taught by tenured professor Cynthia Lepow, a tax expert assigned to teach the course for the first time. Miller found the course sadly lacking. Professor Lepow, he complained, had not ordered class materials on time, had asked students to cover topics through oral presentations instead of teaching them herself, and had changed the time the course was offered without permission from the law school. Moreover, Miller figured, Lepow had covered only "approximately 60% of the Model Rules of Professional Conduct" in her course. Miller also had issues with the quality of Professor Lepow's final exam.[46]

Miller was no stranger to litigation over school-related injuries, having previously sued for negligence after being hit in the head by a sailboat boom during orientation training at the Naval Academy.[47] Unhappy with Loyola's response to his complaints, he sued again, alleging among other things that Loyola was negligent in assigning Lepow, a tax expert, to teach the ethics course and in misrepresenting the course time and content. A New Orleans trial court threw out Miller's lawsuit and a Louisiana appellate court affirmed, holding that it amounted to a nonactionable claim for educational malpractice.[48] But it is not obvious that Miller's lawsuit would have been precluded under the reasoning of *Atria* or recent decisions allowing student suits based on specific contractual promises. Certainly, Miller's core complaint was the academic inadequacy of the Legal Profession course, but he also included some factually specific claims— such as the switch in course time—that were no more "academic" than the question of how to hand back exams or instructors' wasting of class time on personal asides.

Indeed, although two appellate judges in *Miller* affirmed the dismissal of Miller's malpractice claims, a third judge dissented. Judge Steven Plotkin agreed that courts should steer clear of amorphous malpractice claims "which simply attack the general quality of an education," but contended that courts should entertain malpractice claims based on a college's failure to live up to its implied contractual obligation of "good faith and fair dealing."[49] Before the appellate court's decision, Loyola's attorney had suggested to a reporter that Miller was "such a poor law student" that he did not recognize the hopelessness of his legal claims. For his part, Miller said he hoped to establish a precedent upon which all Louisiana students could rely in holding their universities accountable in court.[50] In the end, Miller missed his mark by just one vote. If Judge Plotkin's view had prevailed, the resulting opinion would indeed have permitted judges to weigh in on virtually *every* student–campus dispute (since it is basically possible to tie any grievance to a claim of implied or express contract)— and to pass judgment according to no more definite a legal standard than the court's own ethereal sense of what "good faith and fair dealing" requires.

In all, these cases show a fledgling pattern in which judges claim to preserve the traditional barrier to educational malpractice claims while recognizing distinctions or exceptions that come perilously close to swallowing the rule. Courts have all but crossed the Rubicon and allowed educational malpractice claims outright in a number of cases involving for-profit trade and vocational schools.[51] And these decisions are increasingly setting the tone for court review of similar claims against traditional colleges and universities. A strong theme of recent court decisions involving campus tort claims has been to treat colleges and universities of all stripes increasingly like ordinary businesses. "Overall, there is a tendency to analogize university case law to *business* case law," observed Bickel and Lake, in their survey of campus tort litigation.[52] Although courts continue to subscribe to the general principle of deference when it comes to legal challenges to the exercise of academic judgment, the breadth and strength of that deference is contracting in pace with the "growing trend to view universities in a business category, as selling a product to students as 'consumers.' "[53]

Sticks and Stones: Tort Recovery for Emotional Distress

Govindaswamy Nagarajan is a physics and math professor at Tennessee State University in Nashville. After he was twice deferred for tenure, he declined to reapply and sued, contending that the university had discriminated against him because of his national origin. A federal court ruled in his favor and ordered that he be reinstated as a full professor with $511,000 in back pay.[54] One year after returning to the classroom, twenty-four of the thirty-six students in his Physics 211 course filed a complaint with the chair of Nagarajan's department, alleging that the professor had "failed to attend posted office hours, to return telephone calls from students after repeated attempts to contact him, to correct grading inaccuracies in his grade book, and to address physics problems posed by students." They also complained that he had "discouraged open dialogue with students, used profanity and derogatory remarks, and had degraded and embarrassed students by announcing their overall performance on graded assignments before the entire class."[55] Five students asked the administration to adjust their course grades.

University administrators undertook some inquiry but resolved to take no action. They declined the students' request to change their grades, and they also turned down Nagarajan's demand for an investigation of the students' insurrection. But if the university was prepared to leave things there, Nagarajan was not. He returned to the federal district court that had ordered his reinstatement to the faculty and filed suit against the university, the Tennessee Board of Regents, four university administrators, and the twenty-four students. Among other claims, Nagarajan argued that the affront to his teaching amounted to intentional infliction of emotional distress, entitling him to $60 million in damages.[56] For good measure, he filed a second, "substantially identical" lawsuit in state court, upping the ante of his damage claim to $70 million.[57]

Nagarajan's two lawsuits fared poorly. In both cases, trial courts dismissed the complaints and were upheld on appeal.[58] Nevertheless, the lawsuits illustrate the easy availability of tort law as a basis for converting almost any campus disagreement into a legal dispute. They also illustrate the substantial costs associated even with seemingly frivolous litigation: although he lost at every turn, Nagarajan's lawsuits forced upwards of thirty defendants, including students and administrators, to defend themselves in two court systems in litigation spanning nearly five years. As of 2009, Nagarajan remained on Tennessee State's faculty, though, at least judging by comments posted to an online student forum, continued to have a prickly relationship with some students: two posted comments specifically complained that Nagarajan regularly "threatens to sue" students in class.[59]

The tort claim Nagarajan pressed in court—intentional infliction of emotional distress (IIED)—has become a common resort for academics involved in employment or tenure disputes.[60] The tort provides a remedy when a plaintiff can show that the defendant engaged in "extreme and outrageous" conduct, typically defined as behavior that goes "beyond all possible bounds of decency, and to be regarded as atrocious, and utterly intolerable in a civilized community," intentionally or recklessly causing the victim "severe" emotional distress.[61] As one court observed in a higher-education case, "[i]ntentional infliction of emotional distress claims are often pleaded but rarely get very far."[62] The threshold for "extreme and outrageous" conduct is very high, making it exceedingly difficult to win an IIED claim in the end. But that has not stopped students, faculty, and administrators from trying—and occasionally succeeding—when they feel bruised from campus affronts.[63]

A number of students have sued their professors for IIED based on al-leged inappropriate advances or obnoxious classroom behavior, includ-ing the law student who recovered a $5,000 judgment against her corpo-rations professor for twice calling her a "slut" and making fun of her in class.[64] Others have sued not for dirty words, but for dirty looks. One stu-dent, for example, sued his university for emotional distress after one of his professors "told him in class that he better do well in the program," stated "that his dissertation topic, although worthwhile, was not worth-while as a dissertation," and "on several occasions, failed to acknowledge his presence and silently stared at him."[65]

Another graduate student, Hannah-Ian Faraclas, sued the University of Bridgeport, an associate dean, and three of her classmates for emo-tional distress inflicted by catty remarks and "shunning" behavior in class. Faraclas complained that after she had asked a question in class, one of the student-defendants, Jennifer Botwick, "interjected that the information Faraclas requested was not of interest to her and asked the professor to move on"; Botwick also allegedly "hissed when another stu-dent made an inappropriate joke in class" at Faraclas's expense. Another student-defendant said Faraclas asked too many questions in class and allegedly "fixed Faraclas with an 'angry stare'" in a hallway. The associ-ate dean was sued for causing her distress by, among other things, dis-couraging her complaints, chastising her for missing a mid-term exam, and accusing her of "unprofessional behavior."[66]

A Connecticut court held that almost all of this behavior was not bad enough to qualify as "extreme and outrageous" conduct, but decided that Faraclas could go forward with an IIED claim against one classmate who, besides rude remarks, accused the plaintiff of stealing her lab report.[67] Al-though Botwick dodged trial for her alleged hissing, she was haled into an-other court by her homeowners insurance company, which successfully obtained a declaration that it had no duty to defend her against Faraclas's suit.[68]

With regard to the associate dean, the University of Bridgeport urged the court to bar the claim because "as a matter of public policy imposing tort li-ability based on a university administrator's decisions would be disruptive to the educational process," but the court expressly declined to "bas[e] its decision on that ground." Instead, it ruled that the dean's allegedly callous conduct toward the plaintiff simply fell short of what was necessary to es-tablish liability. "In the educational context, administrators make decisions that may distress students, but more is required to make such distress actionable in tort," the court ruled. "The administrator's decision must be so wrongful that emotional distress involving illness or bodily harm was foreseeable."

Meanwhile, a Yale student's complaint that her faculty advisor "personally disliked her" and that administrators had "referred to her in a demeaning manner by using her initials 'KH' in their email exchange" triggered an emotional-distress suit, though not ultimately liability.[69] This also happened with a University of Pennsylvania graduate student who complained, among other things, that a professor had cut in front of him in line at the campus copy shop;[70] and with a law student's sprawling conspiratorial tort claims, including that she "was called on to speak in her Corporations class six or seven times during the semester while other students were not called on at all."[71] A North Carolina decision, however, provides an example of the sort of administrative behavior that can cross the line. The plaintiff, a top student and president of the senior class, alleged that Saint Augustine's College retaliated against her after she testified in a professor's discrimination lawsuit against the school. She stated that unexplained errors surfaced on her previously unblemished transcript that prevented her from graduating on time and that two professors sought to impeach her as class president; when she met with the college's vice president for academic affairs about the transcript errors she alleged, he laughed at her. A federal appeals court found "ample evidence" to sustain the $180,000 jury award of compensatory and punitive damages in her favor.[72]

Tort law is making inroads not only in the classroom and the dean's suite, but also in the laboratory and other venues for scholarly debate. Besides defamation, tort law is now providing, as the next section shows, a range of additional tools for those who wish to limit or redirect new lines of scholarly inquiry or criticism.

The Research Wars: Repressing Memories and Debate

When Dr. David L. Corwin published a case study of a young woman wrestling with repressed memories of childhood sexual abuse in the scientific journal *Child Maltreatment*, his work was hailed as "an extraordinarily important record" and "a model for how to conduct interviews with children and adolescents about traumatic events."[73] Corwin had first interviewed the subject of his study when, at age six, she was the center of a brutal custody battle in her parents' divorce. At the time, in 1984, the child's allegation that her mother had sexually abused her while bathing her resulted in a court granting custody to her father and cutting off her mother's visitation rights. Corwin interviewed the girl again in 1995. Then seventeen years old, the girl had been troubled by her inability to recall any memory of the abuse she reported at age six, but during her videotaped interview with Dr. Corwin, the memories suddenly came back to her. Corwin then showed her the videotape of the 1984 interview and she responded "that the tapes reinforced her belief that her mother had abused her."[74] Corwin presented Jane Doe's case as dramatic evidence of the recovery of a repressed traumatic memory. It quickly became Exhibit A in what is often called "the memory wars" over the validity of the "recovered memory" phenomenon.

Elizabeth Loftus, an eminent psychologist then at the University of Washington and herself a veteran of the memory wars, thought the story sounded "fishy."[75] Loftus was the author of *Eyewitness Testimony* and *The Myth of Repressed Memory,* and had testified as an expert witness about the unreliability of human recall in a Who's Who list of famous trials, including the Rodney King, O. J. Simpson, Ted Bundy, and McMartin preschool cases.[76] As Loftus and a coauthor, University of Michigan psychologist Melvin Guyer, later wrote: "Corwin's case study was vivid and compelling. Leading scientists were persuaded by it; indeed, emotionally moved by it . . . Few were skeptical that Jane really had been abused by her mother before age six, that her retrieved memories were accurate, or that 'repression' accounted for her forgetting what her mother supposedly had done to her. But we were."[77] Loftus and Guyer were skeptical not only about whether Jane Doe had actually been molested, but also more broadly about the scientific validity of conclusions drawn from narrow case studies. They set out to critically examine the facts of Jane Doe's case, to offer "a case study of a case study."[78]

Loftus and Guyer succeeded in identifying Jane Doe from clues Corwin had given at professional meetings discussing her case. With some additional sleuthing and the help of a private detective, they were able to track down and interview other key players, including Jane's mother, her stepmother, her foster mother, and others involved in her story. Loftus and Guyer became convinced that key parts of Jane Doe's family history had been omitted from Corwin's account, and concluded that the step-mother might have planted, perhaps intentionally, some of Jane's memories of sexual abuse. In their eventual report on their investigation, published fittingly in the journal *Skeptical Inquirer*, Loftus and Guyer offered the women's recollections of key events in Jane Doe's life, including teenaged Jane's happy reunion with her birth mother, her self-doubt before the interview with Corwin when she was seventeen, and her angry, accusing phone call with her mother after Corwin's 1995 visit. Jane Doe became self-destructive and depressed after Corwin's visit, the two authors wrote, quoting her former foster mother.

When Jane Doe got wind of Loftus and Guyer's investigation into her background, she filed an ethics complaint with the University of Washington. The university then launched an investigation of Loftus's project, seized her files, and ordered her not to discuss or publish her research; the University of Michigan similarly put the brakes on Guyer. Nearly two years later, the universities exonerated Loftus and Guyer and lifted the restrictions. In 2002, they published their findings in a two-part article, entitled "Who Abused Jane Doe? The Hazards of the Single Case History." The authors questioned Corwin's methods and hoped that their critical examination would serve as "a cautionary tale" for future researchers who place too much stock in single case histories.

A few months later, Jane Doe shed her anonymity and filed a lawsuit in the hopes of making their case "a cautionary tale" of a different sort for future researchers. Jane Doe, it turned out, was Nicole Taus, then a twenty-something naval officer and aviator. Her complaint included twenty-one separate tort claims for negligent infliction of emotional distress, invasion of privacy, fraud, and defamation. The charges stated that the *Skeptical Inquirer*, Loftus, Guyer, and Carol Tavris, another contributor to the journal, "improperly had invaded plaintiff's privacy and committed other tortious conduct by investigating plaintiff's background and discovering and disclosing information concerning her private life without her consent."[79] What galled many of Loftus's supporters was that Jane Doe had long consented to have Corwin tell her story, and seemed to be using the law to ensure that she could be fodder for only one side of the academic debate. "She wanted her story told her way, as everyone does," observed Tavris, "and when others disputed her version of events, she took out her anger the American way: by suing."[80]

Under California's so-called "anti-SLAPP" law, courts are supposed to dismiss lawsuits directed against First Amendment–protected speech unless a judge finds "a probability that the plaintiff will prevail on the claim."[81] As a result, even before trial, the court hearing Taus's claims first had to decide whether she had "a probability" of winning at trial. The trial court dismissed some of Taus's claims, but allowed others to go forward. On appeal, the court of appeal in San Francisco culled more of Taus's claims, but decided that she had shown a probability of prevailing on several. The disclosures contained in the published articles were themselves "newsworthy," the court wrote, and therefore not grounds for liability. But several events surrounding the articles *could* support liability—including a remark Loftus made during a professional talk suggesting that Jane Doe had engaged in "destructive behavior" after Corwin's 1995 visit, Loftus's reference to Doe's real initials in an earlier deposition, and misrepresentations Loftus allegedly made to gain the trust of Doe's former foster mother.

By now, the academic community had fully taken notice of the case. In 2003, Loftus had written of her "Orwellian nightmare" in *Daedalus,* the journal of the American Academy of Arts and Sciences, warning of "a new and disturbing trend: throughout America, scientists are being sued simply for exercising their constitutional right to speak out on matters of grave public concern." She urged that "[t]hose of us who value the First Amendment and open scientific inquiry must bring these efforts to suppress freedom of speech into the light."[82] The appellate court's decision, finding "a probability" of liability under several legal theories, did nothing to calm these fears, and prominent academics like Harvard's Richard McNally, himself the author of *Remembering Trauma,* wrote to the California Supreme Court, urging it to take the case. When the case reached the supreme court, fifty university professors filed an amicus brief warning that the case posed a "grave threat" to scientific researchers, the scientific method, and free inquiry in general; a large group of national media organizations filed their own brief, expressing concern that the threat of tort liability could be used to suppress investigative journalism. "Legal action against Loftus et al.," McNally wrote to the court, "appears to be little more than an attempt to squelch inquiry into matters of profound social significance."[83]

When California's highest court handed down its decision in 2007, it ruled mostly for the defendants, holding that Loftus's stray remarks at the seminar and deposition were either newsworthy or insufficiently revealing. But it agreed there was a probability that Loftus could be held liable on the claim that she misrepresented herself to gain access to information about Doe. If a jury believed that Loftus had deceived Doe's foster mother into thinking that she was one of Corwin's allies to win her trust— Loftus herself adamantly denied that allegation, insisting that the foster mother's claims to that effect were inspired by "source remorse"—Taus could recover damages for the tort of "intrusion into private matters." "A person's interest in preserving the privacy of [confidential family information] . . . would be substantially undermined," the court wrote, "if a would-be investigator could employ any means whatsoever to extract or obtain such private information from a relative or close friend."[84]

Advocates on both sides of the case claimed victory. Taus's lawyer issued a press release spinning the decision as "a victory for people whose privacy is invaded by unscrupulous means." Indeed, some of Taus's supporters had long insisted that her lawsuit defended, rather than attacked, science. "Science is in jeopardy if the public is not protected by ethics and standards," one advocate told the *Los Angeles Times*. "There is no individual who is above the law, whether they be a very well-respected scientist or the president or a garbage collector."[85]

Although Taus had lost in her claims against publication of the *Skeptical Inquirer* articles, the court's decision left open the possibility of holding researchers liable for using "questionable and unorthodox" means in seeking out even significant and newsworthy information.[86] Moreover, the court's decision, as the *Los Angeles Times* reported, "did not make clear under what circumstances professors and reporters would cross the line."[87]

Faced with the prospect of a trial on the remaining privacy claim, Loftus agreed to a settlement that would pay Taus a modest $7,500 (Taus had once sought $1.3 million in the litigation). Loftus later wrote that she would have preferred to press on for complete vindication, but that her insurance company pressured her to consign herself to a "nuisance settlement."[88] But, if the insurance company considered the matter to be a nuisance, Loftus obviously regarded it as something more. "A researcher might prevail in the end," she noted, "but the pathway to that end can be very long and arduous, and involves great anxiety and, in some instances, considerable expense and possible damage to a person's professional standing."[89] In fact, in Loftus's case, the litigation had dragged on for four years and the costs of the combined legal defense had topped

$450,000.[90] Given such staggering burdens, Loftus writes, "[t]he possibility of being sued into silence delivers an ominous message for all scientists. Baseless litigation not only affects the defendants—it also discourages scientists from speaking out on controversial topics, for fear that they will be next."[91]

Not all litigation concerning academic research is baseless, of course. In 2007, the State of Iowa agreed to pay $925,000 to settle claims arising from a notorious 1939 experiment in which a celebrated University of Iowa speech pathologist tried to induce stuttering in a group of orphan children. The experiment, in which children from a Davenport orphanage were used to test Wendell Johnson's theory that stuttering could be induced through sustained negative social feedback, was said to have damaged a number of the children for life. The episode, dubbed the "Monster Experiment" by Iowa graduate students, came to light only in 2001 after the *San Jose Mercury News* published an investigative report. (Ironically, in light of the California Supreme Court's later ruling in the *Loftus* case, the writer "later resigned for not identifying himself as a reporter to gain access to the U of I documents while he was a graduate student there."[92]) The University of Iowa apologized for the study in 2001, and the state supreme court had held that the surviving research subjects were entitled to go forward with their tort claims.[93]

Other recent court decisions have similarly recognized the availability of tort remedies for research subjects. In one case, a court found a researcher's release agreement unenforceable after a subject experienced severe altitude sickness during the study.[94] In another case, 164 Mulberry Street Corporation v. Columbia University, said to be "the first case in which a plaintiff claim[ed] IIED against a social science researcher," a Columbia University business school professor sent letters to restaurants across the city purportedly from patrons complaining of food poisoning, to test the responsiveness of the restaurants.[95] A New York appellate court ruled that the chagrined restaurateurs had sufficient grounds for asking a jury to award damages for intentional infliction of emotional distress and fraud. The researcher's toying with restaurateurs' livelihoods could be found to be "extreme and outrageous" conduct, the court ruled; and the elements of fraud—"a misrepresentation which was false and known to be false by the defendant, made for the purpose of inducing the other party to rely on it, and justifiable reliance of the other party on the misrepresentation and injury"—also could be found.[96] After the appellate court's ruling, the case settled out of court.

Even if tort litigation arising from academic research is still novel, the threat is sufficiently serious that legal scholars are already at work inventing tailor-made defenses. Many scholars have expressed growing concern about the role of institutional review boards (IRBs) in screening and approving academic research; Elizabeth Loftus, for example, complained that "IRBs often subordinate the pursuit of knowledge to the financial stakes, real or imagined, of the institution in which they operate."[97] And, yet, it is possible that IRB approval might emerge as an effective legal defense against tort claims, in the same way in which compliance with other intensive regulatory regimes sometimes provides a defense in tort law.[98]

With both legal principles and scientific capabilities expanding so rapidly, however, many questions of potential liability are only now beginning to be surface. Some are so novel that even if courts were to recognize an IRB defense, it would provide no help because IRBs are not yet addressing them. One unfolding dilemma, for example, concerns researchers' duties with respect to "incidental findings" (IFs), discoveries that may be of high significance to a research subject though they lie outside the interest of the research that generates them. Some forms of biomedical research, such as genomic microarrays and full-body magnetic resonance imaging, generate very high rates of IFs; some studies suggest that IFs are yielded for nearly half of research subjects. Yet, Susan Wolf, Jordan Paradise, and Charlisse Caga-anan, law and medicine scholars at the University of Minnesota, observe that "[c]urrent law and federal regulations offer no direct guidance on how to deal with IFs in research, nor is there adequate professional or institutional guidance."[99]

It is not hard to imagine the potential tort claims to come. Harvard Medical School professor Charles Nelson relates the story of a student at a major research university who volunteered to submit to an MRI in the early 1990s at a time when the procedure was still experimental. Several years later, the student collapsed from a seizure and was rushed to an emergency room, where it was discovered that she had a brain tumor—a tumor that had gone undetected on the earlier MRI. As Nelson notes, "it is not unreasonable to think that if this scan had been read by a neuroradiologist, the tumor would have been spotted earlier," reducing the student's medical risks.[100] While medical researchers, unlike clinicians, "have until very recently been held to owe research participants few, if any, duties of clinical care enforceable in tort or contract law," Wolf, Paradise, and Caga-anan, in company with some other legal scholars, argue that researchers should have a legal duty to recognize, assess, and report potentially significant IFs to their research subjects.[101] Whatever courts eventually decide, the recent decisions in *Taus,* the Monster Study case, and *164 Mulberry Street* have started to build the foundation that will ensure that these questions will find their way into court.

In charting the future direction of tort law on campus, what is called for is surely not categorical barriers to court review of harmful behavior, such as found in the immunity doctrines that once shielded universities from liability. As with legal remedies for discrimination, speech suppression, and other misfeasance, judicial scrutiny of campus conduct causing injury is entirely compatible with academic freedom—if applied sensitively, with understanding of the competing values at stake. Requiring a university truck driver to obey the speed limit or a medical researcher to refrain from conducting experiments on human subjects without their informed consent poses little danger to the academic enterprise. But expanding tort scrutiny also poses particular risks for academic freedom. Inviting judges or jurors to determine the "reasonableness" of academic instruction, evaluation, research methods, and the like entails direct second-guessing and potentially profound influence over core academic functions. Recognizing expansive new legal duties of care relating to "incidental findings," for example, inevitably would shape academic research agendas by substantially increasing the cost of some kinds of medical research. As in the specific tort context of defamation, differentiating between lawful and negligent research methodologies—or, for that matter, between a highly demanding classroom demeanor and intentional infliction of emotional distress—will sometimes require enormously delicate judgments about appropriate academic conduct.

Fortunately, even under ordinary circumstances, tort law generally contemplates a balancing of costs and benefits in determining liability. Under negligence law, for example, an assessment of "reasonable" conduct ordinarily entails an assessment of the costs to a defendant of investing in greater safety. This framework readily permits courts to take account of the particular costs to academic actors of alternative courses of conduct, such as forgoing potentially valuable research or dampening the sharpness of academic criticism. But this requires that courts understand the ways universities operate and the potential impact and costs of decisions imposing liability. Judging from recent tort litigation involving colleges and universities, and the willingness of some courts to tread ever closer to recognizing a direct remedy for "educational malpractice," such sensitivity is in no way assured.

All of this perhaps casts new light on another of line of experiments reportedly undertaken by some of Professor Loftus's psychology students to demonstrate the malleability of human memory. According to a newspaper profile:

> In an extra-credit homework assignment, . . . Loftus' students went home and said to younger siblings things as simple as "Hey, do you remember the time you got lost in the mall when you were 5 years old?" and then recorded the ways in which the "memory" would take on a life of its own in the succeeding days, becoming more vivid, more detailed, with each conversation.[102]

The way things are going, those younger siblings may soon have lawyers competing for their attention.

CHAPTER **9**

Promises, Promises:
Contracts on Campus

When Professor Aleksandr Makarov began teaching at Cleveland Chiropractic College in Kansas City, he signed a contract that incorporated the college's faculty handbook into its terms. The faculty handbook, for its part, imposed on professors a duty to "treat each student with courtesy, respect, fairness and professionalism."

Professor Makarov likely didn't think twice about that feel-good clause—until a student sued him for violating it.

First-year chiropractic student Leonard Verni argued that, as a student, he was a third-party beneficiary of the contract between the college and its faculty members and, therefore, should be able to sue for an alleged breach of Professor Makarov's employment contract. What is even more surprising than that inventive argument is that Verni prevailed in two out of three Missouri courts.

The dispute started in 1999 when an anonymous fellow student accused Verni of selling Professor Makarov's exam questions to classmates before their impending dermatology exam. The college's student services director investigated and decided that Verni had indeed engaged in theft and academic dishonesty. In an appeals hearing at the school, Verni argued that he had written the questions himself, as Professor Makarov had suggested, and had thrown a copy of his very own questions into the trash. A student must have found those questions, Verni reasoned, and turned them over to the college, thinking that they had been sold to another. The appeals committee did not believe Verni's version of events either, and upheld his dismissal from the college.

So Verni filed suit in a Missouri state court. Among the fourteen counts that he brought against the college and his former professor, Verni charged that Professor Makarov had breached his own contract with the college, especially the part in the faculty handbook about the professor's duty to "treat each student with courtesy, respect, fairness and professionalism." It was the fairness part of the clause on which Verni relied especially. Verni claimed that Professor Makarov had used all of Verni's suggested test questions nearly verbatim but had not told investigators that he had. By not revealing this during the investigation, Verni argued, Makarov had flagrantly breached his contractual duty of "fairness" to students. Professor Makarov, for his part, flatly denied Verni's claims of authorship of his exam. He told the jury that, in fact, he had not received any test questions from Verni and therefore could not have used any of Verni's questions on his test.

It seemed improbable that Verni would win his lawsuit. He had an uphill battle not only because of the story he advanced against his professor's denials, but also because of the improbable legal theory on which he pinned his hopes. A St. Louis attorney who specializes in education law called Verni's third-party beneficiary approach "creative," explaining that he had "never [before] seen it used against a faculty member."[1]

Yet Verni's approach worked startingly well with Missouri jurors. They sided with Verni on his breach-of-contract action based on Professor Makarov's alleged breach of a promise to treat him fairly and awarded Verni $10,000 in damages. On appeal, Verni found the judges at Missouri's intermediate appellate court similarly sympathetic. All three judges who heard the appeal agreed that a student like Verni was legally entitled to sue a faculty member as a third-party beneficiary of the professor's employment contract with the school. The contract obviously was meant to benefit students, the court reasoned, because it included provisions mandating that faculty members spend at least forty hours per week on campus and at least five hours meeting with students during office hours. The judges also focused on the language of "duty" used in the faculty handbook—the duty to treat students with "courtesy, respect, fairness and professionalism"—and found that it, too, was plainly intended to benefit students. Students, therefore, were entitled to sue not only for the more quantifiable failure to hold office hours, but presumably also for the more qualitative failure to treat them with courtesy and respect, fairness and professionalism.

As for the professor's argument that a word like "fairness" wasn't easily defined and was therefore too vague to serve as grounds for a breach-of-contract action, the court was also unpersuaded. "The term 'fairness,'" the appellate court wrote in a sweeping declaration of student rights, "must be construed in the overall context of the employment agreement and the duty of faculty members to serve the interests of the students for whom the College exists." A jury is perfectly capable of deciding what is "fair" in the circumstances of professor–student interactions, the judges reasoned, so Verni's jury award should stand.[2]

The Missouri Supreme Court agreed to hear the case, and in 2007, for the first time in nearly seven years of litigation, Verni lost. Missouri's highest court found that the student was not a third-party beneficiary of Professor Makarov's contract with the college, because of the "strong presumption" in Missouri law that contracts are made solely for the parties named within them, and not to benefit outsiders.[3]

Verni ended up in the win column for colleges and universities, but they could take little comfort from it. For one thing, the first four judges who heard Verni's third-party contract claim, both at trial and first appeal, agreed that it was a winner, suggesting that the theory may yet have legs in other jurisdictions. Equally significant, the Missouri Supreme Court ultimately sided with the college and its professor on notably narrow grounds. The court did not laugh the claim out of court or preclude it on the broad ground that judicial enforcement of professorial "fairness" to students would trench on academic freedom. Instead, the matter was "resolved by examining the contract's language." Even assuming that "the faculty handbook is a binding part of the employment contract," the court ruled, the contract did not sufficiently vest students with standing to enforce its terms.[4] The supreme court's disagreement with the lower courts was therefore quite narrow and it joined them in treating the dispute as if it were any other commercial contract scrape. Moreover, it left open that the contract terms—presumably including the duty of fairness—could be enforced in an action between the parties to the contract.

Whatever the decision's implications for other campuses, it apparently inspired new prudence on the part of Cleveland Chiropractic College. Within a year of the supreme court's decision, any mention of a faculty five-hour office hour minimum or a duty to treat students with courtesy, respect, fairness, and professionalism had disappeared entirely from the online version of Cleveland Chiropractic's Faculty Handbook. Only a less potent version was left: a mention that ethical behavior, quality teaching, and a nurturing environment are all part of the college's "core values."[5]

A Brief History of Academic Contracts

Notwithstanding the novelty of Verni's attempted extension of contract law on campus—a student-as-third-party-beneficiary claim—more straightforward contract disputes have been around since the dawn of higher education in the United States. Given the frequency with which faculty and administrators were dispatched by early legislatures in periodic house-cleanings at state universities, this is not surprising. Disputes over the terms and conditions of faculty appointments—litigated by professors and colleges, rather than third parties—have been knocking around the courts at least since the Rev. John Bracken protested his removal as head of William and Mary's grammar school in 1790.[6] Yet, for most of that history, the courts' reluctance to rule against academic institutions was so strong that it sometimes seemed that faculty employment contracts were not worth the paper they were printed on. Even when a professor was summarily dismissed midway through a fixed-term contract, courts often found no remediable breach.[7] The courts' reluctance to recognize and enforce students' contract rights was even stronger, with many "complain[ing] that contract law is [simply] too inflexible either to capture the complexity of the student–university relationship or to provide sufficient latitude to institutional decision making."[8]

Court opinions today continue to make nods toward academic deference, especially when contract interpretation would invite second-guessing an institution's core "academic" judgments about such matters as tenure or graduation standards.[9] Yet, the wall of deference is crumbling fast, with some courts taking a narrower view of what counts as an "academic" judgment warranting deference and others rejecting the notion of deference altogether. More and more, courts are inclined to enforce academic contracts just as they would any other, with a contract for the delivery of educational services seen as legally no different from one for the sale of a lawn mower. As significant, courts today are often willing to find enforceable contracts leaping from sources that would have been unimaginable to older courts. As Ann Springer, associate counsel to the AAUP, writes, in recent years "[c]ourts have found promises or contracts to be included in documents such as: School catalogs, course catalogs, manuals, bulletins, handbooks, circulars, institutional regulations and policies, registration materials, degree requirements, and syllabi." And the list seems likely to grow. "As higher education institutions act more like corporations," Springer notes, "courts are more willing to see the policies and practices of institutions as 'contracts' with the 'customers' or 'clients' (students) regarding the quality of the 'product' (education)."[10]

The basic outlines of contract law are straightforward. An enforceable contract is formed when a mutually beneficial bargain is offered and accepted—a sum of cash for a car, for example, or a fixed salary for an employee's services. Contracts on some matters, such as the sale of a house, must be in writing, but contract law typically tolerates a good deal of informality. Oral agreements can be binding, for example, even if hard to prove. And even without an agreement in words, an enforceable bargain may be implied by the parties' conduct—as, for example, when a patient goes to see a doctor without first inquiring about the cost.

It is the very looseness of contract law that makes it so easily adapted to so many interactions and disputes. When express or implied contracts underlie dozens of everyday transactions, from purchasing a cup of coffee to borrowing a library book, it is not hard to see the potential for contract claims in virtually any campus dispute. With notions of academic abstention in retreat, the new judicial receptivity is encouraging a proliferation of contract litigation. And with it, academic relationships long governed by loose and pliable internal norms are being remade according to the more rigid and exacting demands of contractual entitlement. Matters once committed to the discretion of university administrators may now be resolved by a judge's eagle-eyed parsing of campus handbooks or policy memoranda.

Faculty Contracts: Minding Your P's and Q's—and S's

In 1999, Dr. Marc Sackman, a music professor, came up for tenure at upstate New York's Alfred University, a school that prides itself on being the second-oldest coeducational college in the United States. Alfred University's tenure-track professors are evaluated on scholarly activity, student advising, campus service, and teaching ability. It was that last category that apparently was Sackman's downfall; his "evaluation indicated a weakness in teaching skills."[11] The votes did not go well for Sackman. The chair of the music department came down against tenure, followed by the promotion and tenure committee and Sackman's dean. Sackman then met with the promotion and tenure committee, which stood by its decision. Sackman appealed to the university's faculty council, which sent the case back to the tenure and promotion committee for further review. The committee, looking at the file for a third time, again found that Sackman's "lack of demonstrated excellent teaching prohibited a recommendation of tenure." The dean again advised the provost to deny tenure and the provost made the same recommendation to the university president, who agreed. The unfortunate process seemed to have run its course.

But Sackman did not give up. Instead he went to court, arguing that the university's action breached his employment contract and was "arbitrary and capricious," in violation of New York administrative law. Sackman's tenure file then landed on the desk of a New York state trial judge, James Euken, formerly the county district attorney. Euken began his opinion with the usual gesture of obeisance to academic authorities. "This court has limited authority to review a tenure decision made by Alfred University in accordance with its [Faculty] Handbook," he wrote. Courts should tread only " 'with the greatest caution and restraint[] in such sensitive areas as faculty appointment, promotion, and tenure,' " Euken emphasized. But here it was appropriate, he warned, for the court to ensure that the university "complied with its own rules," including the provisions of the faculty handbook. "The court may not substitute its judgment for the judgment and discretion of Alfred University, but may determine whether Alfred University's action in denying tenure to Dr. Sackman violated the Handbook and was arbitrary and capricious."[12]

On this basis, Judge Euken concluded that Sackman was entitled to a "do over" of the entire tenure review based on the court's "interpretation of an unambiguous provision in the Handbook." The problem, Euken explained, was that the department chair had based his negative evaluation of Sackman's teaching only on "student responses (written, verbal, and course evaluations); music colleagues; colleagues from the Performing Arts Division; and his own observations including an observation of Dr. Sackman's Fundamentals I class." Yet, "[t]he handbook provides that the chairperson shall, through classroom visitations and other means, keep up-to-date on the capabilities of each member." Sackman, the court observed, had received only one "classroom visitation" from the department chair during the year in which his file was reviewed. "This court cannot rewrite the handbook by providing that no classroom visitation or only one classroom visitation is sufficient for an evaluation," the court wrote. "Classroom visitations," it added definitely, "mean[s] two or more."[13] Though Sackman was not contractually entitled to tenure itself— "[t]enure was not part of the agreement" between Sackman and the university, the court noted—he was entitled to a tenure review based upon more than one "visitation" to the classroom.

The result in *Sackman* was nominally grounded in New York's administrative law, but its reasoning reflects a broader readiness of courts to treat academic handbooks, policies, and guidelines as legally binding and judicially enforceable. Another New York court, for example, found that an internal memorandum from a provost to a dean concerning departmental tenure standards constituted a contract enforceable by a tenure candidate.[14] Even a boast in a promotional brochure or an incautious remark in a faculty meeting or at a recruiting dinner can potentially give rise to an enforceable contract.[15]

Sackman also shows just how wooden judicial understanding of academic policies can be, and shows the potential hazards of turning campus handbooks, bulletins, brochures, and e-mails over to judges for the purpose of contract interpretation. In Sackman's case, an apparent multilayered tenure evaluation, taking into account multiple forms of student feedback, faculty peer review, and the chair's own classroom observations, was deemed legally defective on the basis of an "s" in a single sentence in the faculty handbook. Even if additional class visits might have been the better course in the view of most deans and faculty, the evidence seems thin that Sackman's chair failed in his obligation to keep "up-to-date" on Sackman's abilities "though classroom visits and other means."

Nonetheless, when faculty dismissals are at stake, the resort to contract law is readily understandable and often appropriate. In 2007, for example, five tenured professors at Denver's Metropolitan State University challenged a revision of the faculty handbook that eliminated previously promised protections for tenured faculty in the event of a reduction in force. A Colorado appellate court agreed that the professors had stated a plausible claim for breach of contract and sent the case on for trial. Law professor Matthew Finkin, a leading scholar on tenure and academic freedom, had testified as an expert in the case that the policy change "eviscerate[d] tenure," and contract law provided the hook to resist the diminution of academic freedom.[16] Certainly, if a professor is abruptly fired without cause in the middle of a fixed-term contract, as happened to the unfortunate Bolivar Head at the University of Missouri in 1860, he should have a legal remedy.[17] And, yet, courts have found that opening the door to legitimate faculty contract claims has inevitably encouraged litigation of seemingly more dubious claims of injury.

In Salkin v. Case Western Reserve University, for example, a business school professor sued his university after his department chair assigned him to teach a course he preferred not to teach. The professor, Harvey Salkin, insisted that the course assignment violated what he said was a contractual promise by a former dean that he would only be required to teach "mutually agreeable courses." But an Ohio appeals court ruled that a memorandum the professor had made memorializing his conversation years earlier with the former dean did not constitute an enforceable contract and that the professor would have to teach the courses the school assigned. Since he was already contractually obligated to teach classes at the time he struck his bargain with the former dean, the court decided, he had given no new "consideration" that would make the dean's promise legally binding.[18] In other contexts, negotiations over course assignments *can* give rise to enforceable contracts. An untenured college math instructor in Louisiana, for example, was found to have stated a plausible breach-of-contract claim for the loss of a promised summer teaching assignment. The college's protest that there was no signed agreement evidencing the promise was brushed aside as a matter for the jury.[19]

Determining whether an enforceable contract exists is, of course, only the first challenge; courts can then find themselves facing ticklish questions of interpretation. A California court, for example, was confronted with a dispute over the meaning of a provision in a settlement agreement committing the professor-parties to create a "nurturing environment" within an academic department. The professor-plaintiff argued that his colleagues at the University of California Riverside Graduate School of Management had been far from nurturing: he claimed that they had excluded him from department affairs, had failed to promote him, had awarded him inadequate research funds, and had simply assigned him too much work. (In a surprising twist, both parties to the contract had apparently relied on the clause—the professor's dean had stopped the professor's summer pay as punishment for the professor's own failure to contribute to the department's "nurturing environment.") But the court ultimately managed to dodge the interpretive challenge by finding that the professor first needed to exhaust his remedies within the university, suggesting that the meaning of a contractual term as subjective as "nurturing" was probably best sorted out on campus.[20] In a similar vein, an earlier North Carolina court managed to avoid deciding whether a music professor had lived up to a contract provision requiring college faculty to build an "esprit de corps second to none."[21]

The courts' new willingness to enforce campus obligations through contract law does not, of course, always work to the benefit of employees. In some cases, universities have been the ones to press contract claims for their own advantage. For example, when a philosophy professor sued Yale University for breach of contract after she was denied tenure, Yale turned the argument around, successfully moving to dismiss the suit on the ground that she had breached *her* contractual obligations in the faculty handbook to first exhaust all remedies through the university's grievance process.[22]

Even more aggressively, a California community college in 2008 successfully sued one of its professors for breaching his sabbatical leave agreement. In his application for a sabbatical, the professor had stated his intention to use the year to research and write a book about "the effectiveness of the tactics and strategies used by the United States and the Soviet Union during the Cold War." When the year was up, and the professor was able to produce what the court called only "a minimally revised version" of his decade-old dissertation, the college sued to force him to pay back his sabbatical salary. The California appeals court seemed to relish the chance to decide whether the professor had earned his keep on sabbatical or, as is so often suspected by those outside of academic life, had spent the ten months lounging. The court concluded that the professor had not kept up his end of the sabbatical bargain and ordered him to repay the year's salary.[23]

As expansive as contract law has become in governing university–faculty relations, there is often a genuine contract—the employment contract—lurking somewhere beneath the growing mass of claims. When it comes to student claims, however, putting a finger on the governing contract is often more of a challenge. As law professor Hazel Glenn Beh, herself a proponent of student contract rights, acknowledges, "[t]he complex relationship between the student and the university is largely implied rather than explicitly stated, thus making it difficult for courts to determine the contractual terms of the apparent 'contract.'"[24] Nonetheless, this difficulty has not deterred students from asserting contract claims—or, increasingly, courts from accepting them.

The "$200,000 Contract": Student Contract Rights

In his junior year at Duke University, Andrew Giuliani, son of former New York City mayor Rudy Giuliani, was "shocked" to be suspended from the varsity golf team. True, the coach had accused him of various trifling misconduct—acting disrespectfully to a trainer, throwing clubs, roughing up teammates in a football game, tossing an apple into the face of a teammate, and gunning his car engine and speeding out of the golf course parking lot. He had not "quibble[d]" over these charges and had apologized to his teammates. Yet coach Orrin D. Vincent III nevertheless booted him from the team and forced him to stay off unless all of his teammates supported his return. They did not. Even his parking privileges at the golf course were revoked.[25]

In July 2008, Giuliani hastened to federal court in Durham and sued the university and his former coach. His suspension and loss of golfing privileges, he argued, breached his contract with Duke; Coach Vincent should also be held individually liable for tortiously interfering with Giuliani's contractual relationship with the university. Giuliani demanded damages to compensate him for the impairment of future earning capacity as a professional golfer and an order immediately restoring his golfing privileges now and for the rest of his life.

At the same time, Giuliani's complaint made clear that there was a much larger principle at stake than merely his own interests: "Through this action, Andrew not only seeks to vindicate his rights but also those of his fellow students, so that Duke University may no longer insist that its students do not enjoy the same basic rights of contract that are shared by every other citizen who enters into a contract in this state."[26]

Giuliani, in other words, wanted to establish that the university–student relationship is amenable to judicial policing on precisely the same terms as the ordinary commercial relation between shopkeepers and customers. The implications of his legal theory were large indeed, particularly in light of the diffuse nature of the "contract" he asserted. The source of his claimed rights was what he styled "a $200,000 contract" effectively shared in common with all Duke students. "Upon his enrollment at Duke University, Andrew and Duke University entered into an agreement," his complaint postulated. "The Agreement required Andrew to pay Duke University roughly $200,000 in tuition and fees and by definition required him to forego numerous opportunities at other colleges and universities that compete with Duke for top student-athletes. In exchange, the University promised to provide Andrew with various educational services, lodging, and a right of access to the Athletic Department's Varsity program and facilities."[27] The sprawling "Contract" was said to encompass as well all terms found in the Duke University Student-Athlete Handbook, the Duke University Athletic Department Policy Manual, the Duke University Student Bulletin, and the NCAA Division I Manual.[28]

The university breached this contract, he argued, when it ejected him from the golf squad for petty misconduct; under "the Contract," Giuliani insisted, only "a serious felony" or "certain conduct specifically enumerated in the Contract" can provide grounds for ouster from a varsity sport.[29] Moreover, the coach's "bizarre scheme" to consult Giuliani's teammates about his possible reinstatement was not specifically authorized by any provision of "the Contract or any University handbook, manual, or governing document[]"; indeed, "[t]he only University document that is consistent with O. D. Vincent's scheme," Giuliani added smartly, "is the library's copy of William Goulding's [sic] *The Lord of the Flies.*"[30]

It might be tempting to chalk off Giuliani's lawsuit as simply the antic of one particular high-maintenance, celebrity student. A federal magistrate was clearly unimpressed.[31] But, then again, some seasoned observers have suggested that a similar high-maintenance, entitlement mentality pervades much of the present generation of college students.[32] In fact, some have cited the surging consumer expectations of today's college students as a reason for expanding their contract rights on campus.[33] Whatever becomes of Giuliani's lawsuit, it is worth considering the premise of his legal theory because it reflects the nature of many student contract claims today.

In one sense, Giuliani's invocation of the "$200,000 contract" encompassing the entire implicit bargain between a university and its students is essentially instinctive and free-wheeling. The very looseness of the claim recalls something of the argument advanced by Dennis Denuto, a hopelessly unprepared lawyer in the Australian film *The Castle*. Pressed by a skeptical court to state the legal basis for his improbable claim that an airport authority lacked eminent domain power over neighboring properties, he stammered, "[I]t's the Constitution . . . it's justice, it's law, it's the vibe and—No, that's it. It's the vibe."[34]

Yet, paradoxically, Giuliani's conception of the contract rights of a university and its students is simultaneously breathtakingly rigid and narrow. It would apparently reduce all exercise of university authority to specifically enumerated contractual powers. Coach Vincent, for example, was said to be unable to consult teammates because there was "[n]othing in the Contract or any University handbook, manual, or governing documents" specifically authorizing him to do so. Giuliani found "amazing" Duke's suggestion that the coach's decisions about the golf roster fell within the university's " 'significant authority.' "[35]

Giuliani has company. The rapid flight to ethereal claims of contract rights, and simultaneous readiness to parse policy binders, mission statements, and handbooks to define the precise metes and bounds of campus authority, can be seen in innumerable recent student lawsuits. A University of Pennsylvania law student, for example, sued to enforce an alleged contractual agreement by a professor to allow him to argue *both* sides of a moot court case, contrary to law school convention. The argumentative student fought his battle, unsuccessfully, all the way to the U.S. Supreme Court.[36] The following year, a dental student sued for breach of contract after her professor allegedly demeaned her work in front of other students and "carried on in a conspicuously disgruntled manner" during an exam—all, she said, in violation of the school's code of conduct.[37]

In 2005, a frustrated student sued his alma mater for breach of contract on the ground that some of his professors had reused their old exam questions during his time at the university. Recycling exam questions, the student argued, breached a contractual promise in the school bulletin that faculty would "not tolerate academic dishonesty." After an Ohio court rejected the claim, he apparently sought to litigate it a second time two years later, with no more success.[38] In 2006, a psychology student challenged his dismissal from a Ph.D. program for alleged clinical errors and absences, "egregious plagiarism," failure to disclose two arrests, and misrepresenting his credentials as a breach of the university's contractual promise to give him a degree.[39] And in a possible warning of things to come for universities entering the world of distance learning, a student in 2008 sued her online school for breach of contract when her professors failed to respond to her e-mails as promptly as promised in its course catalog.[40]

Many of these student contract claims still fail, of course. In particular, courts remain wary of " 'any attempt to repackage an educational malpractice claim as a contract claim' because the policy concerns militating against educational malpractice also exist in contract claims which attack the general quality of education."[41] Yet, courts are growing more sympathetic to student legal claims even in this context. As with tort claims involving educational malpractice, courts today are defining the scope of nonjusticiable "academic" matters more narrowly.

In addition, in a significant signal of shifting attitudes, appellate courts have begun reinstating contract claims screened out by trial courts found to have deferred excessively to university authorities. A North Carolina appeals court, for example, reinstated a medical resident's breach of contract action based on a university hospital's failure to give him a promised gynecology rotation.[42] In an Ohio case, a doctoral student in music theory sued the University of Cincinnati for breach of contract after failing all three sections of his comprehensive oral examination. He challenged the theoretical approaches used by faculty members on his committee—contending, for example, that he was "disadvantage[d] because Professor Wheaton's method of Schenkerian analysis was different from the method he had been trained in by Komar"—and protested that one of the five committee members had not attended the session because of a dental emergency. An appeals court reversed a deferential trial court ruling for the university and found that the university had in fact breached a contract with the student, memorialized in the student bulletin, when it conducted the oral exam with only four faculty evaluators. "Here, the contract specified five members for the oral examination board," the court concluded, "but there were only four present to administer the re-examination to appellant." Even though three of the four faculty members believed the student had failed each part of his exam (the fourth faculty member had abstained from voting), the court sent the case back for a new oral exam and for an assessment of the student's monetary damages.[43]

Similarly, when a Columbia University student brought a twenty-six-count, kitchen-sink challenge to his dismissal on plagiarism charges, a federal trial court dismissed the entire action, only to be reversed on appeal. The federal appeals court in Manhattan held that the student was entitled to go forward with claims for contract breaches "resulting from the University's failure to provide a sufficient number of sections of a required course, a . . . professor's failure to grade a late term paper, and because Plaintiff was required to take a final examination although he claims to have been ill."[44]

Course syllabi are yet another new source of student contract claims. In 2007, for example, the University of Massachusetts at Amherst undergraduate Brian Marquis sued the university and his philosophy teaching assistant alleging that the "Defendants breached the contract (course syllabus) when they failed to . . . calculate final letter grades" in the manner suggested by the syllabus.[45] A Howard University law student had made the same claim in 2002. In both cases the claims were unsuccessful (in the Howard case, the court held that even if the syllabus was a contract, the student's claim was barred by the applicable statute of limitations).[46] Yet, the legal danger is palpable enough that the AAUP has advised faculty to "take precautions" to avoid exposing themselves to contractual liability: "When drafting course descriptions, syllabi and other documents, be aware of the way intentions are framed. Reflect that course content and discussion will be flexible to some extent, and try not to set expectations that can't be met . . . [L]anguage providing . . . guarantees ('this course will cover all American history from x to y,' or 'this course will prepare students for x licensing test') creates a sense of entitlement that may be problematic." The AAUP further suggested that "[f]aculty may also want to label their syllabi as 'preliminary' or 'proposed,' and may want to include language explaining the timeframes/order of topics/specific readings/etc. discussed therein may change over the semester as necessary."[47]

And, yet, as Vanderbilt University learned, even the clearest disclaimers may prove incapable of heading off a student and court intent on finding a contract. In Atria v. Vanderbilt University, the pre-med student who argued that a disciplinary hearing finding him guilty of academic dishonesty had breached his contract rights under "the Honor Council's procedural rules, as embodied in the Student Handbook" won the right to a jury trial. He had claimed, in addition to his test-turnback complaints, that he was contractually entitled to present polygraph evidence of his innocence, though the council excluded such evidence as unreliable. Even though the trial court had held that "dismissal of Atria's breach of contract claim was necessary because a federal court is an inappropriate forum in which to challenge academic matters," the U.S. Court of Appeals for the Sixth Circuit "disagree[d] with the district court's characterization of this claim as one challenging academic matters," and held that a jury should decide whether Vanderbilt breached its contractual duties to Atria.

Moreover, *Atria* held that a jury could find a valid contract based on the student handbook notwithstanding that the handbook itself expressly stated that its policies "do not constitute a contract"; the court held that, even so, "its provisions may be enforced" on the theory that it somehow created "an implied contract." The court further held that a jury could find an implied contractual entitlement to present polygraph evidence because "[n]either Vanderbilt's Student Handbook nor the [honor appeals panel's] rules of procedures . . . *expressly prohibit* a petitioner from submitting polygraph evidence."[48] Even though the handbook (which disclaimed being a contract) said nothing about polygraph evidence, and even though the court conceded that "the reliability of polygraph exams is questionable at best," the court held that a jury could infer that the university's allowance of hearsay evidence implied a right to present other forms of unreliable evidence under the noncontract handbook.[49]

The Sixth Circuit's reasoning in *Atria* is a striking demonstration of just how far courts have traveled from their traditional reluctance to find and enforce contract rights in an academic setting. Even so, it is surely not the *most* astonishing demonstration. For all the breaks Nicklaus Atria received from the appellate court in his case, he was still required to go on to medical school, earn his degree, and hold down a job if he wanted to earn a living as a medical doctor. In one notable recent case, however, a Florida court found that an aspiring doctor was contractually entitled to collect his expected standard of living directly from the university that had failed to graduate him.

Great Expectations: Entitlements and Earning Potential

Keith Sharick was a medical student at Florida's Southeastern University of the Health Sciences, studying for a degree in osteopathic medicine. He was in his final few months of school when he failed a rural rotation in general medicine at a community health center. Sharick's superiors noted that he could not identify "fundamental signs and symptoms of diabetes mellititus," had "failed to examine the abdomen and suprapubic area of a woman complaining of abdominal pain," had "raised the skirt of a female patient without informing her" in advance, and had "consistently failed to review charts properly prior to interacting" with patients.[50] Eventually, he was dismissed from the school. The university found that "he didn't have the basic understanding that he should have as a fourth-year medical student," and, as the university's lawyer would explain later, "did not have the requisite skill to become a doctor at that point."[51]

Keith Sharick answered back, in effect, that the university did not have a basic understanding of the new legal environment; he sued for breach of an implied contract to graduate him. He drew the relevant contractual guarantee from a scrap of text found in the preface to the student handbook, stating that the course of study at the school was a "four year curriculum *leading to the DO degree*."[52] Sharick convinced a jury that the decision to dismiss him was arbitrary and capricious—before failing the rotation, he had a grade point average of 83.2 percent and was ranked seventy-fifth in his class of 104 students—and the jury awarded him partial tuition reimbursement.

But Sharick wanted a good deal more than that. He argued that any damages awarded to him should include his future earnings as a doctor, salary that he would have earned as a practitioner had the university delivered on the promised "DO degree." So he appealed his case to the Florida appellate court.

Sharick's fortunes continued to rise. "We agree with Sharick," the appellate court wrote, "that the value of a professional degree, particularly to a prospective physician who has successfully completed the overwhelming majority of the academic and clinical requirements, significantly exceeds the tuition costs expended." Accordingly, Sharick was entitled to ask a jury to determine how much he would have earned in the future as a doctor if only the university had fulfilled its contractual duty to graduate him.

The university attempted a further appeal, asking that the case be reconsidered by all ten judges on the appellate court. But the full court denied review and, in doing so, took the somewhat unusual step of issuing opinions along with its refusal to hear the case. One opinion supporting the denial of rehearing went out of its way to shred the university's argument that courts should review academic decisions deferentially—self-consciously, as one commentator later noted, "plow[ing] over icons that universities have held dear for decades."[53] Judicial deference to universities, the concurring opinion emphasized, is "now disfavored because it no longer represents contemporary values." And, as if to hoist the university on its own academic petard, the opinion drew support from law review articles—pointedly, in the judge's words, "the product of the same university system being sued here"—that were critical of past judges for failing to intervene aggressively in student–university cases: " 'The deeply rooted hostility toward student claims and judicial deference to university conduct becomes increasingly less defensible as bottom-line, commercial concerns motivate university actions and students seek a more consumer friendly product.' "

Given what the judge took to be the new commercial reality of American higher education, he wrote that "[t]he best analogy to Sharick's situation can be found in cases where new businesses assert lost profits as consequential damages for breach of contract."[54]

Florida lawyers readily recognized that *Sharick* had significant implications for future actions brought by students, especially the "unusual" holding permitting students to sue universities for their future earning potential.[55] But Sharick was not yet finished. There was still the matter of calculating damages. At some point after the appeals court's denial of rehearing, the medical school, changing its mind on Sharick's fitness to practice medicine, offered him a deal to drop his case: a settlement that would award him $785,000 and his medical degree. But Sharick would have none of it and believed his would-be future as a doctor had an even greater value. His own attorney asked that the court appoint someone to look after Sharick's interests, implying that only someone who was not in his right mind would reject such an offer,[56] but the guardian *ad litem* found Sharick perfectly competent. Sharick was permitted to renounce the settlement offer and try his luck with a jury.

In February 2008, jurors finally heard evidence on what Sharick could have earned as an osteopathic physician and ordered the medical school to pay him $4.3 million to make good on his lost earning potential.[57] Sharick, it turned out, had been uncommonly shrewd—or just plain lucky—in holding out for more.[58]

By turning down his lawyer's advice, Sharick both padded his bank account and earned a spot on the radar screen of every university general counsel across the country. Sharick's case provided a frightening precedent for campus lawyers on multiple fronts. First, it advanced the trend of finding enforceable contract rights embedded in handbooks and manuals, finding a legal right in a seemingly innocuous line in a handbook preface. Second, it obliterated the traditional distinction between legal claims challenging "academic" judgments and those addressed to nonacademic concerns. Third, it expressly rejected the idea of special judicial deference to university judgments in any context by equating academic and commercial enterprises. And, fourth, it recognized a new and potentially expansive measure of liability, entitling students to recover their expected future incomes from their colleges if their academic aspirations are thwarted.

Even before the final jury award, Scott D. Makar, then a Jacksonville attorney who became Florida's solicitor general, observed that *Sharick* seemed to turn a corner in the law governing student–university relationships. The court's decision "touches on many issues of the day affecting colleges, universities and their students in disciplinary matters: due process, implied contracts, remedies, and the role of the judiciary in academic judgments," he wrote. "It is also (perhaps unknowingly) on the cusp of a judicial trend that views institutions of higher learning as not significantly different from other commercial ventures that serve a consumer dominated society." By tapping into so many developing currents in the field, the case was "an education law professor's dream."

But it was also plainly a university counsel's nightmare. The practical lessons of the case for counsel, Makar suggested, included (1) that "commercialism and formalism" would increasingly define future student–university relations; (2) that colleges and universities face mounting liability costs under expansive new theories of contract damages; and (3) that academic institutions should try as hard as possible to "avoid courts, which increasingly are inhospitable to traditional notions of academic deference."[59]

Yet, as sensible as that advice appears, colleges and universities are likely to find it increasingly difficult to keep themselves out of court. Indeed, campus disputants are learning that it is not even necessary actually to *have* a contractual agreement to make use of contract principles in court. Simply relying on a promise or an established campus custom, under the right circumstances, can give rise to legally enforceable rights.

Promises without Contracts

Even when a contract is never actually formed, the law sometimes allows an equitable remedy—a sort of sympathetic safety net—for people who rely to their detriment on the promises of others. Sometimes described as a "quasi-contract," the doctrine of "promissory estoppel" is both loose and intuitive. If you raise expectations or make promises on which others reasonably rely, the law may hold you to your promise if injustice would otherwise result. In short, "[p]romissory estoppel developed in order to protect reliance on a broken promise in the absence of a contract."[60]

The doctrine has had its critics through the years. Grant Gilmore, a leading theorist of contract law, famously charged that promissory estoppel and similar doctrines were to blame for "the death of contract" by blurring the law of enforceable promises.[61] But the doctrine's very malleability has made it a temptingly useful backstop in sympathetic cases where the elements of an enforceable contract are not quite satisfied. Indeed, all evidence suggests that, like the universe itself, the doctrine of promissory estoppel is constantly expanding.[62] Clearly, promissory estoppel claims have become increasingly popular in campus disputes, opening an important new route for legal regulation of academic life.

Consider the case of Robert Natelson, the conservative University of Montana law professor whose quest to teach constitutional law spurred claims of political viewpoint discrimination. Natelson, who had been hired primarily to teach property law courses, had long desired to branch out into constitutional law. Yet when an opening to teach the course arose, the dean passed him over and opened a nationwide search for a new hire. Natelson complained to the university president that he was the victim of political discrimination, and the university president appointed a Montana lawyer to conduct a hearing on the controversy and issue a recommendation.

The lawyer, Donald Robinson, passed over Natelson's claim of discrimination and ruled in his favor based on the doctrine of promissory estoppel. Robinson found that there had been a loose "custom and practice" at Montana's law school of giving existing faculty members first crack at any course openings. "That promise or assurance was relied upon by Professor Natelson" when he invested his energies over the years in building expertise in constitutional law in the hopes of one day teaching the course, the lawyer explained. Although the "custom and practice" did not amount to an enforceable contract, Robinson reasoned, it sufficiently raised Natelson's expectations to give him an enforceable right to claim the course. The next day, the university president followed Robinson's recommendation and ordered the dean to assign the course to Natelson.[63]

Natelson's claim to teach the constitutional law course was not resolved by a court, but it was resolved by a lawyer on the basis of Montana law—Robinson cited Montana Supreme Court precedent on the doctrine of promissory estoppel—in a quasi-judicial proceeding. And Robinson's rationale for upholding Natelson's claim of entitlement shows clearly the potential power of quasi-contract and other equitable doctrines to encroach deeply into decisions once thought left entirely to the discretion of deans or other campus authorities. Robinson acknowledged that the "custom and practice" on which Natelson relied was "not very extensive, nor had it been applied in any extraordinary number of instances"; yet it was sufficiently well understood to make Natelson's expectations reasonable—and enforceable. In the past, such departmental norms and expectations might operate as a constraint on decanal power, but the sanctions for violating expectations would be purely informal, worked out through the give-and-take of faculty politics. Now, these norms and expectations might give rise to legally enforceable rights through principles of "quasi-contract."

The expansiveness of promissory estoppel doctrine makes it serviceable for nearly any campus dispute. Four examples—involving claims by a dean, a professor, a student, and even college trustees—show its all-around utility.

In the case of the trustees, promissory estoppel featured in the recent battle for control over the future of Dartmouth College. Nearly two centuries after the Supreme Court repelled the New Hampshire legislature's attempt to seize control of Dartmouth's board, some libertarian-minded Dartmouth alumni mounted their own effort to gain control by electing a succession of "insurgent" alumni trustees. Alumni were reportedly unhappy over campus policies they saw as prioritizing research over undergraduate teaching and imposing a "de facto" speech code; some were said to be further exercised because "[s]everal fraternities ha[d] been punished for infractions, and the football team ha[d] done poorly in recent years."[64] In 2007, when the college announced plans to blunt the insurgency by enlarging the size of the board from eighteen to twenty-six trustees, thereby diluting alumni representation, the Dartmouth Association of Alumni fired back with a lawsuit. The group alleged that the college's effort to trim their influence breached an 1891 deal guaranteeing alumni half the seats on the board of trustees. Even if the 1891 arrangement was not an enforceable contract, the alumni argued, the parties' dealings over the next 116 years had established an implied contract fixing alumni influence or amounted to a promise of influence that Dartmouth could not renounce under promissory estoppel. Dartmouth's "promises have induced [alumni] . . . to undertake substantial detriments from which it has benefitted," the alumni argued, "and . . . it would be manifestly unjust to permit the College to disregard its promises at the expense of the settled expectations of its benefactors."[65] The case was dropped the next year only because alumni hostile to the insurgency gained control of the alumni association that filed the suit.

In Nye v. University of Delaware, promissory estoppel was again invoked, this time on behalf of a dean who was not reappointed to a third five-year term. Anticipating his reappointment, the dean and his wife had made plans to build a large new home suitable for entertaining. Before launching construction, the dean had approached the university president and asked about his prospects for reappointment. Based on the president's assurances, the dean and his wife went forward with building plans. Later that year, however, resistance developed and the dean was not reappointed. Still worse, months later, before he could take his promised year of administrative leave, the dean died suddenly of a brain hemorrhage—a tragedy his widow blamed on stress caused by his non-reappointment. His widow sued the university, both for herself and her husband's estate, arguing that she and her husband had reasonably relied on the president's assurances in building their new house. The court initially agreed that these facts supported a possible claim for promissory estoppel and also agreed that she was entitled to press a contract claim to collect her husband's salary for the administrative leave he never enjoyed, based on what she said was an "unwritten policy" at the university guaranteeing displaced deans a year of paid leave as deferred compensation for past administrative service.[66]

Faculty have similarly invoked promissory estoppel in a wide range of disputes over their appointments or job conditions. For example, in

Suddith v. University of Southern Mississippi, the university brought John Suddith to campus with the promise of a tenure-track faculty position and then changed its mind after learning that he had had an affair with a student at his previous college. Suddith sued for promissory estoppel, seeking to hold the university to its earlier promise of the appointment. In 2007, a Mississippi appellate court agreed that the claim had surface appeal but ultimately rejected it, finding that the discovery of the affair made the university's change of heart reasonable.[67]

Finally, promissory estoppel has proved to be an increasingly fertile ground for student claims. In 2008, for example, Yale's art school sought to expel a teen prodigy from its MFA program. Annabel Osberg had enrolled in college at age fourteen and been admitted to Yale's graduate program at age seventeen, but midway through her first year in the program, Yale is said to have concluded that she was too immature for the MFA program after all and sent her home. Osberg sued Yale for promissory estoppel and breach of contract, contending that she had moved across the country in reliance on Yale's implicit representation that she was fit for the program and that Yale had not lived up to certain procedural promises in attempting to expel her.[68] In early 2009, a trial court in Connecticut allowed Osberg's claims based on promissory estoppel and breach of contract to continue over Yale's arguments that they should be stricken.[69]

Even so, Osberg's lawsuit may not ultimately survive. The discovery of any new information about her maturity level and artistic readiness for the program after she arrived on campus, as in Suddith's case, depending on the facts, might be found to justify a change in the university's initial enthusiasm. But her case reflects the sort of claim that commentators believe—and some hope—will be more common in the years ahead: suits to hold colleges and universities to the expectations they raise through their student marketing and promotions. In 2007, as just one example, a front-page story in the *Wall Street Journal* reported on growing pressure on law schools to be more forthright in describing the difficult job prospects their students may face after graduation. The story quoted a number of recent graduates from middle-tier schools who were disgruntled that the big-money Wall Street jobs that lured them to law school were nowhere to be found after graduation. "Now," the *Journal* reported, "debate is intensifying among law-school academics over the integrity of law schools' marketing campaigns."[70]

Indeed, one of the schools mentioned in the story, Brooklyn Law School, had already faced a student lawsuit over placement figures it had reported to *U.S. News & World Report* for the magazine's annual ranking of law schools. While a federal court in New York turned down that suit—one that had alleged fraud and, rather fantastically, a conspiracy in violation of federal racketeering law—lawsuits grounded in contract law or promissory estoppel may well hold greater promise.[71] In fact, some courts have already laid the foundation for future litigation by recognizing that promotional representations, at least if they are not so vague as to be considered mere "puffery," can be legally enforced.[72] Given the explosion of aggressive marketing directed at prospective students, some commentators see this as a particularly ripe area for future legal claims. Even faculty Web-page biographies have recently come under close scrutiny on at least one campus for fear of potential fraud claims by students.[73] "After all, students potentially have foregone other opportunities and purchased an educational product based on promises and on representations that the institution made to induce them to enroll," writes law professor Hazel Glenn Beh. "Ignoring the consumer nature of the relationship allows the institution too much discretion."[74]

The reach of promissory estoppel into college and university life surely will not stop there. Given the enormous versatility of promissory estoppel, and its ready invocation any time a disappointed student, professor, or administrator can claim to have reasonably relied on a promise or shared expectation of a better result, all indications are that promissory estoppel claims will continue to extend into every nook and cranny of campus life.

To some, this ongoing proliferation of contract and quasi-contract claims on campus reflects a deeply troubling trend and a mounting threat to healthy academic relationships and, ultimately, to academic freedom. To others, it comes not a moment too soon. Peter Berkowitz, an assistant professor at Harvard before being denied tenure, wrote in the *Chronicle of Higher Education* after his tenure denial that the real threat to academic freedom came from "the shielding of colleges from the ordinary requirements of contract law." Berkowitz related how the Massachusetts courts had turned aside his own breach-of-contract suit against Harvard based on its rejection of his tenure grievance. Excessive deference to academic institutions had "turn[ed] colleges into islands of lawlessness," he wrote. "For when courts abdicate their responsibility to enforce contracts, the established powers can be counted on to impose their will by rooting out dissenting opinions, rewarding friends and allies, and rigging decisions about who gets what."[75]

Andrew Giuliani couldn't have said it better. And all indications are that courts are coming around.

CHAPTER 10

Looking Forward

Richard Peltz, a tenured law professor at the University of Arkansas in Little Rock, is an expert on the First Amendment and freedom of information law. He has written and lectured widely on laws authorizing public access to government meetings and records and is a coauthor of a volume on the Arkansas Freedom of Information Act. His work to open government doors and keep information flowing won him the Arkansas Press Association's Freedom of Information award in 2006.[1]

Ironically, it was that same freedom of information law that gave the *Arkansas Democrat-Gazette* newspaper access to Peltz's university e-mails, allowing readers an insider's look at his frustration after some of his students accused him of being a racist.

"That I have not already sued my detractors in defamation represents a hearty measure of generosity on my part," Peltz wrote to his associate dean in an undated e-mail.[2] But his generosity did not last.

On March 7, 2008, Professor Peltz filed a defamation lawsuit against two students and the University of Arkansas chapter of the Black Law Students Association (BLSA), arguing that the students and members of the group had wrongly accused him of racism.[3] Peltz asked for punitive damages.

The lawsuit sprang from a standard academic event also mentioned on Peltz's vita: "Panelist, *Affirmative Action, Diversity, and the Constitution*, UALR Black Law Students Association, Oct. 2005." There is, of course, disagreement about what transpired that day and at the events that followed.

It was during the October 2005 panel, BLSA student members alleged, that Peltz expressed his opposition to affirmative action, admitted to having racist friends, and complained that he had been passed over for an internship because of affirmative action.

A few weeks later, BLSA members claimed, Peltz "ranted" about affirmative action in his constitutional law class. During class discussion, according to BLSA members, he displayed an article from the satirical newspaper *The Onion* about civil rights pioneer Rosa Parks, and handed out forms asking for each student's race. If black students scored equal to white students on the exam, the students claimed Peltz told them, he would give black students an extra point.[4]

Peltz raised ire again in 2007, after returning to campus following a year away for sabbatical and a teaching visit to another law school, by supporting a student leader of the law review who was accused of racism for failing to appoint black editorial board members.[5]

The students wrote to the dean of the law school asking that Professor Peltz apologize for his behavior, that he be "openly reprimanded," that he not be allowed to teach any required course so black students would not be forced to take his classes, that an "inability to deal fairly with Black students" be noted in his file, and that he be required to attend diversity training.[6]

Peltz disavows many of the students' claims. That—and the fact that the students took their complaints about Peltz to the law school dean and beyond—was the crux of Peltz's defamation action. "Defendants' false accusations of racism," Peltz's complaint read, "damaged Plaintiff's reputation, character, and integrity in the Arkansas legal community."[7] The students' allegations of racism, he had written in an earlier email, left him feeling "spat on" and "treated as a pariah."[8] In time, the students answered with their own lawsuit, accusing their professor of having defamed *them* with his baseless legal action.[9]

There was, of course, a certain irony in Peltz's resort to the courts to protect his reputation in the Arkansas legal community: inevitably, the lawsuit brought Peltz far more negative attention than the Arkansas BLSA chapter could ever have dreamed of stirring against him. Within a week of Peltz's filing in Pulaski County Circuit Court, a report surfaced in the Little Rock papers; six weeks later, the *New York Times* caught wind of the story; a week after that, Peltz's story had crossed the Atlantic, cropping up in a *Times Higher Education* article musing on the latest American trend-setting. "If developments in US higher education today are an indicator of tomorrow's trends in the UK," the article noted, "students may want to think twice about the way they treat their lecturers."[10]

The blogosphere naturally had a field day. "Suing students! It seems unthinkable," wrote Wisconsin law professor Ann Althouse. "But this is the direction we head when free speech and academic freedom lose their grip on us . . . What a sad, sad story."[11] UCLA law professor Stephen Bainbridge added, "If Professor Peltz behaved as described in the article . . . his conduct was unprofessional and even moronic (in my opinion, a qualification I hasten to add just in case Professor Peltz is feeling really litigious)."[12]

Many, of course, expressed astonishment at the opening of the latest frontier in campus litigation. "Surely every law professor has at some time worried that an ill-considered comment he or she made, or a bad grade he or she conferred, would result in a lawsuit by a student," observed Cornell law professor Michael Dorf, "but I'll bet it had not occurred to most law professors—it certainly had not occurred to me—that we could be the plaintiffs suing our students for, say, lousy course evaluations."[13]

Other observers were less amused. "It is especially shocking that a professor of constitutional law, rather than rely on the First Amendment, rather than rely on academic freedom in an effort to explain why his views on affirmative action are not racist, he sues," Harvey Silvergate, cofounder of the Foundation for Individual Rights in Education, told the *Democrat-Gazette*.[14] *Inside Higher Ed* suggested that the ramifications from Peltz's lawsuit extended "well beyond" the Arkansas dust-up.[15] Jonathan Knight, director of academic freedom and tenure for the American Association of University Professors (AAUP), agreed. He worried that a lawsuit like the one filed by Peltz could effectively limit campus speech. "When you ask a court to become involved in making judgments about the metes and bounds of free expression on campus," Knight warned, "it can be dangerous."[16]

Yet, in reader comments posted at the end of *Inside Higher Ed*'s coverage of Peltz's lawsuit, some academics expressed sympathy for Peltz's sense of injury—and for the idea of turning to the courts. Bitterness over the "travesty" of student course evaluations emerged as a dominant theme:

> I've never wanted to sue students for what they say or write, which seems to me to defeat the whole purpose of teaching academic discourse,

but I have wondered about the possibility of suing a college for soliciting from students anonymous unsigned ratings and comments about their teachers and professors. On many occasions students respond on printed institutional forms with scores and remarks which are not only falsehoods but slander and libel. I don't blame the students. They are led by the institution—which also requires faculty to participate in this travesty by distributing the forms in order to lend to the process an illusion of legitimacy—to believe that their anonymous unsigned criticism and complaints are helpful and somehow improve instruction and education. Nothing could be further from the truth. But each term their remarks are read by secretaries, clerks, administrative assistants, deans, and sometimes even college vice presidents and presidents before faculty ever learn what students have written about them; and because faculty do learn what students have written only weeks and even months after the term is over the faculty have no way of confronting their anonymous accusers. I'd like to see a college sued for this conduct.[17]

Another readily agreed: "My first year, tenure track contract was not renewed this year, largely because a half dozen students didn't think I upheld the standards of my predecessor, who had minimal hands on experience in the field," the professor wrote, "and I have evidence of how the students did this (mostly via those anonymous evaluations)." Three weeks and forty-six posts later in the same thread, the same professor added a final follow-up post: "Met with My Lawyer Yesterday. And we're suing the school, the administration, and, YES, the students. Stay tuned!"[18]

Peltz, for one, dropped his lawsuit in November 2008, eight months after filing it; neither side admitted wrongdoing, though Peltz claimed some vindication in a law school statement finding no evidence that he was racist.[19] He told *Inside Higher Ed* that the experience had led him to despair about free expression in universities today: "When I started teaching 10 years ago, I thought universities were the quintessential market place of ideas. I was so naïve, and so, so wrong," he told a reporter after dropping the lawsuit. "It's not an open market place of ideas—I hope we can get back to that notion because our society desperately needs places where we can have truly free discussion. I just can't say I see that in the American university today."[20]

Peltz, as the plaintiff in an action that has the decided potential to sti-fle student speech, apparently did not intend his statement to be ironic.

From any sober perspective, Peltz's lawsuit against his students was a bad idea. It was poorly calculated to enhance Peltz's reputation in the Arkansas legal community or beyond. It was certainly bad for Peltz's students. "I am shocked and disheartened," acknowledged one, "to learn that I have been sued by one of my professors at the Bowen School of Law."[21] Peltz's dean was forced to reassure students and faculty in an e-mail that the law school remained committed to an environment "in which all members—faculty, students, and staff—are free to openly voice their opinions and concerns."[22] And it was surely bad for higher educa-tion in general, contributing dramatically to the trend toward campus liti-giousness and the public sense that academics have finally gone around the bend.

The "man-bites-dog quality"[23] of Peltz's lawsuit got it plenty of head-lines, but the truth is that it is not a singularly momentous development in the ongoing "legalization" of academia. In fact, the most important feature of that phenomenon is that the vast majority of such lawsuits have become entirely humdrum events that no longer trigger serious no-tice. The trend toward litigating campus disputes, tentatively spotted as a trickle in the 1970s, has grown now into an unmistakable river. The campus workplace, veteran academic lawyers Ann Franke and Lawrence White have observed in a legal guide for new department chairs, is now "a high-risk zone."[24] "In modern higher education, few major decisions are made without considering the legal consequences," higher education law expert Michael Olivas has written. And, "[i]f events continue as in the past, there can be no doubt that higher education will be become in-creasingly legalized."[25]

There are in fact two distinct and independently significant features of the trend line. The first is that those involved in campus disputes, like Peltz and his students, are increasingly willing to resort to the courts to settle scores. What judge and former professor Frank Easterbrook wrote of one relatively early campus lawsuit fairly describes a now much broader phenomenon: litigation has become simply "the extension of ac-ademic politics by other means."[26] It now appears that no slight—the re-moval of faculty dress-up photos from a hallway display case, a tempo-rary curtailment of a fraternity's social activities, omission of a faculty member's accomplishments from a departmental brag list—is too small to warrant the making of "a federal case."

The second, equally important aspect of the trend is that courts are increasingly willing to entertain these lawsuits and to render decisions on the merits. "Colleges and universities enjoyed nearly complete autonomy from legal regulation before the 1950s," writes Peter Byrne, "being seen as a different realm, akin to a religion or the family, more than a marketplace."[27] In former times, if a student or faculty member had the temerity to bring a grievance to court, it was likely to be bounced out in short order, on the basis of some categorical bar or immunity. Now, if the old analogy to family holds at all, it is increasingly to a dysfunctional, divorcing family which courts feel free to enter and reorder from the ground up, parceling out the rights and obligations of each disputant down to the last dollar and school vacation. In recent years, courts have intervened to police the boundaries of permissible criticism in peer review, to weigh how professors should hand back exams, and to direct which of two candidates should be installed as student government president.

Thoughtful observers of higher education have identified several emerging threats to academic freedom: these include the dramatic commercialization of academia, with its realignment of priorities and incentives for the "hoarding and selling" of knowledge[28]; the whittling away of the protections of tenure through growing reliance on nontenured instructors[29]; and mounting pressure, through private monitoring and public oversight and legislation, to police ideological "balance" in college classrooms.[30]

This book has argued for recognizing another threat to academic freedom: the growing "legalization" of academia. By documenting the far-flung academic disputes that have found their way into court in recent years, and the newfound readiness of courts to resolve them, the preceding chapters have shown how law, litigation, and "rights talk" have permeated every crease and wrinkle of academic life. In the gloom of the Cold War, when the menace to academic freedom took the stark and villainous form of a prosecutorial inquisition, Justice Frankfurter wrote eloquently of the indispensability of "free universities" to a "free society" and of the need to ensure "the exclusion of governmental intervention in the intellectual life of the university."[31] In our own day, the government's insinuation into the intellectual life of the university through the courts is more prosaic, but should be no less worrisome.

Taking stock of the phenomenon, and considering what, if anything, can be done about it, requires consideration of both its likely causes and effects. In assessing the factors that have inspired more litigation and eroded judicial inhibitions, it is important to place campus litigation in a broader context. The push for judicial review of campus grievances coincides with a much larger clamor for stepped-up oversight of colleges and universities, stretching back over decades but notably accelerating in recent years.

Early inroads were made in the context of anti-discrimination law. Pioneering litigation in the 1930s and 1940s used the Constitution's guarantee of equal protection to overcome racial exclusion in public colleges and universities. These constitutional gains were extended to cover private colleges and additional forms of discrimination through a series of federal statutes and amendments—Titles VI and VII of the Civil Rights Act of 1964, the Age Discrimination in Employment Act, Title IX of the Education Amendments of 1972, the Rehabilitation Act, the Americans with Disabilities Act—in the 1960s, 1970s, and 1980s. New statutes spawned an even more impressive array of regulations authored by federal agencies to implement Congress's directives.

Against the rising tide of the civil rights movement, the "Second American Revolution," university autonomy buckled.[32] Before the 1960s, "if faculty members did not receive tenure, or were forced to move for another reason, they would simply find another position or fall on their sword," observes Michael Olivas.[33] After the 1960s, new statutes and a sea change in public attitudes encouraged victims of bias to seek protection in the courts. By the 1990s, colleges and universities were fully immersed in "the alphabet and numeric soup of antidiscrimination law."[34]

Resort to the courts was further encouraged during this period by the sea change in the relationship between students and the university. The paternalistic assumptions of the *in loco parentis* doctrine were replaced by a new model that envisaged students as "adults who are members of the college or university community" on more or less equal terms.[35] As Justice Douglas observed in his opinion celebrating the transformation in Healy v. James, the 1972 SDS cases, a new generation refused to accept old notions of "the minds of students as receptacles for the information

which the faculty" saw fit to impart; instead, in the wake of campus up-
risings over racism and the Vietnam War and even enactment of the
Twenty-Sixth Amendment to the Constitution, guaranteeing eighteen-
year-olds the right to vote, students would challenge "the status quo of
the college or university" and assert greater control over their own education.[36] That colleges and universities also resorted to the courts to defend their authority only gave the courts a broader foothold on campus,
as Robert O'Neil had foreseen during the upheaval following the Kent
State tragedy.[37]

Growing student political power in the Vietnam era later combined
with newfound student market power in the 1970s, moreover, to introduce a new dynamic: "the growth of student 'consumerism' in higher
education."[38] The eminent Harvard sociologist David Riesman was one of
the first to spot the development and its implications. Writing in 1980,
after the booming college enrollments of the 1960s had given way to a
new era in which "institutions compete[d] frantically with one another
for body counts," Riesman observed that students had turned "from being supplicants for admission to courted customers."[39] Among the consequences that troubled Riesman were that "faculty members and administrators [would] hesitate to make demands on students in the form of
rigorous academic requirements for fear of losing . . . full-time equivalent students" and that students would slide into "viewing themselves
primarily as passive consumers of education rather than as active pro-
ducers of their own education and as resources for educating each other
and even faculty."[40] This rising sense of entitlement, in turn, was fueling
"students' increased litigation against colleges and increased federal efforts to protect student interests by regulating institutions."[41]

These earlier developments have gathered considerable steam in our
own time. The new watchword driving today's public debates over higher
education is accountability. "A growing chorus of critics—legislators, governors, alumni, students, parents, trustees, and others—is pressuring colleges to increase 'accountability' and 'transparency,'" observes Richard
Vedder, an economics professor at Ohio University and an enthusiastic
voice in the chorus. Vedder, who served on the Bush administration's
Commission on the Future of Higher Education, known as the Spellings
Commission, rattles off a litany of concerns feeding the public perception
that colleges and universities are out of control: rising tuition costs, spend-

ing scandals, lavish executive compensation packages, mind-boggling endowments.[42]

These concerns have driven initiatives to bring new accountability to
higher education on multiple fronts. After a two-year study, the Spellings
Commission in 2007 issued a report calling for colleges and universities
to publicize data concerning their finances, admissions, alumni placement and earnings, and teaching loads, and to develop standardized tests
and other learning measures to permit comparative shopping on academic quality. In 2008, President George W. Bush signed legislation reau-
thorizing the Higher Education Act, "promising consumers greater transparency in the rising costs of college."[43] The Act imposes wide-ranging
disclosure requirements and provides for creation of a "Higher Education
Price Increase Watch List" of schools with fast-rising tuitions. The Act
also pushed universities to broaden campus speech rights by including a
"sense of Congress" resolution about the importance of "free and open"
speech by students. Congress also joined the ranks of nearly three dozen
states by putting pressure on colleges to lower textbook costs by requiring broader disclosure of pricing.[44]

In the meantime, Congress was also pressing for accountability on
other fronts. In 2007, before significant stock market losses, the U.S. Senate Finance Committee held hearings into the growth of university endowments, questioning whether universities were spending enough to
justify their tax-exempt status. Under mounting public pressure, some of
the wealthiest universities, including Harvard and Yale, announced plans
to spend more on scholarships for students from middle- and low-income
families.[45] "Tuition has gone up, college presidents' salaries have gone up,
and endowments continue to go up and up," said Senator Chuck Grassley, ranking Republican on the committee. "We need to start seeing tuition relief for families go up just as fast."[46] At the same time, Congress
was also pressing for increased federal scrutiny of Big Science through the
auspices of Title IX, to root out possible evidence of sex bias in university
research programs.[47]

The not-too-subtle theme underlying all of these initiatives for "accountability" is that colleges and universities must be brought to heel.
The Spelling Commission's Vedder pointedly warns that "if colleges resist calls for accountability and transparency too much, they may pay a
high price: the loss of institutional autonomy. The public and its political

representatives are getting fed up. When that anger passes some threshold, the politicians will probably act, and colleges won't like the imposed solutions."[48]

Beneath the anger is not only a concern with affordability, but also more fundamentally that universities have lost their way and forgotten the public-spiritedness that once set them apart. "[M]any people still regard [universities] as selfless institutions above and beyond the self-serving rules of the marketplace," Columbia University professor Andrew Delbanco wrote in the *New York Times* in 2007, just as Senator Grassley's hearings were getting under way, but that view "is deteriorating fast." Whereas the public mind once imagined faculty "as bumbling bookworms, today's professors are more likely to be seen as jet-setting self-promoters." Now, "[d]riven by big science and global competition, our top universities compete for 'market share' and 'brand-name positioning,' employ teams of consultants and lobbyists and furnish their campuses with luxuries in order to attract paying 'customers'—a word increasingly used as a synonym for students."[49]

As David Kirp observed in *Shakespeare, Einstein, and the Bottom Line:*

> A great deal is at stake in this contest between the values of the market and those of the commons: the commitment to test, not just replicate, the prevailing wisdoms of the day; the pride of place given to need and merit, rather than ability to pay, in determining who is to be educated; the contention that universities should be places for discovering, sharing, and passing on knowledge rather than companies for hoarding and selling it; the idea, to revive the nineteenth-century metaphor, that one can speak of the *soul* of the university.[50]

Lurking beneath the groundswell for accountability are the most basic questions about the academic enterprise: "[W]hat, exactly, are colleges doing to justify their public subsidies?" and "What makes the modern university different from any other corporation?"[51]

Not surprisingly, this environment of mounting cynicism and disappointment shapes the attitudes of judges as well as legislators and op-ed writers. Even judges who are deeply sympathetic to the academic enterprise and steeped in its culture have suggested a role for broader litigation in ensuring the accountability of colleges and universities. Prominent federal appeals court judge José Cabranes, who served as Yale

University's first general counsel before his appointment to the bench, drew on three decades of experience as a trustee at Colgate, Fordham, Yale, and Columbia to conclude in 2007 that it is unrealistic to expect trustees to provide public accountability through aggressive oversight of university administrators. Instead, he suggested, "[t]he most promising source for enhanced oversight of university affairs" lies outside the university campus, in legislative reforms to require broader public disclosure and to expand standing to sue.[52] The impulse to expose campuses to greater scrutiny through private litigation, then, is importantly just one piece of a larger drive for external control of the academic enterprise. Indeed, the Foundation for Individual Rights in Education made the linkage explicit when it celebrated the 2008 "sense of Congress" resolution on campus speech rights by linking the legislative initiative with court action: "Congress' strong words add to those of the federal judiciary in urging universities to live up to their unique and important role in society."[53]

Similarly, it is not only in the halls of Congress and state legislatures that "rising tuition costs have increased public scrutiny of colleges and further undermined the arguments for institutional autonomy."[54] In addition to fueling legislation, rising costs have fueled litigation. The *Wall Street Journal* reported in 2007, for example, that a shortage of high-paying legal jobs has put intense pressure on law students outside the most elite schools to distinguish themselves academically.[55] David Van Zandt, dean of Northwestern University's law school and president of the American Law Deans Association, suggested several months later that spiraling costs may be feeding a new litigiousness over grades and other academic matters because the stakes for students are so much larger. "It certainly is understandable if it's happening because the cost of education is going up," he said. "From some of the [lawsuit] examples, the students seem to be challenging something that is very important to them because their place in school has an impact on their job later."[56] The weakened economy and the tightening job market are likely only to aggravate the resort to litigation.

The phenomenon is not confined to students. Essentially the same anxiety can be seen fueling the turn to law by scholars and teachers. Recent years have seen a shift in teaching responsibilities at colleges and universities to non–tenure track faculty. According to the AAUP, instructors off the tenure track now constitute roughly 70 percent of the faculty teaching at colleges and universities.[57] The growing reliance on adjunct or other contract faculty has been occasioned partly by the rise of for-profit universities that reject the tenure model. But it is also rapidly transforming major research universities, where grant-generating tenured faculty are increasingly dedicated to research and "[t]he slack is picked up by poorly paid graduate students and by non-tenure-track adjuncts with low salaries and no fringe benefits."[58] The resulting stratification of academic employment, with dwindling ranks of privileged tenured faculty far outnumbered by the swelling numbers of low-status, essentially dispensable classroom teachers, has been called "[t]he dirty secret of higher education," but it is hardly a secret.[59] For the have-nots, it has occasioned both resentment and a spreading sense of vulnerability. In *The Last Professors*, Frank Donoghue, an English professor at Ohio State, warns that the victims of the market-driven transformation of academic work will ultimately include not merely individual unfortunates now emerging from graduate programs, but the humanities as disciplines altogether. Professors "are now disappearing from the landscape of higher education," he laments, warranting serious planning for "what universities might look like without professors."[60]

The growing job insecurity of academic employees contributes to the rise in campus litigation in at least two ways. First, the greater turnover in academic employment creates more occasions for potential grievance, and the scarcity of high-value academic jobs raises the stakes of disputes. Two decades ago, an earlier tightening of the academic job market was cited as a "major factor" in the initial spike in litigation over faculty hiring and tenure, and recent years have only intensified the pressure.[61] Second, denying the internal academic-freedom protections afforded by tenure to contract faculty has left instructors who feel aggrieved by campus policies or decisions with "no way to fight back short of engaging in an expensive legal battle."[62] In this sense, the very lack of contract and other legal protections for the new academic labor force has, perhaps ironically, fueled their resort to the courts.

Ideological conflict has provided another pressure point on academic self-governance. Popular suspicions that American college campuses are dominated by leftists bent on indoctrinating young minds and enforcing slavish conformity to "political correctness" have undermined respect for university autonomy both in the political arena and in the courts. Congress's latest resolution promoting campus speech rights in 2008 was motivated by a felt need to strike back at campus orthodoxy. The effort to enact state legislation embodying an Academic Bill of Rights to safeguard "intellectual diversity" on college campuses plainly springs from the same source.[63] And precisely the same concern can be seen driving court decisions casting off traditional restraints of academic deference to dictate the scope of speech and associational rights on campus. As Peter Byrne has observed, "the trend of decisions justif[ies] greater judicial intrusion into academic decision making on the grounds that colleges and universities are places rife with intolerance, although needing maximum liberty."[64]

Finally, of course, the commercialization of higher education has been a significant force in chipping away at judicial deference to academia, just as it has in Congress. "[I]ncreasingly," writes federal appeals court judge and prominent legal scholar Richard Posner, "the outlook of universities in the United States is indistinguishable from that of business firms."[65] "The more similar institutions are to corporations," former AAUP associate counsel Ann Springer has observed, "the less courts will be willing to defer to the professional judgment of educators and the institutional autonomy of colleges and universities."[66] Indeed, some recent court decisions slashing deeply into traditional doctrines of academic deference have been at pains to equate academic and commercial actors. For example, in Sharick v. Southeastern University of the Health Sciences—the Florida case resulting in the $18 million award for lost earning potential for the would-be doctor dismissed in his last year of medical school (discussed in Chapter 9)—a judge emphasized that " 'judicial deference to university conduct toward students becomes increasingly less defensible as bottom-line, commercial concerns motivate university actions and students seek a more consumer friendly product.' "[67]

At a more fundamental level, the threat to academic freedom posed by these developments originates not with greedy college trustees, selfish students, prickly professors, or overzealous judges, but in a breakdown in the basic social compact underlying higher education. "For over nine hundred years," observes former Cornell president Frank Rhodes, "the effectiveness of the university has been dependent upon a social compact under which society supports the university financially and grants it a remarkable degree of autonomy, while the university uses its resources and its freedom to serve the larger public interest."[68] Understandably, news reports of efforts to hoard knowledge, patent human genes, or extract rents from already strapped students fuel perceptions that universities have broken their end of the bargain. A 2009 disclosure that some colleges were helping banks to market credit cards and stood to profit when their students opened accounts and carried a balance—Michigan State University, for instance, was guaranteed a one-half percent slice of all retail purchases charged to the cards—sparked predictable outrage in Congress and calls for new legal controls on campus administrators.[69]

In this new age, university autonomy is seen not, as Rhodes describes it, as an *engine* of beneficial social change, but as a dangerous *obstruction*. In a 2009 op-ed, for example, Columbia University professor Mark Taylor decried what he saw as the self-centered obsolescence of modern higher education and assigned blame squarely on the lack of external controls. A basic "obstacle to change," he contended, "is that colleges and universities are self-regulating or, in academic parlance, governed by peer review."[70] Taylor's prescription, captured in the headline of his essay, was to "End the University as We Know It": "If American higher education is to thrive in the 21st century, colleges and universities, like Wall Street and Detroit, must be rigorously regulated and completely restructured."[71]

Yet, a basic reason for inventive revenue schemes and for spiraling college costs generally is that the public has broken its end of the bargain as well by steadily withdrawing financial support for higher education. State dollars for higher education have shrunk dramatically in recent decades, whether measured in terms of per-student investment or as a percentage of state budgets.[72] Of necessity, public colleges and universities have been forced to turn to tuition and other private revenue sources to make up the shortfall, effectively "privatizing" themselves.[73] The ensuing loss of affordability and access, as well as the seeming abandonment of their public identity and mission, in turn, feeds public cynicism. The result is a vicious cycle unraveling the social compact underlying the university's claim to autonomy and emboldening calls for regulation and accountability.

Given the realities of modern economic trends and tax policy, all indications are that the cycle will only quicken in the years ahead. "Although these trends have been going on for at least 20 years," writes Ami Zusman, "the extraordinary pressures being placed on state revenues and expenditures for competing services today are likely to accelerate the move for reliance on private funding for 'public' higher education."[74] Accordingly, as Robert Berdahl, former chancellor of the University of California–Berkeley and now president of the Association of American Universities, acknowledged in an address to German scholars in 2000, "For American universities, there is no turning back; we will have to continue to raise large amounts of private funds. But we must do so while recognizing that few gifts are free of some obligation, few sources of support are without some strings, and all courses of action contain dangers."[75]

The danger posed by these trends to academic freedom is substantial. The genius of the American system of higher education has been its diffusion of authority and initiative to individual faculty members. Giving individual scholars and researchers the leeway, through tenure and other safeguards of academic freedom, to create, collaborate, and compete for research support has been key to the staggering advances in knowledge over the past century. Entrusting evaluation in hiring, promotions, and research funding to peer-specialists in the relevant field brings both maximal expertise and unique rigor to core academic judgments.[76] Judicial supervision of this enterprise, if it becomes too expansive or aggressive, undermines these essential conditions. George LaNoue and Barbara Lee, studying tenure litigation in 1987 when it was still relatively nascent, suggested that "[p]erhaps when academic administrators learn more about litigation, they will realize they may lose more control of institutional autonomy in the courtroom than in any other arena."[77] Two decades of experience in the courtroom prove the point. In fact, it may not be too much to say, as Peter Byrne wrote in 2004, that "in the past decade or so, judicial and other constitutional decisions have threatened the continued vitality of constitutional academic freedom."[78]

The threat takes several forms. Most obviously, court decisions intervening in a university's intramural affairs, as in *Sharick,* may directly displace the academic judgment of faculty or university officials, substituting that of the judge or jury.

Even in the absence of a court order, the process of litigation or even just its plausible threat may work real damage to the core mission of colleges or other academic organizations. "The mere act of litigation," LaNoue and Lee observed, "may have political, organizational, financial, and emotional consequences."[79] Academic defendants face a potentially staggering toll on their personal resources, possibly spanning many years. "The burden of legal negotiations and litigation on school officials' time and energy," noted one weary dean, "makes it increasingly difficult for them to attend to the regular affairs of the university and to do the necessary planning for the future."[80]

Consider one law student's legal challenge to her failing grade in constitutional law. She sued George Mason University, three deans, and her professor (in their individual capacities), alleging claims under the First Amendment and the Americans with Disabilities Act. Her claims were dismissed at trial, revived on appeal, and eventually dismissed again, a three-year span of litigation. In a statement after the case was finally extinguished, Dean Daniel Polsby observed:

> One of the lessons we teach in law school is that litigation is a serious and expensive business, not to be undertaken lightly and never to be undertaken frivolously. [The student's] bogus lawsuit has inflicted significant dead-weight losses on the individual defendants and on our law school. Many hundreds of hours have been spent dealing with it, hours that could profitably have been spent on productive activities that would have benefited our students and our program.[81]

Aside from the distractions and aggravations, there is, as Dean Polsby alluded, the matter of the expense. In 2007, for example, one university reportedly spent more than $450,000 in legal fees to fire a dean who had been indicted on corruption and fraud charges.[82] Those expenses are daunting enough for large institutions; for an individual academic, they are catastrophic. And yet individual students and scholars regularly find that they are on their own if sued for their scholarly activity or publications.[83] Professors are strongly encouraged to protect themselves by purchasing liability insurance coverage for their scholarly activities, but insurance raises its own concerns for academic freedom. Michael Olivas points out a collateral consequence of the legalization of academic life: as liability and litigation costs loom larger, insurance carriers have greater power to shape academic policies and scholarly initiatives through coverage restrictions and limitations.[84]

Defendants can choose to limit their litigation costs by settling, of course, but settlement carries its own costs. One measure is in dollars. University counsel agree that the financial cost of settling even frivolous, "nuisance" suits continues to rise. In 2006, an informal survey of university lawyers found that most estimated that their colleges would be willing to pay between $5,000 and $10,000 to dispose of a suit they considered baseless. "The price of nuisance does go up," lamented the general counsel for a major academic insurance carrier.[85]

And, of course, the more ominous costs, as far as academic freedom is concerned, may take the form of nonpecuniary submission to the demands of a plaintiff. In University of Oregon professor Merle Weiner's case, the journal that published her disputed article—which made a brief reference to a child custody case involving the plaintiff—agreed to excise offending material from its electronic archives, as "dictated by in-house counsel."[86] Similarly, in 2008, the journal of the College Art Association, *Art Journal,* agreed to ask its subscribers around the world to withdraw portions of a book review that had offended the author whose work was critiqued in the review. The disgruntled subject, chair of the art history department at Hebrew University of Jerusalem, had threatened to sue the journal over a bruising review by Joseph Massad, a controversial Columbia University professor of Arab Studies, that suggested she had not given proper credit to others for ideas contained in her work. In a twist, taking advantage of the journal's international readership, she had threatened to sue in Britain, where libel laws are more plaintiff-friendly than in the United States. The journal consulted with U.S. and British lawyers and "decided that the cost and risk of defending a libel case there looked punishingly high."[87] Again, scholarship was withdrawn because the costs of defending it in court were prohibitive.

"Risk-producing industries," reports law professor Thomas McGarity, regularly use threats of litigation to bully scientists or journal editors into avoiding publishing unwelcome research findings. The "important but unanswered question," he notes, "is how many scientific studies have never seen the light of day because of such borderline extortion."[88] As Wendy Wagner and Rena Steinzor observe, such attacks "cannot help but deter the best and brightest from entering the disciplines where they are needed the most."[89] At the very least, notes Paul Fischer, one medical researcher who learned the hard way, "scientists [must] have a better understanding of the legal implications of their research." Fischer, who endured a bruising legal battle with R. J. Reynolds over tobacco research, writes: "Scientists are the perfect subjects for harassment by litigation. The ultimate goal is to make the process sufficiently painful so that the researcher cannot complete further research and so that other scientists are discouraged from conducting similar studies."[90]

A 2008 study of the effects of political criticism of NIH-funded scientific research supports Fischer's assessment, finding that "[a] majority of the researchers reported that their experience of being targeted by Congressional representatives or the Traditional Values Coalition led them to engage in a number of self-censorship practices."[91] Fischer himself gave up his full professorship at the Medical College of Georgia for family practice.[92] The study that attracted R. J. Reynolds's wrath, published in the *Journal of the American Medical Association* in 1991, had found that Camel cigarettes' cartoon icon "Old Joe" (or "Joe Camel") was as readily recognized by six-year-olds as the logo for the Disney Channel.

In 2007, it was Disney's turn to rattle the sabers, this time at a University of Washington study that found that videos for babies, such as Disney's "Baby Einstein" series, are "more likely to slow language acquisition than to assist with it." The university refused, however, to retract its press release or the study.[93]

Even if research or criticism is not directly suppressed by a court order or settlement agreement, it can be deterred from ever being undertaken by a scholar's own calculation of the litigation risks. Peer reviewers faced with knowledge that whatever they write may be disclosed not only to the subject of their review but to the entire world via the Internet or in a published case reporter, might reasonably elect to temper their criticism or omit comparative references—or even to steer clear of the business altogether. Not surprisingly, some academics report having "had trouble finding people to serve [on tenure and promotion] committees in departments which have been involved in litigation."[94] In their study of tenure litigation, LaNoue and Lee concluded that, "[o]n close calls, some decision makers may feel timid about enforcing standards for fear of dragging the institution through the courts again."[95]

The same hesitation is likely to apply to research and scholarship. As Professor Massad, author of the disputed *Art Journal* review, observed, "If every academic was going to think that any critique of academic scholarship was going to have to be defended in a court of law, the state of academic argumentation would be very different."[96] In fact, Oregon's Professor Weiner says she has already passed over at least one writing project for fear of litigation. "This has impacted my ability to do my job," she said. "I'm very cautious now."[97]

In addition to affecting academic decisions about research and publication, the threat of litigation can also override academic judgments in the evaluation of students. In 2003, Coppin State College in Baltimore reportedly agreed to let eight students graduate with master's degrees, despite the fact that "they did not pass their comprehensive exams or write final papers considered acceptable by the faculty," after the students sued to demand their degrees. According to the *Chronicle of Higher Education*, some professors in the students' department were so appalled they considered boycotting commencement. A classmate who *had* completed the requirements for graduation considered turning to the courts herself; she was said to be contemplating her own lawsuit on the theory that "her degree ha[d] been rendered meaningless by the decision to award the credential to students who did not complete the required course work."[98]

If the rising tide of campus litigation carries troubling implications for the decisions that scholars make individually and collectively about what they will study, publish, critique, and teach—and therefore for academic freedom itself—what, if anything, might be done to turn the tide?

The first thing to acknowledge is that there is obviously no way to put the genie of campus litigation back in the bottle. Nor would we wish to do so, even if it were possible. Statutes such as Title VII and Title IX make emphatically clear that their regulations extend to campus, and the Supreme Court has recognized constitutional protection as well for the benefit of students and faculty of public universities. Very real injustices exist on campuses warranting a judicial remedy.[99] Jerome Karabel's compelling history of admissions at Harvard, Yale, and Princeton, for example, makes clear that the very academic autonomy successfully asserted in recent cases to defend inclusivity and affirmative action on campus was once wielded frankly to exclude Jews and other minorities.[100] Thus scholars on all sides—even those who would privilege institutional academic freedom over the academic freedom of individual professors or students—recognize that we are realistically left with the unavoidable task of setting a balance point between the value of accountability through the courts and the value of limiting intrusions on the autonomy of academic communities.[101] The goal is not, by any means, to exclude all litigation, but rather to push judges and academics alike to a fuller accounting of the costs of campus litigation so that a more accurate balance point between desirable and undesirable claims can be found.

Professor Byrne, who favors a narrow window for individual claims against the university, traces part of the slippage of academic deference to the courts' use of "a vague and confusing doctrinal framework."[102] In searching for causes of the retreat of academic abstention, he writes that "[o]ne cannot discount the extent to which the prevailing doctrine, which could be characterized either as vague or subtle, confuses judges who lack an understanding of the academic context and values."[103] For those who are alarmed by the easy encroachment of the courts on the core academic judgments and operations of colleges and universities, an obvious response would be to clarify or stiffen the doctrine to make clear that deference is still required.

Yet, given the enormous diversity in the campus controversies that find their way into court today, it is implausible to suppose that any single doctrinal formula could strike the right balance in all cases. Rather, in each legal context, courts must find ways of allowing for judicial review while minimizing the risk that judges will trench dangerously on legitimate academic decision making. Courts must, for example, have the capacity to intervene in appropriate cases of discrimination, intellectual suppression, breach of contract, or wrongful personal injury, but under a doctrinal formulation that limits the intervention to cases where the expected benefits outweigh the risks. This is likely to require recognition of a buffer zone in which wrongful action may well have occurred, but not sufficiently clearly to warrant risks of judicial intervention in the intellectual life of the university.

Courts have offered one workable model, for example, in the context of student claims for academic accommodation under federal disability discrimination law. In Wynne v. Tufts University School of Medicine, Steven Wynne challenged his dismissal from the medical program after repeatedly failing basic first-year courses.[104] He contended that his dyslexia entitled him to forgo multiple-choice exams; the university answered emphatically that its multiple-choice exams tested analytical skills essential to the successful practice of medicine. The federal appeals court in Boston recognized that the case presented two important public values, with "the statutory rights of a handicapped individual . . . in tension with concern for the autonomy of an academic institution."[105] The court struck the balance by requiring deference to the rational exercise of academic judgment: "If the institution submits undisputed facts demonstrating that the relevant officials within the institution considered alternative means, their feasibility, cost and effect on the academic program, and came to a rationally justifiable conclusion that the available alternatives would result either in lowering academic standards or requiring substantial program alteration, the court could rule as a matter of law that the institution had met its duty of seeking reasonable accommodation."[106]

Justice Stephen Breyer, then a judge on the appellate court three years before his elevation to the Supreme Court, wrote separately to underscore the propriety of deference to academic judgments that do "not significantly depart from accepted academic norms."[107] Such an approach frankly denies authority to judges to override academic judgment based simply on disagreement, no matter how emphatic it may be, with an academic officer's weighing of the relevant considerations. For Breyer, beefy deference to university officials was warranted by realization that "the designing of tests aimed at screening out those who will not become good doctors is a quintessentially academic task, close to the heart of a professional school's basic mission." Moreover, "the design of proper academic tests . . . is not itself a science, but, rather, is a judgmental matter in respect to which teachers and doctors are far more expert than judges and juries."

At bottom, the deferential standard Breyer endorsed reflected understanding of the limits of judicial review to competently second-guess academic judgment and a basic trust in the good faith of academic actors:

> [C]ircumstances should caution us against applying reasonable-sounding legal standards in a way that, as a practical matter, would force universities to produce the *kinds* of proofs that seem to appeal especially to courts—"hard" evidence, tests of tests, statistical studies—for to do this is to take a basic educational decision away from those who may know the most about it, teachers using their own subjective judgment and experience,

and to place it in the hands of those (say, lawyers) who will have to defend an academic decision in court.[108]

Doctrinal formulations like these may be genuinely useful in steering courts but are probably quite inadequate by themselves to stem the tide of judicial entanglement with academic matters. Doctrine matters, but only so much.

Consider, for example, the contrasting cases of Gordon v. Purdue University,[109] decided by an Indiana appellate court in 2007, and Sharick v. Southeastern University of Health Sciences,[110] decided by an appellate court in Florida a few years earlier. Both cases involved legal challenges by graduate or professional students to their academic dismissals. Richard Gordon was an economics doctoral student at Purdue, who was dismissed by the university after receiving failing grades in his thesis research course. Gordon was given a chance to get his thesis back on track, but his advisor stepped down and Gordon was unable to find another advisor before time ran out. He sued Purdue under a laundry list of contract and tort theories, but the gist of all of them was that Purdue unfairly left him high and dry without an advisor, despite a promise in the student handbook that Purdue would provide doctoral students with "a full or adequate Advisory Committee" and would "ensure that his Major Professor/Advisor . . . [was] competent and/or actually fulfilling [his or her] purpose in directing and supervising [Gordon's] doctoral research." Given that Gordon was given *no* thesis advisor during his crucial final months, he seemed to have at least a plausible contract claim, assuming that the handbook qualified as a contract.

Yet, the Indiana trial court ultimately ruled against Gordon's claims and the appellate court affirmed. Both courts emphasized that courts must tread carefully when reviewing the academic judgments of a university, and so followed a doctrinal test that allowed court intervention *only* if it found that the university's action was "illegal," "arbitrary and capricious," or demonstrated "bad faith." This deferential standard of review, the court explained, would buffer academic decisions from direct second-guessing by the courts into such matters as "the nuances of educational processes and theories." Applying this test, the court readily found that the facts Gordon claimed simply did not show the necessary "bad faith" to allow court intervention.[111] Gordon walked away empty-handed.

Sharick is the medical student who failed his final course, a rural rotation in general medicine, one he needed to graduate from medical school. Sharick, like Gordon, sued the university for various tort and contract theories. Unlike in *Gordon*, the Florida courts allowed Sharick's claim to go before a jury, which found in his favor. On appeal, the appellate court stated the very same deferential standard used in *Gordon*, providing that "judicial review of a private educational institution's determination of academic performance in this context is limited to whether the challenged determination was arbitrary and capricious, irrational, made in bad faith, or in violation of constitution or statute." The court readily upheld the jury's finding of a breach of contract under this test, reasoning that the university had breached a promise made in the student handbook describing the course of study as a "four year curriculum *leading to the DO degree*."[112] Sharick, in other words, had been promised a degree and then had the rug pulled out from under him. After a further trial to determine his damages, Sharick was awarded $4.3 million.[113]

Both cases applied the same doctrinal test to essentially similar facts and yet reached diametrically opposed results. In fact, to the extent there was any material factual difference between the cases, it arguably cut in favor of Gordon, not Sharick. Gordon's handbook promise was, if anything, a more definite promise than was Sharick's. That the cases reached such different legal outcomes appears to confirm Professor Byrne's general observation that "[j]udicial decisions [in this context] often seem the result of purposeful misreadings driven by larger concerns."[114]

The larger concerns that appear to divide the courts in *Gordon* and *Sharick* center on the degree to which each genuinely respects the academic realm as deserving of special judicial solicitude. The *Gordon* court, in short, appears to have meant what it said about the importance of adapting ordinary contract principles to leave appropriate room for "the subjective professional judgment of trained educators"[115]; the *Sharick* court evidently did not. On subsequent petition for rehearing, another member of the appellate court was even more emphatic in this regard—purporting to apply the deferential "arbitrary and capricious" standard to sustain the university's liability even while expressly rejecting judicial deference to academic institutions as "disfavored" and out of step with "contemporary values."[116]

Accordingly, the real driver of liability decisions in the university context appears to be the extent to which the judges involved genuinely understand and respect the complexity and sensitivity of academic evaluations and the academic enterprise more generally. A chief difference, for example, between Justice Breyer, who wrote separately in *Wynne* to emphasize the propriety of academic deference, and Justice Thomas, who wrote separately in Grutter v. Bollinger to mock the University of Michigan's stated academic mission and the concept of academic deference more generally, may well be that Breyer spent more than a quarter century on the faculty of Harvard Law School before his appointment to the bench.[117] If so, this suggests that the biggest priority for universities, today and going forward, must be to work to educate the courts about the importance and social value of higher education to society, and the importance of academic freedom and institutional autonomy to the success of higher education.

A closely related challenge is to educate courts about the breadth and nature of the "academic" role. Recently, a growing stream of court decisions, including *Sharick,* Atria v. Vanderbilt University, and others, reflect a crabbed and shallow understanding of the nature of academic judgment.[118] The challenge of educating the courts will require long, steady engagement, and will not yield immediate results; but given the foundational importance of the understanding of academia to the judgments courts inevitably will be called upon to make, there is no substitute. This will require colleges and universities to seize every significant opportunity, through friend-of-the-court briefs and otherwise, to explain to courts how they operate, and the ways in which "academic" judgment can be implicated even in matters that, to an outside observer, might appear otherwise. Colleges and universities have been regrettably inconsistent in seizing these opportunities in the past.[119] But the success of concentrated efforts in cases such as *Grutter,* the affirmative action case involving the University of Michigan Law School, show that it is possible to have an important impact in this way.[120]

Colleges and universities must also make their case to the public more broadly through public engagement. In an environment in which colleges and universities are increasingly seen as disconnected from the public good and focused on lining their own pockets through profit-making research ventures, big-time athletics, and tending to their eye-popping endowments, sustained outreach and sensible accommodations, such as Harvard's and Yale's recent decisions to divert a larger portion of their endowment funds to promote accessibility, are important steps toward rebuilding confidence in the public-mindedness of American higher education.

Perhaps hardest of all, colleges and universities could constructively reduce the current incentives to litigation by working to restore a sense of community within their often-sprawling institutions. Former Cornell president Frank Rhodes emphasized the importance of this challenge in his thoughtful volume, *The Creation of the Future.* The task will not be easy. Many state and private universities have grown so large, complex, specialized, and diverse, it seems fanciful to speak of building "community." And, yet, Rhodes makes a strong argument that "[i]n the case of universities, loss of community is not a mere misfortune; it is a catastrophe, for it undermines the very foundation on which the universities were established: the conviction that the pursuit of knowledge is best undertaken by scholars, living and working, not in isolation, but in the yeasty and challenging atmosphere of community." Rhodes adds that "community does not imply agreement or even harmony, but it does imply interaction . . . Our present loss of community reflects not a lack of agreement, not even a lack of cohesiveness, but rather a lack of discourse, an absence of meaningful dialogue, and indifference to significant communication. For we are not only a group of individuals sharing a common space; we also share some quite basic common concerns and goals."[121]

Rhodes offers his prescription for community not to reduce litigation, but to enhance the university's ability to address social problems that do not come in "neat disciplinary or professional packages," and to promote the university's engagement with and indispensability to the broader society. Yet, his proposal might well contribute quite constructively to the goal of deterring resort to the courts. Two related features of current campus life that Rhodes seeks to address through community-building are (1) the atomistic isolation of many of its participants; and (2) the lack of communication and dialogue between groups. Both of these features also appear to contribute to the growing tendency of campus combatants to head to court.[122] Once, the communal, "gentlemen's club" quality of academia powerfully discouraged even the most meritorious legal claims.[123] Yet, by 1980, Steven Vago and Charles Marske observed that "[t]he heterogeneous, impersonal and at times, almost alienated quality of the [new] academic climate fosters the utilization of law to assert individual rights and settle grievances in academic situations."[124] Beyond the isolation and lack of communication, there should be added a third factor, a common failure of many campus disputants to keep a sense of perspective about their grievances.

No case better illustrates these features at work than Burnham v. Ianni, the case involving the tussle over the faculty dress-up photographs at the University of Minnesota at Duluth history department.[125] If ever there was a case involving a failure of community, this was it. The case, after all, involved a colleague in a small academic department who had been subjected to very real and very menacing death threats that had roiled the entire campus. Even accepting that her colleagues meant her no distress by posing in their goofy frontier and Roman get-ups, and even allowing that they regarded her alarm as an overreaction, the question remains why Judith Trolander's colleagues could not bring themselves to accept the president's initially gentle suggestion that they voluntarily remove the photos as "an act of collegiality."[126] Their resolve, after the president's heavy-handed removal, to take the case to court and litigate through two appeals, in order to stick it to a hapless president and a colleague facing death threats, is a sad reflection of a deep and malignant atomism, lack of communication, and lack of perspective.

University counsel have long recognized the value in promoting greater communication as a means of keeping disputes from snowballing into court. In their legal guide for new department chairs, veteran campus counsel Ann Franke and Lawrence White emphasize the importance of communication and civility in personal interactions, considerations which are seemingly as often overlooked as they are obvious.[127] Colleges and universities have already taken a number of steps in recent years aimed at finding ways of promoting constructive dialogue and reducing antagonism in dispute resolution. Campus ombudspersons, first employed in the 1960s as a means of defusing student unrest, have since been redeployed successfully to address the grievances of individual students, faculty, staff, and even alumni and to divert them from court.[128] Academic institutions are also making greater use of mediation and other mechanisms of alternative dispute resolution, and some are embracing more ambitious approaches in "restorative justice," an innovative response used in some communities with the goal of reconciling offenders and victims through common understanding and acceptance of responsibility, rather than simply meting out sanctions.[129]

Ultimately, of course, no single one of these steps will turn back the tide of campus litigation. Colleges and universities can never go back to the climate that prevailed before the 1960s. But through sustained, steady engagement aimed at promoting a sense of community on campus, and a deeper, more sensitive understanding of the nature and complexity of the academic enterprise in the courts, colleges and universities have their best hope of rebuilding the norms of mutual accommodation, respect, and toleration that once helped to minimize resort to litigation.

Given the indispensability of higher education to the nation's past and future success, and of academic freedom to the vitality of colleges and universities, it is essential to recognize the danger posed by the creeping legalization of academic life. Courts and universities each have important roles to play—through the articulation of workable doctrines of deference, public and judicial education about the norms and contributions of academic life, and the development of internal mechanisms of dispute resolution—in moderating the trend.

But responsibility for the solution also rests with individual members of university communities, as a final story out of Dartmouth College usefully recalls.

Priya Venkatesan's freshman writing students at Dartmouth were surprised to receive an e-mail from their professor at the end of the Winter 2008 term:

> I regret to inform you that I am pursuing a lawsuit in which I am accusing some of you (whom shall go unmentioned in this e-mail) of violating Title VII of anti-federal discrimination laws . . .
>
> I am also writing a book detailing my experiences as your instructor, which will "name names," so to speak. I have all of your evaluation[s] and these will be reproduced in the book.
>
> Have a nice day.[130]

Venkatesan had clashed repeatedly with her students over such topics as postmodernism and French narrative theory. A breaking point came when students erupted in applause after a white male student challenged a feminist argument she was presenting about science in connection with a discussion of Renaissance witch trials.[131]

"I think I have a good case," she explained to the campus newspaper, "because there were just so many instances—it was almost an incessant barrage—of hostility, nastiness and anti-intellectualism that I may just in fact have a case."[132]

Venkatesan, who was also a researcher in Dartmouth's medical school, told reporters that she was also considering litigation against some faculty members. Among other concerns, she complained that "many of her academic interpretations of science in the context of literary theory during laboratory meetings were received in a 'hostile,' 'demeaning' and 'anti-intellectual' manner by her colleagues."[133]

The threat of litigation understandably put some of Venkatesan's freshman students back on their heels. "You're an 18-year-old away from home," observed Thomas Cormen, director of Dartmouth's writing program, sympathetically, "and your professor's threatening to sue you. I'd be anxious."[134]

In the end, the students had nothing to fear; Venkatesan evidently decided not to go forward with her lawsuit. It emerged fairly quickly that Title VII, a statute prohibiting discrimination by employers, was not a promising vehicle for suing her students.

But, more than that, Venkatesan came to see that "[p]robably . . . courts are [not] the way to address this issue."[135] Having left Dartmouth for a research post at Northwestern University, Venkatesan was ready to move on: "The situation was not handled the way it probably should've been," she told a campus reporter at her new academic home. "I want to put it behind me. I think that'll be healthy for everyone."[136]

Venkatesan's threat to sue her students for creating a hostile environment in the classroom had lit up the blogosphere and news outlets from the syndicated *News of the Weird* to the *Wall Street Journal*. Not surprisingly, the suit was offered up as Exhibit A in the media case for everything that is wrong with modern academia. "Class Action," screamed the characteristically pithy headline in the *New York Post;* "Dartmouth Prof Suing Mean Students."[137]

Yet there was an uplifting coda: Venkatesan thought better of it and never sued. When she first pressed her grievances against her Dartmouth students and colleagues, Venkatesan suggested that she wanted her story to serve as an object lesson for others. Yet, she may have provided her greatest service as a role model not by pressing her claims, but by letting them go.

Her ultimate realization—allowing that "right now, the legal road is probably causing more harm than good"[138]—is a lesson a great many more academics plainly need to hear.

Notes

1. An Introduction

1. John P. Holloway, "Injunctive Orders," in Grace W. Holmes, ed., *Law and Discipline on Campus* (Ann Arbor, Mich.: Institute of Continuing Legal Education, 1971), pp. 115, 124.
2. Richard M. Goodman, "A Trial Lawyer's View of Lawsuits against Schools," in Grace W. Holmes, ed., *Law and Discipline on Campus* (Ann Arbor, Mich.: Institute of Continuing Legal Education, 1971), pp. 173, 174–179.
3. Thomas R. Hensley, *The Kent State Incident: Impact of Judicial Process on Public Attitudes* (Westport, Conn.: Greenwood Press, 1981).
4. Goodman, "A Trial Lawyer's View of Lawsuits against Schools," pp. 175–176.
5. Robert M. O'Neil, "The Litigator's Response," in Grace W. Holmes, ed., *Law and Discipline on Campus* (Ann Arbor, Mich.: Institute of Continuing Legal Education, 1971), pp. 159, 161.
6. Robert M. O'Neil, *The Courts, Government, and Higher Education* (New York: Committee for Economic Development, 1972), pp. 1–2, 10.
7. Ibid., p. 168.
8. Ibid.
9. "Questions and Answers," in Grace W. Holmes, ed., *Law and Discipline on Campus* (Ann Arbor, Mich.: Institute of Continuing Legal Education, 1971), pp. 195, 198–199.
10. Ibid., p. 199.
11. Ibid., p. 198.
12. Ibid., p. 199.
13. Ibid., pp. 198–199.
14. O'Neil, *The Courts, Government, and Higher Education,* p. 11.
15. Christopher J. Lucas & John W. Murry Jr., *New Faculty: A Practical Guide for Academic Beginners,* 2d ed. (New York: Palgrave, 2007), chapter 9, pp. 205–227.

16. Ibid., p. 203.

17. C. K. Gunsalus, *The College Administrator's Survival Guide* (Cambridge, Mass.: Harvard University Press, 2006), p. 163.

18. Patricia A. Hollander, D. Parker Young, & Donald D. Gehring, *A Practical Guide to Legal Issues Affecting College Teachers* (Asheville, N.C.: College Administration Publications, 1985), p. 1.

19. Jeffrey Selingo & Goldie Blumenstyk, "At Meeting of College Lawyers, They Talk of Costlier Settlements and Whistle-Blowers," *Chronicle of Higher Education,* July 7, 2006, p. A29.

20. "Pressing Legal Issues: 10 Views of the Next 5 Years," *Chronicle of Higher Education,* June 25, 2004, p. 4; *see also* Alvin P. Sanoff, "Catholic U. Preaches, and Practices, Preventive Law," *Chronicle of Higher Education,* Jan. 27, 2006, p. B13.

21. *See* Josie Cantu-Weber, "Harassment and Discrimination; Litigation and Complaints Involving Higher Education," 3 *Change* 38 (1999); Elizabeth F. Farrell, "Colleges' Risk Managers Face a Rising Tide of Litigation," *Chronicle of Higher Education,* Nov. 16, 2001, p. 29; Lelia B. Helms, "Patterns of Litigation in Postsecondary Education: A Case Law Study," 14 *Journal of College and University Law* 99, 101–103 (1987).

22. Tillinghast-Towers Perrin, *A Summary of Findings from the 1997 Educators Legal Liability Coverage Survey* (New York: Tillinghast-Towers Perrin, 1998).

23. On the rise to prominence of in-house counsel, such that "the legal counsel is now crucial to the operation of a university," *see* Sara Lipka, "The Lawyer Is In: Alligators, Athletics, and the Internet: General Counsels' Growing Role Covers a Range of Issues," *Chronicle of Higher Education,* July 1, 2005, p. A19. On the use of outside counsel, *see* Peter H. Ruger, "The Practice and Profession of Higher Education Law," 27 *Stetson Law Review* 175, 181 (1997).

24. *See* Terry L. Leap, *Tenure, Discrimination, and the Courts,* 2d ed. (Ithaca, N.Y.: ILR Press, 1995).

25. "By the Numbers: The Rise in Race Discrimination Claims, 1991 to 1997," 2 *Employment Action* 3 (United Educators Insurance Risk Retention Group, Winter 1999).

26. *See* Corynne McSherry, *Who Owns Academic Work? Battling for Control of Intellectual Property* (Cambridge, Mass.: Harvard University Press, 2001); Steven G. Poskanzer, *Higher Education and the Law: The Faculty* (Baltimore: Johns Hopkins University Press, 2002), pp. 34–55; David Glenn & Goldie Blumenstyk, "Patent Disputes with Professors Lead to Judgment for Yale U., Lawsuit by UMass," *Chronicle of Higher Education,* Feb. 25, 2005, p. A27.

27. Frederick Schauer, "Is There a Right to Academic Freedom?" 77 *Colorado Law Review* 907, 914–915 (2006).

28. Ibid., p. 915 n.38; *see also* Helms, "Patterns of Litigation," p. 118 (concluding, in a study of Iowa court decisions involving higher education between 1850 and 1987, that the substantial "increase in the volume of litigation is largely

due to suits by faculty, staff or students," which had been essentially nonexistent before 1960).

29. Piggee v. Carl Sandburg College, 464 F.3d 667, 668 (7th Cir. 2006).

30. *See* John R. Thelin, *A History of American Higher Education* (Baltimore: Johns Hopkins University Press, 2004), p. 343. Writing of the period between 1970 and 2000, Thelin observed that "[a]n interesting wrinkle in the growing amount of litigation that involved colleges and universities as defendants was that the plaintiffs varied, ranging from disgruntled outsiders to insiders who as members of the campus community felt that the administration and board had treated them improperly." Ibid.

31. *See* ibid.

32. William A. Kaplin & Barbara A. Lee, *The Law of Higher Education*, 4th ed. (San Francisco: Jossey-Bass, 2006), p. 9.

33. Harry T. Edwards & Virginia Davis Nordin, *Higher Education and the Law* (Cambridge, Mass.: Harvard University Institute for Educational Management, 1979), p. 4.

34. Ibid., pp. 4–5.

35. Helen Gouldner, "The Social Impact of Campus Litigation," 51 *Journal of Higher Education* 329, 331 (1980).

36. *See* Equal Employment Opportunity Act of 1972, § 2, Pub. L. No. 92-261, 86 Stat. 103 (1972). Previously, Title VII exempted educational institutions "with respect to the employment of individuals to perform work connected with the educational activities of such institution[s]." 42 U.S.C. § 2000e-1 (1970).

37. *See* Pub. L. No. 92-318, Title IX, § 901 (1972), *now codified at* 20 U.S.C. § 1681.

38. *See* Pub. L. No. 93-112, § 504 (1973), *now codified as amended at* 29 U.S.C. § 794. In 1992, the Act was amended to substitute the term "disability" for "handicap." *See* Rehabilitation Act Amendments of 1992, § 102(p)(32), Pub. L. No. 102-569,

39. *See* Educational Amendments of 1974, Pub. L. No. 93-380, 88 Stat. 484 (1974), *now codified at* 20 U.S.C. § 1232g. Thus, writing in 1984, Michael Olivas and Kathleen McCartan Denison observed that "the judiciary has become a major interpreter and guarantor of educational outcomes, not because courts have sought this role, but because the increasing legislation affecting education ultimately requires an active role by the courts." Michael A. Olivas & Kathleen McCartan Denison, "Legalization in the Academy: Higher Education and the Supreme Court," 11 *Journal of College and University Law* 1, 1–2 (1984).

40. *See* Civil Rights Restoration Act of 1987, § 4(2), Pub. L. No. 100-259 (1988), *now codified at* 29 U.S.C. § 794(b)(2)(A).

41. Leap, *Tenure, Discrimination, and the Courts*, p. 55.

42. Ibid., p. 47.

43. Lawrence White, "Judicial Threats to Academe's 'Four Freedoms,'" *Chronicle of Higher Education,* Dec. 1, 2006, p. 6 (quoting a 2005 presentation by Donna Euben to the National Association of College and University Attorneys).

44. Cases reported in 2006, for example, included Leibowitz v. Cornell Univ., 445 F.3d 586 (2d Cir. 2006); Cox v. Shelby State Cmty. College, 194 Fed. Appx. 267 (6th Cir. 2006); Atkinson v. Lafayette College, 460 F.3d 447 (3d Cir. 2006); Smith v. Bd. of Trustees, 2006 U.S. Dist. LEXIS 39811 (N.D. Fla. May 27, 2006); Payne v. Univ. of Arkansas, 2006 U.S. Dist. LEXIS 52806 (W.D. Ark. July 26, 2006); Gorres v. Univ. of Rhode Island, 2006 U.S. Dist. LEXIS 63877 (D.R.I. Aug. 21, 2006); Jacobsen v. Illinois Cmty. College, 2006 U.S. Dist. LEXIS 85330 (N.D. Ill. Nov. 21, 2006); Tyler v. Univ. of Louisville, 2006 U.S. Dist. LEXIS 85728 (W.D. Ky. Nov. 27, 2006); Spector v. Community-Technical Colleges, 463 F. Supp. 2d 234 (D. Conn. 2006); Turner v. Sullivan Univ., 420 F. Supp. 2d 773 (W.D. Ky. 2006); Rudebusch v. Arizona, 436 F. Supp. 2d 1058 (D. Ariz. 2006); and Conney v. Univ. of California, 2006 Cal. App. Unpub. LEXIS 8561 (Cal. Ct. App. Sept. 26, 2006). From 2000 through 2005, there were more than 65 such cases.

45. Kaplin & Lee, *The Law of Higher Education,* p. 4.

46. J. Peter Byrne, "The Threat to Constitutional Academic Freedom," 31 *Journal of College & University Law* 79 (2004).

47. Ibid.

48. Atria v. Vanderbilt University, 142 Fed. Appx. 246 (6th Cir. 2005).

49. Ibid., pp. 249–250.

50. Ibid., p. 250.

51. Ibid., p. 255.

52. Ibid., p. 251 n.2 (citation omitted).

53. Ibid., p. 255 (quoting Doherty v. Southern College of Optometry, 862 F.2d 570, 577 (6th Cir. 1988)).

54. Ibid.

55. *See* ibid.

56. Ibid., p. 256.

57. Ibid.

58. *See* United States v. Sheffer, 523 U.S. 303 (1998) (holding that a *per se* ban on the admission of polygraph evidence does not violate a criminal defendant's rights to a fair trial); Richard D. Friedman, "Prior Statements of a Witness: A Nettlesome Corner of the Hearsay Thicket," 1995 *Supreme Court Review* 277, 282–283 (discussing a case in which polygraph evidence was refused while hearsay was admitted).

59. *Atria,* 142 Fed. Appx. at 255.

60. "Pressing Legal Issues," p. 4. Olivas wrote that "[s]uch issues from the business world are leaching slowly into higher-education law . . . The first federal case overturning a grade occurred in 1997, and more litigation is on its way." Ibid.

61. Frank H. T. Rhodes, *The Creation of the Future: The Role of the American University* (Ithaca, N.Y.: Cornell University Press, 2001), p. 1.

62. Ibid.

63. Derek Bok, *Universities in the Marketplace: The Commercialization of Higher Education* (Princeton, N.J.: Princeton University Press, 2003), p. 1.

64. Rhodes, *The Creation of the Future*, xi.

65. Richard Hofstadter & Walter P. Metzger, *The Development of Academic Freedom in the United States* (New York: Columbia University Press, 1955), p. 3.

66. Ibid., p. 6.

67. *See* Byrne, "The Threat to Constitutional Academic Freedom," p. 85. Byrne, for example, observed that the widespread acceptance of the robust concept of academic freedom advanced by the AAUP in first half of the twentieth century "paralleled the success of the American model of higher education in which faculty are expected to pursue research and publication, as well as teach and manage the academic standards for the institution, and individual schools compete for faculty, students, research grants, and philanthropy." Ibid.

68. Rhodes, *The Creation of the Future*, p. 215; *see also* Matthew W. Finkin & Robert C. Post, *For the Common Good: Principles of American Academic Freedom* (New Haven, Conn.: Yale University Press, 2009), pp. 40–41.

69. Ibid., p. 13.

70. Edwards & Nordin, *Higher Education and the Law*, p. 5.

71. Ibid., p. 3.

72. Rhodes, *The Creation of the Future*, p. 14.

73. "Pressing Legal Issues," p. 4 (comments of Peter D. Kushibab, general counsel of the Maricopa County Community College District).

74. Ibid.

75. Byrne, "The Threat to Constitutional Academic Freedom," p. 85.

76. Finkin & Post, *For the Common Good*, p. 7.

77. Bok, *Universities in the Marketplace*, p. 189.

78. Fischbach v. Trustees of California State Univ., 2004 Cal. App. Unpub. LEXIS 987 (Cal. Ct. App. Jan. 30, 2004).

79. Adelman-Reyes v. St. Xavier Univ., 2006 U.S. Dist. LEXIS 24558 (N.D. Ill. Apr. 28, 2006).

80. Ibid., pp. **22–23. Relevantly, on appeal, the court upheld the trial court decision, finding that there was no evidence that the dean had acted recklessly or with a direct intent to injure the professor or sabotage her career. Adelman-Reyes v. St. Xavier Univ., 500 F.3d 662, 669 (7th Cir. 2007).

81. DeJohn v. Temple Univ., 2006 U.S. Dist. LEXIS 64911 (E.D. Pa. Sept. 11, 2006).

82. Byrne, "The Threat to Constitutional Academic Freedom," p. 85.

83. *See* Stacey M. Berg & Montgomery K. Fisher, "Liability of Individuals Who Serve on Panels Reviewing Allegations of Misconduct in Science," 37 *Villanova*

Law Review 1361, 1362 (1992); Thomas H. Wright Jr., "The Faculty and the Law Explosion: Assessing the Impact—A Twenty-Five Year Perspective (1960–85) for College and University Lawyers," 12 *Journal of College & University Law* 363, 378 (1985).

84. Finkin & Post, *For the Common Good*, pp. 7, 43.
85. Tinker v. Des Moines Indep. Community Sch. Dist., 393 U.S. 503, 506 (1969). On the appearance of this phrase, "the bromide of all bromides of academic freedom law," as boilerplate in such decisions of the lower courts, *see* Alan K. Chen, "Bureaucracy and Distrust: Germaneness and the Paradoxes of the Academic Freedom Debate," 77 *University of Colorado Law Review* 955, 955–956 (2006).
86. In one recent case, two staff members, dismissed for conducting an exorcism over the cubicle of an absent colleague they considered possessed, sued the University of Texas at Arlington for violating their rights to religious freedom. *See* Andrew Mytelka, "Fired for Exorcism, 2 Workers Sue College," *Chronicle of Higher Education*, Jan. 5, 2007, p. A26.
87. *E.g.*, Axson-Flynn v. Johnson, 356 F.3d 1277, 1290 (10th Cir. 2004) (quoting Hazelwood Sch. Dist. v. Kuhlmeier, 484 U.S. 260, 273 (1988)); Bishop v. Aronov, 926 F.2d 1066, 1074 (11th Cir. 1991); Head v. Board of Trustees of California State Univ., 2006 WL 2355209, at *6 (N.D. Ill. Aug. 14, 2006). *See* Rebecca Gose Lynch, Note, "Pawns of the State or Priests of Democracy? Analyzing Professors' Academic Freedom Rights Within the State's Managerial Realm," 91 *California Law Review* 1061 (2003).
88. *Axson-Flynn*, 356 F.3d at 1290.
89. Brown v. Li, 308 F.3d 939, 949 (9th Cir. 2002), *cert. denied*, 538 U.S. 908 (2003).
90. *Bishop*, 926 F.2d at 1074.
91. Byrne, "The Threat to Constitutional Academic Freedom," p. 99.
92. Silva v. University of New Hampshire, 888 F. Supp. 293, 316 (D.N.H. 1994).
93. Ibid., p. 313.
94. *See* ibid., p. 300.
95. Robert M. O'Neil, *Free Speech in the College Community* (Bloomington: Indiana University Press, 1997), pp. vii–ix.
96. Bok, *Universities in the Marketplace*, p. 2. For an account of Stanford University's strategic development of academic–industry research partnerships in the 1930s, *see* Thelin, *A History of American Higher Education*, pp. 243–245.
97. Ibid., p. 2. On Saban's hiring, *see* William C. Rhoden, "Paying the Price While Coaches Cash In," *New York Times*, Jan. 9, 2007; Jodi Upton, "Contract Could Bring Congressional Inquiry, Administrators Worried about Rollover Effect," *USA Today*, Jan. 4, 2007, p. 9C. For a perceptive early account of "The Rise of Football" in higher education, *see* Frederick Rudolph, *The American College and University: A History*, rev. ed. (Athens: University of Georgia Press, 1990), p. 373.

98. Ibid. For other accounts assessing the commercialization of academia, *see* Eric Gould, *The University in a Corporate Culture* (New Haven, Conn.: Yale University Press, 2003); David L. Kirp, *Shakespeare, Einstein, and the Bottom Line: The Marketing of Higher Education* (Cambridge, Mass.: Harvard University Press, 2003); Donald G. Stein, ed., *Buying In or Selling Out? The Commercialization of the American Research University* (New Brunswick, N.J.: Rutgers University Press, 2004); Jennifer Washburn, *University, Inc.: The Corporate Corruption of American Higher Education* (New York: Basic Books, 2005).

99. Lawrence White, "Judicial Threats to Academe's 'Four Freedoms,'" *Chronicle of Higher Education*, Dec. 1, 2006, p. 6.

100. Ibid.

101. This book does not seek to compare directly litigation in higher education with litigation rates in the United States more generally; indeed *any* litigation in higher education is noteworthy because of past legal protections and campus and societal norms. Nonetheless, it is interesting to note that while instances of higher education litigation in the United States seem to be rising, not all types of claims have increased in U.S. courts generally. Tort claims in the United States, for example, fell 21 percent in the period from 1997 through 2007. Robert C. LaFountain, Richard Y. Schauffler, Shauna M. Strickland, William E. Raftery, Chantel G. Bromage, Cynthia G. Lee, & Sarah A. Gibson, "Examining the Work of State Courts, 2007: A National Perspective from the Court Statistics Project," (Williamsburg, VA: National Center for State Courts, 2008). Automobile tort cases fell 23 percent, medical malpractice claims fell 8 percent, and product liability filings fell 4 percent, though contracts claims rose by 23 percent (Ibid). And while there is certainly a clear difference between filed civil claims (which may ultimately settle before trial) and civil trials, the Bureau of Justice Statistics found a 50 percent decline in the number of civil trials between 1992 and 2005. Lynn Langton & Thomas H. Cohen, *Civil Bench and Jury Trials in State Courts 2005* (Washington, DC: U.S. Department of Justice, Office of Justice Programs, 2008).

102. *See* Robert A. Kagan, *Adversarial Legalism: The American Way of Law* (Cambridge, Mass.: Harvard University Press, 2001); Mary Ann Glendon, *Rights Talk: The Impoverishment of Political Discourse* (New York: Free Press, 1991).

103. Clark Kerr, *The Uses of the University*, 4th ed. (Cambridge, Mass.: Harvard University Press, 1995), p. 1.

104. *See* Rhodes, *The Creation of the Future*, pp. 8–11, 45–48.

105. *See* White, "Judicial Threats to Academe's 'Four Freedoms,'" p. 6.

106. *See* Donna Euben, "Legal Contingencies for Contingent Professors," *Chronicle of Higher Education*, June 16, 2006, p. 8 (noting that "[a]s the ranks of contingent faculty members expand, so too does the amount of litigation involving them").

107. *See* "Pressing Legal Issues," p. 4 (comments of Martin Michaelson, a partner in Hogan & Hartson in Washington, D.C.).

108. *See* ibid. (comments of Beverly E. Ledbetter, vice president and general counsel of Brown University, noting that "[t]he distinction between the academic world and the corporate sector is dissolving," and "[a]s regulators try to sort out which hat we are wearing, tax consequences will surely follow"); Scott D. Makar, "Litigious Students and Academic Disputes," *Chronicle of Higher Education,* Nov. 8, 2002, p. 20 (noting that "courts and juries increasingly view colleges as no different from commercial businesses"—"a trend that could have frightening implications for higher education").

109. *See Atria,* 142 Fed. Appx. at 251 n.2.

110. Sharick v. Southeastern Univ. of Health Sci., 780 So.2d 142, 142 (Fla. Ct. App. 2001) (Ramirez, J., concurring in denial of reh'g) (quoting Hazel Glenn Beh, "Student versus University: The University's Implied Obligation of Good Faith and Fair Dealing," 59 *Maryland Law Review* 183, 196 (2000)).

111. Ibid.

112. Ibid., p. 4; *see also* Hofstadter & Metzger, *The Development of Academic Freedom in the United States,* pp. 7–11. As Peter Byrne has noted, "[l]aw played no positive role in the development or initial enforcement of academic freedom. The principles and procedures were developed by academics, adopting German principles, for internal governance and to make up for the lack of authority or protection extended to faculty by law." Byrne, "The Threat to Constitutional Academic Freedom," p. 85.

113. *See* Robert M. O'Neil, "Academic Freedom and the Constitution," 11 *Journal of College & University Law* 275, 278 (1984).

114. Peter Byrne has traced "[t]he first appearance of the words 'academic freedom' in a reported judicial opinion" to a 1940 decision by a New York trial court—ironically, ordering "City College not to employ Bertrand Russell as a professor because of his bad moral character, evidenced by his writings on sex." Byrne, "The Threat to Constitutional Academic Freedom," p. 86 (citing Kay v. Bd. of Higher Educ., 18 N.Y.S.2d 821 (N.Y. Sup. Ct. 1940)).

115. 354 U.S. 234 (1957).

116. Ibid., p. 250.

117. Ibid., p. 262 (Frankfurter, J., concurring) (internal citations omitted).

118. *See* J. Peter Byrne, "Academic Freedom: A 'Special Concern of the First Amendment,'" 99 *Yale Law Journal* 251 (1989).

119. *See* Grutter v. Bollinger, 539 U.S. 306, 328–329 (2003); Regents of the Univ. of California v. Bakke, 438 U.S. 265, 312 (1978) (opinion of Powell, J.).

120. Robert M. O'Neil, "Academic Freedom in the Post–September 11 Era: An Old Game with New Rules," in Evan Gerstmann & Matthew J. Streb, eds., *Academic Freedom at the Dawn of a New Century: How Terrorism, Governments, and Culture Wars Impact Free Speech* (Stanford, Calif.: Stanford University Press, 2006), p. 43.

121. *Sweezy,* 354 U.S. at 262 (Frankfurter, J., concurring).

122. Ibid.

123. Ibid., p. 250.

124. *See, e.g.,* Johnson v. Heimbach, 2003 WL 22838476 (E.D. Pa. Nov. 25, 2003) (ultimately rejecting a professor's First Amendment claim to be free from negative peer evaluations containing " 'false perceptions' from in-class observations, 'derogatory written comments,' and 'conclusions of teaching effectiveness without first discussing their classroom observations with [Plaintiff]' "), *aff'd,* 112 Fed. Appx. 866 (3d Cir. 2004).

125. Urofsky v. Gilmore, 216 F.3d 401 (4th Cir. 2000).

126. Byrne, "The Threat to Constitutional Academic Freedom," p. 111.

127. O'Neil, "Academic Freedom and the Constitution," p. 278.

128. *See* David M. Rabban, "A Functional Analysis of 'Individual' and 'Institutional' Academic Freedom," 53 *Law & Contemporary Problems* 227 (1990).

129. Matthew Finkin, "Intramural Speech, Academic Freedom, and the First Amendment," 66 *Texas Law Review* 1323, 1343 (1988).

130. Matthew Finkin, "On Institutional Academic Freedom," 61 *Texas Law Review* 817, 843 (1983).

131. Ibid., p. 845.

132. *Statement on Academic Freedom,* May 25, 2005, First Annual Global Colloquium of University Presidents. The statement emerged from a discussion on academic freedom by participating presidents of more than 40 universities from around the world, chaired by Columbia University president Lee Bollinger, himself a leading scholar on academic freedom and the First Amendment, in January 2005. Of course, given that the discussants were themselves university presidents, it is perhaps not surprising that "[a]s participants wrestled with the meaning of academic freedom, institutional autonomy quickly emerged as a critical enabling condition." Report on the First Annual Colloquium of University Presidents, available at www.columbia .edu.

133. O'Neil, "Academic Freedom and the Constitution," p. 281.

134. O'Neil, "The Litigator's Response," 170; O'Neil, *The Courts, Government, and Higher Education,* pp. 38–39.

135. *See* Rhodes, *The Creation of the Future,* pp. 45–57.

136. *See* Gunsalus, *The College Administrator's Survival Guide,* pp. 147–150.

137. O'Neil, "The Litigator's Response," p. 169.

138. *See* Eugene McCormack, "Socratic Guidance for Faculty Grievances: More Institutions Are Asking Ombudsmen to Handle Professors' Complaints before They Escalate," *Chronicle of Higher Education,* Feb. 3, 2006, p. A10; Makar, "Litigious Students and Academic Disputes," p. A20.

139. *See* Christine Des Gerennes, "Changes Made to Online Education Proposal," *(Champaign-Urbana, Ill.) News-Gazette,* Jan. 9, 2007, p. A1; "U of I Plans For-Profit Online 'Campus,' " *Crain's Chicago Business,* Sept. 6, 2006. Original plans

to organize the virtual "campus" as a limited liability corporation were dropped in January 2007 in response to objections from university faculty. *See* Des Gerennes, "Changes Made to Online Education Proposal," p. A1.

140. Paul Wood, "UI Board of Trustees Votes to Reboot Global Campus," *(Champaign-Urbana, Ill.) News-Gazette,* May 22, 2009.

141. Karen W. Arenson, "At Universities, Plum Post at Top Is Now Shaky," *New York Times,* Jan. 9, 2007.

142. Report on the First Annual Colloquium of University Presidents on academic freedom, available at www.columbia.edu.

143. Poskanzer, *Higher Education and the Law: The Faculty,* pp. 259–260.

144. Holmes v. Poskanzer, 2007 U.S. Dist. LEXIS 3216 (N.D.N.Y. Jan. 3, 2007) (memorandum decision and order).

145. Press release, "Judge Grants Preliminary Injunction to Students," SUNY–New Paltz, Jan. 5, 2007, available online at www.newpaltz.edu/.

146. The trial court dismissed the plaintiff's complaint in February 2008, mostly on qualified immunity grounds. Holmes v. Poskanzer, 2008 U.S. Dist. LEXIS 13545 (N.D.N.Y. Feb. 21, 2008).

2. A World Apart

1. David W. Robson, *Educating Republicans: The College in the Era of the American Revolution* (Westport, Conn.: Greenwood Press, 1985), p. 104.

2. Ibid., pp. 104–105; Willis Rudy, *The Campus and the Nation in Crisis: From the American Revolution to Vietnam* (Madison, N.J.: Fairleigh Dickinson University Press, 1996), pp. 31–32.

3. *The National Cyclopedia of American Biography,* vol. 3 (New York: James T. White & Co., 1893), pp. 233–234.

4. Rudy, *Campus and Nation,* p. 33.

5. Ibid., pp. 33–34; *see also* Jennings L. Wagoner Jr., *Jefferson and Education* (Charlottesville, Va.: Thomas Jefferson Foundation, 2004), pp. 39–41.

6. Bracken v. Visitors of William & Mary College, 7 Va. 573 (1790).

7. Ibid., p. 599.

8. *See* Bracken v. William & Mary College, 5 Va. 161, 164 (1797).

9. *See* Matthew C. Finkin & Robert C. Post, *For the Common Good: Principles of American Academic Freedom* (New Haven, Conn.: Yale University Press, 2009), pp. 11–24.

10. *See* John R. Thelin, *A History of American Higher Education* (Baltimore: Johns Hopkins University Press, 2004), pp. 11–12 (contrasting governance at Oxford and Cambridge and the early colonial colleges); Finkin & Post, *For the Common Good,* pp. 24–25; Judith Areen, "Government as Educator: A New Understanding of First Amendment Protection of Academic Freedom and Governance," 97 *Georgetown Law Journal* 945, 951–953 (2009); Matthew W. Finkin, "On 'Institutional' Academic Freedom," 61 *Texas Law Review* 817,

822–825 (1983) (contrasting collegiate governance in Germany and the United States); Jurgen Herbst, *From Crisis to Crisis: American College Government, 1639–1819* (Cambridge, Mass.: Harvard University Press, 1982).

11. Rudy, *Campus and Nation,* p. 35.

12. *See* Robert M. O'Neil, "Academic Freedom and the Constitution," 11 *Journal of College and University Law* 275, 278–279 (1984) (observing that scholarly interest in legal protection for the academic freedom of faculty was only "nascent" by the late 1930s, and that as late as 1961, " '[a] reading of hundreds of cases . . . yielded very few opinions which pay any attention to the subject of academic freedom, and, much less, show any genuine appreciation of either its meaning or substance' ") (quoting David Fellman, "Academic Freedom in American Law," 61 *Wisconsin Law Review* 3, 17 (1961)).

13. Bracken v. William & Mary College, 5 Va. 161 (1797).

14. *National Cyclopedia of American Biography,* vol. 3, p. 234. For the proximity of the church and president's house, and the continued interactions of Madison and Bracken as Episcopal leaders, see David L. Holmes, *A Brief History of the Episcopal Church* (Valley Forge, Pa.: Trinity Press International, 1993), p. 19.

15. Trustees of Dartmouth College v. Woodward, 17 U.S. 518 (1819).

16. Daniel Walker Howe, "Religion and Education in the Young Republic," in Wilfred M. McClay, ed., *Figures in the Carpet: Finding the Human Person in the American Past* (Grand Rapids, Mich.: William B. Eerdmans Publishing Co., 2006), p. 386.

17. The Trustees issued a bill of particulars justifying Wheelock's dismissal, including that Wheelock had "claim[ed] to exercise the whole executive authority of the college, which the Charter has expressly committed to the Trustees," and that he had "libeled" the Trustees and led others to believe that "the real cause of the dissatisfaction of the Trustees with him was a diversity of religious opinions between him and them." Baxter Perry Smith, *The History of Dartmouth College* (Boston: Houghton, Osgood & Co., 1878), pp. 96–97 (quoting Trustees' statement of grounds for dismissal).

18. Ibid., p. 100.

19. Howe, "Religion and Education," pp. 386–387; Francis N. Stites, *Private Interest and Public Gain: The Dartmouth College Case, 1819* (Amherst: University of Massachusetts Press, 1972).

20. Smith, *History of Dartmouth College,* p. 103 (reproducing remonstrance of Trustees Thomas Thompson, Elijah Paine, and Asa M'Farland, June 19, 1816).

21. Trustees of Dartmouth College v. Woodward, 1 N.H. 111, 135–136 (1817).

22. Ibid.

23. Trustees of Dartmouth College v. Woodward, 17 U.S. 518 (1819).

24. Writing for the Court, Marshall did allow that the Trustees might qualify as third-party beneficiaries of the College's charter, with "a freehold right in

the powers confided to them," giving them a personal stake in objecting to the state's impairment of the contract. Ibid., pp. 653–654.

25. Ibid., p. 630; *see Bracken*, 7 Va. 573 (contending that William & Mary was "a private, not a public institution," "completely Eleemosynary").

26. Trustees of Dartmouth College v. Woodward, 17 U.S. at 653.

27. Ibid., pp. 646–647.

28. The prevailing view is stated, for example, by Guy Padula: "In the annals of American constitutional law very few cases approach the importance of *Dartmouth College*. By ruling that charters of incorporation are to receive constitutional protection against legislative infringement, the Marshall Court left an indelible stamp on the development of the American economy." Guy Padula, *Madison v. Marshall: Popular Sovereignty, Natural Law, and the United States Constitution* (Lanham, Md.: Lexington Books, 2001), p. 131.

29. Finkin, " 'Institutional' Academic Freedom," p. 832.

30. Ibid., p. 833.

31. *See* Sage v. Dillard, 54 Ky. 340 (1854) (reaching the same conclusion as *Dartmouth College* on remarkably similar facts, while acknowledging that "the legislature may amend the charters of public corporations").

32. Thelin, *History of American Higher Education*, pp. 71–72. Frederick Rudolph, in his classic history of American higher education, also emphasizes the porousness of the public–private distinction in the establishment and early experience of Harvard, William and Mary, and Yale. *See* Frederick Rudolph, *The American College and University: A History* (Athens: University of Georgia Press 1990), pp. 13–15.

33. *See* Alumni of Dartmouth College v. Trustees of Dartmouth College, N.H. Super. Ct., Grafton Co., No. 07-E-0289 (Respondent's Motion to Dismiss, Oct. 26, 2007); Statement on Termination of Lawsuit Against Dartmouth College (Dartmouth College press release, June 27, 2008) (available at www.dart mouth.edu); Annie Karni, "Dartmouth May Face Lawsuit over Trustees," *New York Sun*, Sept. 13, 2007.

34. Sterling v. Regents of the Univ. of Michigan, 68 N.W. 253, 255 (Mich. 1896) (quoting Select Committee Report, Mich. House Doc. 1840, p. 470).

35. Ibid., p. 256 (quoting Mich. Const. of 1850, art. 13).

36. The century-long struggle between homeopathy and mainstream medicine is placed in a broader context in John S. Haller Jr., *The History of American Homeopathy: The Academic Years, 1820–1935* (New York: Pharmaceutical Products Press, 2005).

37. In truth, unconventional medical theories were not altogether alien to the Michigan faculty. An early history of the University recalled that one of the founding members of the medical school faculty, a Dr. Denton, was "long remembered by his students because of his high hat and his buck-board wagon, as well as his belief in the medical efficiency of alcohol." Wilfred Shaw, *The University of Michigan* (New York: Harcourt, Brace & Howe, 1920), p. 124.

38. People *ex rel.* Drake v. Regents of the Univ. of Mich., 4 Mich. 98 (1856).

39. People *ex rel.* Regents of the Univ. of Mich. v. Auditor-General, 17 Mich. 161, 168 (1868) (quoting 1867 statute); Shaw, *University of Michigan,* p. 58.

40. Shaw, *University of Michigan,* pp. 143–144.

41. *Sterling,* 68 N.W. at 256.

42. Ibid.

43. Haller, *History of American Homeopathy,* pp. 122–123.

44. Professor Peter Byrne counted nine states whose public universities enjoyed constitutional status (California, Georgia, Hawaii, Idaho, Michigan, Minnesota, Montana, Nebraska, and Oklahoma), though he noted that the courts' generosity in "interpret[ing] often ambiguous constitutional language as imposing limitations on the legislature," made it difficult to identify all such jurisdictions. J. Peter Byrne, "Academic Freedom: A 'Special Concern of the First Amendment,'" 99 *Yale Law Journal* 251, 327 n.303 (1989).

45. *History of Boone County, Missouri* (St. Louis: Western Historical Co., 1882), pp. 274–286 (quoting Columbia *Statesman* article of Oct. 5, 1849); *see also* Marshall Solomon Snow, *Higher Education in Missouri* (Washington, D.C.: Government Printing Office, U.S. Bureau of Education, Circular of Information No. 2, 1898) p. 20.

46. Snow, *Higher Education in Missouri,* pp. 20–21.

47. Head v. The University, 86 U.S. 526, 528 (1873).

48. Ibid., pp. 529–531.

49. *See* Matthew W. Finkin, "'A Higher Order of Liberty in the Workplace': Academic Freedom and Tenure into the Vortex of Employment Practices and Law," 53 *Law and Contemporary Problems* 357 (1990).

50. Darrow v. Briggs, 169 S.W. 118, 123–124 (Mo. 1914).

51. 138 F. 372, 376–377 (8th Cir. 1905); *see also* People *ex rel.* Kelsey v. New York Postgraduate Med. Sch. & Hosp., 51 N.Y.S. 420 (App. Div. 1898) (finding that medical college had authority to dismiss faculty without notice or grounds notwithstanding bylaws provision specifying detailed procedure for "removal" of faculty members for grounds).

52. 58 N.W. 1042, 1044–1045 (Wis. 1894).

53. Byrne, "Academic Freedom," p. 325.

54. 38 S.E. 698, 698–700 (W. Va. 1901). For a discussion of modern interpretation of "good cause" limitations in employment contracts, *see* Isidore Silver, *Public Employee Discharge and Discipline,* 3rd ed., vol. 1, § 21.02 (New York: Panel Publishers, 2001).

55. People *ex rel.* Pratt v. Wheaton College, 40 Ill. 186, 187 (1866). In another "secret society" case, the Indiana Supreme Court surprisingly invalidated Purdue University's policy of refusing admission to students who would not disavow membership in fraternities, bizarrely distinguishing the *Wheaton College* case on the ground that it established only the university's power to dismiss students once admitted, not to deny them admission in the first

instance. State *ex rel.* Stallard v. White, 82 Ind. 278 (1882). The opinion's author, Justice William Ellis Niblack, was himself a member of the Sons of the
American Revolution, a fraternal order, and was reported to harbor hopes of
running for governor.

56. Waugh v. Board of Trustees of University of Mississippi, 237 U.S. 589, 596–597
(1915) (upholding University's enforcement of state law banning fraternal organizations on the ground that "whether such membership makes
against discipline was for the state of Mississippi to determine" and "[i]t is
not for us to entertain conjectures in opposition to the views of the state,
and annul its regulations upon disputable considerations of their wisdom or
necessity").

57. Robert D. Bickel & Peter F. Lake, *The Rights and Responsibilities of the Modern
University* (Durham, N.C.: Carolina Academic Press, 1999), p. 22.

58. As Bickel and Lake observed, before about 1960, "a university was rarely, if
ever, subject to a lawsuit. It was a time of *insularity* from legal scrutiny, and
like governments, charities and families of that era, the college was considered to be another institution outside the safety rules of the legal system,
and in a sense above the law." Ibid., p. 7 (emphasis in original).

59. *See* ibid., pp. 17–33; David A. Hoekema, *Campus Rules and Moral Community:
In Place of* In Loco Parentis (Lanham, Md.: Rowman & Littlefield Publishers,
1994), pp. 21–26.

60. *See* Barbara Bennett Woodhouse, "Child Abuse, the Constitution, and the
Legacy of *Pierce v. Society of Sisters,*" 78 *University of Detroit-Mercy Law Review*
479 (2001); State v. Wilder, 748 A.2d 444 (Me. 2000) (holding that courts
must consider deferentially parents' reasons for inflicting corporal punishment in any criminal prosecution for child abuse).

61. *See* Elizabeth M. Schneider, "The Violence of Privacy," 23 *Connecticut Law Review* 973 (1991); Reva B. Siegel, "'The Rule of Love': Wife Beating as Pre-
rogative and Privacy," 105 *Yale Law Review* 2117 (1996); Barbara Bennett
Woodhouse, "'Who Owns the Child?' *Meyer* and *Pierce* and the Child as
Property," 33 *William and Mary Law Review* 995 (1992).

62. John B. Stetson Univ. v. Hunt, 102 So. 637 (Fla. 1924).

63. Tanton v. McKenney, 197 N.W. 510, 511–513 (Mich. 1924).

64. Anthony v. Syracuse Univ., 231 N.Y.S. 435, 440 (App. Div. 1928); *see also*
West v. Board of Trustees, 181 N.E. 144 (Ohio Ct. App. 1931) (deferring to
Miami University's dismissal of a student for failing grades).

65. *Hartigan,* 38 S.E. at 699; *see also Gillan,* 58 N.W. at 1044.

66. *Stetson Univ.,* 102 So. at 641.

67. Byrne, "Academic Freedom," p. 323.

68. *See* Harry T. Edwards & Virginia Davis Nordin, *Higher Education and the Law*
(Cambridge, Mass.: Harvard University Institute for Educational Manage-
ment, 1979), pp. 14–17; Neil W. Hamilton, *Zealotry and Academic Freedom: A
Legal and Historical Perspective* (New Brunswick, N.J.: Transaction Press,

1995), pp. 215–217; Lelia B. Helms, "Patterns of Litigation in Postsecondary Education: A Case Law Study," 14 *Journal of College and University Law* 99, 102–103 (1987); Terrence Leas, "Evolution of the Doctrine of Academic Abstention in American Jurisprudence" (Ph.D. diss., Florida State University, 1989); *compare* William A. Kaplin & Barbara A. Lee, *The Law of Higher Education,* 4th ed. (San Francisco: Jossey-Bass, 2006), pp. 9–11 (describing same phenomenon as a product of "judicial hands-off attitudes").

69. *See* John Bellamy Foster, "The Commitment of an Intellectual: Paul M. Sweezy (1910–2004)," 56 *Monthly Review* (Oct. 2004); Christopher Phelps, "An Interview with Paul M. Sweezy—Founding Editor of the 'Monthly Review,'" *Monthly Review* (May 1999); Louis Uchitelle, "Paul Sweezy, 93, Marxist Publisher and Economist, Dies," *New York Times,* Mar. 2, 2004.

70. Sweezy v. New Hampshire, 354 U.S. 234, 236–237 (1957) (quoting New Hampshire statute).

71. Ibid., p. 250.

72. Ibid., pp. 261–262 (Frankfurter, J., concurring in the judgment).

73. *See* Adler v. Board of Educ. of the City of New York, 342 U.S. 485, 508 (1952) (Douglas, J., dissenting); Wieman v. Updegraff, 344 U.S. 183, 195–197 (1952) (Frankfurter, J., concurring); *see also* William W. Van Alstyne, "Academic Freedom and the First Amendment in the Supreme Court of the United States: An Unhurried Historical Review," 53 *Law and Contemporary Problems* 79, 105–109 (1990). Ironically, the very first invocation of "academic freedom" in a judicial opinion is found in an infamous New York trial court decision trashing the concept. In *In re Kay,* 18 N.Y.S.2d 821 (Sup. Ct. 1940), the court sided with a legal challenge to the appointment of Bertrand Russell to a chair of philosophy at City College of New York based upon his "bad moral character" as evidenced by "the filth which is contained in [his] books." The court set aside concerns for academic freedom on the rationale that "[a]cademic freedom does not mean academic license[;] [i]t is the freedom to do good and not to teach evil." Ibid., pp. 826–829. Fortunately, the *Kay* decision stood then, as it does today, as a notorious outlier in a case law otherwise stacked heavily against such interventions.

74. Finkin, "'A Higher Order of Liberty,'" p. 357.

75. Matthew Finkin and Robert Post provide a comprehensive and compelling account of the AAUP's pivotal role in Finkin & Post, *For the Common Good.*

76. Van Alstyne, "Academic Freedom and the First Amendment," p. 79. Of course, Sweezy's own unhappy experience in the academy illustrates just how "soft" these protections were. As Robert O'Neil points out, "[d]uring the McCarthy era of the 1950s, at least a hundred tenured or continuing professors at American colleges and universities were dismissed, mainly for suspect political associations or even for refusing to expose or accuse colleagues when asked to do so by legislative committees." Robert O'Neil, *Academic Freedom in*

the Wired World: Political Extremism, Corporate Power, and the University (Cambridge, Mass.: Harvard University Press, 2008), p. 23.

77. Walter P. Metzger, "The 1940 Statement of Principles on Academic Freedom and Tenure," 53 *Law and Contemporary Problems* 3, 7 (1990).
78. Van Alstyne, "Academic Freedom and the First Amendment," p. 80.
79. Keyishian v. Board of Regents of the Univ. of the State of N.Y., 385 U.S. 589, 603 (1967) (quoting United States v. Associated Press, 52 F. Supp. 362, 372 (S.D.N.Y. 1943)). For a compelling "inside" account of the *Keyishian* litigation, *see* Robert M. O'Neil, "The Story of *Keyishian v. Board of Regents:* Loyalty Oaths, Academic Freedom and Free Speech in the University Community," in Michael A. Olivas & Ronna Greff Schneider, eds., *Education Law Stories* (New York: Foundation Press, 2008), p. 285.
80. Regents of the University of California v. Bakke, 438 U.S. 265, 312–313 (1978) (opinion of Powell, J.).
81. *Sweezy,* 354 U.S. at 262–263 (Frankfurter, J., concurring in the judgment).
82. *Bakke,* 438 U.S. at 313.
83. Grutter v. Bollinger, 539 U.S. 306, 329 (2003) (quoting *Bakke,* 438 U.S. at 318–319); *see also* Paul Horwitz, "*Grutter*'s First Amendment," 46 *Boston College Law Review* 461 (2005).
84. Board of Curators of the University of Missouri v. Horowitz, 435 U.S. 78, 90–92 (1978).
85. Ibid., p. 96 n.6 (Powell, J., concurring).
86. Regents of the University of Michigan v. Ewing, 474 U.S. 214, 225 (1985).
87. Ibid., p. 226.
88. Byrne, "Academic Freedom," p. 326.
89. Healy v. James, 408 U.S. 176, 172–176 & nn. 4 & 6 (1972). For an account of the growing militancy of the SDS at the time of the Connecticut controversy, *see* David Barber, *A Hard Rain Fell: The SDS and Why It Failed* (Oxford: University of Mississippi Press, 2008).
90. Healy v. James, 445 F.2d 1122, 1123 (2d Cir. 1971).
91. *Healy,* 408 U.S. at 185–193.
92. Ibid., pp. 195–196 (Burger, C.J., concurring).
93. Ibid., pp. 196–197 (Douglas, J., concurring).
94. Paul Horwitz, "Universities as First Amendment Institutions: Some Easy Answers and Hard Questions," 54 *UCLA Law Review* 1497, 1503 (2007).
95. As Professor Judith Areen observed, "[t]he academic freedom decisions of the Supreme Court naturally fall into two distinct periods. In the early period, which began in 1952, the Court protected the academic freedom of faculty from intrusions by state legislatures . . . After 1968, most Court cases involved internal rather than external challenges to academic freedom." Areen, "Government as Educator," p. 967.
96. *See* O'Neil, "Academic Freedom and the Constitution," p. 281.
97. *Grutter,* 539 U.S. at 328.

98. Ibid., pp. 328, 343.
99. Ibid., pp. 379–380 (Rehnquist, C.J., dissenting).
100. Ibid., pp. 362–364 (Thomas, J., concurring in part and dissenting in part).
101. Ibid., p. 350.
102. Ibid., pp. 362, 363.
103. Ibid., p. 377 (Thomas, J., concurring in part and dissenting in part).

3. Battles over Bias

1. McLaurin v. Oklahoma State Regents for Higher Education, 339 U.S. 637, 640 (1950).
2. *See* State of Missouri *ex rel.* Gaines v. Canada, 305 U.S. 337 (1938).
3. Sipuel v. Board of Regents of University of Oklahoma, 332 U.S. 631 (1948).
4. *See McLaurin,* 339 U.S. at 639–640 & n.1; Mark V. Tushnet, *Making Civil Rights Law: Thurgood Marshall and the Supreme Court, 1936–1961* (New York: Oxford University Press, 1994), pp. 129–130.
5. *See* Richard Kluger, *Simple Justice: The History of* Brown v. Board of Education *and Black America's Struggle for Equality* (New York: Vintage Books, 1977), pp. 268–269; Tushnet, *Making Civil Rights Law,* p. 130.
6. *McLaurin,* 339 U.S. at 640–641.
7. Brown v. Board of Education, 347 U.S. 483 (1954).
8. *See* Tushnet, *Making Civil Rights Law,* pp. 126–127; Mark V. Tushnet, *The NAACP's Legal Strategy Against Segregated Education, 1925–1950* (Chapel Hill: University of North Carolina Press, 1987); Plessy v. Ferguson, 163 U.S. 537 (1896).
9. Sweatt v. Painter, 339 U.S. 629 (1950).
10. Sweezy v. New Hampshire, 354 U.S. 234, 263 (1957) (Frankfurter, J., concurring) (quoting Remonstrance of the Open Universities in South Africa).
11. Ada Lois Sipuel Fisher, *A Matter of Black and White: The Autobiography of Ada Lois Sipuel Fisher* (Norman: University of Oklahoma Press, 1996), p. 92. At the University of Oklahoma, President George Lynn Cross had actually been sympathetic and quietly helpful to both McLaurin and Sipuel, but navigated a narrow space cabined by state statutes. For example, "[t]he university president told [a prominent Oklahoma civil rights advocate] that he would put whatever 'you feel will get you into court' in the letter rejecting Sipuel's application." Tushnet, *Making Civil Rights Law,* p. 129. Sipuel herself described the designation of the president as a defendant as "purely legalistic." "From the very beginning," she wrote, "I realized that resistance was coming primarily from certain elected officials, the legislature, and the Constitution and laws of the State of Oklahoma." Fisher, *A Matter of Black and White,* p. 92. For President Cross's own account, *see* George Lynn Cross, *Blacks in White Colleges: Oklahoma's Landmark Cases* (Norman: University of Oklahoma Press, 1975).
12. Berea College v. Commonwealth of Kentucky, 211 U.S. 45, 46 (1908) (quoting 1904 Kentucky statute). The centrality of integrated education to the

college's mission, and the remarkable courage of its founders in pursuing that mission in antebellum Kentucky, is told in John A. Rogers, *The Birth of Berea College: A Story of Providence* (Philadelphia: Henry T. Coates & Co., 1902), published two years before the enactment of the Kentucky statute mandating segregation. As Professor William Van Alstyne observes, "[i]n modern terms, [Berea's] would be called a strong institutional academic freedom claim." William W. Van Alstyne, "Academic Freedom and the First Amendment in the Supreme Court of the United States: An Unhurried Historical Review," 53 *Law and Contemporary Problems* 79, 91 (1990) (emphasis omitted).

13. Matthew W. Finkin, "On 'Institutional' Academic Freedom," 61 *Texas Law Review* 817, 836 (1983).

14. *See* William M. Wiecek, *The Birth of the Modern Constitution: The United States Supreme Court, 1943–1951* (New York: Cambridge University Press, 2006) (volume XII of the Oliver Wendell Holmes Devise History of the Supreme Court), pp. 685–687; Kluger, *Simple Justice,* pp. 280–291.

15. Michael J. Klarman, *From Jim Crow to Civil Rights: The Supreme Court and the Struggle for Racial Equality* (New York: Oxford University Press, 2004), p. 205; *see also* Leland B. Ware, "The Story of *Brown v. Board of Education:* The Long Road to Racial Equality," in Michael A. Olivas & Ronna Greff Schneider, eds., *Education Law Stories* (New York: Foundation Press, 2008), pp. 19, 35–36.

16. Fisher, *A Matter of Black and White,* pp. 100, 144–145; Sherman P. Willis, "Bridging the Gap: A Look at Higher Public Education Cases between *Plessy* and *Brown,*" 30 *Thurgood Marshall Law Review* 1, 36–37 (2004).

17. Fisher, *A Matter of Black and White,* pp. 145–146.

18. Canavan v. College of Osteopathic Physicians and Surgeons, 166 P.2d 878 (Cal. Ct. App. 1946).

19. As the Supreme Court explained, in crafting an award of retroactive job seniority to a victim of employment discrimination under Title VII of the Civil Rights Act of 1964: "To effectuate this 'make whole' objective, Congress in § 706(g) vested broad equitable discretion in the federal courts to 'order such affirmative action as may be appropriate, which may include, but is not limited to, reinstatement or hiring of employees, with or without back pay . . . , or any other equitable relief as the court deems appropriate.'" Franks v. Bowman Transportation Co., 424 U.S. 747, 763 (1976).

20. Section 702 of Title VII of the Civil Rights Act of 1964, 78 Stat. 255, quoted in University of Pennsylvania v. EEOC, 493 U.S. 182, 189–190 (1990). Title VII, as amended, now appears at 42 U.S.C. §§ 2000e *et seq.*

21. *See* Note, "Questioning Age-Old Wisdom: The Legality of Mandatory Retirement of Tenured Faculty under the ADEA," 105 *Harvard Law Review* 889 (1992). The Age Discrimination in Employment Act, as amended, now appears at 29 U.S.C. §§ 621 *et seq.*

22. Terry L. Leap, *Tenure, Discrimination, and the Courts,* 2d ed. (Ithaca, N.Y.: ILR Press, 1995), p. 27.

23. *See* Roy Lavon Brooks, *Rethinking the American Race Problem* (Berkeley: University of California Press, 1990), p. 63; J. Peter Byrne, "Academic Freedom: A 'Special Concern of the First Amendment,'" 99 *Yale Law Journal* 251, 325 (1989). The historical influence of these rationales in limiting judicial review of academic decisions is explored more fully in Chapter 2.

24. Note, "Questioning Age-Old Wisdom," pp. 890–891; *see also* Richard A. Epstein, *Forbidden Grounds: The Case against Employment Discrimination Laws* (Cambridge, Mass.: Harvard University Press, 1992), pp. 459–463 (contending that abolition of mandatory retirement under the ADEA carries special risks for academic self-governance).

25. U.S. House of Representatives, Education and Labor Committee, H.R. Rep. No. 92–238, 92d Cong., 2d Sess., 1972; *United States Code & Administrative News* 2137, 2155 (June 2, 1971).

26. Title IX of the Education Amendments of 1972, 20 U.S.C. §§ 621 *et seq.;* Rehabilitation Act of 1973, § 504, 29 U.S.C. § 794; *see* William A. Kaplin & Barbara A. Lee, *The Law of Higher Education,* vol. 1, 4th ed. (San Francisco: Jossey-Bass, 2006), pp. 386–389, 391–399.

27. Americans with Disabilities Act, 42 U.S.C. §§ 12101 *et seq.; see* Kaplin & Lee, *Law of Higher Education,* vol. 1, pp. 391–399.

28. *University of Pennsylvania,* 493 U.S. at 190.

29. Lawrence Solotoff & Henry S. Kramer, *Sex Discrimination and Sexual Harassment in the Work Place* (New York: Law Journal Press, 2006), § 4.04[2], pp. 4-14.1 through 4-14.2; *see also* Leap, *Tenure, Discrimination, and the Courts,* pp. 55–56.

30. Elizabeth Bartholet, "Application of Title VII to Jobs in High Places," 95 *Harvard Law Review* 945 (1982).

31. Faro v. New York University, 502 F.2d 1229 (2d Cir. 1974); *see also* Note, "Title VII on Campus: Judicial Review of University Employment Decisions," 82 *Columbia Law Review* 1206, 1220–1227 (1982) (examining rationales for courts' early reluctance to review academic judgment).

32. George R. LaNoue & Barbara A. Lee, *Academics in Court: The Consequences of Faculty Discrimination Litigation* (Ann Arbor: University of Michigan Press, 1987), p. 235.

33. Leap, *Tenure, Discrimination, and the Courts,* p. 56.

34. Harry T. Edwards & Virginia Davis Nordin, *Higher Education and the Law* (Cambridge, Mass.: Harvard University Institute for Educational Management, 1979), p. 14.

35. LaNoue & Lee, *Academics in Court,* pp. 30, 34.

36. Powell v. Syracuse University, 580 F.2d 1150, 1153 (2d Cir. 1978).

37. Brown v. Trustees of Boston University, 891 F.2d 337 (1st Cir. 1989), *cert. denied,* 496 U.S. 937 (1990).

38. University of Pennsylvania v. EEOC, 493 U.S. 182, 198–199 (1990) (quoting Regents of University of Michigan v. Ewing, 474 U.S. 214, 225 (1985)).

39. Lelia B. Helms, "Patterns of Litigation in Postsecondary Education: A Case Law Study," 14 *Journal of College and University Law* 99, 109 (1987) (citing Christensen v. State of Iowa, 563 F.2d 353 (8th Cir. 1977)).

40. Martha Chamallas, "Jean Jew's Case: Resisting Sexual Harassment in the Academy," 6 *Yale Journal of Law and Feminism* 71, 73 (1994).

41. Ibid., p. 74.

42. Jew v. The University of Iowa, 749 F. Supp. 946, 947–948 (S.D. Iowa 1990) (quoting Dean John W. Eckstein).

43. Chamallas, "Jean Jew's Case," p. 74.

44. *Jew,* 749 F. Supp. at 949–951.

45. Ibid., pp. 951–952; Chamallas, "Jean Jew's Case," p. 75.

46. *Jew,* 749 F. Supp. at 953.

47. Ibid., pp. 953–961 & n.7.

48. Ibid., pp. 960–963 & n.7.

49. Deborah Woo, *Glass Ceilings and Asian Americans: The New Face of Workplace Barriers* (Walnut Creek, Calif.: AltaMira Press, 2000), p. 136.

50. *See* ibid.; Chamallas, "Jean Jew's Case," pp. 81–89.

51. *University of Pennsylvania,* 493 U.S. at 198 (emphasis in original).

52. *Jew,* 749 F. Supp. at 958; Chamallas, "Jean Jew's Case," p. 74.

53. As one federal court observed: "Disputes over tenure and promotion in universities are often bitterly fought, and qualification for promotion often turns on highly subjective and contested evaluations of academic work in environments where factional rivalries are endemic. Accusations that purportedly objective decisions are based on discrimination or personal hostility are not uncommon. Rivalries and vendettas may last for years, and questions of ideology, professional methodology, personal relationships, racism, and sexism often overlap. Disentangling these strands is difficult, as is distinguishing objective evidence from suspicion, rumor, and speculation." Hinton v. City College of New York, 2008 U.S. Dist. LEXIS 16058 (S.D.N.Y. Feb. 29, 2008). Nonetheless, the court disentangled those particular strands to its satisfaction and ruled in part for the plaintiff in her discrimination action. The plaintiff had argued in part that she had been mistreated with regard to classroom space, classroom equipment, teaching schedules, hiring committee membership, sabbatical leave, funding, and sick leave requests.

54. Bennun v. Rutgers, the State University of New Jersey, 737 F. Supp. 1393, 1396 (D.N.J. 1990), *aff'd,* 941 F.2d 154 (3d Cir. 1991), *cert. denied,* 502 U.S. 1066 (1992).

55. Petition for Writ of Certiorari, Bennun v. Rutgers, No. 91–819 (U.S. Nov. 19, 1991).

56. *Bennun,* 737 F. Supp. at 1400.

57. Ibid., pp. 1402–1408.

58. Rutgers' Petition for Certiorari, n.2.

59. *Bennun,* 737 F. Supp. at 1404–1409.

60. Bennun v. Rutgers, 941 F.2d 154, 177 (3d Cir. 1991).

61. Ibid., p. 181 (Sloviter, C.J., dissenting from denial of rehearing en banc).

62. Rutgers' Petition for Certiorari; Brief of *Amici Curiae* American Council on Education, New York University, the Regents of the University of California, the Trustees of Princeton University, the University of Michigan, and the University of Pennsylvania in Support of Petitioners, Rutgers, State University v. Bennun, No. 91–819 (Dec. 19, 1991).

63. Hinton v. City College of New York, 2008 U.S. Dist. LEXIS 16058. (S.D.N.Y. Feb. 29, 2008).

64. Laura Hinton, *The Perverse Gaze of Sympathy: Sadomasochistic Sentiments from Clarissa to* Rescue 911 (Albany, N.Y.: SUNY Press, 1999).

65. *Hinton,* 2008 U.S. Dist. LEXIS 16058.

66. *See* ibid.

67. Ibid.

68. *See* Barbara A. Lee & Judith A. Malone, "As the Professoriate Ages, Will Colleges Face More Legal Landmines?" *Chronicle of Higher Education,* Nov. 30, 2007 (noting rise in requests for disability accommodations as average faculty age increases, and attendant risks of litigation). Litigation is encouraged by the uncertainty surrounding both the definition of what counts as a "disability" and the extent of colleges' legal duty to make "reasonable accommodation" for disabled students, staff, and faculty. In Betts v. Rector of the University of Virginia, for example, a federal appeals court concluded that a pre-med student who had been diagnosed at the university's student learning center as having "a mild learning disability" requiring double time on examinations could not be considered "disabled" under the ADA because even if the condition interfered with his success in an elite medical program, "his impairment does not substantially limit his ability to learn in comparison to the general population." Still, the court held that the student was protected against discrimination based on his learning impairment because the university *perceived* him to be disabled, triggering the protections of the ADA. Betts v. Rector and Visitors of the University of Virginia, 18 Fed. Appx. 114 (4th Cir. 2001). (In a subsequent appeal four years later, the court concluded that the university had sufficiently accommodated his perceived disability by allowing him double time on some exams and giving him opportunities for additional preparatory coursework. Betts v. Rector and Visitors of the University of Virginia, 145 Fed. Appx. 7 (4th Cir. 2005)).

    In another case, the same court ruled that a law student was entitled to challenge her failing grade on a constitutional law exam under the ADA on the ground that the law school had failed to reasonably accommodate her "intractable migraine syndrome" by giving her extra time on the exam. Constantine v. Rector and Visitors of George Mason University, 411 F.3d 474, 498–499 (4th Cir. 2005). In 1987, before the enactment of the ADA, the Iowa Supreme Court had refused to second-guess the University of Iowa's decision not to

readmit a schizophrenic medical student, emphasizing its "extreme[] reluc-
tan[ce] to involve itself in the discretionary function of officials of academic
institutions who must daily decide who should be admitted, who should be
readmitted, who should be graduated, and how the performance of students
should be measured." North v. State of Iowa, 400 N.W.2d 566, 571 (Iowa
1987). Two decades later, the question whether a student with migraines is
entitled to extra time on her final exams is more likely to be decided by a jury.

Yet, not all questions of disability discrimination will be put before jurors,
as *Hinton* itself reflects. The Vermont Supreme Court declined to order the
University of Vermont to readmit a medical student who admitted repeatedly falsifying his academic credentials, despite the student's plea that his
Tourette's Syndrome was to blame. Bhatt v. University of Vermont, 958 A.2d
637 (Vt. 2008). A federal appeals court drew the line when a professor sued
his college for failing to accommodate his need to work from home because
of agoraphobia, panic attacks, and stress caused by his department chair—
impairments that the professor said "substantially limited . . . his ability to
think and interact with others." Even if his impairments could qualify as a
disability, the court observed, "[t]he fact that the ability to think and interact
with others are prerequisites for a college professor should be self-evident."
Lloyd v. Washington & Jefferson College, 288 Fed. Appx. 786 (3d Cir. 2008).
For a discussion of the significant role that higher education cases have
played in developing federal disability discrimination law, *see* Laura Roth-
stein, "The Story of *Southeastern Community College v. Davis:* The Prequel to the
Television Series 'ER,'" in Olivas & Schneider, eds., *Education Law Stories,*
pp. 197, 212.

69. 42 U.S.C. § 2000e-3(a); *see also* CBOCS West, Inc. v. Humphries, 128 S. Ct.
1951 (2008) (interpreting 42 U.S.C. § 1981); Gomez-Perez v. Potter, 128 S.
Ct. 1931 (2008) (interpreting the ADEA); Jackson v. Birmingham Board of
Education, 544 U.S. 167 (2005) (interpreting Title IX).

70. *Hinton,* 2008 U.S. Dist. LEXIS 16058.

71. Ibid.

72. Somoza v. University of Denver, 513 F.3d 1206, 1214–1215 (10th Cir. 2008).

73. Kant v. Seton Hall University, 2008 U.S. Dist. LEXIS 638, at *47–48 (D.N.J.
Jan. 4, 2008). A jury would later award the professor $80,000 on his retali-
ation claim and an appellate court upheld that award. Kant v. Seton Hall
University, 279 Fed. Appx. 152 (3d Cir. 2008).

74. Recio v. Creighton University, 521 F.3d 934, 939–941 (8th Cir. 2008).

75. Whaley v. City University of New York, 555 F. Supp. 2d 381 (S.D.N.Y. 2008).

76. Ibid.

77. *See* Smith v. Board of Trustees of the University of Florida, 2006 U.S. Dist.
LEXIS 39811 (N.D. Fla. May 27, 2006).

78. *See* Deborah Ball, "Professor Awarded $150K in Suit vs. UF," *Gainesville Sun,*
Sept. 2, 2006.

79. Grutter v. Bollinger, 539 U.S. 306, 361 (2003) (Thomas, J., concurring in part and dissenting in part).

80. *See* ibid., p. 360 (asserting that "[t]he Law School's decision to be an elite institution does little to advance the welfare of the people of Michigan or any cognizable interest of the State of Michigan"); ibid., pp. 368–369 (observing that "there is nothing ancient, honorable, or constitutionally protected about 'selective' admissions").

81. Ibid., p. 363 (quoting Sweezy v. New Hampshire, 354 U.S. 234, 262 (1957) (Frankfurter, J., concurring)).

82. "Job Bias Charges Rise 9% in 2007, EEOC Reports," EEOC press release, Mar. 5, 2008, available at www.eeoc.gov.

83. Josie Cantu-Weber, "New Stories Show Litigation on the Rise," *Change*, May 1, 1999 (study of news coverage of campus litigation found about half related to discrimination); Employment Action, Survey Shows ELL Claims and Costs up Sharply, Winter 1999 (insurance newsletter for campus administrators reported that half of all campus claims were founded on alleged discrimination and that race discrimination claims brought against its insured had risen from 54 in 1991 to 191 in 1997); "Employment Disputes at Schools," *Wall Street Journal*, Dec. 4, 1995 (reporting that discrimination claims against higher education defendants had risen 190% from 1992 to 1995).

84. AAUW Educational Foundation, *Tenure Denied: Cases of Sex Discrimination in Academia* (Washington, D.C.: AAUW Educational Foundation, 2004), p. 18.

85. Leland Ware, "People of Color in the Academy: Patterns of Discrimination in Faculty Hiring and Retention," 20 *Boston College Third World Law Journal* 55 (Winter 2000). Professor Olivas also acknowledges that minority faculty face discriminatory actions involving academia's "merit badges"—those foundations of tenure and promotion like named lecture invitations, honorary degrees, and membership in certain societies. He argues that they are distributed in a racially significant and discriminatory way. Michael A. Olivas, "Reflections on Academic Merit Badges and Becoming an Eagle Scout," 41 *Houston Law Review* 81, 84 (2000). In this way, they can provide the basis both for plaintiff's discrimination claims and for arguments from academic employers that plaintiffs simply did not have an impressive enough curriculum vitae.

86. Janice Drakich & Penni Stewart, "After 40 Years of Feminism, How Are University Women Doing?" *Academic Matters*, Feb. 2007, p. 6; "Academic Discrimination Still a Factor for Women: Report," *City News*, www.citynews.ca.

87. "To Prohibit Academic Discrimination against Students Because of Their Service in the Armed Forces," www.petitiononline.com.

88. Hammer v. Board of Regents of the University of Michigan, Michigan Court of Appeals, No. 272801 (Appellee's Reply Brief on Appeal, p. 15) (Jan. 15, 2007). Briefs in the case are available at http://www.wayneoutlaws.org.

89. Betts v. Rector and Visitors of the University of Virginia, 18 Fed. Appx. 114 (4th Cir. 2001).

90. Scott Jaschik, "Tracking Bias or Guilt by Association?" *Inside Higher Ed* (Dec. 19, 2007), www.insidehighered.com.
91. *See* Lindy Stevens, "Former Law Prof Claims Anti-Gay Bias Influenced Tenure Decision," *The Michigan Daily,* Mar. 7, 2008.
92. Jaschik, "Tracking Bias."
93. Hammer v. Board of Regents of the University of Michigan, No. 04-241 MK, Michigan Court of Claims (Plaintiff's Brief in Opposition to Defendant's Amendment Motion for Summary Judgment, pp. 22–27) (Oct. 11, 2007).
94. Jaschik, "Tracking Bias."
95. Hammer v. Board of Regents of the University of Michigan, Michigan Court of Appeals, No. 272801 (Defendant/Appellant Board of Regents of The University of Michigan's Brief on Appeal, pp. 15–17) (Dec. 6, 2006).
96. Hammer v. Board of Regents of the University of Michigan, Michigan Court of Appeals, No. 272801 (Appellee's Reply Brief on Appeal, pp. 29–31) (Jan. 15, 2007).
97. National Pride at Work, Inc. v. Granholm, Michigan Court of Appeals, No. 265870 (Brief of American Association of University Professionals as *Amicus Curiae* in Support of Plaintiffs-Appellees, pp. 12–13) (Dec. 14, 2005).
98. National Pride at Work, Inc. v. Governor of Michigan, 732 N.W.2d 139, 152 (Mich. Ct. App. 2007) (quoting Branum v. Board of Regents of University of Michigan, 145 N.W.2d 860, 862 (Mich. App. 1966)), *aff'd*, 748 N.W.2d 524 (Mich. 2008).
99. National Pride at Work v. Governor of Michigan, 748 N.W.2d 524, 539 (Mich. 2008).

4. Free Speech Free-for-All

1. Iota Xi Chapter of Sigma Chi Fraternity v. George Mason University, 993 F.2d 386, 388 (4th Cir. 1993).
2. *See* Anthony DePalma, "U.S. Judge Upholds Speech on Campus," *New York Times,* Aug. 29, 1991.
3. Appellee's Brief, George Mason University v. Iota Xi Chapter of Sigma Chi Fraternity, No. 91-2684 (4th Cir. Dec. 17, 1991), pp. 2–3 & n.2.
4. Iota Xi Chapter of Sigma Chi Fraternity v. George Mason University, 773 F. Supp. 792, 793–794 (E.D. Va. 1991).
5. Appellant's Reply Brief, George Mason University v. Iota Xi Chapter of Sigma Chi Fraternity, No. 91-2684 (4th Cir. Jan. 3, 1992), pp. 5–7.
6. *Iota Xi Chapter,* 993 F.2d at 392–393.
7. *Iota Xi Chapter,* 773 F. Supp. at 795.
8. Tanton v. McKenney, 197 N.W. 510, 511–513 (Mich. 1924) (quoting Pugsley v. Sellmeyer, 250 S.W. 538, 539 (Ark. 1923)).
9. Waugh v. Board of Trustees of the University of Mississippi, 237 U.S. 589, 596 (1915).

10. *See* Gitlow v. New York, 268 U.S. 652 (1925) (holding that the First Amendment's substantive guarantees of free speech and press are applicable against state government through incorporation into the Fourteenth Amendment's Due Process Clause).

11. Healy v. James, 408 U.S. 169 (1972).

12. *Iota Xi Chapter*, 993 F.2d at 393–394 (Murnaghan, J., concurring in the judgment).

13. Ibid., p. 395.

14. Robert O'Neil, *Academic Freedom in the Wired World: Political Extremism, Corporate Power, and the University* (Cambridge, Mass.: Harvard University Press, 2008), p. 49.

15. Regents of University of California v. Bakke, 438 U.S. 265, 312–313 (1978) (opinion of Powell, J.).

16. *Healy*, 408 U.S. at 180–189.

17. Steven M. Teles, *The Rise of the Conservative Legal Movement: The Battle for Control of the Law* (Princeton, N.J.: Princeton University Press, 2008), p. 232; *see also* John K. Wilson, *The Myth of Political Correctness: The Conservative Attack on Higher Education* (Durham, N.C.: Duke University Press, 1995).

18. Teles, *Conservative Legal Movement*, pp. 232–235 (quoting internal CIR documents).

19. Stanley Fish, "The Free-Speech Follies," *Chronicle of Higher Education*, June 13, 2003.

20. Silva v. University of New Hampshire, 888 F. Supp. 293, 298–299 (D.N.H. 1994).

21. Ibid., pp. 299–306.

22. Ibid., pp. 313–314.

23. "Professor Accused of Harassment Reinstated," *New York Times*, Dec. 4, 1994.

24. "CIR's Greatest Courtroom Victories," Center for Individual Rights, www.cir -usa.org.

25. Two years before *Silva*, in another CIR-backed case, a federal court of appeals in New York had held that City College could not create shadow sections of a philosophy professor's course or investigate his writings (the most notorious of which had professed that blacks, on average, are intellectually inferior to whites) as conduct unbecoming a faculty member. The appellate court agreed that such action could create "a chilling threat of discipline." Levin v. Harleston, 966 F.2d 85 (2d Cir. 1992).

26. Vanderhurst v. Colorado Mountain College District, 208 F.3d 908, 911 (10th Cir. 2000).

27. Cohen v. San Bernardino Valley College, 92 F.3d 968 (9th Cir. 1996).

28. Kenneth L. Marcus, "Higher Education, Harassment, and First Amendment Opportunism," 16 *William & Mary Bill of Rights Journal* 1025, 1028–1029 (2008); Frederick Schauer, "The Speech-ing of Sexual Harassment," *Directions*

in Sexual Harassment Law 347 (Catherine A. MacKinnon & Reva B. Siegel, eds., 2004).

29. *See* O'Neil, *Academic Freedom in a Wired World,* pp. 71–74.

30. Hardy v. Jefferson Community College, 260 F.3d 671 (6th Cir. 2001).

31. Gee v. Humphries, 141 F.3d 1189 (11th Cir.) (order summarily affirming district court), *cert. denied,* 525 U.S. 869 (1998); *see* Brief of the American Association of University Professors as Amicus Curiae, Gee v. Humphries, No. 97–2265 (11th Cir. Sept. 17, 1997), p. 3.

32. Dambrot v. Central Michigan University, 55 F.3d 1177 (6th Cir. 1995).

33. Bonnell v. Lorenzo, 241 F.3d 800, 820–821 (6th Cir. 2001); *see also* Rubin v. Ikenberry, 933 F. Supp. 1425 (C.D. Ill. 1996) (upholding instigation of disciplinary proceedings against education professor for using "sexual commentary, inquiries, and jokes during class," despite professor's insistence that the use was "pedagogically correct").

34. O'Neil, *Academic Freedom in the Wired World,* p. 74; *see also* Chris Jay Hoofnagle, "Matters of Public Concern and the Public University Professor," 27 *Journal of College and University Law* 669 (2001) (suggesting that courts have looked at very similar facts and have arrived at opposite conclusions); Amy H. Candido, "A Right to Talk Dirty? Academic Freedom Values and Sexual Harassment in the University Classroom," 4 *University of Chicago Law School Roundtable* 85 (1996–1997).

35. Hayut v. State University of New York College at New Paltz, 352 F.3d 733, 749–752 (2d Cir. 2003).

36. Head v. Board of Trustees of California State University, 2007 Cal. App. Unpub. LEXIS 393 (Cal. Ct. App. Jan. 18, 2007).

37. Axson-Flynn v. Johnson, 356 F.3d 1277 (10th Cir. 2004).

38. Mindy Sink, "Lawsuit Cites Collision of Religious and Speech Rights," *New York Times,* May 8, 2004.

39. Paul Ketzle, "The 'A' Word," 15 *Continuum: The Magazine of the University of Utah* 2 (Fall 2005).

40. Ibid.

41. Burnham v. Ianni, 119 F.3d 668, 671 (8th Cir. 1997) (en banc).

42. William H. Honan, "Court Upholds 2 Professors' Right to Strike a Pose," *New York Times,* July 30, 1997.

43. *Burnham,* 119 F.3d at 681 (McMillian, J., dissenting).

44. Ibid., pp. 681–682.

45. Honan, "Court Upholds 2 Professors' Right to Strike a Pose."

46. *Burnham,* 119 F.3d at 684 (McMillian, J., dissenting).

47. Burnham v. Ianni, 98 F.3d 1007, 1012 (8th Cir. 1996), vacated on rehearing en banc, 119 F.3d 668 (8th Cir. 1997).

48. Burnham v. Ianni, 899 F. Supp. 395, 403 (D. Minn. 1995), *aff'd,* 119 F.3d 668 (8th Cir. 1997) (en banc).

49. "Political Correctness and Academic Freedom at the University of Minnesota," Center of the American Experiment Luncheon Forum, Minneapo-

lis, Minnesota, Oct. 26, 1994 (comments of Professor Ian Maitland), www
.americanexperiment.org.

50. *See* "Prof. Maitland Settles His Case against U. Minnesota," CIR press release
    (June 12, 2003), www.cir-usa.org; Maitland v. University of Minnesota, 260
    F.3d 959 (8th Cir. 2001), *cert. denied,* 535 U.S. 929 (2002).

51. *Burnham,* 899 F. Supp. at 401–404 (quoting Lawrence Tribe, *American Consti-
    tutional Law,* 2d ed. (St. Paul, Minn.: West Publishing Co., 1988), p. 852.

52. *Burnham,* 98 F.3d at 1015–1016.

53. Ibid., p. 1020 (Beam, J., dissenting).

54. *Burnham,* 119 F.3d at 675–680.

55. Ibid., p. 684 (McMillian, J., dissenting).

56. Lawrence Ianni, *A Plague on Both Their Houses* (New York: iUniverse, 2006).

57. Close v. Lederle, 424 F.2d 988, 989–991 (1st Cir. 1970).

58. Piarowski v. Illinois Community College District 515, 759 F.2d 625, 629–630
    (7th Cir.), *cert. denied,* 474 U.S. 1007 (1985).

59. O'Connor v. Washburn University, 416 F.3d 1216 (10th Cir. 2005), *cert. de-
    nied,* 547 U.S. 1003 (2006).

60. O'Neil, *Academic Freedom in a Wired World,* p. 145. For a fuller exploration of
    the status of First Amendment protection for art, *see* Randall Bezanson, *Art
    and the Freedom of Speech* (Champaign: University of Illinois Press, 2009).

61. *See Burnham,* 119 F.3d at 674.

62. *See* Department of History Faculty, University of Minnesota at Duluth, www
    .d.umn.edu.

63. Eric Athas, "Student Files Lawsuit against UMass, Claims He Received Un-
    just Grade," *The Daily Collegian,* Feb. 7, 2007, www.dailycollegian.com.

64. Jonathan Saltzman, "Student Takes His C to Court; Judge Dismisses Suit
    against UMass," *Boston Globe,* Oct. 4, 2007.

65. *E.g.,* Steinhauer v. Arkins, 69 P. 1075 (Colo. 1902) (rejecting student's de-
    mand for diploma based on claim that faculty had given him a failing grade
    on final exam based solely on personal hostility).

66. Head v. Board of Trustees of California State University, 2007 Cal. App. Un-
    pub. LEXIS 393 (Cal. Ct. App. Jan. 18, 2007).

67. *See* Yohn v. University of Michigan Board of Regents, 39 Fed. Appx. 225 (6th
    Cir.), *cert. denied,* 537 U.S. 1018 (2002), rehearing denied, 537 U.S. 1149
    (2003); Yohn v. University of Michigan Board of Regents, 2005 Mich. App.
    LEXIS 992 (Mich. Ct. App. Apr. 19, 2005), appeal denied, 706 N.W.2d 28
    (Mich. 2005), reconsideration denied, 711 N.W.2d 300 (Mich. 2006).

68. Petition for Writ of Certiorari, Yohn v. University of Michigan Board of Re-
    gents, No. 02-191 (U.S. July 15, 2002), p. 10.

69. Yohn v. University of Michigan Board of Regents, 537 U.S. 1018 (2002), re-
    hearing denied, 537 U.S. 1149 (2003).

70. Stronach v. Virginia State University, 2008 U.S. Dist. LEXIS 2914 (E.D. Va.
    Jan. 15, 2008).

71. Parate v. Isibor, 868 F.2d 821, 827–828 (6th Cir. 1989).

72. *Stronach*, 2008 U.S. Dist. LEXIS 2914. A later discrimination action brought by the professor based in part on the grade change matter also failed at the trial level. Stronach v. Virginia State University, 2008 U.S. Dist. LEXIS 41184 (E.D. Va. May 23, 2008).

73. Urofsky v. Gilmore, 216 F.3d 401, 415 (4th Cir. 2000).

74. *Stronach*, 2008 U.S. Dist. LEXIS 2914.

75. Lawrence White, "Does Academic Freedom Give a Professor the Final Say on Grades?" *Chronicle of Higher Education*, Apr. 25, 2008.

76. Charles S. Johnson, "Natelson Seeks Regents' Help in Clash with UM Law School," *The Missoulian*, June 20, 2004; Robert G. Natelson faculty biography, University of Montana Law School Web site, www.umt.edu/law/ (noting Natelson's "colorful life").

77. Johnson, "Natelson Seeks Regents' Help"; Jennifer Jacobson, "Professor Accuses U. Montana's Law School of Viewpoint Discrimination," *Chronicle of Higher Education*, July 6, 2004.

78. Findings of Fact & Opinion, *In re* Grievance and Appeal of Robert G. Natelson & University of Montana School of Law, University of Montana (Donald D. Robinson, hearing officer; Aug. 25, 2004), available at www.law.ucla.edu/volokh/.

79. Memorandum from G. M. Dennison to E. E. Eck, Aug. 25, 2004, available at www.law.ucla.edu/volokh/.

80. Betsy Cohen, "Natelson Wins UM Dispute," *The Missoulian*, Aug. 27, 2004.

81. Keyishian v. Board of Regents of State University of New York, 385 U.S. 589, 603 (1967).

82. Robert M. O'Neil, *Free Speech in the College Community* (Bloomington: Indiana University Press, 1997), p. vii.

83. Memorandum of G. M. Dennison to E. E. Eck, p. 2; Findings of Fact & Opinion, *In re* Grievance and Appeal of Robert G. Natelson, pp. 6–8.

84. Eugene Volokh, *The Volokh Conspiracy*, http://volokh.com/archives/archive_2004_07_00.shtml #1088706514 (blog post, July 1, 2004).

85. *See* William W. Van Alstyne, "Academic Freedom and the First Amendment in the Supreme Court of the United States: An Unhurried Historical Review," 53 *Law and Contemporary Problems* 79 (1990).

86. J. Peter Byrne, "Racial Insults and Free Speech within the University," 79 *Georgetown Law Journal* 399, 399–400 (1991).

87. O'Neil, *Academic Freedom in a Wired World*, pp. 58–59. In this regard, a recent decision of the U.S. Supreme Court limiting First Amendment protection for the work-related speech of public employees generally has raised alarm over its possible implications for academic freedom. In Garcetti v. Ceballos, 547 U.S. 410 (2006), the Court rejected a First Amendment claim by a deputy district attorney disciplined by his supervisors for challenging their judgment in a particular prosecution, reasoning that "when public employees make statements pursuant to their official duties, the employees are not speaking as citi-

zens for First Amendment purposes, and the Constitution does not insulate their communications from employer discipline." Ibid., p. 421. Some, including dissenters in *Garcetti* itself, have expressed concern over the Court's failure to distinguish a broader freedom for the professional speech of scholars and teachers of public colleges and universities. *See* ibid., p. 438 (Souter, J., dissenting); *see also* Judith Areen, "Government as Educator: A New Understanding of First Amendment Protection of Academic Freedom and Governance," 97 *Georgetown Law Journal* 945, 976, 988 (2009) (warning that "[t]he *Garcetti* official-duty test threatens to terminate all constitutional protection for [faculty governance speech], and for academic freedom generally"). "University classroom speech and professorial scholarship, [being] unique kinds of high value speech," argues First Amendment scholar Sheldon Nahmod, "merit maximum First Amendment protection as befits their extraordinary contribution to democracy." Sheldon Nahmod, "Academic Freedom and the Post-*Garcetti* Blues," 7 *First Amendment Law Review* 54, 74 (2008).

88. O'Neil, *Free Speech in the College Community*, pp. 91–92; Michael J. Friedman, "Dazed and Confused: Explaining Judicial Determinations of Traditional Public Forum Status," 82 *Tulane Law Review* 929, 970–971 (2008); Gilles v. Blanchard, 477 F.3d 466, 473–474 (7th Cir.) (Posner, J.), *cert. denied*, 128 S. Ct. 127 (2007).

89. Marcus, "Higher Education," p. 1047.

90. *See* Areen, "Government as Educator," pp. 992–993; Matthew W. Finkin & Robert C. Post, *For the Common Good: Principles of American Academic Freedom* (New Haven, Conn.: Yale University Press, 2009), pp. 43–44.

91. Frank S. Ravitch, "Intelligent Design in Public University Science Departments: Academic Freedom or Establishment of Religion," 16 *William and Mary Bill of Rights Journal* 1061 (2008).

92. Byrne, "Racial Insults," pp. 416–417.

93. O'Neil, *Free Speech in the College Community*, p. x.

94. Areen, "Government as Educator," pp. 994–997.

95. Churchill, a professor of ethnic studies, became the target of widespread outrage after writing an essay describing some victims of the September 11, 2001, attack on the World Trade Center as "little Eichmanns." After he was later fired by the University of Colorado in 2007, following an investigation that found him guilty of shoddy scholarship and academic misconduct, Churchill sued the University for violating his First Amendment rights. In April 2009, a jury awarded Churchill one dollar in damages, a judgment his attorney hailed as "a great victory for the First Amendment and for academic freedom." Kirk Johnson & Katharine Q. Seelye, "Author of Sept. 11 Essay Was Wrongly Fired, Jury Says," *New York Times*, Apr. 3, 2009. Churchill continued to seek reinstatement, contending that only regaining his tenured professorship would "repair the damages that his dismissal did to his reputation and to the greater cause of academic freedom." Peter Schmidt, "Ward

Churchill Asks Judge to Make U. of Colorado Take Him Back," *Chronicle of Higher Education*, May 15, 2009, p. 9.

96. Marcus, "Higher Education," p. 1027.

97. Flint v. Dennison, 488 F.3d 816 (9th Cir. 2007), *cert. denied*, 128 S. Ct. 882 (2008); George F. Will, "The $114.69 Speech Police," *Washington Post*, Oct. 25, 2007. The University of Montana's general counsel later observed that even in rejecting the student's claim, the appeals court's analysis may well have paved the way for a new swath of student lawsuits. *See* David Aronofsky, "Higher Education Student Elections and Other First Amendment Student Speech Issues: What *Flint v. Dennison* Portends," 34 *Journal of College and University Law* 637, 670 (2008) (suggesting that "in adopting the limited public forum approach to decide [*Flint*], the Ninth Circuit has undoubtedly created a new panoply of student expressive rights at public higher education institutions"). But Flint's suit was not the first to challenge the outcome of a student election. In 2005, the runner-up in a hotly contested race for student government president filed suit after a university appeals board refused to disqualify her rival for violating campaign-spending rules. A state judge ordered the University of Kentucky to recognize the plaintiff as president, over Kentucky's strong protest that "[t]he university ought to be allowed to govern itself and to govern the institutions that comprise it." It was not exactly *Bush v. Gore*, the *Chronicle of Higher Education* observed, but the court's willingness to police voting rights on campus encourages campus politicos to think of themselves in that light. Sara Lipka, "State Judge Who Decided the Winner in U of Kentucky Student-Government Case Declines to Reconsider," *Chronicle of Higher Education*, Sept. 23, 2005, p. A44.

98. Brown v. Li, 308 F.3d 939 (9th Cir. 2002), *cert. denied*, 538 U.S. 908 (2003).

99. *See* Steve Bauer & Julie Wurth, "Judge Denies Students' Case against UI," *The (Champaign-Urbana) News-Gazette*, Feb. 16, 2007, p. A1; "Appeals Court Rejects Chief Illiniwek Lawsuits," *(Bloomington, Ill.) Pantagraph*, May 8, 2008; Illinois Native American Bar Ass'n v. Board of Trustees of University of Illinois, 856 N.E.2d 460 (Ill. Ct. App. 2006). In 2004, however, Illinois students and faculty prevailed in a First Amendment lawsuit challenging a campus directive barring them from contacting prospective athletic recruits to engage them in the debate over the mascot. *See* Crue v. Aiken, 370 F.3d 668 (7th Cir. 2004).

100. Pugel v. University of Illinois, 378 F.3d 659 (7th Cir. 2004).

101. Wirsing v. Board of Regents of University of Colorado, 739 F. Supp. 551 (D. Colo. 1990).

102. Johnson-Kurek v. Abu-Absi, 423 F.3d 590 (6th Cir. 2005).

103. Wozniak v. Conry, 236 F.3d 888 (7th Cir.), *cert. denied*, 533 U.S. 903 (2001).

104. Barrow v. Arizona Board of Regents, 761 P.2d 145, 148 (Ariz. Ct. App. 1988).

105. Faculty Rights Coalition v. Shahrokhi, 204 Fed. Appx. 416 (5th Cir. 2006).

106. De Mino v. Sheridan, 2006 Tex. App. LEXIS 3137 (Tex. Ct. App. Apr. 20, 2006).

107. Paul R. Abramson, *Romance in the Ivory Tower: The Rights and Liberty of Conscience* (Cambridge, Mass.: MIT Press, 2007), p. 50.
108. Iota Xi Chapter of Sigma Chi Fraternity v. Patterson, 538 F. Supp. 2d 915, 928–929 (E.D. Va. 2008).
109. Noon Salih, "Sigma Chi Sues Mason Administrators," *Broadside Online,* Oct. 22, 2007, www.broadsideonline.com.

5. Prerogative and Profit

1. William Townsend Porter, *Physiology at Harvard* (Cambridge, Mass.: Harvard Medical School, 1903), pp. 5–7.
2. Harvard College v. Harvard Bioscience, Inc., 204 F. Supp. 2d 134, 136–137 (D. Mass. 2002).
3. "President Eliot on Football," 28 *American Educational Review* 953–954 (April 1907).
4. *Harvard Bioscience,* 204 F. Supp. 2d at 136 (quoting 1906 letter from Jerome Greene, Secretary to President Eliot and Harvard Corporation, to a member of the Board of Overseers).
5. "43rd APS President (1970–1971) A. Clifford Barger," The American Physiological Society, http://www.the-aps.org/about/pres/introacb.htm; A. Clifford Barger, "The Meteoric Rise and Fall of William Townsend Porter, One of Carl J. Wiggers' 'Old Guard,'" 25 *Physiologist* 407–413 (1982).
6. Harvard Bioscience, 2008 Annual Report, p. 2, available at http://harvard bioscience.com.
7. *Harvard Bioscience,* 204 F. Supp. 2d at 136–137.
8. "Make the Bold Choice: Harvard Needs a Visionary President, Not a Consensus Pick," *Harvard Crimson,* Jan. 31, 2007; *see also* James L. Fisher & James V. Koch, *The Entrepreneurial College President* (Westport, Conn.: Praeger Publishers, 2004), p. 120; Regina E. Herzlinger, "Vision Less: The Ivy League without Larry Summers," *The New Republic,* July 7, 2007.
9. *See* Sheila Slaughter & Gary Rhoades, *Academic Capitalism and the New Economy: Markets, State, and Higher Education* (Baltimore: Johns Hopkins University Press, 2004).
10. *See* "Summers Speaks," 21 *The International Economy* 12 (Fall 2007).
11. "College Men in Industry," 28 *American Educational Review* 941 (April 1907).
12. David L. Kirp, *Shakespeare, Einstein, and the Bottom Line: The Marketing of Higher Education* (Cambridge, Mass.: Harvard University Press, 2003), p. 2.
13. Derek Bok, *Universities in the Marketplace: The Commercialization of Higher Education* (Princeton, N.J.: Princeton University Press, 2003), pp. 2–3.
14. Frank H. T. Rhodes, *The Creation of the Future: The Role of the American University* (Ithaca, N.Y.: Cornell University Press, 2001), p. 49.
15. Kirp, *Shakespeare, Einstein, and the Bottom Line,* pp. 4–5.

16. Michael A. Olivas, "Introduction: Intellectual Property on Campus, Computers, Copyright, and Cyberspace," 27 *Journal of College and University Law* 1, 1 (2000).

17. Arti K. Rai, "The Increasingly Proprietary Nature of Publicly Funded Biomedical Research," in Donald G. Stein, ed., *Buying In or Selling Out? The Commercialization of the American Research University* (New Brunswick, N.J.: Rutgers University Press, 2004), pp. 117, 118.

18. University Technology Managers Survey, www.autm.net.

19. Association of University Technology Managers 2006 Survey Summary, www.autm.net; Margo A. Bagley, "Academic Discourse and Proprietary Rights; Putting Patents in Their Proper Place," 47 *Boston College Law Review* 217, 217–218 (2006).

20. In 2006, for example, Ohio State University earned $5.7 million on the sale of licensed clothing and memorabilia after a very successful football season. Ohio State University press release, Dec. 18, 2006, www.osu.edu.

21. Kirp, *Shakespeare, Einstein, and the Bottom Line*, p. 3.

22. Jennifer Washburn, *University, Inc.: The Corporate Corruption of American Higher Education* (New York: Basic Books, 2005), p. x.

23. William A. Kaplin & Barbara A. Lee, *The Law of Higher Education*, 4th ed. (San Francisco: Jossey-Bass, 2006), p. 1640.

24. Corynne McSherry, *Who Owns Academic Work? Battling for Control of Intellectual Property* (Cambridge, Mass.: Harvard University Press, 2001), p. 24.

25. In March 2009, the trial court judge lowered the amount awarded Cornell to $43,494,282. Cornell University v. Hewlett-Packard, 2009 U.S. Dist. LEXIS 28125 (N.D.N.Y. March 31, 2009). As of late spring 2009, an appeal was pending.

26. Donial Dastgir, "Cornell Wins $184 Million in Lawsuit against Hewlett-Packard," *Cornell Daily Sun*, June 5, 2008.

27. Aaron Munzer, "Hewlett Packard Plans Appeal of CU's Patent Lawsuit," *Ithaca Journal*, June 3, 2008.

28. John B. Fenn, "Autobiography," in *Les Prix Nobel: The Nobel Prizes, 2002* (Stockholm: Nobel Foundation, 2003).

29. David Glenn, "Federal Judge Awards $1-Million in Damages to Yale U. in Patent Dispute with Nobel Laureate," *Chronicle of Higher Education*, Feb. 14, 2005.

30. Fenn v. Yale University, 283 F. Supp. 2d 615, 625–626 (D. Conn. 2003).

31. Marilyn Alva, "Leaders and Success," *Investor's Business Daily*, Apr. 11, 2006, p. A4.

32. *Fenn*, 283 F. Supp. 2d at 639 (quoting Nobel Foundation press release).

33. Ibid., pp. 629–632; Fenn v. Yale University, 2005 U.S. Dist. LEXIS 1827 (D. Conn. Feb. 8, 2005).

34. Fenn v. Yale University, 184 Fed. Appx. 21 (2d Cir. 2006).

35. Analytica of Branford, Inc. v. Fenn, 2007 U.S. Dist. LEXIS 54534 (D. Conn. July 27, 2007).

36. Kirp, *Shakespeare, Einstein, and the Bottom Line*, p. 5.

37. Saint Louis University v. Meyer, 2008 U.S. Dist. LEXIS 29371, at *4 (E.D. Mo. Apr. 10, 2008)

38. *See, e.g.*, University of Pittsburgh v. Townsend, 2007 U.S. Dist. LEXIS 56860 (E.D. Tenn. Aug. 3, 2007); Madey v. Duke University, 413 F. Supp. 2d 601 (M.D.N.C. 2006); Shaw v. University of California, 67 Cal. Rptr. 2d 850 (Cal. Ct. App. 1997);

39. Bosch v. Ball-Kell, 2006 U.S. Dist. LEXIS 62351, at *8–*9 (C.D. Ill. Aug. 31, 2006).

40. Weinstein v. University of Illinois, 811 F.2d 1091, 1094 (7th Cir. 1987).

41. "Intellectual property created, made, or originated by a faculty member shall be the sole and exclusive property of the faculty, author, or inventor, except as he or she may voluntarily choose to transfer such property, in full, or in part." AAUP 1999 Statement on Copyright, www.aaup.org; *see also* Pittsburg State University v. Kansas Board of Regents, 122 P.3d 336, 421 (Kan. 2005); McSherry, *Who Owns Academic Work?* pp. 107–108.

42. Robert C. Denicola, "Copyright and Open Access: Reconsidering University Ownership of Faculty Research," 85 *Nebraska Law Review* 351, 373 (2006).

43. Professor Denicola argues that university-retained copyright, however, would lead to more access to published articles. Denicola, "Copyright and Open Access," p. 353.

44. "College Men in Industry," p. 941.

45. "Temporary Stars: An Interesting Observation at Litchfield Observatory," *New York Times*, Dec. 25, 1876 (reprinting Dec. 21, 1876, letter of C. H. F. Peters to the *Utica Morning Herald*).

46. National Academy of Sciences, *Biographical Memoirs*, vol. 76 (Washington, D.C.: National Academy Press, 1999), p. 289.

47. "At War about the Stars," *New York Times*, Feb. 1, 1889.

48. Simon Newcomb, *The Reminiscences of an Astronomer* (Boston: Houghton, Mifflin & Co., 1903), p. 270.

49. "A Catalogue of the Stars: Suit Brought by Dr. C. H. F. Peters," *New York Times*, July 9, 1888.

50. National Academy of Sciences, *Biographical Memoirs*, vol. 76, p. 297.

51. Newcomb, *Reminiscences*, pp. 271–272.

52. Peters v. Borst, 9 N.Y.S. 789, 798 (N.Y. Sup. Ct. 1889).

53. National Academy of Sciences, *Biographical Memoirs*, vol. 76, p. 306.

54. "Prof. Borst Accepts," *New York Times*, June 7, 1888; "Johns Hopkins University," *New York Times*, Feb. 21, 1892 (announcing that Borst had observed several large and small sun spots).

55. Root v. Borst, 36 N.E. 814, 816 (N.Y. 1894).

56. *Peters*, 9 N.Y.S. at 798.

57. Newcomb, *Reminiscences*, p. 268.

58. Ibid., pp. 268–269.

59. John Noble Wilford, "Ex-Colleagues Turn Combatants," *New York Times,* May 22, 1990.
60. Weissmann v. Freeman, 684 F. Supp. 1248, 1252 (S.D.N.Y. 1988), *rev'd,* 868 F.2d 1313 (2d Cir.), *cert. denied,* 493 U.S. 883 (1989).
61. Wilford, "Ex-Colleagues Turn Combatants."
62. *Weissmann,* 684 F. Supp. at 1251.
63. Wilford, "Ex-Colleagues Turn Combatants."
64. *Weissmann,* 684 F. Supp. at 1250 ("uncommon controversy"); *Weissmann,* 868 F.2d at 1315 ("long relationship").
65. *Weissmann,* 684 F. Supp. at 1258–1263.
66. *Weissmann,* 868 F.2d at 1327 (Pierce, J., concurring).
67. Ibid., pp. 1316–1326 (majority opinion of Cardamone, J.).
68. McSherry, *Who Owns Academic Work?* p. 88.
69. *Weissmann,* 684 F. Supp. at 1259.
70. McSherry, *Who Owns Academic Work?* p. 97.
71. Fred Faust, "A Research Chemist Wins $300,000," *St. Louis Post-Dispatch,* July 6, 1998.
72. Nemani v. Saint Louis University, 33 S.W.3d 184, 186 (Mo. 2000).
73. Bill Bell, "SLU and Research Clash before High Court," *St. Louis Post-Dispatch,* Sept. 8, 2000.
74. McSherry, *Who Owns Academic Work?* p. 71 (discussing Ron Grossman, "In Academe, the Serfs Are Toppling the Lords," *Chicago Tribune,* Aug., 24, 1997, p. C1).
75. One well-known example involves Professor Betty Dong of the University of California-San Francisco who, in the late 1980s, signed a research contract with a pharmaceutical company agreeing that all research findings would be confidential and were "not to be published or otherwise released" without the company's consent. Dong would eventually publish the results of her study that showed generics were just as effective as the company's drug, but she had to fend off company complaints to her university (with two resulting investigations), the company's warnings of liability, and the university's suggestion that Dong would have to defend herself in court if the company sued her for violating the contract. Sheldon Krimsky, *Science in the Public Interest* (New York: Rowman & Littlefield, 2004), pp. 14–17; *see also* BASF AG v. Great American Assurance Co., 522 F.3d 813, 816 (7th Cir. 2008).
76. Brief of Appellants, *In re* Klopfenstein, No. 03-1538 (Fed. Cir. Oct. 27, 2003), pp. 1–2.
77. *In re* Klopfenstein, 380 F.3d 1345 (Fed. Cir. 2004).
78. *See* Massachusetts Institute of Technology v. Harman International Industries, Inc., 530 F. Supp. 2d 369 (D. Mass. 2007) (thesis defense); *In re* Cronyn, 890 F.2d 1158 (Fed. Cir. 1989) (thesis defense); *In re* Hall, 781 F.2d 897 (Fed. Cir. 1986) (filing and indexing thesis in university library).

79. *Massachusetts Institute of Technology,* 530 F. Supp. 2d at 378–379. In September 2008, a federal trial court ruled in favor of MIT's patent over Harman's claims of public use. 584 F. Supp. 2d 297 (D. Mass. 2008).

80. *Klopfenstein,* 380 F.3d at 1351.

81. Ibid.

82. Margo A. Bagley, "Academic Discourse and Proprietary Rights: Putting Patents in Their Proper Place," 47 *Boston College Law Review* 217, 221 (2006).

83. Ibid., pp. 239–241; Jeremy M. Grushcow, "Measuring Secrecy: A Cost of the Patent System Revealed," 33 *Journal of Legal Studies* 59, 75–79 (2004); Washburn, *Universities, Inc.,* p. xi (noting that "[s]ecrecy and delays of publication have become routine since 1980").

84. Bagley, "Academic Discourse," pp. 239–241.

85. Ibid., p. 219; *see also* Rai, "Increasingly Proprietary Nature," pp. 118–121.

86. Bagley, "Academic Discourse," pp. 218–219.

87. Washburn, *University, Inc.,* p. xi.

88. Rai, "Increasingly Proprietary Nature," p. 117.

89. Rochelle Cooper Dreyfuss, "Collaborative Research: Conflict on Authorship, Ownership, and Accountability," 53 *Vanderbilt Law Review* 1161, 1163 (2000)

90. Kenneth L. Marcus, "Higher Education, Harassment, and First Amendment Opportunism," 16 *William & Mary Bill of Rights Journal* 1025 (2008); *see also* Frederick Schauer, "First Amendment Opportunism," in Lee C. Bollinger & Geoffrey R. Stone, eds., *Eternally Vigilant: Free Speech in the Modern Era* (Chicago: University of Chicago Press, 2002), p. 176. Professor Barry McDonald discusses First Amendment protection for scientific research, inquiry, and expression, in McDonald, "Government Regulation or Other 'Abridgments' of Scientific Research: The Proper Scope of Judicial Review under the First Amendment," 54 *Emory Law Journal* 979 (2005).

91. *Weissmann,* 684 F. Supp. at 1258.

92. McSherry, *Who Owns Academic Work?* p. 72.

93. Ibid., p. 86.

94. Manco v. University of the Sciences, 2005 U.S. Dist. LEXIS 16059 (D.N.J. July 29, 2005); Vincent v. City Colleges of Chicago, 485 F.3d 919 (7th Cir. 2007).

95. *Vincent,* 485 F.3d at 923.

96. Fromer v. Freedom of Information Commission, 875 A.2d 590, 595 (Conn. Ct. App. 2005). *But see* Russo v. Nassau County Community College, 623 N.E.2d 15 (N.Y. 1993) (upholding freedom of information act request for classroom materials).

97. Associated Press, "Creator Demands Chief Logo Back from Board of Trustees," *Daily Illini,* Apr. 6, 2007.

98. Steve Bauer, "Judge Says Federal Court Doesn't Have Jurisdiction in Logo Case," *(Champaign-Urbana, Ill.) News-Gazette,* July 8, 2008.

99. Story told in Williams v. Weisser, 78 Cal. Rptr. 542, 547 (Cal. Ct. App. 1969), citing Abernethy v. Hutchinson, 3 L.J. (Ch.) 209 (1825).

100. Ryan Singel, "Lawsuit Claim: Students' Lecture Notes Infringe on Professor's Copyright," *Wired Blog Network,* Apr. 4, 2008, http://blog.wired.com/27bstroke6/2008/04/prof-sues-note.html.

101. Catherine Rampell, "A Professor Who Has Problems with a Company that Profits from His Lectures," *Chronicle of Higher Education,* May 23, 2008, p. 11.

102. University of Florida v. KPB, Inc., 89 F.3d 773, 775 (11th Cir. 1996).

103. Goldie Blumenstyk, "Putting Class Notes on the Web: Are Companies Stealing Lectures?" *Chronicle of Higher Education,* Oct. 1, 1999, p. A31.

104. "The Future of Higher Ed: Lawsuit Information Page," www.thefutureofhighered.org.

105. McSherry, *Who Owns Academic Work?* pp. 102, 110; *see* Williams v. Weisser, 78 Cal. Rptr. 542 (Cal. Ct. App. 1969) (upholding right of UCLA professor to stop commercial distribution of student notes from his lectures).

106. Sweezy v. New Hampshire, 354 U.S. 234, 262 (1957) (Frankfurter, J., concurring).

107. "The Future of Higher Ed: Lawsuit Information Page," www.thefutureofhighered.org.

6. Privacy in Peril

1. *See* Minutes of February 20, 2002, Tenured Faculty Meeting, University of Michigan Law School, http://wayneoutlaws.org/hammer_v_umich/about/.

2. E-mail from Dean Jeffrey Lehman to Tenured Faculty, February 22, 2002, available at http://wayneoutlaws.org/hammer_v_umich/about/.

3. Affidavit of Peter J. Hammer, Hammer v. Board of Regents of the University of Michigan, Michigan Court of Claims, No. 04-241 MK (June 19, 2006), ¶ 73, pp. 27–28, available at http://wayneoutlaws.org/hammer_v_umich/about/.

4. For sample solicitation letters promising confidentiality, *see, e.g.,* Appendix to Procedures for Peer Review Committee for Library Faculty at the University of Illinois, www.library.uiuc.edu; University of Idaho Sample Request for Outside Peer Review Letter of Evaluation, University of Idaho College of Agriculture, www.ag.uidaho.edu; University of Washington Promotion and Tenure Review Letter Request: An Example, www.depts.washington.edu.

5. Appendix to Peter J. Hammer's University of Michigan Law School Grievance Form, August 20, 2002 (Grievance Five), available at http://home.comcast.net/~peterhammer/grievance.html.

6. The quotation is from Doe v. Abington Friends School, 480 F.3d 252, 256 (3d Cir. 2007).

7. Hammer's grievance and supporting documents are available at http://home.comcast.net/~peterhammer/grievance.html; briefs and supporting documentation relating to Hammer's lawsuit are available at http://wayneoutlaws.org/hammer_v_umich/about/.

8. *See* Report to the Faculty of the Standing Tenure Committee: Peter J. Hammer, University of Michigan Law School, available at http://wayneoutlaws .org/hammer_v_umich/about/.

9. Letter from Dean Jeffrey S. Lehman to Provost Paul Courant, February 28, 2002, available at http://wayneoutlaws.org/hammer_v_umich/about/.

10. Jack Chin, "If You Want to Know What Your Colleagues Think About You, Take Their Deposition: Tenure Litigation at Michigan," *Concurring Opinions,* Nov. 15, 2007, www.concurringopinions.com.

11. *See, e.g.,* Qamhiyah v. Iowa State University, 245 F.R.D. 393 (S.D. Iowa 2007) (ordering university to produce forty-one documents to a discrimination plaintiff, including draft committee reports, notes, and e-mails of those involved in the faculty member's tenure appeal).

12. J. Peter Byrne, "Academic Freedom: A 'Special Concern of the First Amendment,'" 99 *Yale Law Journal* 251, 319 (1989).

13. Frank H. T. Rhodes, *The Creation of the Future: The Role of the American University* (Ithaca, N.Y.: Cornell University Press, 2001), p. 23.

14. Byrne, "Academic Freedom," p. 319.

15. University of Pennsylvania v. EEOC, 493 U.S. 182, 185–186 (1990).

16. For discussion of the previous split of authority in the federal courts over the availability of a qualified academic privilege, *see* Terry L. Leap, *Tenure, Discrimination, and the Courts,* 2d ed. (Ithaca, N.Y.: ILR Press, 1995), pp. 163–172.

17. Byrne, "Academic Freedom," p. 320.

18. *University of Pennsylvania,* 493 U.S. at 193.

19. Ibid. (quoting EEOC v. Franklin & Marshall College, 775 F.2d 110, 116 (3d Cir. 1985), *cert. denied,* 476 U.S. 1163 (1986)).

20. Ibid., pp. 197, 199–200.

21. Linda Greenhouse, "Universities Lose Shield of Secrecy in Tenure Disputes," *New York Times,* Jan. 10, 1990.

22. *University of Pennsylvania,* 493 U.S. at 200–201.

23. Ibid., p. 199 (emphasis in original).

24. Timothy G. Yeung, "Comment: Discovery of Confidential Peer Review Materials in Title VII Actions for Unlawful Denial of Tenure: A Case against Redaction," 29 *University of California Davis Law Review* 167, 195 (1995); *cf.* Leap, *Tenure, Discrimination, and the Courts,* p. 177 (suggesting that allowing colleges and universities wide latitude in redacting evaluations would effectively amount to "a limited de facto qualified privilege").

25. James v. Ohio State University, 637 N.E.2d 911, 913 (Ohio 1994).

26. *See* Petition for Certiorari, Rutgers, The State University v. Bennun, No. 91–819 (U.S. Nov. 19, 1991), p. 4 (available at 1991 WL 11178984).

27. Weinstock v. Columbia University, 1996 U.S. Dist. LEXIS 16779 (S.D.N.Y. Nov. 12, 1996).

28. Bennun v. Rutgers, 727 F. Supp. 1373, 1404–1408 (D.N.J. 1990), *aff'd,* 941 F.2d 154 (3d Cir. 1991), *cert. denied,* 502 U.S. 1066 (1992).

29. Waggaman v. Villanova University, Civ. No. 04–4447, 2008 U.S. Dist. LEXIS 42740 (E.D. Pa. June 2, 2008).

30. Ibid.

31. Waggaman v. Villanova University, 2008 U.S. Dist. LEXIS 67254 (E.D. Pa. Sept. 3, 2008). Judge Pollak ruled in the university's favor.

32. Steve Dale, "My Pet World: See a Veterinary Neurologist," *Sun-Sentinel*, Aug. 21, 2006, p. 2D.

33. *See* www.michaelpodelldvm.com.

34. David Lore, "OSU Research that Involves Killing Cats OK, USDA Says," *Columbus Dispatch*, Mar. 22, 2002, p. 6B.

35. David Lore, "Meth Speeds Spread of Virus in Cats, OSU Researchers Say," *Columbus Dispatch*, June 5, 2002, p. 3C; Catherine E. Shoichet & Piper Fogg, "Cat Researcher Says Animal-Rights Activists Hounded Him Out of Academe," *Chronicle of Higher Education*, July 26, 2002, p. 10.

36. Leah Thorson, "Group Sues NIH for Documents on Cat Experiments," *Washington Post*, Jan. 14, 2002, p. A15.

37. PCRM News Release, "Doctors File Three New Complaints over Controversial Cat Experiments," Feb. 20, 2002, www.pcrm.org.

38. Ibid.

39. Physician's Committee for Responsible Medicine, Complaint and Request for Investigation to the USDA Animal and Plant Health Inspection Service, Feb. 21, 2002, pp. 3–4 (stating that "[o]n page 4 of the application, entitled 'Budjet [*sic*] Justification Page,' his total direct costs are rounded off, and his sum of total costs is incorrect by a factor of one thousand").

40. PCRM Letter, "Doctors Sue NIH over Controversial Cat Experiments," *Townsend Letter for Doctors and Patients*, Apr. 1, 2002.

41. Physicians Committee for Responsible Medicine v. NIH, 326 F. Supp. 2d 19, 21, 25–26 (D.D.C. 2004).

42. Ibid., p. 23 (quoting Washington Research Project, Inc. v. Department of Health, Education & Welfare, 504 F.2d 238, 244–245 (D.C. Cir. 1974)).

43. PCRM News Release, "Doctors Declare Victory as Cruel Drug Abuse Experiments on Cats Are Halted," June 13, 2002, www.pcrm.org.

44. David Lore, "Embattled Researcher Leaving," *Columbus Dispatch*, June 12, 2002, p. 1C.

45. News Release, Foundation for Biomedical Research, "Foundation for Biomedical Research Reacts to Researcher Leaving Ohio State University," June 12, 2002.

46. Soichet & Fogg, "Cat Researcher," p. 10.

47. Andrew Goldsteing, "A Win for the Kitties," *Time*, June 24, 2003, p. 20.

48. Ibid.

49. David Lore, "OSU Researcher's Departure Isn't End to Animal Battles," *Columbus Dispatch*, June 26, 2002, p. 7B; Sheryl Gay Stolberg, "Debate over Whether to Defend Animal Tests," *New York Times*, July 23, 2002, p. A1.

50. Ron Southwick, "Researchers Face More Federal Scrutiny on Animal Experimentation," *Chronicle of Higher Education,* June 28, 2002, p. 23.

51. *See* Lawrence K. Altman, "H.I.V. Study Finds Rate 40% Higher Than Estimated," *New York Times,* Aug. 3, 2008; Press release, "Study Offers New Insight on HIV Transmission Risk of Men Who Have Sex with Men," *Eurekalert,* Aug. 7, 2008, www.eurekalert.org.

52. "Help End the Use of Live Pigs for Trauma Training at the University of Medicine and Dentistry of New Jersey," www.pcrm.org.

53. P. J. v. Utah, 247 F.R.D. 664 (D. Utah 2007) (granting subpoena); *In re* Welding Rod Products Liability Litigation, 2005 U.S. Dist. LEXIS 23913 (N.D. Ohio Oct. 18, 2005) (denying subpoena).

54. Wu v. National Endowment for Humanities, 460 F.2d 1030, 1034 (5th Cir. 1972).

55. Kahn v. Superior Court, 233 Cal. Rptr. 662, 674 (Ct. App. 1987)

56. Ibid., p. 673.

57. *University of Pennsylvania,* 493 U.S. at 200.

58. Ibid., p. 193.

59. *Kahn,* 233 Cal. Rptr. at 670.

60. Michael Cusumano, official Web page, www.web.mit.edu.

61. Biography, *David B. Yoffie,* www.drfd.hbs.edu.

62. Steve Hamm, "A Book at the Center of the Microsoft Case," *Business Week,* Nov. 2, 1998, p. 16.

63. Steve Lohr, "Expert for Microsoft Helps Fight One of Its Subpoenas," *New York Times,* Sept. 30, 1998, p. C2.

64. Hiawatha Bray, "Microsoft Loses Bid for Research Notes," *Boston Globe,* Dec. 16, 1998, p. C2.

65. Branzburg v. Hayes, 408 U.S. 665 (1972).

66. *University of Pennsylvania,* 493 U.S. at 201.

67. *In re* Cusumano, 162 F.3d 708, 710, 714, 717 (1st Cir. 1998).

68. Steve Lohr, "Microsoft Denied Access to Scholars' Tapes," *New York Times,* Dec. 16, 1998, p. C5.

69. *In re* Subpoena to Michael Witzel, 2008 U.S. App. LEXIS 14470 (1st Cir. July 7, 2008).

70. Haigley v. Department of Health and Mental Hygiene, 736 A.2d 1185 (Md. 1999); Progressive Animal Welfare Society v. University of Washington, 884 P.2d 592 (Wash. 1994); Murphy v. Phillip Morris, Inc., 2000 U.S. Dist. LEXIS 21128 (C.D. Cal. Mar. 17, 2000).

71. Wright v. Jeep Corporation, 547 F. Supp. 871 (E.D. Mich. 1982)

72. *In re* Grand Jury Subpoena, 750 F.2d 223 (2d Cir. 1984) (the court skeptically remanded the case, however, to allow the researcher to show why his notes should be protected).

73. Mt. Sinai School of Medicine v. American Tobacco Company, 880 F.2d 1520 (2d Cir. 1989).

74. Burka v. Department of Health and Human Services, 87 F.3d 508, 521 (D.C. Cir. 1996).

75. Paul M. Fischer, "Science and Subpoenas: When Do the Courts Become Instruments of Manipulation?" in Wendy Wagner & Rena Steinor, eds., *Rescuing Science from Politics* (Cambridge: Cambridge University Press, 2006), pp. 86–97.

76. *In re* Bextra and Celebrex, 2008 U.S. Dist. LEXIS 21098 (N.D. Ill. Mar. 14, 2008).

77. *In re* Bextra and Celebrex, 249 F.R.D. 8, 13–14 (D. Mass. 2008).

78. Lila Guterman, "Journals Win a Round in Defense of Peer Review," *Chronicle of Higher Education,* Apr. 4, 2008, p. 4; Lila Guterman, "Journals Resist a Drug Company's Subpoenas, Citing Threat to Peer Review," *Chronicle of Higher Education,* Mar. 28, 2008.

7. War of the Words

1. Frank J. Sulloway curriculum vitae, available at www.sulloway.org.

2. Gary R. Johnson, "Science, Sulloway, and Birth Order: An Ordeal and an Assessment," 19 *Politics and the Life Sciences* 212, 213 (Sept. 2000).

3. Frank J. Sulloway, "*Born to Rebel* and Its Critics," 19 *Politics and the Life Sciences* 182 (Sept. 2000).

4. Frank J. Sulloway, "Chronology of a Conflict: Unethical Editorial Conduct and Abuse of Power at Politics and the Life Sciences," 2004, www.sulloway .org.

5. Susan Goldsmith, "Frank's War: How a Berkeley Scholar's Groundbreaking Research Sparked One of the Nastier Academic Debates in Recent Memory," *East Bay Express,* Apr. 28, 2004, available at www.eastbayexpress.com.

6. Johnson, "Science, Sulloway, and Birth Order," p. 240.

7. *E.g.,* "Full House: Three Is the New Two," *Boston Globe Magazine,* May 28, 2006, p. 18.

8. Frederic Townsend, "Birth Order and Rebelliousness: Reconstructing the Research in *Born to Rebel,*" 19 *Politics and the Life Sciences* 135 (Sept. 2000).

9. Frederic Townsend, "Robert Citron and the Orange County Smokescreen," 24 *Futures* 12 (Nov. 1995).

10. Roger Ebert, "Movie Answer Man," June 23, 2006, available at www .rogerebert.com.

11. "Darts and Laurels," *Columbia Journalism Review,* Mar./Apr. 1996.

12. *See, e.g.,* "Banned Words for 2007: TomKat, Awesome," *Chicago Tribune,* Jan. 1, 2007, p. A8.

13. "In retrospect, I should not have agreed to participate in this exchange, because the deck was stacked from the beginning." Sulloway, "Chronology of a Conflict."

14. Johnson, "Science, Sulloway, and Birth Order," p. 212.

15. Ibid.

16. Ibid.
17. Ibid.
18. Ibid., p. 213.
19. Ibid., p. 214.
20. Ibid., p. 217.
21. Ibid., p. 219.
22. Sulloway, "Chronology of a Conflict."
23. Ibid.
24. Ibid.
25. Ibid.
26. Ibid.
27. Ibid.
28. Jim Ritter, "Sun-Times Insight," *Chicago Sun-Times,* May 20, 2004, p. 16.
29. Ibid.
30. Johnson, "Science, Sulloway, and Birth Order," p. 211.
31. Ibid., p. 241.
32. Ibid.
33. Ibid., p. 214.
34. Ibid., p. 241.
35. Ibid.
36. Ibid.
37. Ibid., p. 241. Johnson wrote that Sulloway's actions had caused "virtual terror" and suggested that "[s]cholars, scientists, and publishers cannot focus properly on what should be their principal concerns if the threat of catastrophic legal costs hangs over them and their organizations and journals."
38. For accounts of the long-running battle between Newton and Hooke, see Gale E. Christianson, *Isaac Newton* (Oxford: Oxford University Press, 2005); James Gleick, *Isaac Newton* (New York: Pantheon Books, 2003).
39. Christianson, *Isaac Newton,* p. 68. Newton added, "I found it so formerly, and now am no sooner come near her again, but she gives me warning." Ibid.
40. Restatment of Torts (Second) § 559 (1977).
41. Instead, academics' defamation actions were all directed against those outside academia—newspapers, for example, or popular magazines—charging that the publications had printed falsehoods, with sexual misconduct outside the university a frequent fact pattern. *E.g.,* Edwards v. National Audubon Soc'y, 556 F.2d 113 (2d. Cir. 1977) (libel case based on magazine article about bird population); Maclean v. Scripps, 17 N.W. 815 (Mich. 1883) (libel case based on report that medical professor had engaged in "illicit relations" and an "obscene correspondence" with a patient); *see also* Sanford v. Howard, 95 P.2d 644 (Okla. 1939) (finding no libel in college president's report of illicit activity between grounds supervisor and "matron" to Board of Regents because information stemmed from police report). Perhaps the earliest reported

defamation claim by a professor in the United States is Maurice v. Worden, 54 Md. 233 (Md. 1880).

42. Michael Traynor, "Defamation Law: Shock Absorbers for Its Ride into the Groves of Academe," 16 *Journal of College & University Law* 373, 374 (1990).

43. Neary v. Regents of Univ. of Cal., 230 Cal. Rptr. 281 (Ct. App. 1986). The award was reduced to $3 million in a later settlement between the rancher and the university while the case was pending on appeal. *See* Neary v. Regents of Univ. of Cal., 10 Cal. Rptr. 2d 859 (Cal. 1992).

44. Traynor, "Defamation Law," 374–375, 376.

45. Ibid., p. 379.

46. Francine T. Bazluke, *Defamation Issues in Higher Education* (Washington, D.C.: National Association of College & University Attorneys, 1990), p. 1.

47. Ibid., pp. 1, 25.

48. Martin v. Press Publishing Co., 87 N.Y.S. 859 (App. Div. 1904).

49. Ollman v. Evans, 750 F.2d 970 (D.C. Cir. 1984).

50. Traynor, "Defamation Law."

51. Dilworth v. Dudley, 75 F.3d 307 (7th Cir. 1996).

52. Ibid., p. 308.

53. Ibid., p. 309.

54. Ibid., p. 310.

55. Ibid.

56. Ibid.

57. Katz v. Goldstone, 673 F. Supp. 76, 79 (D. Conn. 1987).

58. Ibid., p. 81.

59. Ibid., p. 82 (citing Preveden v. Croation Fraternal Union of America, 98 F. Supp. 784, 786 (W.D. Pa. 1951)).

60. Ibid., p. 83.

61. Ibid., p. 82.

62. Among other appointments, Lott's sixty-two-page curriculum vitae lists visiting professorships at the University of Chicago, Texas A&M, Rice, SUNY-Binghamton, UCLA, and Pennsylvania's Wharton School, and fellowships or research-scholar appointments at Chicago, Cornell, Stanford, and Yale. From 2001 to 2006, Lott was a resident scholar at the American Enterprise Institute. *See* http://johnrlott.tripod.com/Lott_CV_03_08.pdf.

63. *See* John R. Lott Jr., "Affirmative Action Has Mixed Results for Cops," Foxnews.com, Mar. 28, 2005; Kevin A. Hassett & John R. Lott Jr., "Partisan Bias in Newspapers? A Study of Headlines Says Yes," *Philadelphia Inquirer*, Oct. 6, 2004; John R. Lott Jr., "'Sentencing Fairness' Rules Backfired in Martha's Case," *Investor's Business Daily*, Mar. 11, 2004, p. A15. Lott's op-ed pieces are collected on his Web site, www.johnrlott.blogspot.com.

64. For Lott's interjections on the 2000 presidential election, *see*, for example, John R. Lott Jr., "Gore Rewrites the Rules to Win," *Wall Street Journal*, Nov. 20, 2000, A26 (with Stephen Bronars); John R. Lott Jr., "Gore Might Lose a

Second Round: Media Suppressed the Bush Vote," *Philadelphia Inquirer*, Nov. 14, 2000. Lott's curriculum vitae notes that he "[w]rote the Statistical Report for the Minority members of the *U.S. Commission on Civil Rights* on the 'Probe of Election Practices in Florida During the 2000 Presidential Election.'" For Lott's interjections on the murder rate in Baghdad, *see* John R. Lott Jr., "Baghdad's Murder Rate Irresponsibly Distorted," *Investor's Business Daily*, Dec. 12, 2003, p. A14; John R. Lott Jr., "Armed, and Safer, Iraqis," *New York Post*, June 26, 2006, p. 31.

65. John R. Lott Jr., *More Guns, Less Crime: Understanding Crime and Gun-Control Laws* (Chicago: University of Chicago Press, 1998).

66. John R. Lott Jr., *The Bias against Guns: Why Almost Everything You've Heard about Gun Control Is Wrong* (Washington, D.C.: Regnery Books, 2003).

67. *See* www.johnlott.org.

68. *See, e.g.,* Ted Goertzel, "Myths of Murder and Multiple Regression," 26 *Skeptical Inquirer* 19–23 (Jan./Feb. 2002); Chris Mooney, "Double-Barreled Double Standards," *Mother Jones*, Oct. 13, 2003; Julian Sanchez, "The Mystery of Mary Rosh," *Reason*, May 2003. For a more restrained evaluation, concluding that "the statistical evidence that these [concealed-carry] laws have reduced crime is limited, sporadic, and extraordinarily fragile," *see* Ian Ayres & John J. Donohue III, "Shooting Down the 'More Guns, Less Crime' Hypothesis," 55 *Stanford Law Review* 1193, 1201 (2003).

69. *See* Michael W. Lynch & Jacob Sullum, "Cold Comfort: An Interview with John R. Lott," *Reason*, Jan. 2000.

70. Ibid.

71. *See* Richard Morin, "Scholar Invents Fan to Answer His Critics," *Washington Post*, Feb. 1, 2003, p. C1; Sanchez, "The Mystery of Mary Rosh."

72. Lott admitted to the "Mary Rosh" persona when confronted by a reporter for the *Washington Post*. He attributed a rave review of *More Guns, Less Crime* posted by "Mary Rosh" on Amazon.com to his son and wife. *See* ibid.

73. *See* "100 People Who Shape Our World," *Time*, Apr. 30, 2006.

74. Steven D. Levitt & Stephen J. Dubner, *Freakonomics: A Rogue Economist Explores the Hidden Side of Everything* (New York: HarperCollins, 2005). In its eighty-fifth week on the *New York Times* best-seller list in January 2007, Dwight Garner described *Freakonomics* as "clinging, like snow that won't melt, to the nonfiction list in hardcover." Dwight Garner, "Inside the List," *New York Times*, Jan. 7, 2007, p. 26.

75. Jim Holt, "Everything He Always Wanted to Know," *New York Times*, May 15, 2005.

76. Levitt & Dubner, *Freakonomics*, pp. 133–134.

77. Lott v. Levitt, 469 F. Supp. 2d 575 (N.D. Ill. 2007).

78. Ibid.

79. David Glenn, "Federal Judge Allows Defamation Lawsuit against Best-Selling Economist to Proceed," *Chronicle of Higher Education*, Jan. 16, 2007.

80. *Lott,* F. Supp. 2d at 579.
81. Ibid. (quoting complaint, ¶ 12).
82. Ibid., p. 580.
83. Ibid.
84. Haberstroh v. Crain Publications, Inc., 545 N.E.2d 295 (Ill. App. Ct. 1989).
85. Ibid., pp. 271–272.
86. Ibid., p. 271.
87. Ibid.
88. *Lott,* 469 F. Supp. 2d at 584.
89. Ibid.
90. Ibid.
91. David Glenn, "Dueling Economists Reach Settlement in Defamation Lawsuit," *Chronicle of Higher Education,* Aug. 10, 2007, p. A10.
92. Briefs available at www.ca7.uscourts.gov.
93. Lott v. Levitt, 556 F.3d 564, 570 (7th Cir. 2009).
94. *See* Scott Carlson, "2 Instructors Drop Their Lawsuit against Web Site that Criticized Them," *Chronicle of Higher Education,* Oct. 20, 2000, p. A44; "ACLU Asks San Francisco Court to Dismiss Lawsuit by Professor against Student Website Reviewing Teachers," *Ascribe Newswire,* Jan. 31, 2000.
95. Lisa Fernandez, "Teacher's Legal Case Could Redefine Internet's Nature," *San Jose Mercury News,* Mar. 7, 2000.
96. Morin, "Scholar Invents Fan to Answer His Critics," p. C1.
97. Tanya Schevitz, "Teacher Review Web Site Escapes Suit, S.F. City College Professors Drop Defamation Case," *San Francisco Chronicle,* Oct. 4, 2000, p. A17.
98. *See* ibid.
99. *See* Milkovich v. Lorain Journal Co., 497 U.S. 1 (1990).
100. *See* Byars v. Kolodziej, 363 N.E.2d 628, 629–630 (Ill. App. Ct. 1977). The Pennsylvania Supreme Court similarly held that statements made by a department chair and outside reviewer to a college provost disparaging an untenured professor's teaching and student interactions reflected merely the speakers' "opinion as to the continued value of the [professor] to the Art Department and the College." Baker v. Lafayette College, 532 A.2d 399, 402–403 (Pa. 1987).
101. Ibid., p. 630.
102. *See* Maynard v. Daily Gazette Co., 447 S.E.2d 293, 296–298 (W. Va. 1994).
103. Chemerinsky, *Constitutional Law: Principles and Policies,* p. 1011.
104. *See* ibid.
105. An Alabama court actually entered a $25,000 default judgment in the plaintiff's favor, but the supreme court in Minnesota, where the defendant resided, refused to enforce it on the ground that the Alabama court lacked personal jurisdiction over the absent defendant. *See* Griffis v. Luban, 646 N.W.2d 527 (Minn. 2002), *cert. denied,* 538 U.S. 906 (2003); Scott Carlson, "Minnesota Court Rules in Online-Libel Case," *Chronicle of Higher Education,* Aug. 2, 2002, p. A29.

106. Baxter v. Scott, 847 So.2d 225, 234 (La. Ct. App. 2003), set aside on procedural grounds, 860 So. 2d 535 (La. 2003).

107. Smith v. Atkins, 622 So.2d 795, 799 (La. Ct. App. 1993) (holding that statement is defamatory *per se*).

108. Schumacher v. Argosy Educ. Group, 2006 U.S. Dist. LEXIS 88608, at *46 (D. Minn. Dec. 6, 2006) (holding that "[s]uch a vague and imprecise reference cannot be verified as a fact").

109. *Lott,* 469 F. Supp. 2d at 585.

110. Ibid.

111. Glenn, "Federal Judge Allows Defamation Lawsuit against Best-Selling Economist to Proceed."

112. *Lott,* 469 F. Supp. 2d at 580.

113. *E.g.,* Nike, Inc. v. Kasky, 539 U.S. 654, 676 (2003) (Stevens, J., concurring); Time, Inc. v. Hill, 385 U.S. 374, 388–389 (1967); New York Times v. Sullivan, 376 U.S. 254, 272 (1964).

114. Fischbach v. Trustees of Cal. St. Univ., 2004 Cal. App. Unpub. LEXIS 987 (Cal. Ct. App. Jan. 30, 2004).

115. Ibid.

116. *See* Peter Geier, "Legal Affairs," *The (Baltimore, MD) Daily Record,* May 25, 2001 (discussing a case in which "[a]n associate professor at the University of Maryland Medical School is suing the school's Baltimore Foundation Inc. and its institutional review board director, alleging that his appointment was not renewed due to the IRB director's defamatory remarks").

117. Ibid.

118. Ibid.

119. *See* Piper Fogg, "A Battle for the Ages," *Chronicle of Higher Education,* Sept. 30, 2005, p. 10 (describing the defamation lawsuit brought against S. Jay Olshansky, a professor at the University of Illinois at Chicago). For yet another recent scholar-to-scholar defamation case—one that resulted in a $3.5 million verdict for the plaintiff—*see* Shawn Day & Angela Forest, "Jury Awards Ex-Professor $3.5M in HU Lawsuit," *Daily Press (Newport, Va.),* Aug. 12, 2006 (former psychology chair, fired for alleged financial irregularities, holds Hampton University liable for failing to prevent a rival colleague from passing out fliers at commencement ceremony accusing plaintiff of "moral defectiveness").

120. *See* "Student Charges Miami U. Sorority Chapter with Defamation," *Chronicle of Higher Education,* May 23, 1997. For a small sample of administrator defamation claims, *see, e.g.,* Baxter, 847 So.2d 225 (suit by university vice president against faculty critic); Lenita Powers, "Ex-Research Vice President Sues UNR," *Reno Gazette-Journal,* Apr. 15, 2005 (defamation claim by former vice president against university president). Even colleges are now suing for institutional defamation. *See* "College Files Defamation Suit against Environmental Group," *Chronicle of Higher Education,* Mar. 21, 2003, p. A29 (describing suit by the Stevens Institute of Technology alleging that "the Fund

for a Better Waterfront damages Stevens's reputation by spreading false information about one of its construction projects").

121. Paul Lannon, *Words Like Swords: Defamation Claims at Colleges and Universities* (2002), available on the Web site of Holland & Knight, www.hklaw.com.

122. Lisa K. Garcia, "Paper at Va. Tech Is Sued," *Roanoke Times*, May 15, 1996, p. A1.

123. Jew v. University of Iowa, 749 F. Supp. 946 (S.D. Iowa 1990).

124. Ibid., pp. 949 n.3, 961.

125. Smith v. Atkins, 622 So.2d 795 (La. Ct. App. 1993).

126. Ibid., p. 803 (Barry, J., concurring).

127. *Jew,* 749 F. Supp. at 961 (footnote omitted).

128. Restatement (Second) of Torts, ch. 25, topic 2, title b, Introductory Note (1977).

129. "Twisting in the Wind," *Inside Higher Ed,* Nov. 30, 2005, available at www .insidehighered.com.

130. Ibid. Weiner reportedly received the same advice—to withdraw the article in order to avoid a costly legal fight—from counsel at Oregon. Ibid.

131. *See* Peter Monaghan, "Professors Settle Suit with U. of Denver over Retracted Article," *Chronicle of Higher Education,* Sept. 7, 2001, p. A25; Peter Monaghan, "A Journal Article Is Expunged and Its Authors Cry Foul," *Chronicle of Higher Education,* Dec. 8, 2000, p. A14.

132. *See* Monaghan, "Professors Settle Suit with U. of Denver over Retracted Article." In similar fashion, the *Journal of Studies on Alcohol* at Rutgers University was caught between opposing threats of legal action over a disputed article. *See* Kim A. McDonald, "Rutgers Journal Forced to Publish Paper Despite Threats of Libel Lawsuit," *Chronicle of Higher Education,* Sept. 13, 1989.

133. Underwager v. Salter, 22 F.3d 730, 735 (7th Cir. 1994). Longtime media lawyer Michael Traynor, too, notes that "[t]he chill on [academic] research [from defamation actions] would be far more consequential than that on common errant journalism." Traynor, "Defamation Law," p. 375.

134. *See* Philadelphia Newspapers, Inc. v. Hepps, 475 U.S. 767, 779 n.4 (1986); Hutchinson v. Proxmire, 443 U.S. 111, 133 n.16 (1979).

135. Traynor, "Defamation Law," p. 376.

136. "Twisting in the Wind."

137. Ibid.

138. Keyishian v. Board of Regents of Univ. of State of N.Y., 385 U.S. 589, 603 (1967).

139. Ibid., p. 961 n.8.

140. *See* ibid., p. 961.

141. *See* ibid., p. 967 (Appendix D, Iowa jury instruction on immunity).

142. Maria von Bolschwing, *Dancing Through the God's Eye, Holas Amigos* (1992), reprinted in Current Comments, Huichol Art and Culture, available at www

.garfield.library.upenn.edu. "It is hardly surprising . . . to find that as individuals the Huichols take responsibility for the creation of their own realities."

143. The facts for this section are taken from Fikes v. Furst, 81 P.3d 545 (N.M. 2003) and Fikes v. Furst, 61 P.3d 855 (N.M. Ct. App. 2002).

144. *Fikes,* 81 P.3d at 547.

145. Simon Romero, "Peyote's Hallucinations Spawn Real-Life Academic Feud," *New York Times,* Sept. 16, 2003, p. F-2.

146. Fikes, 61 P.3d 855.

147. Fikes, 81 P.3d 545.

148. Ibid. at 550.

149. Robert M. O'Neil, *Free Speech in the College Community* (Bloomington: Indiana University Press, 1997), vii.

150. *Fikes,* 81 P.3d at 551.

8. Of Injuries and Insults

1. Kenneth S. Abraham, *The Forms and Functions of Tort Law,* 3d ed. (New York: Foundation Press, 2007).

2. Gary A. Menneke, *How to Succeed in Law School,* 3d ed. (New York: Barron's Educational Services, 2001), p. 15.

3. *See* Garratt v. Dailey, 279 P.2d 1091 (Wash. 1955).

4. Jennifer Jacobson, "So Sue Me!" *Chronicle of Higher Education,* July 6, 2001.

5. Complaint, DiFede v. Pace University, www.findlaw.com.

6. Nick Chapin, "U. Virginia Student Sues Law Professor," *Cavalier Daily,* Mar. 27, 2002.

7. Justin Park, "Student Sues Professor," *Virginia Law Weekly,* Mar. 22, 2002, p. 1 (quoting attorney Steven D. Rosenfield).

8. *See* Helen Peterson, "Law Student Has Court Retort for Taking Fall," *New York Daily News,* June 26, 2001 (reporting that "[a] law professor whose specialty is torts got a lesson in negligence yesterday from a former student").

9. James Taranto, "Best of the Web Today: 'Let's Sue All the Lawyers,'" *Wall Street Journal* (online edition), Mar. 28, 2002.

10. Letter to the Editor, *Virginia Law Weekly,* Apr. 5, 2002, p. 3.

11. Ibid. (letter to editor by professors Rosa Ehrenreich Brooks, Daryl Levinson, Elizabeth Magill, and Jennifer Mnookin).

12. *The Paper Chase* (1973), www.imdb.com.

13. McAlpin v. Burnett, 185 F. Supp. 2d 730, 735–736 (W.D. Ky. 2001).

14. Robert D. Bickel & Peter F. Lake, *The Rights and Responsibilities of the Modern University: Who Assumes the Risks of College Life?* (Durham, N.C.: Carolina Academic Press, 1999), p. 5.

15. Ibid., p. 30.

16. *See* ibid., pp. 9–12, 65, 76–104.

17. Peter F. Lake, "Higher Education and the Courts: 1999 in Review," 27 *Journal of College and University Law* 255, 310 (2000).

18. *See, e.g.,* Branum v. Michigan, 145 N.W.2d 860 (Mich. Ct. App. 1966) (university may be held liable for negligence of its truck driver); Duarte v. California, 151 Cal. Rptr. 727 (Ct. App. 1979) (university may be held liable as a landlord for injury to student in dormitory).

19. *See* Moustafa Ayad, "Woman Sues PSU over Loose Moose Head," *Pittsburgh Post-Gazette,* Jan. 27, 2007. In another case illustrating the wide-ranging physical hazards of university life, that same academic year a student sued Florida Gulf Coast University after she was allegedly "chased down by wild pigs" while traversing the campus. *See* Samantha Henig, "Hogs on the Quad," *Chronicle of Higher Education,* Sept. 15, 2006, p. A6.

20. *See* Bickel & Lake, *Rights and Responsibilities,* p. 151 (observing that "[w]ith the fall of charitable and governmental immunity, duties to provide reasonably safe classroom instruction (physical injuries only—courts routinely reject educational malpractice claims) became readily enforceable, even if instances of injury and lawsuits were rare").

21. Shelton v. Trustees of Columbia University, 2005 U.S. Dist. LEXIS 26480 (S.D.N.Y. Nov. 1, 2005) (quoting Gally v. Columbia University, 289 F. Supp. 2d 199, 207 (S.D.N.Y. 1998)), *rev'd* in part on other grounds, 236 Fed. Appx. 648 (2d Cir. 2007).

22. Ross v. Creighton University, 957 F.2d 410, 414–415 (7th Cir. 1992).

23. Zack's employment prospects appear not to have been aided by the fact that he was evidently fired and escorted from the offices of the Delaware law firm where he worked as a summer associate during his final summer before graduation. *See* Complaint, Zachariasewycz v. Morris, Nichols, Arsht & Tunnell, LLP, Delaware Chancery Court, No. CA 2312-N (filed Nov. 21, 2006), ¶ 9, available at http://kevinunderhill.typepad.com/Documents/bad_typist_lawsuit.pdf.

24. Ibid., ¶ 18.

25. Ibid., ¶ 23.

26. Ibid., ¶¶ 25, 26.

27. Stephanie Gottschlich, "Student Sues Law School, Says Others Cheated," *Dayton Daily News,* Nov. 23, 2007; Complaint, Valente v. University of Dayton School of Law, No. 3:07-CV-0473 (S.D. Ohio Dec. 21, 2007). As of early 2009, the case was continuing in federal court. *See* Valente v. University of Dayton, 2009 U.S. Dist. LEXIS 7403 (S.D. Ohio Feb. 3, 2009) (preliminary motions decision).

28. Lord v. Meharry Medical College School of Dentistry, 2005 Tenn. App. LEXIS 486 (Tenn. Ct. App. Aug. 12, 2005).

29. Ibid. (citing Regents of University of Michigan v. Ewing, 474 U.S. 214 (1985); Board of Curators of University of Missouri v. Horowitz, 435 U.S. 78 (1978)).

30. *In re* Susan M., 556 N.E.2d 1104, 1005 (N.Y. 1990); *see also, e.g.,* Redman v. Michigan State University, 1987 U.S. Dist. LEXIS 15619, at *13 (W.D. Mich.

Mar. 24, 1987); Hull v. Yale University, 2003 Conn. Super. LEXIS 1583 (Conn. Super. Ct. May 21, 2003); Hutchings v. Vanderbilt University, 55 Fed. Appx. 308 (6th Cir. 2003).

31. Allison v. Howard University, 209 F. Supp. 2d 55, 61 (D.D.C. 2002).

32. Mostaghim v. Fashion Institute of Technology, 2002 U.S. Dist. LEXIS 10968 (S.D.N.Y. June 19, 2002).

33. Cullen v. University of Bridgeport, 2003 Conn. Super. LEXIS 3430 (Conn. Sup. Ct. Dec. 10, 2003).

34. Chira v. Columbia University, 289 F. Supp. 2d 477 (S.D.N.Y. 2003).

35. McAlpin v. Burnett, 185 F. Supp. 2d 730, 734 (W.D. Ky. 2001).

36. Doe v. Yale University, 748 A.2d 834, 847–849 (Conn. 2000).

37. Ian Fisher, "Yale Must Pay $12.2 Million to a Physician Who Got H.I.V.," *New York Times*, Dec. 18, 1997. The case settled shortly thereafter for what the plaintiff's lawyer termed "a substantial amount." Telephone interview with Michael Koskoff, July 25, 2008.

38. Atria v. Vanderbilt University, 142 Fed. Appx. 246, 251 & n.2 (6th Cir. 2005).

39. Atria's professor, B. A. Hess, testified that he rebuffed a suggestion by a university administrator that he revise his method of handling exams because "I felt that they were encroaching on my academic freedom, and I'm pretty strong on academic freedom." Ibid., p. 252 n.3.

40. *See, e.g.,* Swartley v. Hoffner, 734 A.2d 915 (Pa. Super. Ct. 1999) (allowing graduate student to challenge the conduct of her dissertation committee under a breach-of-contract theory).

41. Gupta v. New Britain General Hospital, 687 A.2d 111, 120 (Conn. 1996).

42. Hull, 2003 Conn. Super. LEXIS 1583.

43. Alsides v. Brown Institute, Ltd., 592 N.W.2d 468, 472–474 & n.3 (Minn. Ct. App. 1999).

44. Lake, "Higher Education and the Courts," p. 309.

45. Bittle v. Oklahoma City University, 6 P.3d 509 (2000).

46. Miller v. Loyola University of New Orleans, 829 So. 2d 1057, 1058 (La. Ct. App. 2002).

47. Miller v. United States, 42 F.3d 297, 307 (5th Cir. 1995).

48. *Miller,* 829 So.2d at 1060–1061.

49. Ibid., pp. 1064–1065 (Plotkin, J., dissenting).

50. Curie Veronica Jones, "Law Student Sues Loyola," *Loyola Maroon,* Feb. 22, 2002.

51. In Collins v. Minnesota School of Business, 655 N.W.2d 320, 323 (Minn. 2003), for example, students enrolled in a trade school's sports medicine program sued, claiming they were misled in their studies by its advertisement that claimed a growing "need for qualified sports medicine technicians"; after the trial court rejected the school's argument that the students' claims should be barred as ones for "educational malpractice," the school settled for $200,000. *See also* Jamieson v. Vatterott Educational Center, 473

F. Supp. 2d 1153 (D. Kan. 2007) (allowing students to sue on claim that occupational classes offered by college did not match courses of study that the college had promised).

52. Bickel & Lake, *Rights and Responsibilities*, p. 149 (emphasis in original); *see also* ibid., p. 139 (noting that recent court decisions "are charting a 'business' tort path for colleges, rightly or wrongly").

53. Lake, "Higher Education and the Courts," p. 309.

54. Nagarajan v. Tennessee State University, 1999 U.S. App. LEXIS 16950 (6th Cir. July 19, 1999).

55. Nagarajan v. Scheick, 2003 Tenn. App. LEXIS 888, at *4 (Tenn. Ct. App. Dec. 19, 2003).

56. Ibid., p. *4; Nagarajan v. Scheick, 8 Fed. Appx. 336 (6th Cir. 2001).

57. *Nagarajan*, 2003 Tenn. App. LEXIS 888, at *5.

58. Ibid.; *Nagarajan*, 8 Fed. Appx. at 338. In separate lawsuits, Nagarajan also unsuccessfully claimed to have been the victim of discrimination in the revocation of his driver's license; *see* Nagarajan v. Williams, 1998 U.S. App. LEXIS 31977 (6th Cir. Dec. 22, 1998), and in a dispute with a Methodist church board, *see* Nagarajan v. Jones, 33 Fed. Appx. 791 (6th Cir. 2002).

59. Rate My Professors, www.ratemyprofessors.com.

60. *See, e.g.,* Ismael v. Ali, 276 Fed. Appx. 156 (3d Cir. 2008) (organizer of academic conference sued two fellow faculty participants in dispute over conference finances); Martin v. Howard University, 275 Fed. Appx. 2 (D.C. Cir. 2008) (visiting professor sued for intentional infliction of emotional distress when not hired for tenure-track position); Barefield v. Board of Trustees of California State University, Bakersfield, 500 F. Supp. 2d 1244 (E.D. Cal. 2007) (tenure-track counselor passed over for position of Director of Student Activities); Reardon v. Allegheny College, 926 A.2d 477 (Pa. Super. Ct. 2007) (student disciplined for plagiarism sued college, professor, and two classmates for intentional infliction of emotional distress).

61. Restatement (Second) of Torts § 46 comment d (1965).

62. Grigorenko v. Pauls, 297 F. Supp. 2d 446, 450 (D. Conn. 2003).

63. *See, e.g.,* Edsall v. Assumption College, 367 F. Supp. 2d 72 (D. Mass. 2005) (holding that a visiting professor who was allegedly passed over for a tenure-track vacancy had not stated a valid IIED claim, but could seek to hold the college president and provost individually liable for tortiously interfering with his prospective employment relationship with the college; the court also allowed the professor's wife to sue the president and provost for her own emotional loss of her husband's "society and companionship" following his disappointment).

64. Smith v. Atkins, 622 So.2d 795 (La. Ct. App. 1993); *see also* Hayut v. State University of New York, 352 F.3d 733 (2d Cir. 2003) (student sued for IIED and other claims based on professor's alleged classroom comments likening her to Monica Lewinsky); Frederick v. Simpson College, 149 F. Supp. 2d 826

(S.D. Iowa 2001) (student sued for IIED and other claims based on professor's allegedly inappropriate comments and advances inside and outside of classroom).

65. Martin v. University of New Haven, 2006 Conn. Super. LEXIS 3214 (Conn. Super. Ct. Oct. 24, 2006).

66. Faraclas v. Botwick, 2005 Conn. Super. LEXIS 217 (Conn. Super. Ct. Jan. 25, 2005).

67. Ibid.

68. Sentry Claims Service v. Botwick, 2004 Conn. Super. LEXIS 1521 (Conn. Super. Ct. June 8, 2004).

69. Hull, 2003 Conn. Super. LEXIS 1583.

70. Seaton v. University of Pennsylvania, 2001 U.S. Dist. LEXIS 19780 (E.D. Pa. Nov. 30, 2001).

71. Richards v. Duke University, 480 F. Supp. 2d 222, 228 (D.D.C. 2007).

72. Ross v. Saint Augustine's College, 103 F.3d 338, 343 (4th Cir. 1996).

73. *See* Taus v. Loftus, 2005 Cal. App. Unpub. LEXIS 3048, at *13 (Cal. Ct. App. Apr. 1, 2005) (quoting Paul Ekman, clinical psychologist at University of California, San Francisco), *aff'd* in part & *rev'd* in part, 151 P.3d 1185 (Cal. 2007); David Corwin & Ema Olafson, "Videotaped Discovery of a Reportedly Unrecallable Memory of Child Sexual Abuse: Comparison with a Childhood Interview Taped 11 Years Before," 2 *Child Maltreatment* 91 (May 1997).

74. *Taus*, 151 P.3d at 1191.

75. Elizabeth F. Loftus, "On Science under Legal Assault," 132 *Daedalus* 84, 85 (Fall 2003).

76. *See* Sasha Abramsky, "Memory and Manipulation," *LA Weekly,* Aug. 20, 2004, p. 32; Elizabeth F. Loftus, *Eyewitness Testimony* (Cambridge, Mass.: Harvard University Press, 1996); Elizabeth F. Loftus, *The Myth of Repressed Memory: False Memories and Allegations of Sexual Abuse* (New York: St. Martin's Press, 1994).

77. Elizabeth F. Loftus & Melvin J. Guyer, "Who Abused Jane Doe? The Hazards of the Single Case History," 26 *Skeptical Inquirer* 24 (May/June 2002).

78. Ibid., p. 26.

79. *Taus*, 151 P.3d at 1189.

80. Carol Tavris, "Whatever Happened to 'Jane Doe'?" 32 *Skeptical Inquirer* (Jan. 2008).

81. Ibid., p. 1197 (quoting California Code of Civil Procedure § 425.16(b)(1)).

82. Loftus, "On Science under Legal Assault," pp. 84–86.

83. Letter from Professor Richard J. McNally to Chief Justice Ronald M. George, June 3, 2005.

84. *Taus*, 151 P.3d at 1207–1221.

85. Maura Dolan, "High Court to Review Privacy Rights," *Los Angeles Times,* June 23, 2005, p. B4 (quoting Joyanna Silberg, clinical psychologist and executive vice president of the Leadership Council on Child Abuse and Interpersonal Violence).

86. *Taus,* 151 P.3d at 1220.

87. Maura Dolan, "Ruling May Constrain Researchers; State High Court Says Journalists and Scholars Can Be Held Liable for Privacy Intrusion if They Misrepresent Themselves to Obtain Information," *Los Angeles Times,* Feb. 27, 2007, p. B3.

88. Elizabeth F. Loftus, "Perils of Provocative Scholarship," *Association for Psychological Science Observer,* May 2008.

89. Ibid.

90. Tavris, "Whatever Happened to 'Jane Doe'?"

91. Loftus, "On Science under Legal Assault," p. 86.

92. Abby Simons, "State to Pay $925,000 to End Stutter Lawsuit," *Des Moines Register,* Aug. 18, 2007.

93. *See* Nixon v. Iowa, 704 N.W.2d 643 (Iowa 2005).

94. Vodopest v. MacGregor, 913 P.2d 779 (Wash. 1996).

95. Kevin M. Samuels, Note, "Institutional Review Boards and the Statutory Compliance 'Defense' to Intentional Tort Liability," 56 *Case Western Reserve Law Review* 799, 800 (2006).

96. 164 Mulberry Street Corp. v. Columbia University, 771 N.Y.S.2d 16, 22–24 (N.Y. App. Div. 2004).

97. Loftus, "Perils of Provocative Scholarship." *See also* Special Issue, "Symposium on Censorship and Institutional Review Boards," 101 *Northwestern University Law Review* 339 *et seq.* (2007).

98. Samuels, "Institutional Review Boards," pp. 800–802 (arguing that courts should recognize IRB compliance as creating a rebuttable presumption of due care in tort cases arising from academic research).

99. Susan M. Wolf, Jordan Paradise, & Charlisse Caga-anan, "The Law of Incidental Findings in Human Subjects Research: Establishing Researchers' Duties," 36 *Journal of Law, Medicine and Ethics* 361, 362–363 (2008).

100. Charles A. Nelson, "Incidental Findings in Magnetic Resonance Imaging (MRI) Brain Research," 36 *Journal of Law, Medicine and Ethics* 315, 316 (2008).

101. Wolf et al., "The Law of Incidental Findings," pp. 362–363; *see also* Alan Milstein, "Research Malpractice and the Issue of Incidental Findings," 36 *Journal of Law, Medicine and Ethics* 356 (2008).

102. Abramsky, "Memory and Manipulation," p. 32.

9. Promises, Promises

1. John DeMoor, "MO Court of Appeals, Western District Upholds Student's Claims against Private College," *Missouri Lawyers Weekly,* Oct. 31, 2005.

2. Verni v. Cleveland Chiropractic College, 2005 Mo. App. LEXIS 1544 (Mo. Ct. App. Oct. 25, 2005).

3. Verni v. Cleveland Chiropractic College, 212 S.W.3d 150, 153 (Mo. 2007).

4. Ibid., p. 153.

5. Cleveland Chiropractic College Faculty Handbook, www.cleveland.edu.

6. *See* Bracken v. Visitors of William & Mary College, 7 Va. 573 (1790); *see also, e.g.,* University of Alabama v. Walden, 15 Ala. 655 (Ala. 1849) (salary); Butler v. Regents of the University of Wisconsin, 32 Wis. 124 (Wis. 1873) (appointment).

7. *See* Head v. The University, 86 U.S. 526 (1873) (discussed in Chapter 2).

8. Hazel Glenn Beh, "Student versus University: The University's Implied Obligations of Good Faith and Fair Dealing," 59 *Maryland Law Review* 183, 186 (2000).

9. *See, e.g.,* Shepard v. Temple University, 948 A.2d 852 (Pa. Super. Ct. 2008) (holding that "the evaluation of the performance of a college professor and his or her suitability to the educational needs, goals, and philosophies of a particular institution necessarily involves many subjective, nonquantifiable factors," and is "best performed by those closely involved in the life of the institution, not by judges") (internal citation omitted).

10. Ann D. Springer, "AAUP: Legal Issues for Faculty" (2004), available at www.aaup.org.

11. Sackman v. Alfred University, 717 N.Y.S.2d 461, 463 (N.Y. Sup. Ct. 2000).

12. Ibid., p. 464 (quoting Pace College v. Commission on Human Rights of City of New York, 339 N.E.2d 880 (N.Y. 1975)).

13. Ibid., p. 465.

14. Roufaiel v. Ithaca College, 660 N.Y.S.2d 595 (App. Div. 1997).

15. *See* Guckenberger v. Boston University, 974 F. Supp. 106, 150–152 (D. Mass. 1997) (finding breach of contract formed by assurances given to prospective students by university officials; also assuming arguendo that enforceable contract could be formed by prospective students' reliance on statements made in promotional brochure). In Johns Hopkins University v. Ritter, 689 A.2d 91 (Md. Ct. App. 1996), a Maryland appellate court upheld a jury finding that a department chair's oral assurances while recruiting two lateral hires that they would be granted tenure became part of their employment contract. It overturned an $822,000 award in their favor, however, on the ground that the chair lacked the authority to bind the university to a promise of tenure. An assurance within the chair's authority, however, such as lab space or other job conditions, presumably would have been enforceable as a contract.

16. Saxe v. Board of Trustees of Metropolitan State College of Denver, 179 P.3d 67, 76 (Colo. Ct. App. 2007).

17. *See* Head v. The University, 86 U.S. 526 (1873).

18. Salkin v. Case Western Reserve University, 2007 Ohio App. LEXIS 1077 (Ohio Ct. App. Mar. 15, 2007).

19. Oyefodun v. Dillard University, 2004 U.S. Dist. LEXIS 12756 (E.D. La. July 8, 2004); Oyefodun v. Dillard University, 2003 U.S. Dist. LEXIS 26175 (E.D. La. June 26, 2003). The *Oyefodun* court further held that the instructor was

entitled to press a second breach-of-contract claim for violations of the faculty handbook when he was later removed from teaching because of student allegations of sexual harassment. Whether university employment manuals constitute enforceable contracts, the court ruled, must be decided "on a case by case basis."

20. Khoury v. University of California, 2008 Cal. App. Unpub. LEXIS 888 (Cal. Ct. App. Jan. 31, 2008).

21. Thomas v. Catawba College, 104 S.E.2d 175 (N.C. 1958). The court ducked the "esprit de corps" analysis by finding that the professor had accepted what was, in effect, severance pay, and thereby had agreed to a resolution without court intervention.

22. Neiman v. Yale University, 851 A.2d 1165 (Conn. 2004).

23. Chaffey Community College District v. Tatum, 2008 Cal. App. Unpub. LEXIS 3392 (Cal. Ct. App. Apr. 24, 2008).

24. Beh, "Student versus University," pp. 197–198.

25. *See* Complaint, Giuliani v. Duke University, No. 1:08-CV-00502 (M.D.N.C. filed July 23, 2008); Alison Leigh Cowan, "Forced Off Duke's Varsity Golf Team, Giuliani's Son Files a Lawsuit," *New York Times,* July 25, 2008.

26. Complaint, Giuliani v. Duke University, subheading K, p. 15 (boldface and capitals omitted).

27. Ibid., ¶ 15; *see also* ibid., ¶ 59.

28. Ibid., ¶ 60.

29. Ibid., ¶¶ 62–64.

30. Ibid., ¶¶ 68, 70.

31. Alison Leigh Cowan, "Dismissal Urged in Lawsuit Brought by Giuliani's Son," *New York Times,* May 21, 2009.

32. Jeffrey Zaslow, "The Most-Praised Generation Goes to Work," *Wall Street Journal,* Apr. 20, 2007.

33. *See* Beh, "Student versus University," pp. 193–194 (observing that "the typical college student is less and less characterized as wide-eyed and innocent and is more often regarded as a savvy shopper" and that "[t]oday, many students expect the school to accommodate the student's schedule and interests and not vice versa").

34. *The Castle* (Working Dog 1997).

35. Complaint, Giuliani v. Duke University, p. 1 & ¶ 68.

36. Altschuler v. University of Pennsylvania Law School, 1997 U.S. Dist. LEXIS 3248 (S.D.N.Y. Mar. 21, 1997), *aff'd,* 201 F.3d 430 (3d Cir. 1999), *cert. denied,* 530 U.S. 1276 (2000).

37. Gally v. Columbia University, 22 F. Supp. 2d 199 (S.D.N.Y. 1998).

38. Leiby v. University of Akron, 2005 Ohio Misc. LEXIS 517 (Ohio Ct. Cl. Nov. 9, 2005), *aff'd,* 2006 Ohio App. LEXIS 2649 (Ohio Ct. App. June 6, 2006); Leiby v. University of Akron, 2007 Ohio Misc. LEXIS 282 (Ohio Ct. Cl. July 19, 2007).

39. McCawley v. Universidad Carlos Albizu, 461 F. Supp. 2d 1251 (S.D. Fla. 2006).

40. Chepak v. Walden University, 2008 U.S. Dist. LEXIS 14085 (S.D.N.Y. Feb. 26, 2008).

41. Jamieson v. Vatterott Educational Center, 473 F. Supp. 2d 1153, 1160 (D. Kan. 2007) (quoting Ross v. Creighton University, 957 F.2d 410, 416 (7th Cir. 1992)).

42. Ryan v. University of North Carolina Hospitals, 494 S.E.2d 789 (N.C. Ct. App. 1998). Later, the court would uphold a finding in favor of the university based on the breach of contract claim. 2005 N.C. App. LEXIS 402 (N.C. Ct. App. Mar. 1, 2005).

43. Elliott v. University of Cincinnati, 730 N.E.2d 996 (Ohio Ct. App. 1999).

44. Shelton v. Trustees of Columbia University, 2005 U.S. Dist. LEXIS 26480, at *10 (S.D.N.Y. Nov. 1, 2005), *rev'd in relevant part,* 236 Fed. Appx. 648 (2d Cir. 2007).

45. Complaint, Marquis v. University of Massachusetts, Civ. Action No. 07-30015-KPN (D. Mass. filed Jan. 31, 2007), ¶ 59.

46. Allison v. Howard University, 209 F. Supp. 2d 55, 60 (D.D.C. 2002).

47. Springer, "AAUP: Legal Issues for Faculty."

48. Atria v. Vanderbilt University, 142 Fed. Appx. 246, 254–256 (6th Cir. 2005) (emphasis added).

49. Ibid., p. 256 (stating that "[a] reasonable juror could conclude that Vanderbilt's decision to accept some forms of unreliable evidence but not others was an arbitrary decision and a breach of its implied contract with Atria").

50. Sharick v. Southeastern University of the Health Sciences *(Sharick II),* 780 So. 2d 142, 146 (Fla. Ct. App. 2001) (dissenting opinion).

51. Brian Villalobos, "Expelled Student Sues University in Florida," *Daily Texan,* Aug. 15, 2002.

52. Sharick v. Southeastern University of the Health Services *(Sharick I),* 780 So. 2d 136, 139 (Fla. Ct. App. 2000) (emphasis added).

53. Scott D. Makar, "What Can Be Learned from *Sharick v. Southeastern University?*" (unpublished paper, 2002), available at www.law.stetson.edu.

54. *Sharick II,* 780 So.2d at 144–145 (Ramirez, J., concurring) (quoting Hazel Glenn Beh, "Student versus University: The University's Implied Obligation of Good Faith and Fair Dealing," 59 *Maryland Law Review* 183 [2000]).

55. Villalobos, "Expelled Student Sues."

56. Sharick v. Southeastern University of the Health Services *(Sharick III),* 891 So. 2d 562 (Fla. Ct. App. 2004).

57. "Digest: Ex-NSU Student Wins Case against School," *Sun-Sentinel,* Feb. 7, 2008.

58. An appeal is pending.

59. Makar, "What Can Be Learned from *Sharick v. Southeastern University?*"

60. John J. Chung, "Promissory Estoppel and the Protection of Interpersonal Trust," 56 *Cleveland State Law Review* 37, 38 (2008).

61. Grant Gilmore, *The Death of Contract* (Columbus: Ohio State University Press, 1974).

62. Richard A. Lord, 4 *Williston on Contracts*, 4th ed., § 8:1 (Eagen, Minn.: Thomson West, 2008) (describing "the ever-expanding doctrine of promissory estoppel").

63. *See* Findings of Fact, Conclusions, Recommended Action of President, and Opinion, *In re* Grievance and Appeal of Natelson and University of Montana School of Law (University of Montana, Aug. 25, 2004); Memorandum of President G. M. Dennison to Dean E. E. Eck, Aug. 25, 2004.

64. Marcella Bombardieri, "College Trustees Clash on Key Values," *Boston Globe*, Apr. 3, 2007; *see also* Tamar Lewin, "Battle over Board Structure at Dartmouth Raises Passion of Alumni," *New York Times*, Sept. 8, 2007; Paul Fain, "Trustee Election at Dartmouth Is Seen as 'Battle for Academic Freedom,'" *Chronicle of Higher Education*, May 5, 2005.

65. Plaintiffs' Opposition to Motion to Dismiss, Association of Alumni of Dartmouth College v. Trustees of Dartmouth College, No. 07-E-0289 (Grafton County, N.H., Super. Ct.), pp. 42–43.

66. *See* Nye v. University of Delaware, 2003 Del. Super. LEXIS 325 (Del. Super. Ct. Sept. 17, 2003). The trial court later found insufficient evidence to support the claims, but Delaware's highest court sent back for trial the part of the lawsuit based on administrative leave pay. 897 A.2d 768 (Del. 2006).

67. Suddith v. University of Southern Mississippi, 977 So. 2d 1158, 1180 (Miss. Ct. App. 2007). In another case involving faculty, the court rejected the professor's promissory estoppel claim to teach only the courses that he preferred. *Salkin*, 2007 Ohio App. LEXIS 1077, at *24.

68. *See* Harrison Korn, "Yale: Former Art Student's Allegations of Improper Expulsion Have 'No Merit,'" *Yale Daily News*, July 23, 2008; Complaint, Osberg v. Yale University (Conn. Super. Ct., filed July 10, 2008).

69. Osberg v. Yale University, 2009 Conn. Super. LEXIS 473 (Conn. Super. Ct. Feb. 11, 2009).

70. Amir Efrati, "Hard Case: Job Market Wanes for U.S. Lawyers," *Wall Street Journal*, Sept. 24, 2007, p. A1.

71. *See* Bank v. Brooklyn Law School, 2000 U.S. Dist. LEXIS 16180 (E.D.N.Y. Oct. 6, 2000) (noting that student's sixty-five-page complaint charging violations of the federal Racketeer Influenced and Corrupt Organizations Act "is exactly the sort of complaint that has given the private right of action under RICO a bad name").

72. *See, e.g., Guckenberger*, 974 F. Supp. 2d at 150–152 (finding possible breach of contract based on statements made by admissions officers to prospective students and recognizing possibility of contract claims based on promotional brochures); Ross v. Creighton University, 957 F.2d 410 (7th Cir. 1992) (disallowing educational malpractice claims, but allowing a student-athlete to sue for breach of promises made in recruiting him to university).

73. In 2008, officials at California State University at Long Beach began scrutinizing the accuracy of faculty biographies after a film professor accused some of his colleagues of padding their credentials. "Students may decide to come to this department based on what they read in those bios," the film department chair told the *Chronicle of Higher Education,* "and in that case, we may be getting into something like fraud." Thomas Bartlett, "Cal State-Long Beach Investigates Allegations of Bogus Claims in Professors' Bios," *Chronicle of Higher Education,* May 6, 2008.
74. Beh, "Student versus University," p. 224; *see also* Michael Zolandz, Note, "Storming the Ivory Tower: Renewing the Breach of Contract Claim by Students against Universities," 69 *George Washington Law Review* 91 (2000).
75. Peter Berkowitz, "Colleges Must Not Be above the Law," *Chronicle of Higher Education,* Oct. 10, 2003.

10. Looking Forward

1. Peltz curriculum vitae, available at www.law.ualr.edu.
2. Michelle Hillen, "Experts Watch as Professor Sues Students," *Arkansas Democrat-Gazette,* Apr. 27, 2008.
3. BLSA was later dismissed from the suit.
4. Memo from BLSA to Dean Goldner, attachment to Peltz v. Nation complaint, available at www.pulaskiclerk.com; *see also* Lynnley Browning, "Law Professor Accuses Students of Defamation," *New York Times,* May 1, 2008.
5. Hillen, "Experts Watch as Professor Sues Students."
6. Ibid.
7. Peltz v. Nation complaint, www.pulaskiclerk.com.
8. Hillen, "Experts Watch as Professor Sues Students."
9. *See* John Lynch, "Student-Professor Legal Clash Concludes; UALR Law Teacher Drops Defamation Suit," *Arkansas Democrat-Gazette,* Nov. 13, 2008.
10. John Gill, "At Writ's End, Lecturers May See Students in Court," *Times Higher Education,* May 8, 2008; *see also* Browning, "Law Professor Accuses Students of Defamation"; John Lynch, "Law Professor Sues Black Groups; Lawyers', Students' Associations Called Him Racist, UALR Expert Says," *Arkansas Democrat-Gazette,* Mar. 13, 2008.
11. Althouse blog, www.althouse.blogspot.com (Apr. 30, 2008).
12. Stephen Bainbridge, "Man Bites Dog: Law Professor Sues Students," www.stephenbainbridge.com (Apr. 29, 2008).
13. Michael Dorf, "Why Didn't I Think of That?" *Dorf on Law,* www.michaeldorf.org (May 1, 2008).
14. Hillen, "Experts Watch as Professor Sues Students."
15. Scott Jaschik, "A Professor Sues His Students," *Inside Higher Ed,* Apr. 30, 2008.
16. Ibid.

17. Ibid.

18. Ibid.

19. John Lynch, "Student–Professor Legal Clash Concludes."

20. Scott Jaschik, "What You Can't Win in Court," *Inside Higher Ed*, Nov. 17, 2008.

21. Hillen, "Experts Watch as Professor Sues Students."

22. Jaschik, "A Professor Sues His Students."

23. Dorf, "Why Didn't I Think of That?"

24. Ann H. Franke & Lawrence White, "Responsibilities of Department Chairs: Legal Issues," American Council on Education Department Leadership Project (rev. ed. 2002), available at www.acenet.edu.

25. Michael A. Olivas, "The Legal Environment: The Implications of Legal Change on Campus," in Philip G. Altbach et al., eds., *American Higher Education in the Twenty-first Century: Social, Political, and Economic Challenges* (Baltimore: Johns Hopkins University Press, 1999), pp. 216, 236.

26. Weinstein v. University of Illinois, 811 F.2d 1091, 1096 (7th Cir. 1987).

27. J. Peter Byrne, "The Threat to Constitutional Academic Freedom," 31 *Journal of College and University Law* 79, 133 (2004).

28. David L. Kirp, *Shakespeare, Einstein, and the Bottom Line: The Marketing of Higher Education* (Cambridge, Mass.: Harvard University Press, 2003), p. 261.

29. *See* Alan Finder, "Decline of the Tenure Track Raises Concerns," *New York Times*, Nov. 20, 2007; "New Book Discussion—*Academic Freedom in the Wired World: Political Extremism, Corporate Power, and the University*," Woodrow Wilson International Center for Scholars, Mar. 19, 2008 (comments of veteran university counsel Ann H. Franke), available at www.wilsoncenter.org; "Pressing Legal Issues: 10 Views of the Next 5 Years," *Chronicle of Higher Education*, June 25, 2004, p. 4.

30. Robert O'Neil, *Academic Freedom in the Wired World: Political Extremism, Corporate Power, and the University* (Cambridge, Mass.: Harvard University Press, 2008), pp. 235–267; J. Peter Byrne, "Constitutional Academic Freedom after *Grutter:* Getting Real about the 'Four Freedoms' of a University," 77 *Colorado Law Review* 929, 943–944 (2006); AAUP Report, *Freedom in the Classroom* (Sept.–Oct. 2007), p. 60.

31. Sweezy v. New Hampshire, 354 U.S. 234, 262 (1957) (Frankfurter, J., concurring).

32. *See* Anthony Lewis, *Portrait of a Decade: The Second American Revolution* (New York: Random House, 1964).

33. Olivas, "The Legal Environment," p. 231.

34. Steven G. Poskanzer, *Higher Education Law: The Faculty* (Baltimore: Johns Hopkins University Press, 2002), p. 174.

35. Healy v. James, 406 U.S. 169, 196 (1972) (opinion of Douglas, J.).

36. Ibid., pp. 196–197.

37. *See* Chapter 1.

38. David Riesman, *On Higher Education: The Academic Enterprise in an Era of Rising Student Consumerism* (San Francisco: Jossey-Bass, 1980), p. xiii.

39. Ibid., p. xiv.

40. Ibid.

41. Ibid., p. xiii.

42. Richard K. Vedder, "Colleges Should Go beyond the Rhetoric of Accountability," *Chronicle of Higher Education*, June 27, 2008, p. 64.

43. Anne Marie Chaker, "Congress Passes College-Oversight Bill," *Wall Street Journal*, Aug. 1, 2008, p. A10.

44. Ylan Q. Mui & Susan Kinzie, "Break on Cost of Textbooks Unlikely before Last Bell, 2010," *Washington Post*, Aug. 20, 2008, p. A1.

45. Alan Finder, "Yale Plans to Increase Spending from Its Endowment," *New York Times*, Jan. 8, 2008.

46. Karen W. Arenson, "Senate Looking at Endowments as Tuition Rises," *New York Times*, Jan. 25, 2008.

47. John Tierney, "A New Frontier for Title IX: Science," *New York Times*, July 15, 2008. Yet another "accountability" measure "require[s] colleges and lobbyists to report their political contributions and certify that they have complied with a new ban on gifts to members of Congress," as well as report other spending, in an effort to scrutinize college lobbying. Kelly Field, "New Rules, More Scrutiny for Colleges and Their Lobbyists," *Chronicle of Higher Education*, Aug. 1, 2008, p. 14.

48. Vedder, "Colleges Should Go beyond the Rhetoric of Accountability," p. 64.

49. Andrew Delbanco, "Academic Business," *New York Times*, Sept. 30, 2007.

50. Kirp, *Shakespeare, Einstein, and the Bottom Line*, pp. 260–261.

51. Delbanco, "Academic Business."

52. José A. Cabranes, "Myth and Reality of University Trusteeship in the Post-Enron Era," 76 *Fordham Law Review* 955, 976–978 (2007). Specifically, Judge Cabranes suggested that "legislatures might be well-advised to modify their nonprofit corporation statutes to provide private rights of action for donors to enforce the terms of their gifts where they have explicitly reserved the right to do so." Ibid., p. 978. Noting well-publicized recent litigation by the Robertson family against Princeton University for misuse of gift funds, Cabranes concluded that "[w]hatever one might think about the merits of the Robertson litigation, it is undeniable that such litigation, or the threat of such litigation, will cause universities to think twice before disregarding the wishes of donors who are, after all, the lifeblood of any private academic institution." Ibid., pp. 978–979.

53. Press Release, "Congress Recognizes Importance of Free Speech, Due Process in Higher Education," Foundation for Individual Rights in Education, Aug. 15, 2008, available at www.thefire.org.

54. Vedder, "Colleges Should Go beyond the Rhetoric of Accountability," p. 64.

55. Amir Efrati, "Hard Case: Job Market Wanes for U.S. Lawyers," *Wall Street Journal,* Sept. 24, 2007, p. A1.

56. Vesna Jaksic, "Don't Like Your Grade? Sue Your Law School," Law.com, Dec. 18, 2007, available at www.law.com.

57. Robin Wilson, "Adjuncts Fight Back over Academic Freedom," *Chronicle of Higher Education,* Oct. 3, 2008, p. A1.

58. Richard A. Posner, "The University as Business," *The Atlantic Monthly,* June 2002, p. 21.

59. Mark C. Taylor, "End the University as We Know It," *New York Times,* Apr. 27, 2009.

60. Frank Donoghue, *The Last Professors: The Corporate University and the Fate of the Humanities* (New York: Fordham University Press, 2008), p. xi.

61. E. R. Shipp, "The Litigious Groves of Academe," *New York Times,* Nov. 8, 1987.

62. Wilson, "Adjuncts Fight Back over Academic Freedom," p. A1.

63. *See* O'Neil, *Academic Freedom,* pp. 250–256.

64. Byrne, "The Threat to Constitutional Academic Freedom," p. 82.

65. Posner, "The University as Business," p. 21.

66. Ann D. Springer, "AAUP: Legal Issues for Faculty (2004)," Feb. 2004, available at www.aaup.org.

67. Sharick v. Southeastern University of the Health Sciences, 780 So.2d 142, 145 (Fla. Ct. App. 2001) (Ramirez, J., concurring in denial of rehearing) (quoting Hazel Glenn Beh, "Student versus University: The University's Implied Obligation of Good Faith and Fair Dealing," 59 *Maryland Law Review* 183, 196 (2000)). As Florida solicitor general Scott Makar observes, *Sharick* "reflects the judiciary's growing tendency to view colleges as similar to commercial ventures—a trend that could have frightening implications for higher education." Scott D. Makar, "Litigious Students and Academic Disputes," *Chronicle of Higher Education,* Nov. 8, 2002, p. 20.

68. Frank H. T. Rhodes, *The Creation of the Future: The Role of the American University* (Ithaca, N.Y.: Cornell University Press, 2001), p. 215; *see also* Matthew W. Finkin & Robert C. Post, *For the Common Good: Principles of American Academic Freedom* (New Haven, Conn.: Yale University Press, 2009), p. 42 (observing that "[a]cademic freedom rests on a covenant struck between the university and the general public, not on a contract between particular scholars and the general public").

69. *See* Jonathan D. Glater, "Colleges Profit as Banks Market Credit Cards to Students," *New York Times,* Jan. 1, 2009.

70. Taylor, "End the University as We Know It."

71. Ibid.

72. *See* Ami Zusman, "Challenges Facing Higher Education in the Twenty-First Century," in Altbach et al., *American Higher Education in the Twenty-first Century,* pp. 115–120; Jeffrey Selingo, "The Disappearing State in Public Higher Education," *Chronicle of Higher Education,* Feb. 28, 2003.

73. *See* Zusman, "Challenges Facing Higher Education in the Twenty-First Century," pp. 119–120.

74. Ibid., p. 119.

75. Address by Robert Berdahl, "The Privatization of Public Universities," Erfurt University, Erfurt, Germany (May 23, 2000), available at http://cio.chance .berkeley.edu/chancellor/sp/privatization.htm.

76. Rhodes, *The Creation of the Future*, p. 23; J. Peter Byrne, "Academic Freedom: A 'Special Concern of the First Amendment,' " 99 *Yale Law Journal* 251, 273–288, 319–320 (1989).

77. George R. LaNoue & Barbara A. Lee, *Academics in Court: The Consequences of Faculty Discrimination Litigation* (Ann Arbor: University of Michigan Press, 1987), p. 246.

78. Byrne, "The Threat to Constitutional Academic Freedom," p. 91; *see also* Olivas, "The Legal Environment," p. 237 (noting that "[o]ur timeless values, such as academic freedom, tenure, institutional autonomy, and due process are in danger of being legislated or litigated away, if we do not remain vigilant and alert and if we do not self-police").

79. LaNoue & Lee, *Academics in Court*, p. 40.

80. Helen Gouldner, "The Social Impact of Campus Litigation," 3 *Journal of Higher Education* 329, 331 (1980); *see also* LaNoue & Lee, *Academics in Court*, p. 230 (observing that "discrimination litigation that drags on for several years is bad for institutional morale" and "the costs in time and money are substantial").

81. "Message from Dean Polsby: Former Student's Lawsuit against Mason Law Dismissed," Feb. 21, 2006, available at www.docketonline.com.

82. "Quick Takes: Cost of Firing Dean," *Inside Higher Ed,* June 5, 2007.

83. Julie H. Margetta, "Guarding the Ivory Tower: The Duty of the University to Defend and Indemnify Faculty Publications," 12 *Texas Journal of Civil Liberties and Civil Rights* 133, 134 (2006) (finding that "current legal protections available to professors at public universities are inadequate to guarantee a legal defense or indemnification in suits arising from their scholarly publications," and that "professors at private universities are similarly exposed to the prohibitive costs of lawsuits arising from their publications"); Kevin Oates, "Professor Defend Thyself: The Failure of Universities to Defend and Indemnify Their Faculty," 39 *Willamette Law Review* 1063 (2003); Scott Jaschik, "Twisting in the Wind," *Inside Higher Ed,* Nov. 30, 2005 (reporting case of University of Oregon law professor Merle Weiner, who was forced to mount her own legal defense to a libel claim arising from a law review article).

84. Michael A. Olivas, "The Rise of Nonlegal Legal Influences on Higher Education," in Ronald G. Ehrenberg, ed., *Governing Academia* (Ithaca, N.Y.: Cornell University Press, 2004), pp. 258, 260–262.

85. Jeffrey Selingo & Goldie Blumentsyk, "At Meeting of College Lawyers, They Talk of Costlier Settlements and Whistle-Blowers," *Chronicle of Higher Educa-*

tion, July 7, 2006, p. 29 (quoting Robb Jones, senior vice president and general counsel for claims management at United Educators Insurance).

86. Jaschik, "Twisting in the Wind."

87. Jennifer Howard, "Scholarly Association Settles 'Libel Tourism' Case," *Chronicle of Higher Education,* June 18, 2008.

88. Thomas O. McGarity, "Defending Clean Science from Dirty Attacks by Special Interests," in Wendy Wagner & Rena Steinzor, eds., *Rescuing Science from Politics: Regulation and the Distortion of Scientific Research* (Cambridge: Cambridge University Press, 2006), pp. 24, 31.

89. Wendy Wagner & Rena Steinzor, "Conclusion: The Imperative of the Principles," in Wagner & Steinzor, *Rescuing Science,* pp. 281, 282.

90. Paul M. Fischer, "Science and Subpoenas: When Do Courts Become Instruments of Manipulation?" in Wagner & Steinzor, *Rescuing Science,* pp. 86, 95, 97.

91. Joanna Kempner, "The Chilling Effect: How Do Researchers React to Controversy?" 5 *PLoS Medicine* 6 (Nov. 2008).

92. Wagner & Steinzor, *Rescuing Science,* p. ix.

93. Gwendolyn Bradley, "Disney Tells University to Retract Release," *Academe Online* (Nov.–Dec. 2007), available at www.aaup.org.

94. LaNoue & Lee, *Academics in Court,* p. 246 (quoting a university counsel).

95. Ibid., p. 230.

96. Howard, "Scholarly Association Settles."

97. Jaschik, "Twisting in the Wind."

98. Megan Rooney, "Coppin State College to Let Failing Students Graduate, Critics Charge," *Chronicle of Higher Education,* May 15, 2003.

99. *See* Harry T. Edwards, *Higher Education and the Unholy Crusade against Governmental Regulation* (Cambridge, Mass.: Institute for Educational Management, 1980).

100. Jerome Karabel, *The Chosen: The Hidden History of Admission and Exclusion at Harvard, Yale, and Princeton* (Boston: Houghton Mifflin, 2005).

101. *See* Byrne, "The Threat to Constitutional Academic Freedom," pp. 90–91.

102. Ibid., p. 79.

103. Ibid., p. 122.

104. Wynne v. Tufts University School of Medicine, 932 F.2d 19 (1st Cir. 1991).

105. Ibid., p. 26.

106. Ibid.

107. Ibid., p. 29 (Breyer, C. J., dissenting).

108. Ibid., pp. 30–31.

109. Gordon v. Purdue University, 862 N.E.2d 1244 (Ind. Ct. App. 2007).

110. Sharick v. Southeastern University of Health Sciences, 780 N.E.2d 136 (Fla. Ct. App. 2000).

111. *Gordon,* 862 N.E.2d at 1246–1253.

112. *Sharick,* 780 So.2d at 138–140 (emphasis in original).

113. An appeal is pending.

114. Byrne, "The Threat to Constitutional Academic Freedom," p. 122.

115. *Gordon,* 862 N.E.2d at 1251.

116. *Sharick,* 780 So.2d at 142–143.

117. *Compare Wynne,* 932 F.2d at 29–31 (Breyer, C. J., dissenting), *with* Grutter v. Bollinger, 539 U.S. 306, 354–366 (2003) (Thomas, J., concurring in part and dissenting in part).

118. Byrne, "The Threat to Constitutional Academic Freedom," p. 89 (noting that "federal judges . . . have trouble distinguishing among valid academic and invalid ideological arguments in intramural disputes"); ibid., p. 90 n.75 (observing that "judges . . . do not understand academic freedom and will tend to substitute generic First Amendment concepts in its place").

119. Ibid., p. 141; O'Neil, *Academic Freedom,* pp. 276–277; William W. Van Alstyne, "Academic Freedom and the First Amendment in the Supreme Court of the United States: An Unhurried Historical Review," 53 *Law and Contemporary Problems* 79, 132–133 (1990) (noting influence of AAUP *amicus* brief on Justice Douglas's opinion in Board of Regents v. Roth, 408 U.S. 564 (1972)).

120. Grutter v. Bollinger, 539 U.S. 306 (2003).

121. Rhodes, *The Creation of the Future,* p. 47.

122. *See* A. Ryor, "Who Killed Collegiality?" 10 *Change* 11 (June/July 1978) (contending that the traditional campus culture of collegiality has been displaced by a new era of liability).

123. Olivas, "The Legal Environment," p. 231 (quoting William Kaplin).

124. Steven Vago & Charles E. Marske, "Law and Dispute Processing in the Academic Community," 64 *Judicature* 165, 168 (1980).

125. Burnham v. Ianni, 119 F.3d 668 (8th Cir. 1997).

126. Ibid., p. 681 (McMillian, J., dissenting).

127. Franke & White, "Responsibilities of Department Chairs"; *see also* "Faculty Communication 101," *Inside Higher Ed,* July 20, 2007.

128. *See* William C. Warters, "The History of Campus Mediation Systems: Research and Practice" (1999), available at http://law.gsu.edu/cncr/pdf/papers/99-1Warterspap.pdf; William C. Warters, *Mediation in the Campus Community: Designing and Maintaining Effective Programs* (San Francisco: Jossey-Bass, 1999); Carolyn Stieber, "Resolving Campus Disputes: Notes of a University Ombudsman," 37 *Arbitration Journal* 5 (1982).

129. *See* Selingo & Blumenstyk, "Meeting of College Lawyers" (noting that majority of campus counsel reported making more use of mediation); Eugene McCormack, "Socratic Guidance for Faculty Grievances: More Institutions Are Asking Ombudsmen to Handle Professors' Complaints before They Escalate," *Chronicle of Higher Education,* Feb. 3, 2006; David R. Karp & Thom Allena, *Restorative Justice on the College Campus: Promoting Student Growth and Responsibility, and Reawakening the Spirit of Campus Community* (Springfield, Ill.: Charles C. Thomas, 2004); Bill Warters et al., "Making Things Right:

Restorative Justice Comes to Campuses," 1 *Conflict Management in Higher Education Report* 1 (Jan./Feb. 2000).

130. Helen Kennedy, "Dartmouth Professor Threatens Students with Discrimination Suit," *New York Daily News,* Apr. 30, 2008.
131. Tyler R. Brace, "TDR Interview: Priya Venkatesan, Writing 5 Professor," *Dartmouth Review,* May 5, 2008.
132. Allyson Bennett, "Prof Threatens Lawsuit against Her Students," *The Dartmouth,* Apr. 28, 2008.
133. Ibid.
134. "Dartmouth Students Get E-mails from Former Teacher Claiming Disrespect," *Boston.com,* May 1, 2008, http://www.boston.com.
135. Brace, "TDR Interview."
136. Brian Rosenthal, "Venkatesan Trying to Move on at NU; Dartmouth Lecturer Who Threatened Suit Enjoying Work at NU," *Daily Northwestern,* May 16, 2008.
137. Emma Haberman & Cynthia R. Fagen, "Class Action: Dartmouth Prof Suing 'Mean' Students," *New York Post,* Apr. 30, 2008.
138. Brace, "TDR Interview."

Index

Note: Some of the cases listed below are described in the text, although they are named in full only in the corresponding footnote. The entries below refer readers to the pages where these cases appear in the main text. The full case citation will be found in the footnote.